Farm Management

FARM MANAGEMENT

PLANNING, CONTROL, AND IMPLEMENTATION

RONALD D. KAY

Texas A&M University

McGraw-Hill Book Company

New York   St. Louis   San Francisco   Auckland   Bogotá   Hamburg
Johannesburg   London   Madrid   Mexico   Montreal   New Delhi
Panama   Paris   São Paulo   Singapore   Sydney   Tokyo   Toronto

This book was set in Times Roman by Waldman Graphics, Inc.
The editors were James E. Vastyan, Carol Napier, and Scott Amerman;
the production supervisor was Diane Renda.
The drawings were done by ECL Art Associates, Inc.
R. R. Donnelley & Sons Company was printer and binder.

FARM MANAGEMENT
Planning, Control, and Implementation

4 5 6 7 8 9 0   DODO   8 9 8 7 6 5 4 3 2

Library of Congress Cataloging in Publication Data

Kay, Ronald D
    Farm management.

    Includes bibliographies and index.
    1. Farm management. I. Title.
S561.K36   630'.68   80-18565
ISBN 0-07-033462-5

Contents

2
PLANNING

3

CONTROL

4

IMPLEMENTATION—ACQUIRING AND MANAGING RESOURCES

5

ADDITIONAL MANAGEMENT TOPICS

Preface

This book has been written for students of farm and ranch management, and many reading it will be sophomores or juniors taking their first college course in farm and ranch management. However, we are always students, or should be, regardless of age or occupation. Students of farm and ranch management may be found not only learning in the college classroom but operating their own farm or ranch, managing one for someone else, lending money to farmers and ranchers, or providing them with the many products and services they need in their business. I hope that everyone interested in farm and ranch management, whether in a formal classroom or in the "classroom of the world," will find this book interesting, stimulating, and above all, useful.

As with many textbooks, this one grew out of my experience teaching an introductory farm and ranch management course first at Iowa State University and, for the last nine years, at Texas A&M University. My teaching notes, which have seen many additions, deletions, revisions, and modifications over the years, provided much of the material for writing this book. However, farm and ranch management is a well-developed discipline, and I cannot claim any originality of material. My aim in writing this book was to provide its users with something new in terms of organization, selection of topics, clarity of presentation, and learning aids. To fulfill the last aim, each chapter contains a list of chapter objectives, a summary, and questions and problems for review.

This book is organized around three basic functions of management—planning, implementation, and control. The various management topics are grouped according to the function with which they relate. While the normal sequence of carrying out these three functions would be planning, implementation, and control, the last two have been switched in order of presentation. A review of more than a dozen course outlines at as many colleges and universities around the country revealed most farm management instructors follow my practice of covering the topics relating to the control function before those relating to implementation. However, the book is flexible enough to permit changing the order of presentation to follow any course outline. Some instructors prefer to cover records first, which can be done without any loss of continuity. No particular prerequisites are assumed or needed to use this book, although introductory courses in agricultural economics, animal science, and agronomy might be helpful, particularly for students without a farm or ranch background.

Part One provides an introduction to management, its importance, and the role of decision making in the management process. The planning function is covered in Part Two, with two chapters on economic principles and three chapters on the various types of budgeting. Material in these first six chapters provides the basic decision-making tools needed by a farm manager and takes up one-third or more of the time in many farm management courses. The reader will find applications of economic principles and budgeting throughout the remainder of the book, particularly in Part Four.

Part Three introduces the concepts necessary for a manager to control and monitor the farm business activities. The emphasis is on business management and financial control utilizing farm records. Chapters 7 and 8 cover the balance sheet and income statement and their analysis. Procedures and methods to complete a whole farm business analysis are covered in Chapter 9. Other records useful in business management and analysis are discussed and illustrated in Chapter 10.

The implementation function, including the acquisition and managing of the resources necessary to implement production decisions, is the subject of Part Four. This part contains chapters on business organization, capital and credit, investment analysis, land, labor, and machinery. Part Five includes several chapters on subjects which do not readily fit under any of the three management functions. Chapter 17 discusses income taxes and tax management, Chapter 18 introduces decision making under risk and uncertainty, and Chapter 19 provides a brief discussion of professional farm management services.

I would not expect the entire book to be covered in a three-semester-hour course which includes a laboratory session. Most instructors will want to include Chapters 1 to 6 in their course outline. The remainder of the book provides sufficient flexibility for different instructors to design their own course outline. For example, Part Three can be omitted if the students have had or will take a course in farm records. Chapters 12 and 13 can be omitted if the same material is covered in an agricultural finance course which the students will take later. For additional flexibility, an understanding of the material in each chapter in Parts Four and Five depends only upon the subject matter in Chapters 1 to 6. Therefore, any or all of them can be covered in any order without loss of continuity or understanding.

It is impossible to mention the many people who have contributed directly and indirectly to my interest and education in farm management and hence to this book. Many of you have encouraged me to write this book, and I shall be forever appreciative of your support, encouragement, and faith that I would some day finish the task. Special recognition should be given to Carl F. Hertz of Hertz Farm Management, Inc., of Nevada, Iowa, who gave an inexperienced college graduate a job and to Robert E. Walters and Thomas E. Rittgers of the same organization who shared their farm management experiences with me. I owe much of my practical education and interest in farm management to these individuals.

Many students at both Iowa State University and Texas A&M University have contributed to this book with their thoughts, ideas, and comments both in and out of the classroom. I doubt if many students fully appreciate how much they contribute to the education of their instructor. Special thanks must also go to the many staff members in the Department of Agricultural Economics at Texas A&M University for their encouragement and for the time many took to read and comment on the various chapters in this book.

I am also grateful for the support and encouragement from the women in my life, Diana, Cynthia, Beth, and Rhonda. Not only did they help by typing and proofreading, they put up with a husband and father who was often absent or preoccupied. Finally, to Ruth Ann Moore who cheerfully and accurately typed and retyped more versions of some chapters than she probably cares to remember—thank you.

Ronald D. Kay

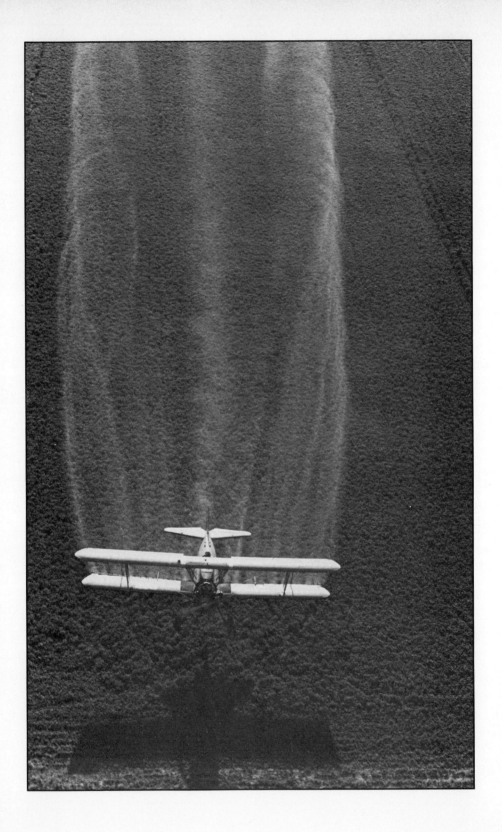

Part 1
MANAGEMENT

HIGHLIGHTS

Management is the key ingredient. The manager "makes" or "breaks" a business. Brains are more important than brawn. How often have you heard these or similar statements or read them in farm magazines? They all emphasize an important factor in the operation of a farm or ranch in today's world. *Management is important*. This does not mean that management was not important in the past. However, in an agriculture which is highly mechanized, uses many technological innovations, and operates with large amounts of borrowed capital, management takes on a new dimension and importance.

Why do some farmers make more money than others? Why do some farm businesses grow and expand while others struggle to maintain their current size? Good or bad luck cannot explain all the differences observed in the profitability of farms and ranches even among those which have about the same amount of land and capital available. Farm business records from many states show the top one-third of the farms to be highly profitable while the bottom one-third are often operating at a loss. Why the difference? Observation and analysis often lead to the same conclusion. The difference is due to management.

1

If management is so important, we must ask even more questions. What exactly is management? What do managers do? What is the difference between management and labor? What knowledge and skills are needed to become a better manager? The answers to the first several questions are discussed in Chapter 1. The last question forms the basis for the remainder of this book.

Chapter 1

The Role
and Functions
of Management

CHAPTER OBJECTIVES

   1   To discuss some definitions of management
   2   To explore some unique characteristics of farm and ranch management
and develop a definition
   3   To note the types and characteristics of farm and ranch management
problems and management decisions
   4   To analyze the steps in the decision-making process
   5   To show how the particular environment in agriculture affects decision
making on farms and ranches
   6   To identify planning, control, and implementation as the three most
important functions of management

Farm and ranch management is becoming an increasingly complex task. Our
nation's farms are becoming larger and larger, their capital requirements have
increased dramatically, and they are affected by frequent changes in many
factors. In recent years, price changes for agricultural commodities have been
frequent, wide, and often abrupt in response to similar changes in supply and
demand. New technology has been a source of other changes. Consider, for
example, the development of new seed varieties and new fertilizer products,
the use of crossbreeding in the livestock industry, the introduction of new
breeds of cattle into the United States, the development of new chemicals for

pest and weed control, new animal health products, and the many changes which have taken place in tractors, machinery, and irrigation equipment.

These are some examples of the changing environment affecting the farm manager of today. Managers have responded to these economic and technological changes in many ways. In the past 30 years, average farm size has nearly doubled, with a corresponding decrease in farm numbers. Corn and wheat production have approximately doubled, while cotton production has shown little change. In this same time, soybean production increased nearly six times. There have also been changes in livestock production, with the number of beef cows on farms and ranches increasing about 2½ times while the number of dairy cows declined by 50 percent.

These changes in agricultural production have resulted from the collective effects of thousands of decisions made by farm and ranch managers over time in response to change in technology, prices, and other economic factors. Continual change is perhaps one of the few things which can be counted on in the future. As new changes come about, farm and ranch managers must be prepared to identify them and make the correct decisions in response. Without a timely and correct response, a manager cannot expect to survive in a dynamic economy. Present and future managers will need to improve and update their management skills continually in order to make the correct decisions when faced with new and changing problems.

DEFINITION OF MANAGEMENT

A discussion of the role and functions of management in a changing and complex environment needs to begin with a definition of management. What are managers supposed to do? How should their efforts be directed? How does management differ from labor? These are questions which cannot be briefly and easily answered. Management is a widely used term but one which is subject to many individual definitions. Textbooks contain a number of definitions, but there is little evidence the authors agree on a common definition.

Perhaps a dictionary definition of management will provide a starting point. One such definition is[1]:

man · age · ment / 'man-ij-mənt / n   1: the act or art of managing: the conducting or supervising of something (as a business) 2: judicious use of means to accomplish an end

The second part of this definition is similar to a definition of economics, which is often defined as "the study of the allocation of scarce resources." These definitions of management and economics imply or require the establishment or identification of goals and objectives, the existence of limited resources, and the need to allocate these limited resources among a number of alternative uses. Implicit in these definitions is the need for decision making in the proper allocation of scarce resources.

[1]By permission. From Webster's New Collegiate Dictionary © 1979 by G. & C. Merriam Co., Publishers of the Merriam-Webster Dictionaries.

Business management and managerial economics are subjects taught in many business schools. Textbooks in these areas often contain a general definition of management applicable to a nonfarm business. These definitions often contain phrases such as "the organization of resources to reach goals" and "the process which directs actions toward some goal." Both these phrases imply a definition of management which is similar to the second dictionary definition discussed previously.

Other authors discuss management in terms of what management does or how it functions. There is little uniformity in the functions discussed, but the more common ones are planning, organizing, coordinating, controlling, directing, supervising, communicating, and implementing. A discussion of these functions does not lead directly to a definition of management, but it does serve to illustrate the broad scope of management and its complexity.

FARM AND RANCH MANAGEMENT

There are some differences in the management of a farm or ranch and the management of a nonfarm business corporation. The obvious differences are in size, type of business, and the products or services produced. Other differences include the relationship between labor and management and the setting of goals.

In a corporation, the board of directors sets policies and goals and hires managers to achieve them. It is generally easy to separate corporation employees who are managers from those who provide the labor necessary to produce a product or provide a service. On a typical farm or ranch, one individual or a family group sets the goals, provides the management, and performs much or all of the labor required. This makes it difficult to separate the management activity from labor because the same individual(s) are involved and both tasks may be performed at the same time. For example, a farmer may be mentally planning a marketing strategy or developing next year's cropping program while operating a tractor or combine. When one person performs both the management and labor functions, there is a danger that the immediate need for labor to perform some task will place management in a secondary role, with management decisions postponed or delayed.

These differences are not readily apparent when definitions of business management and farm and ranch management are compared, but they are nevertheless important. There are many different textbook definitions of farm and ranch management, but several common points run through all of them. One of the more concise definitions is "Farm management is concerned with the decisions which affect the profitability of the farm business."[2] This is a very broad definition, but it contains several important points. First, it identifies profitability as the objective of the business but not necessarily to the

[2]Emery N. Castle, M. H. Becker, and F. J. Smith, *Farm Business Management*, 2d ed., The Macmillan Company, New York, 1972, p. 3.

exclusion of other objectives. Second, this definition specifically identifies decisions and decision making as part of the management process.

Other farm management texts contain different definitions but with many of the same concepts or ideas. The first is some reference to *decisions* or *decision making* as being part of the management process. Second, some mention is made of *goals* or *objectives*. This may be done in general terms, or a more specific goal such as profit maximization may be identified as being an important end to which the management effort is directed. Third, some mention of the *organization* and *operation* of the farm or ranch business is included in many definitions.

Farm and ranch management can be thought of, then, as being a decision-making process. It is a continual process because of the continual changes taking place in our economy and in an individual business. The decisions are concerned with allocating the limited resources of land, labor, and capital among alternative and usually competing uses. This allocation process forces the manager to identify goals and objectives to guide and direct the decision making.

In this text, the following definition will be adopted: *Farm and ranch management* is *the decision-making process whereby limited resources are allocated to a number of production alternatives to organize and operate the business in such a way as to attain some objective(s)*. While this definition is somewhat long, it does identify most of the characteristics of the management activities found on farms and ranches.

PROBLEM TYPES AND CHARACTERISTICS

The aforementioned definition suggests that management is a problem-solving and decision-making activity. What types of problems require a decision on a farm or ranch? What are the basic characteristics of a management or economic problem? Many farm management problems fall into one of three types, each of which can be put into the form of a question:

How much to produce? Production is determined primarily by the number of inputs used and input levels. A manager is faced with the problems of how much fertilizer and irrigation water to use, seeding rates, feeding levels, labor and machinery use, and determining rates and levels for other inputs. The level of production and profit will be determined by the input levels selected.

How to produce? Many agricultural products can be produced in a number of ways. Beef can be produced with a high-grain ration or a high-roughage ration. Hogs can be produced with a large capital investment in buildings and little labor or with less investment but more labor. Crops can be produced with large machinery and little labor, or smaller machinery and more labor. A manager must select the appropriate combination of inputs which will minimize the cost of producing a given quantity of some commodity.

What to produce? This problem involves selecting the combination of crops and livestock to be produced. Should the business produce only crops, only livestock, or some combination? Which crops or crop rotation? Which livestock? The manager must select from among the many alternatives that combination which will maximize profit or best meet some other goal.

Every production decision with which a farm manager is confronted relates to one or a combination of these three questions or problem types. They are also economic problems, and an economic problem has three characteristics:

1   Goals or objectives to be attained
2   A limited amount of resources to use in reaching these goals and objectives
3   A number of alternative ways to use the limited resources in attempting to attain the goals and objectives

Problem solving is a continual process because of the many changes that affect these problem characteristics over time. Goals may change as the business owner grows older and with changes in the financial condition of the business. Resource limits change as more land and capital are acquired. The number of production alternatives may increase as additional capital is acquired and new technology becomes available. Many problem solutions must therefore be viewed as only short-term solutions, and the problem along with its potential solutions will need to be reconsidered as changes occur in the future.

Identification of Goals and Objectives

A manager's first job is to establish goals and objectives for the business. In the case of a hired manager, the business owner may establish and communicate them to the manager. Whether the manager establishes goals or receives them from the business owner, it is important that they exist and be fully understood. Without goals there is no way to measure the results of management decisions or to make proper decisions. Goals provide the guidelines for decision making.

Individuals are different and have their own particular sets of goals and objectives. While different individuals may have the same two or three goals, the relative weights placed on them or their ordering may be different. Most farms and ranches are still individually owned, so it is not surprising to find different goals being used in their operation. Some of the more common goals are profit maximization; attaining a particular output level or business size; reserving a certain amount of time for leisure activities; business growth; business survival; and maintaining a stable income over time.

Each of the above goals may be of primary importance to some individuals, depending upon the time and circumstances. Goals can and do change with age and financial condition. Multiple goals often exist and may be in conflict. Maximizing family consumption expenditures and maximum business growth are examples of conflicting goals. Where multiple goals exist, the manager must place them in the order of their relative importance. As one goal is met, effort can then be directed to the next most important one.

Goals should be completely specified because they provide the yardstick which can be used to measure success. It is also useful to establish goals for the next year or two as well as long-run goals or those to be reached in 5 or 10 years. These long-run goals provide direction to long-run decision making.

Profit maximization is a widely accepted goal, particularly as it contributes to other potential goals such as growth and survival of the business. Throughout this text profit maximization will be the assumed primary goal in both short-term and long-run planning. This selection was made because it has the advantage of being easily measured and quantified; however, the reader should always remember that the establishment of goals is very much an individual process. Goals other than profit maximization can be of special importance to some individuals. In fact, surveys of farm managers show profit maximization is often ranked below other goals such as business survival.

Limited Resources

A manager must consider the resources available for attaining the goals which have been set. Limits are placed on goal attainment because most managers are faced with a limited amount of resources. In a farm or ranch business, goal attainment is confined within some limits set by the amount of land, labor, and capital available. These resources may change over time, but they are never available in infinite amounts. The level of management skills available or the expertise of the manager may be another limiting resource. Identifying current resource limits and acquiring additional resources, including management skills, are continual problems confronting a farm manager.

Alternative Uses

If the limited resources could only be used one way to produce one agricultural product, the manager's job would be much easier. The usual situation allows the limited resources to be used several different ways to produce each of a number of different products. In other words, the manager is faced with a number of alternative uses for the limited resources and must make decisions on how to allocate them among the alternatives to maximize profit from the total business. The emphasis should be on maximizing profit for the entire business and not for just one of the alternatives.

In the more arid regions of the western United States, the land resource is such that the only alternative may be to use it as pasture for livestock production. But even in this situation, the manager must still decide whether to use the pasture for cow/calf production, for grazing stocker steers during the summer, or in some areas, for sheep and goat production. Other areas of the country have land suitable for both crop and livestock production, and a larger number of alternatives exist. As the number of alternative uses for the limited resources increase, so does the size of the manager's problem.

THE DECISION-MAKING PROCESS

The allocation of limited resources among a number of alternative uses requires a manager to make decisions. This is one of the reasons, if not the most important one, for some mention of decisions or decision making in a definition of farm and ranch management. Without decisions nothing would happen. Even allowing things to continue as they are implies a decision, perhaps not a good decision but a passive decision nevertheless.

The process of making a decision can be formalized into a logical and orderly series of steps. Important steps in the decision-making process are

1 Identify and define the problem.
2 Collect relevant data, facts, and information.
3 Identify and analyze alternative solutions.
4 Make the decision—select the best alternative.
5 Implement the decision.
6 Observe the results and bear responsibility for the outcome.

Following these steps will not ensure a perfect decision. It will, however, ensure that the decision is made in a logical and organized manner.

Identify and Define the Problem

Many problems confront a farm or ranch manager. Earlier in this chapter some problems were identified in terms of deciding how much to produce, how to produce, and what to produce. These are basic problems faced by all managers. Problems also result from identifying something that is not as it should be. This may be a goal that is not being attained or a deficiency in the organization or operation of the business identified by finding a difference between *what is* and *what should be*. For example, a farmer may find that his cotton yield is 100 pounds per acre lower than the average for other farmers in the same county on the same soil type. This difference between what is, the farm yield, and what it should be, at least the county average yield, identifies a problem that needs attention.

A manager must constantly be on the alert to identify problems and to identify them as quickly as possible. Most problems will not go away by themselves and represent an opportunity to increase the profitability of the business through wise decision making. Once identified, the problem should be concisely defined. Good problem definition will minimize the time required to complete the remainder of the decision-making steps.

Collecting Data and Information

Once a problem has been identified and properly defined, the next step should be to gather data, information, and facts and to make observations which pertain to the specific problem. A concise definition of the problem will help identify the type of data needed and prevent time being wasted gathering information which is not useful to the particular problem. Data may be obtained from a number of sources, including the local county extension office; bulletins and pamphlets from state experiment stations and agricultural colleges; dealers; salespersons of agricultural inputs; radio; TV; farm magazines; and neighbors. An important source of data and information is an accurate and complete set of past records kept for an individual business. When available this is often the best source. Whatever the source, the relative accuracy and reliability of the information obtained should be considered.

It is important to make a distinction between data and information. Data can be thought of as an unorganized collection of facts and numbers obtained from various sources. In this form, the data may have very little use. To be useful, these data and facts need to be organized, sorted, and analyzed and some calculations made. Information can be thought of as the final product obtained from analyzing data in such a way that useful conclusions and results are obtained. Not all data need to be organized and summarized into useful information, but most are not useful until some type of analysis is made.

Gathering data and facts and transforming them into information can be a never-ending task. A manager may never be satisfied with the accuracy and reliability of the data and the resulting information. However, this step must be terminated at some point to make it possible to move to the third step. It is important to remember that gathering data has a cost in terms of both time and money. Too much time spent gathering and analyzing data may result in a cost which cannot be justified by the extra income received from continual refinement of data collection and information processing.

Identifying and Analyzing Alternatives

Once the relevant information is available, the manager can begin listing alternatives which are potential solutions to the problem. Several may become apparent during the process of collecting data and transforming data into information. Others may take considerable time and thought, and all possible alternatives should be considered. This is the time to brainstorm and list any idea which comes to mind. Custom, tradition, or habit should not restrict the number or types of alternatives which are considered.

Each alternative should be analyzed in a logical and organized manner to ensure accuracy and to prevent something from being overlooked. The principles and procedures discussed in the next five chapters provide the basis for sound analytical methods. In some cases, additional information may be needed to complete the analysis. Good judgment and practical experience may have to substitute for information which is unavailable or available only at an additional cost that is greater than the additional return from its use.

Making the Decision

Choosing the best solution to a problem is not always easy, nor is the best solution always obvious. Sometimes the best solution is to do nothing or to go back, redefine the problem, and go through the decision-making steps again.

These are legitimate decisions, but they should not be used as a way to avoid making a decision when a promising alternative is available.

After all the pros and cons of each alternative are weighed, one may not appear to be definitely better than any other. The one showing the greatest increase in expected profit would normally be selected. However, this selection is often complicated by uncertainty about the future, particularly future prices. If several alternatives have nearly the same potential effect on profit, the manager must then assess the chances or probability that each will have the expected or identified outcome and the risk associated with it.

Implementing the Decision

Selecting the best alternative will not give the desired results unless the decision is correctly and promptly implemented. Resources may need to be acquired and organized, which requires some physical action to be taken. Of course, doing nothing is an alternative and a potential solution to a problem. However, the manager who decides to do nothing or to implement no new alternative should do this only after enough analysis of the problem to be sure that this is the correct decision. Too often doing nothing results from not allocating enough time to the decision-making process or a reluctance to make a decision.

Observing and Bearing Responsibility

Responsibility for the outcome of a decision rests with the decision maker. A reluctance to bear responsibility may explain why some individuals find it so difficult to make a decision. However, since it is difficult for managers to avoid decision making, it follows that they must bear the responsibility. It goes along with the job.

Not every decision will be a perfect one. For this reason the results of each decision should be carefully observed to gather any data or information which can be used to modify the decision and to assist in making better decisions. Careful observation and analysis will result in additional information, allow corrections to be made, and improve future decisions. Managers who learn from their past mistakes may soon find people talking about their "good luck." While good luck may occasionally bless some managers, most is the result of hard work and good decisions.

CLASSIFYING DECISIONS

The decisions made by farm and ranch managers can be classified in a number of ways. One classification system would be to consider decisions as either *organizational* or *operational* in nature. Organizational decisions are those in the general areas of developing plans for the business, acquiring the necessary resources, and implementing the overall plan. Examples of such decisions are how much land to purchase or lease, how much capital to borrow, and what types of crops and livestock to raise. Organizational decisions tend to be long-run decisions which are not modified or reevaluated more than once a year.

Operational decisions are made more frequently than organizational decisions and relate to the many details necessary to implement the farm business plans. They may need to be made on a daily, weekly, or monthly basis and are repeated more often than organizational decisions as they follow the routines and cycles of agricultural production. Examples of operational decisions are selecting fertilizer and seeding rates for a given field and year, making changes in a livestock feed ration, selecting planting and harvesting dates, marketing decisions, and daily work schedules.

Decisions can have one of a number of characteristics, which provides another classification system. One list of decision characteristics is[3]

1 Importance
2 Frequency
3 Imminence
4 Revocability
5 Number of available alternatives

Each of these characteristics may affect how the decision is made and how the manager applies the steps in the decision-making process to a particular problem.

Importance   Given the many decisions made by farm and ranch managers, some will be more important than others. Importance can be measured in several ways, but the most common would be in terms of the number of dollars involved in the decision or the size of the potential gain or loss. Decisions involving a few dollars might be made rather routinely, with little time spent gathering data and proceeding through the steps in the decision-making process.

Decisions involving a large amount of capital and potential profit or loss need to be analyzed carefully. They can easily justify more time spent on gathering data and analyzing possible alternatives. Examples would be the purchase of additional land, establishing an irrigation system, and constructing a new total-confinement hog building.

Frequency   Some decisions may be made only once in a lifetime, such as the decision to choose farming or ranching as a vocation. Other decisions must be made almost daily, such as livestock feeding times, milking times, and the amount of feed to be fed each day. Such frequently made decisions should be based on some rule of thumb or other predetermined method. If much time was allocated to making these routine decisions, the manager would accomplish very little else. Even though some sort of standard routine, rule of thumb,

[3]Emery N. Castle, M. H. Becker, and F. J. Smith, *Farm Business Management*, 2d ed., The Macmillan Company, New York, 1972, p. 9.

or other method is used, the manager must be aware of the cumulative effects of a small error in these decisions. Because these decisions do occur frequently, a small error in the decision-making process because some rule of thumb was used could accumulate into a substantial amount over a period of time.

Imminence   A manager is often faced with making some decisions before a certain deadline or very quickly to avoid a potential loss. Other decisions may have no deadline, and there may be little or no penalty for delaying the decision until more information is obtained and more time spent analyzing the alternatives. When prompt action is required, the manager may have to proceed through the decision-making steps quickly and without complete information. A livestock disease outbreak or a crop infested with insects requires a prompt decision on treatment to avoid a large potential loss. Other decisions such as whether or not to build a new machine shed can be easily postponed with little or no cost until a more complete study and analysis can be done. The approach to any decision will depend on the time element involved.

Revocability   Some decisions can be easily reversed or changed if observation indicates the first decision was not correct. An example would be a livestock feed ration, which could be changed rather quickly and easily as long as the change was not so abrupt as to upset the livestock. Managers may spend very little time on making the initial decision in these situations, as future observation may allow corrections to be made quickly and at very little cost.

Other decisions may not be reversible or can be changed only at a very high cost. Examples would be the decision to dig a new irrigation well or to construct a new building. Once the decision is made to go ahead with these projects, the choice is either to use them or abandon them. It may be very difficult or impossible to recover the money invested. These nonreversible decisions justify much more of the manager's time moving through the steps in the decision-making process.

Number of Available Alternatives   Some decisions have only two possible alternatives. They are of the yes or no and buy or not buy type. The manager may find these decisions easier and less time-consuming than others which have a large number of alternative solutions or courses of action. Where a large number of alternatives exist, the manager may be forced to spend considerable time identifying the alternatives and analyzing each one.

THE DECISION-MAKING ENVIRONMENT

The manager of any business is faced with the problem of making decisions, but the manager of a farm or ranch makes decisions in a somewhat unique environment. Perhaps most important is the limitation placed on a manager's decisions by the biological and physical laws of nature. Farm and ranch managers soon find there are some things that cannot be changed by their decisions. Nothing can be done to shorten the gestation period in livestock production, and there is a physical limit on the amount of feed livestock can consume in a day. The time it takes for a particular crop to grow and mature can be changed somewhat by the choice of variety, but once this decision is made little else can be done. The manager must be aware of the limits placed on decision making by these biological and physical factors.

Production on farms and ranches is perhaps affected more by weather than production in any other type of business. Although efforts have been made to prevent hail and to induce rainfall, there is still little a manager can do to influence the weather and its effect on the business. Crop yields and prices received for them are strongly influenced by weather conditions in the local area and in other areas of the country.

Production agriculture is often used as an example of a perfectly competitive industry. Simply stated, this means that each individual farm or ranch is only one of many and represents such a small part of the total industry that the decisions made affect neither the prices paid for resources nor the prices received for products sold. Prices are determined by national and worldwide supply and demand factors over which individual farmers have very little control except possibly through some type of collective action. Other businesses typically have more control over the prices received for their products.

Weather, insects, disease, and variable prices are examples of factors which place the farm manager in a position of making decisions in an environment of risk and uncertainty. Future yields and prices cannot be predicted with a great deal of accuracy, yet they are important in nearly every management decision. While there is a certain amount of risk and uncertainty in every business endeavor, the farm manager's decision-making environment contains more factors creating risk and uncertainty than most types of business.

MANAGEMENT FUNCTIONS

Earlier in this chapter, management was discussed in terms of the functions performed by managers. Included were the functions of planning, implementation, and control which some consider to be the three basic or primary functions of management.[4] The other functions can be easily included as subfunctions under one of these three. Figure 1-1 is a flowchart which summarizes the management process utilizing these three functions.

Planning

In this simplified flowchart, the planning function contains a number of steps, including the identification and definition of the problem, acquiring the initial information, and identifying alternative solutions. Planning may be taking place

[4]C. S. Barnard, and J. S. Nix, *Farm Planning and Control,* Cambridge University Press, Cambridge, England, 1973, pp. 14–16.

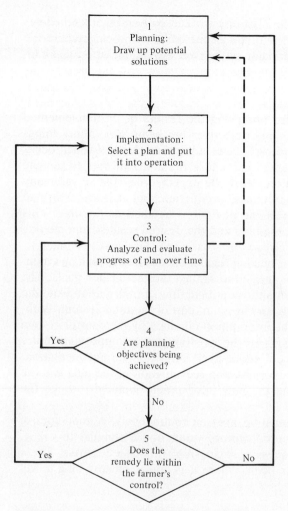

Figure 1-1 Management flowchart. (*Adapted from C. S. Barnard and J. S. Nix, Farm Planning and Control, Cambridge University Press, Cambridge, England, 1973.*)

for a number of problems at the same time. This requires a manager to be able to shift thought processes quickly while watching for information which may be useful in solving more than one problem. Planning is a continual process as new problems and opportunities arise and as new information becomes available from outside or within the system. New information obtained from the control function and fed back into the planning stage is an important feature of the complete system.

Implementation

Once the planning process is completed, the best alternative must be selected and action taken to place the plan into operation. There may be resources to purchase, lease, or reorganize, details to be worked out, and work schedules to be organized. Implementation may not occur quickly and can require the coordination, directing, and supervising of the necessary land, labor, and capital over a period of time.

Control

The control function provides for observing the results of the implemented plan to see if the specified goals and objectives are being met. Many things can cause a plan to go "off its track." Price and other changes which occur after the plan has been implemented can cause the actual results to deviate from the expected. Some deviation should be expected because of the many uncertainties connected with agricultural production, but it is necessary to identify the type and magnitude of the deviations as soon as possible. This information can be used to keep the plan and the desired results from moving outside an acceptable range.

Control requires a system for making regular checks on the plan and monitoring its progress and results as measured against the established goals. The dashed line in Figure 1-1 represents the continual flow of information from the control function back to planning, an important part of the total system. Without some feedback procedure, the information obtained by the control system is of no use in making corrections to the existing plan or improving future plans. This feedback sets up a continuous cycle of planning, implementation, monitoring, and recording progress back to a reevaluation of the plan and the implementation procedures using the new information obtained through the control function.

The importance of control must be stressed continuously. A good control system requires an accurate record-keeping system and the ability to use it. Without detailed records, a business is like a ship without a compass. There is no way to know where it has been, where it is going, or how long it will take to get there.

SUMMARY

The definition, role, and function of management were discussed from several viewpoints in this chapter. Decision making was identified as an important part of management, and the types of decisions and the decision-making process were discussed at some length.

Management was also discussed in terms of the functions to be performed. The three primary functions were identified as planning, implementation, and control. These functions provide the basic organization of this text, and each is discussed in more detail in the following chapters. The planning function is discussed first, followed by control and implementation. While this order is not the normal sequence of events in the management process, it more nearly fits the usual sequence of topics presented in a farm management course.

QUESTIONS FOR REVIEW AND FURTHER THOUGHT

1 Develop your own definition of farm management.
2 Do farm and ranch managers need different management skills than managers of other businesses? What skills? Or do they need the same basic skills?
3 Identify several managers you consider to be above average and several you consider to be below average in management skills. Are there differences in the two groups with respect to their personality? Education? Training? Experience? Other factors?
4 Why are goals important? Give some examples of both short-term and long-term goals for a farm or ranch.
5 What are your personal goals for the next year? Next 5 years? Next 10 years?
6 Why is control an important part of the management process?

REFERENCES

Barnard, C. S., and J. S. Nix: *Farm Planning and Control,* Cambridge University Press, Cambridge, 1973, chap. 1.
Castle, Emery N., Manning H. Becker, and Frederick J. Smith: *Farm Business Management,* 2d ed., The Macmillan Company, New York, 1972, chap. 1.
Herbst, J. H.: *Farm Management Principles, Budgets, Plans,* 4th ed., Stipes Publishing Co., Champaign, Ill., 1976, chap. 1.
Osburn, Donald D., and Kenneth C. Schneeberger: *Modern Agriculture Management,* Reston Publishing Co., Reston, Va., 1978, chap. 1.

Part 2
PLANNING

HIGHLIGHTS

A successful farm or ranch business is not a result of chance. Good weather and good prices certainly help, but a profitable and growing business is the product of good *planning*. But what is planning? Why is it important? How does a manager plan? What tools or skills are necessary to develop a profitable plan?

Planning is primarily making choices and decisions: selecting the most profitable alternative from among all possible alternatives. The alternative selected becomes the plan for this year, next year, or the next 5 to 10 years. There are both short-run and long-run plans and planning procedures.

Planning is also organizing, as a plan represents a particular way of combining or organizing resources to produce some combination and quantity of agricultural products. Land, labor, and capital do not automatically produce corn, wheat, cotton, beef cattle, or any other product. These resources must be organized into the proper combinations, the proper amounts, and at the proper time for the desired production to occur. This organization or plan can be developed for an individual enterprise such as corn production or beef cattle production, or the plan can be for the entire business. Both types of plans are needed.

The tools and skills a manager needs to develop good plans are discussed in this part. Chapters 2 and 3 cover the economic principles important in planning and their application in agriculture. Economic principles are important because they provide a systematic and organized procedure to simplify making choices and decisions when profit maximization is the goal. They provide the guidelines and rules needed to choose the alternative that will maximize profit.

Four types of budgeting are explored in Chapters 4, 5, and 6. Budgeting

19

is a method of comparing alternatives on paper before committing resources to a particular plan or course of action. It is a forward planning tool, as budgeting is used to develop plans for the future and can be applied to a single enterprise, a part of the farm business, or the whole farm business. Economic principles combined with enterprise, partial, whole farm, and cash flow budgeting provide the manager with a powerful set of tools for performing the planning function of management.

Chapter 2

Marginal Analysis and Economic Principles

CHAPTER OBJECTIVES

1 To explain the concept of marginalism
2 To show the relationship between a variable input and an output by use of a production function and the calculation of average physical product and marginal physical product
3 To illustrate the law of diminishing returns and its importance
4 To show how to find the profit-maximizing amount of a variable input using the concepts of marginal value product and marginal input cost
5 To show how to find the profit-maximizing amount of output to produce using the concepts of marginal revenue and marginal cost
6 To demonstrate the importance of input substitution and how to find the least-cost combination of two inputs to produce a given amount of output
7 To describe the competitive, supplementary, and complementary enterprise relationships and how to use them to find the profit-maximizing combination of two enterprises

The discussion in Chapter 1 identified planning as an important function in the management process. To perform this function, some procedures and methods are needed to guide the decision maker. A knowledge of economics provides a manager with a set of principles and rules for decision making which are useful when making plans to organize and operate a farm or ranch business.

A simplified flowchart shows the sequence of events in the decision-making process:

Once a problem is identified, a manager should begin to acquire data and process them into useful information. Using the available information, the manager must make a choice or decision which will maximize profit.

A knowledge of economics is useful in each of these steps. After identifying the economic principle which will help solve the problem, the manager can use economic principles to identify the appropriate physical, biological, and price data required to solve the problem. Economics also provides a guide for processing data into useful information and a set of rules which assure that the choice or decision made will result in maximum profit.

The above sequence of events should be kept in mind when each new economic principle is introduced in this chapter. For each principle, the same procedure is followed: (1) acquire physical or biological data and process them into useful information, (2) acquire price data and process them into useful information, and (3) apply the appropriate economic decision-making rule to maximize profit.

MARGINALISM

Much of economics is related to the concept of marginalism or marginality. The economist and the manager are often interested in what changes will result from a change in one or more factors under their control. For example, they may be interested in how cotton yield changes from using an additional 50 pounds of fertilizer, or how 2 additional pounds of grain in the daily feed ration affects milk production from a dairy cow, or the change in profit from raising an additional 20 acres of corn and reducing soybean production by 20 acres.

The term *marginal* will be used extensively throughout this chapter. It refers to incremental changes, increases or decreases, which occur at the edge or the margin. Until the reader thoroughly understands the use of the term, it may be useful to substitute "extra" or "additional" mentally whenever the word marginal is used (remembering that the "extra" can be a negative amount or zero). It is also important to remember that any marginal change being measured or calculated is a result of or caused by a small marginal change in some other factor.

To calculate a marginal change of some kind, it is necessary to find the difference between an original value and the new value which resulted from the change in the controlling factor. In other words, the change in some value *caused by* the marginal change in another factor is needed. Throughout this text, a small triangle (actually the Greek letter delta) will be used as shorthand for "the change in." For example, Δ *corn yield* would be read as "the change in corn yield'' and would be the difference in corn yield before and after some change in an input affecting yield such as seed, fertilizer, or irrigation water. Although other inputs may also be necessary, there is an assumed fixed or constant amount being used. This does not mean they are unimportant, but this assumption serves to simplify the analysis.

THE PRODUCTION FUNCTION

A basic concept in economics is the *production function*. It is a systematic way of showing the relationship between different amounts of a resource or input that can be used to produce a product and the corresponding output or yield of that product. In other agricultural disciplines, the same relationship may be called a response curve, yield curve, or input/output relationship. By whatever name, a production function shows the amount of output that would be produced by using different amounts of a variable input. It can be presented in the form of a table, graph, or mathematical equation.

The first two columns of Table 2-1 are a tabular presentation of a production function. Different levels of the input which can be used to produce the product are shown in the first column, assuming all other inputs are held fixed. The amount of production expected from using each input level is shown in the second column labeled total physical product. In economics, output or yield is generally called total physical product, which will be abbreviated TPP.

Average and Marginal Physical Products

The production function provides the basic data which can be used to derive additional information about the relationship between the input and TPP. It is possible to calculate the average amount of output or TPP produced by each unit of input at each input level. This value is called average physical product

Table 2-1 Production Function in Tabular Form

Input level	Total physical product, TPP	Average physical product, APP	Marginal physical product, MPP
0	0	0	
			12.0
1	12	12.0	
			18.0
2	30	15.0	
			14.0
3	44	14.7	
			10.0
4	54	13.5	
			8.0
5	62	12.4	
			6.0
6	68	11.3	
			4.0
7	72	10.3	
			2.0
8	74	9.3	
			−2.0
9	72	8.0	
			−4.0
10	68	6.8	

(APP) and is shown in the third column of Table 2-1. APP is calculated by the formula

$$APP = \frac{\text{total physical product}}{\text{input level}}$$

In this example at 4 units of input, the APP is $54 \div 4 = 13.5$. The production function in Table 2-1 has an APP which increases over a short range and then decreases as more than 2 units of input are used. This is only one example of how APP may change with input level. Other types of production functions have an APP which declines continuously after the first unit of input, which is a common occurrence.

The first marginal concept to be introduced is marginal physical product (MPP), shown in the fourth column of Table 2-1. Remembering that marginal means additional or extra, MPP is *the additional or extra TPP produced by using an extra unit of input.* It requires measuring changes in both output and input.

Marginal physical product is calculated as

$$MPP = \frac{\Delta \text{ total physical product}}{\Delta \text{ input level}}$$

The numerator is the *change* in TPP caused by a *change* in the variable input, and the denominator is the actual amount of change in the input. For example, Table 2-1 indicates that using 4 units of input instead of 3 causes TPP to *increase* or change $+10$ units. Since this change was caused by a 1 unit increase or change in the input level, MPP would be found by dividing $+10$ by $+1$ to arrive at an MPP of $+10$. Observing the results of using 9 units of input instead of 8 shows that the change in TPP is *negative* or -2 units. Dividing this result by the 1 unit increase $(+1)$ in input causing the change in TPP, the MPP is -2. Marginal physical product can be positive or negative. It can also be zero if changing the input level causes no change in TPP. A negative MPP indicates too much variable input is being used *relative to* the fixed input(s) and this combination depresses TPP.

The example in Table 2-1 has the input increasing by increments of 1, which simplifies the calculation of MPP. Other examples and problems may show the input increasing by increments of 2 or more. In this case, the denominator in the formula for MPP must be the actual total change in the input. For example, if the input is changing by increments of 4, the denominator in the equation would be 4. The result is not an exact determination of MPP for the *last* unit of input but an average MPP for the 4 units in the change. Many times this will provide sufficient information for decision making unless the change in input between two possible input levels is fairly large. In this case, either more information should be obtained about expected output levels for

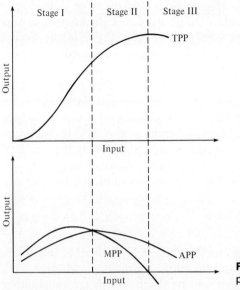

Figure 2-1 Graphical illustration of a production function.

intermediate levels of the variable input or more sophisticated mathematical techniques should be used.[1]

A Graphical Analysis

A production function and its corresponding APP and MPP can also be shown in graphical form. Figure 2-1 is a production function with the same general characteristics as the data in Table 2-1. Notice that TPP or output increases at an increasing rate as the input level is increased from zero. As the input level is increased further, TPP continues to increase, but now at a decreasing rate, and eventually begins to decline absolutely as too much variable input is used relative to the amount of fixed input(s) available.

Both Table 2-1 and Figure 2-1 illustrate several important relationships between TPP, APP, and MPP. Notice that as long as TPP is increasing at an increasing rate, MPP is increasing along with APP. At the point where TPP changes from increasing at an increasing rate to increasing at a decreasing rate, MPP reaches a maximum and then declines continuously, having a value of zero where TPP reaches its maximum. Where TPP is at its maximum, a very small change in the input level neither increases nor decreases output, and therefore MPP is zero.

APP increases over a slightly longer range than MPP before beginning to decline, which serves to illustrate an interesting relationship between APP and MPP. Notice that whenever MPP is above APP, APP will be increasing and

[1]The reader who has had a course in calculus will recognize that for a production function which is known and expressed as a continuous mathematical function, the exact MPP can be found by taking the first derivative of TPP with respect to input.

vice versa. This can be explained by remembering that to raise (lower) any average value, the additional or marginal value used in calculating the new average must be above (below) the old average. The only way baseball players can raise their batting averages is to have a daily batting average (the marginal or additional value) which is above their current season average.

The relationships between TPP, APP, and MPP are often used to divide this particular type of production function into three stages, as shown in Figure 2-1. Stage I begins at the zero input level and continues to the point where APP is maximum and equal to MPP. Stage II begins where APP is maximum and ends where MPP is zero (or TPP is maximum). Stage III is the range of input levels where MPP is negative and TPP is declining absolutely. The importance of these stages in determining the proper amount of input to use will be discussed later.

Law of Diminishing Returns

Table 2-1 and Figure 2-1 can be used to illustrate a law which is important from both a theoretical and practical standpoint in economics and other agricultural disciplines. Diminishing returns can be discussed in terms of either physical production or economic returns, but the discussion here will be limited to physical production.

The term *diminishing returns* as it relates to physical production can be applied to TPP, APP, or MPP. All three of these values begin to diminish or decline after some point as more of the variable input is used. However, the law of diminishing returns states that, *as additional units of a variable input are used in combination with one or more fixed inputs, the marginal physical product will eventually begin to decline.* Notice that this law is expressed in terms of marginal physical product or marginal production and not in terms of average or total production.

Two points in this definition need to be emphasized. First, for diminishing marginal returns to exist, one or more fixed inputs must be used in the production process in addition to the variable input. One acre of land or one head of livestock is often the fixed input used in defining a production function and illustrating diminishing marginal returns. Second, the definition does not preclude diminishing marginal returns from beginning with the first unit of input in agricultural production, which they often do. The importance and practical significance of diminishing marginal returns in the choice of an input level or output level will become apparent in the next two sections.

HOW MUCH INPUT TO USE

An important use of the information derived from a production function is in determining how much of the variable input to use. Given a goal of maximizing profit, the manager must select from all possible input levels the one which will result in the greatest profit.

Some help in this selection process can be found by referring back to the three stages in Figure 2-1. Any input level in Stage III can be eliminated from consideration as additional input causes TPP to decrease and MPP to be negative. For any input level in Stage III, the same output can be obtained with less input in one of the other stages. Choosing an input level in Stage III is clearly irrational, and a manager should not use these input levels even if the input is available at no cost.

Stage I covers the area where adding additional units of input causes the average physical product to increase. In this stage, adding another unit of input increases the productivity of all previous inputs as measured by average productivity or APP. If any input is to be used, it seems reasonable that a manager would want to use at least that input level which gives the greatest average physical product per unit of input. This point is at the boundary of Stage I and Stage II and represents the greatest efficiency in the use of the variable input. However, as will be shown shortly, profit can often be increased further by using more input even though APP is declining.

The above discussion effectively eliminates Stage I and Stage III from consideration in determining the profit-maximizing input level. This leaves only Stage II, which is the logical stage of production. Using only the physical information available at this point, it is not possible to determine which input level in Stage II will actually maximize profit. More information, specifically price information, is needed.

Marginal Value Product

Table 2-2 contains the same production function data as Table 2-1 with APP eliminated. As will be shown, APP is of little or no value in determining the profit-maximizing input level once Stage I is eliminated from consideration. Two additional columns of information needed to determine the optimum input level have been added to the table using an input price of $12 per unit and an output price of $2 per unit. *Marginal value product (MVP)* is the *additional or marginal income received from using an additional unit of input.* It is calculated by using the equation

$$MVP = \frac{\Delta \text{ total value product}}{\Delta \text{ input level}}$$

Total value product (TVP) for each input level is found by simply multiplying the quantity of output (TPP) times its selling price.[2] For example, the MVP for moving from 2 to 3 units of inputs is found by subtracting the total value product at 2 units of input ($60) from the total value product at 3 units ($88) and dividing by the change in input (1) to get MVP of $28. The other MVP values are obtained in a similar manner.

[2]Total value product is the same as total income or gross income. However, TVP is the term used in economics when discussing input levels and input use.

Table 2-2   Marginal Value Product, Marginal Input Cost, and the Optimum Input Level

(Input Price = $12 per Unit; Output Price = $2 per Unit)

Input level	Total physical product, TPP	Marginal physical product, MPP	Total value product, TVP ($)	Marginal value product, MVP ($)	Marginal input cost, MIC ($)
0	0		0		
		12		24	12
1	12		24		
		18		36	12
2	30		60		
		14		28	12
3	44		88		
		10		20	12
4	54		108		
		8		16	12
5	62		124		
		6		12	12
6	68		136		
		4		8	12
7	72		144		
		2		4	12
8	74		148		
		−2		−4	12
9	72		144		
		−4		−8	12
10	68		136		

Marginal Input Cost

Marginal input cost (MIC) is defined as *the change in total input cost or the addition to total input cost caused by using an additional unit of input*. It is calculated from the equation

$$MIC = \frac{\Delta \text{ total input cost}}{\Delta \text{ input level}}$$

Total input cost is equal to the quantity of input used times its price. For example, the MIC for moving from 2 to 3 units of input is found by subtracting the total input cost at 2 units ($24) from the cost at 3 units ($36) and dividing by the change in input (1) to find the MIC of $12.

Table 2-2 indicates that MIC is constant for all input levels. This should not be surprising if the definition of MIC is reviewed. The additional cost of acquiring and using an additional unit of input is equal to the price of the input, which is equal to MIC. This conclusion will always hold *provided* the input price does not change as more or less input is purchased.

The Decision Rule

The MVP and MIC values can now be compared and used to determine the optimum input level. The first few lines of Table 2-2 show MVP to be greater than MIC. In other words, the additional income received from using one more unit of input exceeds the additional cost of that input. Therefore, additional profit is being made. These relationships exist until the input level reaches 6 units. At this point the additional income from and additional cost of another unit of input are just equal. Using more than 6 units of input causes the additional income (MVP) to be less than additional cost (MIC), which causes profit to decline as more input is used.

The profit-maximizing input level is therefore at the point where MVP = MIC. If MVP is greater than MIC, additional profit can be made by using more input. When MVP is less than MIC, more profit can be made by using less input. Note that the profit-maximizing point is *not* at the input level which maximizes TVP or total income. Profit is maximized at a lower input level.

Obviously the profit-maximizing input level can also be found by calculating the total value product (total income) and total input cost at each input level and then subtracting cost from income to find the level where profit is greatest. This procedure has two disadvantages. First, it conceals the marginal effects of changes in the input level. Notice how diminishing marginal returns affect MVP as well as MPP causing MVP to decline until it finally equals MIC. Second, it takes more time to find the new optimum input level if the price of either the input or output changes. Using the MVP and MIC procedure requires only recalculating MVPs if output price changes before the MVP = MIC rule is applied. Similarly, a change in input price requires only substituting the new MIC values for the old. The reader should experiment with different input and output prices to determine their effect on MVP, MIC, and the optimum input level.

HOW MUCH OUTPUT TO PRODUCE

The discussion in the previous section concentrated on finding the input level which maximized profit. There is also a related question. How much output should be produced to maximize profit? To answer this question directly requires the introduction of two new marginal concepts.

Marginal Revenue

Table 2-3 is the same as the previous table except for the last two columns. *Marginal revenue (MR)* is defined as *the change in income or the additional income received from selling one more unit of output.* It is calculated from the equation

$$MR = \frac{\Delta \text{ total revenue}}{\Delta \text{ total physical product}}$$

where total revenue is the same as total income. Total revenue (TR) is used in place of total value product when discussing output levels. It is apparent from Table 2-3 that MR is constant and equal to the price of the output. This should not be surprising given the definition of MR presented above. *Provided the output price does not change as more or less output is sold,* which is typical for an individual farmer or rancher, MR will always equal the price of the output. The additional income received from selling one more unit of output will equal the price received for that output. However, if the selling price

Table 2-3 Marginal Revenue, Marginal Cost, and the Optimum Output Level
(Input Price = $12 per Unit; Output Price = $2 per Unit)

Input level	Total physical product, TPP	Marginal physical product, MPP	Total revenue, TR ($)	Marginal revenue, MR ($)	Marginal cost, MC ($)
0	0		0		
		12		2.00	1.00
1	12		24.00		
		18		2.00	0.67
2	30		60.00		
		14		2.00	0.86
3	44		88.00		
		10		2.00	1.20
4	54		108.00		
		8		2.00	1.50
5	62		124.00		
		6		2.00	2.00
6	68		136.00		
		4		2.00	3.00
7	72		144.00		
		2		2.00	6.00
8	74		148.00		
		-2			
9	72		144.00		
		-4			
10	68		136.00		

varies with changes in either quantity or quality of the output, MR must be calculated using the equation above.

Marginal Cost

Marginal cost (MC) is defined as *the change in cost or the additional cost incurred from producing another unit of output*. It is calculated from the equation

$$MC = \frac{\Delta \text{ total input cost}}{\Delta \text{ total physical product}} \quad \ni \$12 \text{ per unit Input cost}$$

where total input cost is the same as previously defined. In Table 2-3 marginal cost decreases slightly and then begins to increase as additional input is used. Notice the inverse relationship between MPP and MC. When MPP is declining (diminishing returns), MC is increasing, as it takes relatively more input to produce an additional unit of output.

The Decision Rule

In a manner similar to analyzing MVP and MIC, MR and MC are compared to find the profit-maximizing output level. When MR is greater than MC, the additional unit of output increases profit as the additional income exceeds the additional cost. Conversely, if MR is less than MC, producing the additional unit of output will decrease profit. *At the output level where MR = MC, profit will be at its maximum level.* In Table 2-3 this occurs at 68 units of output.

It should be no surprise that the optimum output level of 68 units is produced by the optimum input level of 6 units found in the previous section. There is only one profit-maximizing combination of input and output for a

Table 2-4   Determining the Profit-maximizing Nitrogen Fertilizer Level for Grass Hay Production

(Nitrogen at 20¢ per lb; Hay at 3¢ per lb)

Nitrogen fertilizer (lbs)	T T P Hay yield (lbs)	Marginal physical product, MPP	Marginal value product, MVP (¢)	Marginal input cost, MIC (¢)	Marginal revenue, MR (¢)	Marginal cost, MC (¢)
200	8,550					
250	9,375	16.5	49.5	20	3	1.2
300	10,050	13.5	40.5	20	3	1.5
350	10,575	10.5	31.5	20	3	1.9
400	10,950	7.5	22.5	20	3	2.7
450	11,175	4.5	13.5	20	3	4.4
500	11,250	1.5	4.5	20	3	13.3

given production function and a given set of prices. Once either the optimum input or output level is found the other value can be determined from the production function.

APPLYING THE MARGINAL PRINCIPLES

A common management problem is how much fertilizer to apply per acre for a certain crop. Table 2-4 illustrates the solution for this problem using the principles from the last two sections. The problem is how much nitrogen fertilizer to apply to a grass hay crop to maximize profit given certain prices for both nitrogen fertilizer and hay. The first two columns of Table 2-4 contain the production function data, which can often be obtained from experimental trials. Marginal physical product is calculated from these data and represents the additional pounds of hay produced by an additional pound of fertilizer within each 50-pound increment.

An examination of MVP and MIC shows they are never exactly equal. However, if the fertilizer can be applied only in 50-pound increments, the profit-maximizing level will be 400 pounds. The next 50-pound increment causes MVP to be less than MIC, and profit will be less because each additional pound of fertilizer will cost more than the additional income it generates. A similar conclusion can be drawn from examining marginal revenue and marginal cost, which indicates the profit-maximizing output level is 10,950 pounds of hay which is produced by using 400 pounds of fertilizer.

Several interesting questions can be asked and answered using the data in Table 2-4. For example, what is the effect of a change in the price of fertilizer if hay price is unchanged? The MVP and MIC columns indicate that the price of fertilizer (MIC) must fall to 13.5 cents per pound before 450 pounds would be the profit-maximizing level. Similarly, a fertilizer price above 22.5 cents (but not above 31.5 cents) would cause 350 pounds to be optimum.

What is the effect of a change in the price of hay given the 20-cent cost of fertilizer? MR and MC columns show that the price of hay would have to increase to 4.4 cents per pound before 11,175 pounds becomes the profit-maximizing output level. A hay price below 2.7 cents per pound (but not below 1.9 cents) would make 10,575 pounds the optimum production.

Price changes are common in agriculture, and they affect the optimum input and output levels as in this example. An increase in the input price or a decrease in the output price tends to lower the profit-maximizing input and output levels. Price increases for the output or price decreases for the input tend to increase the profit-maximizing input and output levels.

INPUT SUBSTITUTION

One of the basic decisions a farm or ranch manager must make is *how to produce* a given product. Most products require two or more inputs in the production process, but the manager can often choose the input combination or ratio to be used. The problem is one of determining if more of one input can be economically substituted for less of another and what is the least-cost combination of inputs to produce a given amount of output.

Substitution of one input for another occurs frequently in agricultural production. One grain can be substituted for another or forage for grain in a livestock ration, herbicides substitute for mechanical cultivation, and larger machinery saves labor. The manager must select that combination of inputs which will produce a given amount of output or do a certain task for the least cost. In other words, the problem is to find the least-cost combination of inputs, as this will maximize the profit from producing a given amount of output. The alert manager is always asking the question: Will a different input combination do the same job and do it for less cost?

Input Substitution Ratio

The first step in analyzing a substitution problem is to determine if it is physically possible to make a substitution and at what rate. Figure 2-2 illustrates three types of physical substitution ratios. In Figure 2-2a, the line *PP'* is an isoquant (from isoquantity) and shows the various combinations of the two inputs which will produce the same quantity of output. The substitution ratio, or the rate at which one input will substitute for another, is determined from the equation

$$\text{Substitution ratio} = \frac{\text{amount of input replaced}}{\text{amount of input added}}$$

where both the numerator and denominator are the differences or changes in the amount of inputs being used at two different points on the isoquant *PP'*.

In Figure 2-2a, moving from point A to point B means 4 units of input 1 are replaced by 2 additional units of input 2 in order to maintain the same level

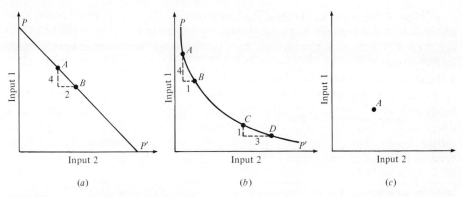

Figure 2-2   Three types of substitution.

of output. The substitution ratio is 4 ÷ 2 = 2. Since *PP'* is a straight line, the substitution ratio will always be 2 between any two points on this line. This is an example of a *constant rate of substitution.* Whenever the substitution ratio is equal to the same numerical value over the full range of possible input combinations, the inputs exhibit a constant rate of substitution.

A *decreasing rate of substitution* is illustrated in Figure 2-2*b*. The substitution ratio is 4 ÷ 1 = 4 when moving from point *A* to point *B* on isoquant *PP'*, but it is 1 ÷ 3 = ⅓ when moving from point *C* to point *D*. Many agricultural substitution problems will have a decreasing substitution ratio. As more of one input is substituted for another, it becomes increasingly difficult to make the substitution and still maintain the same level of output. More and more of the added input is needed to substitute for a unit of the input being replaced which causes the substitution ratio to decrease.

Figure 2-2*c* is an example where *no substitution* is possible. The desired output can be produced only by the input combination shown at point *A*. No substitution is possible, as no other combination will produce this amount of output. More of one input alone will not increase output. Both inputs must be increased, and increased the same proportion, to increase output.

The Decision Rule

Identifying the type of physical substitution which exists and calculating the substitution ratio are necessary steps, but they alone do not permit a determination of the least-cost input combination. Input prices are needed, and the ratio of the input prices is compared with the substitution ratio. The price ratio is calculated from the equation

$$\text{Price ratio} = \frac{\text{price of input being added}}{\text{price of input being replaced}}$$

A least-cost input combination is determined by finding the point where the substitution ratio and price ratio are equal.

Table 2-5   Selecting a Least-Cost Feed Ration
(Price of Grain = 4.4¢ per lb; Price of Hay = 3.0¢ per lb)*

Feed ration	Grain (lbs)	Hay (lbs)	Substitution ratio	Price ratio
A	825	1,350		
			2.93	1.47
B	900	1,130		
			2.60	1.47
C	975	935		
			2.20	1.47
D	1,050	770		
			1.87	1.47
E	1,125	630		
			1.47	1.47
F	1,200	520		
			1.07	1.47
G	1,275	440		

*Each ration is assumed to put the same weight gain on a feeder steer with a given beginning weight.

Table 2-5 is an application of this procedure. Each of the feed rations is a combination of grain and forage which will put the same pounds of gain on a feeder steer. The problem is to select the ration which provides this gain for the least cost. The fourth and fifth columns of Table 2-5 contain the substitution ratio and price ratio for each feed ration. The substitution ratio is declining and the price ratio is constant for the given prices.

If the substitution ratio is greater than the price ratio, the total cost of the feed ration can be reduced by moving to the next lower ration in the table. The converse is true if the substitution ratio is less than the price ratio. This can be verified by calculating the total cost of two adjacent rations for each situation. The least-cost ration in this example is found by moving to ration F, where the substitution ratio is equal to the price ratio.

In any substitution problem, the least-cost input combination depends on both the substitution ratio and the price ratio. The substitution ratios will remain the same over time provided the underlying physical and/or biological relationships do not change. However, the price ratio will change as the relative input prices change, which may result in a different input combination becoming the new least-cost combination. As the price of one input increases relative to the other, the new least-cost input combination will tend to have less of the higher-priced input and more of the now relatively less-expensive input.[3]

ENTERPRISE COMBINATIONS

The third basic decision to be made by a farm or ranch manager is *what to produce* or what combination of enterprises will maximize profit. A choice must be made from among all possible enterprises, which may include corn, wheat, soybeans, cotton, beef cattle, hogs, poultry, and others. Climate, soil,

[3]The reader should note that it is the price *ratio* and not the absolute prices which determine the least-cost combination. If both input prices double, the price ratio and least-cost combination are unchanged. However, profit will obviously decrease in this case.

range vegetation, and limits on other available inputs may restrict the list of possible enterprises to only a few on some farms and ranches. On others, the manager may have a large number of possible enterprises from which to select the profit-maximizing combination.

Competitive Enterprises

The first step in determining profit-maximizing enterprise combinations is to determine the existing physical relationships between the enterprises. Given a limited amount of land, capital, or some other input, the production from one enterprise can often be increased only by decreasing production from another enterprise. There is a trade-off or substitution to be considered when changing the enterprise combination. These are called *competitive* enterprises, as they are competing for the use of the same limited input at the same time.

Figure 2-3 illustrates two types of competitive enterprises. In the first graph, corn and soybeans are competing for the use of the same 100 acres of land. Planting all corn would result in the production of 12,000 bushels of corn and planting all soybeans would produce a total of 4,000 bushels. Other combinations of corn and soybeans totaling 100 acres would produce the combinations of corn and soybeans shown on the line connecting the above points. This line is called a *production possibility curve* (PPC), as it shows all combinations of corn and soybeans which can be produced from the given 100 acres.

Beginning with producing all corn, replacing an acre of corn with an acre of soybeans results in a loss of 120 bushels of corn and a gain of 40 bushels of soybeans. The trade-off or substitution ratio is 3, as 3 bushels of corn must be given up to gain 1 bushel of soybeans. With a straight-line production-possibility curve, this substitution ratio is the same between any two points on the PPC. This is an example of competitive enterprises with a *constant substitution ratio*.

Over a period of time a combination of crop enterprises may benefit each other because of better weed, disease and insect control, erosion control, and timeliness in planting and harvesting large acreages. This situation is shown in the second graph in Figure 2-3. The curved production-possibility curve causes

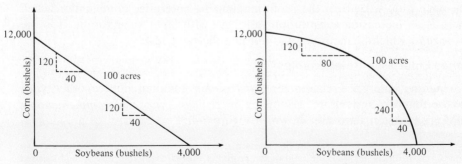

Figure 2-3 Production possibility curves for competitive enterprises.

the substitution ratio to be different for different combinations of the two enterprises. The substitution ratio is $120 \div 80 = 1.5$ near the top of the curve, and increases to $240 \div 40 = 6.0$ near the bottom of the curve. The enterprises are still competitive but have an *increasing substitution ratio*.

The most profitable combination of two competitive enterprises can be determined by comparing the substitution ratio and the price ratio. Each substitution ratio is calculated from the equation

$$\text{Substitution ratio} = \frac{\text{quantity of output lost}}{\text{quantity of output gained}}$$

where the quantities gained and lost are the *changes* in production between two points on the PPC. The price ratio is found from the equation

$$\text{Price ratio} = \frac{\text{unit price of the output being gained}}{\text{unit price of the output being lost}}$$

Profit is maximized by producing that enterprise combination where the substitution ratio is just equal to the price ratio.[4]

The procedure for determining the profit-maximizing enterprise combination is basically the same as for determining the least-cost input combination but with one exception. For enterprise combinations, when the price ratio is greater than the substitution ratio, substitution should continue by moving downward and to the right on the PPC. Conversely, a substitution ratio greater than the price ratio means too much substitution has taken place and the adjustment should be upward and to the left on the PPC. These decision rules are just another way of comparing the additional income with the income which will be lost from more substitution. If the additional income is greater than the income which is lost, the substitution should take place and vice versa.

When the enterprises have a constant substitution ratio, the profit-maximizing solution will be to produce all of one or the other enterprise and not a combination. An increasing substitution ratio will generally result in the production of a combination of the enterprises, with the combination depending on the current price ratio. Any change in the price(s) of the output that changes the price ratio will affect the profit-maximizing enterprise combination when there is an increasing substitution ratio. As with input substitution, it is the price *ratio* which is important and not just the price level.

Other Enterprise Relationships

Competitive enterprise relationships are the most common, but two other types can be found in agriculture. Examples of *supplementary* and *complementary* enterprise relationships are shown in Figure 2-4. Two enterprises are supple-

---

[4]This rule assumes total production costs are the same for any combination of the two enterprises. If this is not true, the ratio of the profit per unit of each enterprise should be used instead of the price ratio.

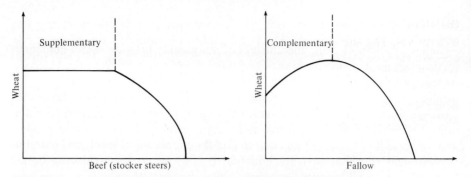

Figure 2-4 Supplementary and complementary enterprise relationships.

mentary if the production from one can be increased without affecting the production level of the other. In the first graph of Figure 2-4, beef production from stocker steers run on winter wheat pasture can be increased over a range without affecting the amount of wheat produced. The relationship eventually becomes competitive, as beef production cannot be increased indefinitely without affecting wheat production. In states such as Texas where landowners can lease hunting rights to hunters, the leasing of hunting rights is often a supplementary enterprise to livestock and crop production.

A manager should take advantage of supplementary relationships by producing both enterprises at least up to the point where they become competitive. If the supplementary enterprise shows any profit, however small, total profit will be increased by producing some of this product, since production of the primary enterprise does not change. The most profitable combination of the two enterprises may be in the competitive range, with the exact combination found by applying the rules for competitive enterprises.

A third type of enterprise relationship is complementary, where increasing the production level of one enterprise causes the production of the other to increase also. The second graph in Figure 2-4 illustrates a possible complementary relationship between wheat production and land left fallow. In many dryland wheat-production areas with limited rainfall, some land is left fallow or idle each year as a way to store part of one year's rainfall to be used by a wheat crop the following year. Leaving some acres fallow reduces the acres in wheat, but the per acre yield may increase enough that total production is actually greater than from planting all acres to wheat year after year.

A complementary enterprise should be increased at least up to the point where production from the primary enterprise (wheat in the example) is at maximum. This is true even if the complementary enterprise has no value, as production from the other enterprise is increasing at the same time. Enterprises are usually not complementary for all combinations and eventually become competitive. As with supplemental enterprises, the profit-maximizing combination may be in the competitive range as determined by the substitution and price ratios.

SUMMARY

Economic principles using the concept of marginality provide useful guidelines for managerial decision making. They have direct application to the basic decisions of how much to produce, how to produce, and what to produce. The production function which describes the relationship between input levels and corresponding output levels provides the basic information needed to determine the profit-maximizing input and output levels. Marginal value product and marginal input cost are equated to find the proper input level, and marginal revenue and marginal cost are equated to find the profit-maximizing output level. These are all marginal concepts which measure the changes in revenue and cost resulting from small changes in either input or output.

Substitution is an important concept when making decisions on how to produce and what to produce. Least-cost input combinations to produce a given amount of output are found by calculating substitution and price ratios, and the profit-maximizing combination of enterprises is found in a similar manner. Marginality plays an important role here, as the substitution ratios are calculated from small or marginal changes in the inputs or outputs.

The manager will seldom have sufficient information to use fully the economic principles of this chapter. This does not detract from the importance of these principles, but their application and use are often hindered by insufficient physical and biological data. Prices must also be estimated before the product is available for sale, which adds more uncertainty to the decision-making process. However, a complete understanding of the economic principles permits making changes in the right direction in response to price and other changes. The manager should continually search for better information to use in refining the decisions made through the use of these basic economic principles.

QUESTIONS FOR REVIEW AND FURTHER THOUGHT

1   In Table 2-2, assume the price of both the input and output have doubled. Calculate the new MVPs and MICs, and determine the profit-maximizing input level for the new prices. Now assume both prices have been cut in half and repeat the process. Explain your results. *Hint:* Think in terms of the relationship between the prices or their ratio.

2   Use several other price combinations for the production function data in Tables 2-2 and 2-3 and find the profit-maximizing input and output for each price combination.

3   Find an extension service or experiment station publication for your state which shows the results of a fertilizer or irrigation rate experiment. Do the results exhibit diminishing returns? Use the concepts of this chapter to find the profit-maximizing amount of fertilizer or irrigation water to use.

4   First double and then halve both prices used in Table 2-5 and find the new least-cost input combination in each case. Why is there no change? What would happen to profit in each case?

5   Identify some additional examples of crop and/or livestock enterprises which would have competitive, supplementary, and complementary relationships. Which type is the easiest to identify and therefore the most common?

REFERENCES

Barnard, C. S., and J. S. Nix: *Farm Planning and Control,* Cambridge University Press, Cambridge, 1973, chap. 2.

Doll, John P., and Frank Orazem: *Production Economics: Theory with Applications,* Grid, Inc., Columbus, Ohio, 1978, chaps. 2 and 3.

Heady, Earl O.: *Economics of Agricultural Production and Resource Use,* Prentice-Hall, Inc., Englewood Cliffs, N.J., 1952, chaps. 2, 4, 5, 6, and 7.

Osburn, Donald D., and Kenneth C. Schneeberger: *Modern Agriculture Management,* Reston Publishing Co., Reston, Va., 1978, chap. 2.

Vincent, Warren H. (ed.): *Economics and Management in Agriculture,* Prentice-Hall, Inc., Englewood Cliffs, N.J., 1962, chap. 3.

Chapter 3

Cost Concepts
in Economics

CHAPTER OBJECTIVES

    1 To demonstrate the use of the equal marginal principle in the allocation of limited resources

    2 To explain the importance of opportunity cost and its use in managerial decision making

    3 To clarify the difference between fixed and variable costs

    4 To identify the fixed costs and how to calculate them

    5 To show the use of fixed and variable costs in making short-run and long-run production decisions

    6 To explore economies of size and how they help explain changes in farm size and profitability

    7 To understand how the principle of comparative advantage explains the location of agricultural production

In Chapter 2, the profit-maximizing amount of a variable input was found by setting MVP = MIC. While this is true, it assumes sufficient input is available to set MVP = MIC for *all* possible uses of the input. In other words, this rule assumes the variable input can be purchased or is available in whatever quantity necessary to reach the profit-maximizing point in all possible uses. However, a manager often has only a limited amount of the input or a limited amount of capital available to purchase it and a large number of potential uses. This situation requires the use of another economic principle.

EQUAL MARGINAL PRINCIPLE

As capital and other inputs are often limited, managers must decide how a limited amount of input should be allocated or divided among many possible uses or alternatives. Decisions must be made on the best allocation of fertilizer between many acres or fields and different crops, irrigation water between fields and crops, and feed between different types of livestock. In addition, limited capital must first be allocated to the purchase of fertilizer, water, feed, and any other inputs. The *equal marginal principle* provides the guidelines and rules to ensure that the allocation is done in such a way that profit is maximized from the use of any limited input including capital.

The equal marginal principle can be stated as follows: *A limited input should be allocated among alternative uses in such a way that the marginal value products of the last unit are equal in all uses.*

Table 3-1 is an application of this principle where irrigation water must be allocated among three crops in three fields of equal size. The MVPs are obtained from the production function relating water use to the yield of each crop and from the respective crop prices.

Assume a maximum of 2,400 acre-inches of water is available and can be applied only in increments of 4 acre-inches. The limited supply of water would be allocated among the three crops in the following manner using the MVPs to make the decisions. The first 400 acre-inches (4 acre-inches on 100 acres) would be allocated to cotton, as it has the highest MVP. The second 400 acre-inches would be allocated to grain sorghum, as it has the second highest MVP. In a similar manner, the third 400 acre-inches would be used on cotton and the fourth, fifth, and sixth 400 acre-inch increments on wheat, grain sorghum, and cotton, respectively. Each successive 400 acre-inch increment is allocated to the field which has the highest MVP remaining after the previous allocations.

The final allocation is 4 acre-inches on wheat, 8 on grain sorghum, and 12 on cotton. Each final 4 acre-inch increment on each crop has an MVP of $1,200, which satisfies the equal marginal principle. If more water was avail-

Table 3-1   Application of the Equal Marginal Principle to the Allocation of Irrigation Water*

Irrigation water (acre-inches)	Marginal value products ($)		
	Wheat (100 acres)	Grain sorghum (100 acres)	Cotton (100 acres)
4	1,200	1,600	1,800
8	800	1,200	1,500
12	600	800	1,200
16	300	500	800
20	50	200	400

* Each application of 4 acre-inches on a crop is a total use of 400 acre-inches (4 acre-inches times 100 acres).

able, the final allocation would obviously be different. For example, if 3,600 acre-inches were available, it would be allocated 8 acre-inches to wheat, 12 to grain sorghum, and 16 to cotton. This equates the MVPs of the last 4 acre-inch increment on each crop at $800, which again satisfies the equal marginal principle.

The profit-maximizing property of this principle can be demonstrated for the 2,400 acre-inch example above. If the 4 acre-inches on wheat were allocated to grain sorghum or cotton, $1,200 of income would be lost and $800 gained for a net loss of $400. The same loss would be incurred if the last 4 acre-inch increment was removed from either grain sorghum or cotton and reallocated to another crop. When the MVPs are equal, profit cannot be increased by a different allocation of the limited input. If the MVPs are not equal, profit can be increased by reallocating the limited input until they are.

The equal marginal principle can also be presented in graphical form as in Figure 3-1, where there are only two alternative uses for the limited input. The problem is to allocate the input between the two uses, keeping the MVPs equal, so that input quantity $0a$ plus quantity $0b$ just equals the total amount of input available. If $0a$ plus $0b$ is less than the total input available, more should be allocated to each use, again keeping the MVPs equal, until the input is fully used. There would have to be a decrease in the input used on both alternatives if $0a$ plus $0b$ exceeded the total input available.

The equal marginal principle applies not only to purchased inputs but also to those which are already owned or available, such as land, the manager's labor, and machinery time. It also prevents making the mistake of maximizing profit from one enterprise by using the input until MVP = MIC and not having enough to use on other enterprises. Maximizing profit from the *total* business requires the proper allocation of limited inputs, which will not necessarily result in maximizing the profit from any *single* enterprise.

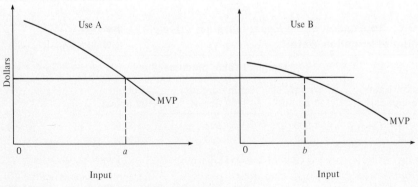

Figure 3-1 Illustration of equal marginal principle.

OPPORTUNITY COST

Opportunity cost is an economic concept closely related to the equal marginal principle. It is a basic concept but one which can be easily overlooked when making managerial decisions. Opportunity cost recognizes the fact that every input has an alternative use even if the alternative is nonuse. Once an input is committed to a particular use, it is no longer available for any other alternative, and the income from the alternative must be foregone.

Opportunity cost is defined as *the value of the product not produced because an input was used for another purpose.* It may also be defined as *the income that could have been received if the input had been used in its most profitable alternative use.* These definitions of opportunity cost should be kept in mind as a manager makes decisions on input use. The *real* cost of an input may not be its purchase price. Its real cost in any one use is the income it would have earned in its next best alternative use, or its *opportunity cost.* If this is greater than the income expected from the planned use of the input, the manager should reconsider the decision.

The concept can be illustrated by referring back to Table 3-1. If the first 400 acre-inches of water is put on the 100 acres of wheat, the opportunity cost is $1,800. This income would be lost by not putting the water to its best alternative use, which is on cotton. Since the expected return from wheat is $1,200, the higher opportunity cost indicates this first unit of water is not earning its greatest possible income. If the first 400 acre-inches was used on cotton, the opportunity cost is $1,600 (from grain sorghum), indicating there is no more profitable use for this water, as the expected income exceeds the opportunity cost. The same line of reasoning can be used to determine the most profitable use of each successive 400 acre-inch increment of water.

Opportunity cost is also useful in selecting the most profitable enterprise combination. Whenever the opportunity cost of land, labor, machinery, or capital is greater in some other enterprise than the return from their current use, some of these inputs should be reallocated to the alternative enterprise. This reallocation should continue until their opportunity costs are equal to or less than the present earnings. A little thought will reveal this to be just another way of applying the equal marginal principle.

A problem facing many managers is how to place a value on owned inputs for planning and decision-making purposes. Items such as land, buildings, breeding stock, machinery, and the owner's labor and management may not be purchased each year, so that no purchase price is available. These inputs can be valued at the opportunity cost of their most profitable alternative use outside the farm or ranch business. This is the real or true cost of using them to produce agricultural products.

It is difficult to evaluate directly the opportunity cost of inputs such as land, fences, buildings, and machinery in terms of nonagricultural alternative uses. These items may have a very low opportunity cost in their present form, but they represent a substantial capital investment. This capital investment is generally used to estimate their opportunity cost. First, the total dollar value of these types of owned assets is estimated along with the opportunity cost of capital. An interest rate equal to the return on savings accounts or the current cost of borrowed capital is often used as a conservative opportunity cost for capital. The next step is to multiply this interest rate by the total value of the owned assets to find their opportunity cost.

This procedure estimates the opportunity cost indirectly by converting the assets into their dollar value, and it will be used in several different applications throughout this text. However, it cannot be applied to noncapital inputs such as labor and management. The opportunity cost for these inputs is estimated directly as the income they would earn in their best nonagricultural alternative use.

COSTS

A number of cost concepts are used in economics. Marginal input cost was studied in Chapter 2. Seven additional cost concepts and their abbreviations are:

1 Total fixed cost (TFC)
2 Average fixed cost (AFC)
3 Total variable cost (TVC)
4 Average variable cost (AVC)
5 Total cost (TC)
6 Average total cost (ATC)
7 Marginal cost (MC)

All these costs are output-related. Marginal cost, which was also studied in Chapter 2, is the additional cost of producing an additional unit of output. The others are either the total or average costs for producing a given amount of output.

Short Run and Long Run

Before these costs are discussed in some detail, it is necessary to distinguish between what economists call the short run and the long run. These are time concepts, but they are not defined as fixed periods of calendar time. The short run is that period of time during which one or more of the production inputs is fixed in amount and cannot be changed. For example, at the beginning of the planting season it may be too late to increase or decrease the amount of cropland owned or rented. The current crop production cycle would be a short-run period, as land is fixed in amount.

Over a longer period of time, land may be purchased, sold, or leased or leases may expire and the amount of land available may be increased or decreased. The long run is defined as that period of time during which the quantity of all necessary productive inputs can be changed. In the long run, a business can expand by acquiring additional inputs or go out of existence by selling all its inputs. The actual calendar length of the long run as well as the short run will vary considerably depending upon the situation and circumstances. Depending on which input(s) are fixed, the short run may be anywhere from several days to several years. One year or one crop or livestock production cycle are common short-run periods in agriculture.

Fixed Costs

The costs associated with owning a fixed input or resource are called fixed costs. These are the costs that are incurred even if the input is not used, and there may be additional costs if it is actually used in producing some product. Fixed costs do not change as the level of production changes in the short run but can change in the long run as the quantity of the fixed input changes. Since there need not be any fixed inputs owned in the long run, fixed costs exist only in the short run and are equal to zero in the long run.

Another characteristic of fixed costs is that they are not under the control of the manager in the short run. They exist and at the same level regardless of how much or how little the resource is used. The only way they can be avoided is to sell the item, which can be done in the long run.

Total fixed cost (TFC) is simply the summation of the several types of fixed costs. Depreciation, insurance, repairs, taxes (property taxes, not income taxes), and interest are the usual components of TFC. They are easily remembered as the "DIRTI 5" costs, where DIRTI is derived from the first letter of each of the fixed cost items. Repairs may not always be included as a fixed cost, as they tend to increase with increased use of the resource. However, some minimum level of repairs may be needed to keep a resource in working order even if it is not used. For this reason, some of the repair expenditure is sometimes included as a fixed cost, particularly for buildings.

The capital invested in a fixed resource has an opportunity cost, and interest is included as a fixed cost to account for this cost. The interest component of total fixed cost is commonly calculated by the formula

$$\text{Interest} = \frac{\text{purchase price} + \text{salvage value}}{2} \times \text{interest rate}$$

where the interest rate is the opportunity cost of capital. This equation gives the interest charge for the average value of the item over its life and reflects the fact that it is decreasing in value over time because depreciation is also being charged.[1]

---

[1]This equation is widely used but only approximates the actual opportunity cost of the investment in the asset. For a more accurate method of determining total fixed cost see Ronald D. Kay, "An Improved Method for Calculating Ownership Costs," *Journal of the American Society of Farm Managers and Rural Appraisers,* vol. 38, no. 1, April 1974.

Average fixed cost (AFC) is found by the equation

$$AFC = \frac{TFC}{output}$$

where output is measured in physical units. Since TFC is a fixed or constant value by definition, AFC will decline continuously as output is increased. One way to lower the cost of producing a given product is to get more output from the fixed resource. This will always lower the AFC per unit of output.

Fixed costs can be either cash or noncash expenses. They can be easily overlooked or underestimated because a large part of total fixed cost can be noncash expenses as shown in the following chart.

Expense item	Cash expense	Noncash expense
Depreciation		X
Interest on the investment	X	X
Repairs	X	
Taxes, property	X	
Insurance	X	X

Depreciation is always a noncash expense, as there is no annual cash outlay for this fixed cost. Repairs and property taxes are always cash expenses, and interest and insurance may be either. If money is borrowed to purchase the asset, there will be some cash interest expense. When the item is purchased with the buyer's own capital, the interest charge would be opportunity cost on this capital, and there is no cash payment to a lender. Insurance would be a cash expense if insurance is carried with an insurance company or noncash if the risk of loss is assumed by the owner. In the latter case, there would be no annual cash outlay, but the insurance charge should still be included in fixed costs to cover the possibility of damage to or loss of the item from fire, windstorm, etc.

This distinction between cash and noncash expenses does not imply that noncash expenses are any less important than cash expenses. In the short run, noncash expenses do mean less cash is needed to meet current expenses. However, income must be sufficient to cover all expenses in the long run if the business is to survive and prosper.

Variable Costs

Variable costs are those which the manager has control over at a given point in time. They can be increased or decreased at the manager's discretion and will increase as production is increased. Items such as feed, fertilizer, seed, chemicals, fuel, and livestock health expenses are examples of variable costs. A manager has control over these expenses in the short run, and they will tend to increase as total production is increased.

Total variable cost (TVC) can be found by summing each of the individual variable costs, each of which is equal to the quantity of the input purchased times its price. Average variable cost (AVC) is calculated from the equation

$$AVC = \frac{TVC}{output}$$

where output is again measured in physical units. Average variable cost may be either increasing or decreasing depending upon the underlying production function and the output level. For the production function illustrated in Figure 2-1, AVC will initially decrease as output is increased and then will increase beginning at the point where average physical product starts to decline.

Variable costs exist in both the short run and the long run. As there need not be any fixed inputs, all costs are considered to be variable costs in the long run. The distinction between a fixed and variable cost also depends on the exact point in time where the next decision is to be made. Fertilizer is generally a variable cost. Yet once it has been purchased and applied, the manager no longer has any control over the size of this expenditure. It must be considered a fixed cost for the remainder of the crop season, and future decisions must be made accordingly. Labor cost and cash rent for land are similar examples. After a labor or lease contract is signed, the manager cannot change the amount of money obligated, and the salary or rent must be considered a fixed cost for the duration of the contract.

Total and Marginal Costs

Total cost (TC) is the sum of total fixed cost and total variable cost (TC = TFC + TVC). In the short run, it will increase only as TVC increases, as TFC is a constant value.

Average total cost (ATC) can be found by one of two methods. For a given output level it is equal to AFC + AVC. It can also be calculated from the equation

$$ATC = \frac{TC}{output}$$

which will give the same result. Average total cost will typically be decreasing at low output levels because AFC is decreasing rapidly and AVC may be decreasing also. At higher output levels, AFC will be decreasing less rapidly and AVC will eventually increase and be increasing at a faster rate than the rate of decrease in AFC. This combination causes ATC to increase.

Marginal cost (MC) is defined as the change in total cost divided by the change in output.

$$MC = \frac{\Delta\ TC}{\Delta\ output} \qquad or \qquad MC = \frac{\Delta\ TVC}{\Delta\ output}$$

It is also equal to the change in total variable cost divided by the change in output. Since TC = TFC + TVC and TFC is constant, the only way TC can change is from a change in TVC. Therefore, MC can be calculated either way with the same result.

Cost Curves

Relationships among the seven output-related cost concepts can be illustrated graphically by a series of curves. The shape of these cost curves depends upon the characteristics of the underlying production function. Figure 3-2 contains cost curves representative of the general production function shown in Figure 2-1. Other types of production functions would have cost curves with different shapes.

The relationships among the three total costs are shown in the top portion of Figure 3-2. Total fixed cost is constant and unaffected by output level. Total variable cost is always increasing, first at a decreasing rate and, past the dashed line, at an increasing rate. Because it is the sum of total fixed cost and total variable cost, the total cost curve has the same shape as the total variable cost curve. However, it is always higher by a vertical distance equal to total fixed cost.

The general shape and relationship of the average and marginal cost curves are shown in the bottom portion of Figure 3-2. Average fixed cost is always

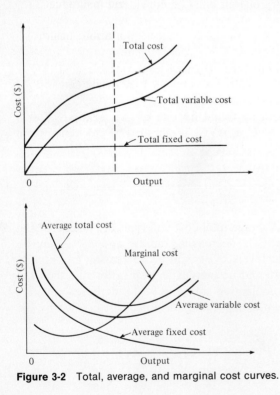

Figure 3-2 Total, average, and marginal cost curves.

declining but at a decreasing rate. The other two average curves are U-shaped, declining at first, reaching a minimum, and then increasing at higher levels of output. Notice that they are not an equal distance apart. The vertical distance between them is equal to average fixed cost, which changes with output level. This accounts for their slightly different shape and for the fact that their minimum points are at two different output levels.

The marginal cost curve will generally be increasing. However, for this particular production function it decreases over a short range before starting to increase. Notice that the marginal cost curve crosses both average curves at their minimum points. As discussed earlier, as long as the marginal value is below the average value, the latter will be decreasing and vice versa. For this reason, the marginal cost curve will always cross the average cost curves at their minimum point if such a point exists.

Application of Cost Concepts

Table 3-2 is an example of some cost figures for the common problem of determining the profit-maximizing stocking rate for a pasture which is fixed in size. It is illustrative of many similar problems where an understanding of the different cost concepts is an aid to good planning and decision making.

Total fixed costs are assumed to be $3,000 in the example. This would cover the annual opportunity cost on the land and improvements, depreciation on fences and water facilities, repairs on the same items, and insurance. Variable costs are assumed to be $295 per steer (steers are the variable input in this example). This includes the cost of the steer, transportation, health expenses, interest on the investment in the steer, and any other expenses which increase along with the number of steers purchased.

Since the size of the pasture and the amount of forage available are both

Table 3-2   Illustration of Cost Concepts Applied to a Stocking-Rate Problem*

Number of steers	Output (hundred-weight of beef)	MPP	TFC ($)	TVC ($)	TC ($)	AFC ($)	AVC ($)	ATC ($)	MC ($)	MR ($)
0	0		3,000	0	3,000	—	—	—		
		7.2							40.97	50.00
10	72		3,000	2,950	5,950	41.67	40.97	82.64		
		7.6							38.82	50.00
20	148		3,000	5,900	8,900	20.27	39.86	60.13		
		7.7							38.31	50.00
30	225		3,000	8,850	11,850	13.33	39.33	52.66		
		7.0							42.14	50.00
40	295		3,000	11,800	14,800	10.17	40.00	50.17		
		6.5							45.38	50.00
50	360		3,000	14,750	17,750	8.33	40.97	49.30		
		6.0							49.17	50.00
60	420		3,000	17,700	20,700	7.14	42.14	49.28		
		5.5							53.64	50.00
70	475		3,000	20,650	23,650	6.32	43.47	49.79		
		5.0							59.00	50.00
80	525		3,000	23,600	26,600	5.71	44.95	50.66		
		4.5							65.56	50.00
90	570		3,000	26,550	29,550	5.26	46.58	51.84		
		4.0							73.75	50.00
100	610		3,000	29,500	32,500	4.92	48.36	53.28		

*Total fixed cost is $3,000 and variable costs are $295 per steer. Selling price of the steers is assumed to be $50 per hundredweight.

limited, running more and more steers will eventually cause the average weight gain per steer to decline. This is reflected in diminishing returns and a declining MPP when more than 30 steers are placed in the pasture. Total beef sold off the pasture still increases but at a decreasing rate as more steers compete for the limited amount of forage.

The cost figures in Table 3-2 have the usual or expected pattern as production or output is increased. TFC remains constant while both TVC and TC are increasing. AFC declines rapidly at first and then continues to decrease but at a slower rate. AVC, ATC, and MC decline initially, reach a minimum at some output level, and then begin to increase.

The profit-maximizing output level was defined in Chapter 2 to be where MR = MC. A point of exact equality does not exist in Table 3-2, but 60 steers and 420 hundredweight of beef produced would be the profit-maximizing levels. At this point, MC is slightly less than MR while MC is greater than MR at 70 steers. This indicates that the additional cost of another 10 steers is greater than the additional income and that less profit would be made with 70 steers than with 60.

However, the profit-maximizing point depends upon the selling price and the variable cost per steer. Looking at the MC column, if the selling price was expected to be $53.64 or higher, the most profitable number of steers would be 70 but it would be 50 if the selling price was expected to be $45.38 or lower. A change in the variable cost per steer (primarily from a change in the cost of the steer) will cause MC to change also and may result in a different profit-maximizing point.

At a price of $50 and running 60 steers, the profit is $300 (total income of $21,000 minus total cost of $20,700). For a price of $45.38, the profit-maximizing point would be 50 steers. However, the ATC per hundredweight at this point is $49.30. This means a loss of $3.92 per hundredweight or a total loss of $1,411. Should any steers be purchased if the expected selling price is less than the ATC?

The answer to this question is yes for some situations. Referring again to Table 3-2, notice there would be a loss equal to TFC ($3,000) if no steers were purchased. This loss would exist in the short run but could be avoided in the long run by selling the land, which would eliminate the fixed costs. However, the fixed costs exist in the short run and the relevant question is: Can a profit be made or the loss reduced to less than $3,000 in the short run by purchasing some steers? Steers should not be purchased if it would result in a loss greater than $3,000, since the loss could be minimized at $3,000 by not purchasing any.

Variable costs are under the control of the manager and can be reduced to zero by not purchasing any steers. Therefore, no variable costs should be incurred unless the selling price is at least equal to or greater than AVC. This will provide sufficient income to cover the total variable costs. If the selling price is greater than AVC but less than ATC, the income would cover variable costs with some left over to pay part of the fixed costs. There would be a loss, but it would be less than $3,000. In other words, for some prices the loss can be minimized by producing some beef.

If the expected selling price is less than the lowest possible AVC, income would be less than TVC and the loss greater than $3,000. No steers should be purchased in this situation in order to minimize the loss at $3,000. In Table 3-2, the lowest AVC is $39.33 and the lowest ATC is $49.28. The loss would be minimized by not purchasing steers when the expected selling price is less than $39.33 and by purchasing steers when the expected selling price is between $39.33 and $49.28. In the last situation, the loss is minimized by following the MR = MC rule.

Each of the above short-run situations can be summarized in the following set of rules:

1 *Expected selling price is greater than ATC.* A profit can be made and is maximized by producing where MR = MC.

2 *Expected selling price is less than ATC but greater than AVC.* A loss is expected, but the loss will be less than total fixed cost and minimized by producing at a point where MR = MC.

3 *Expected selling price is less than AVC.* A loss is expected but can be minimized by *not* producing anything. The loss will be equal to TFC.

A long-run expected selling price which is less than ATC will result in continual losses. In this case, the fixed asset(s) should be sold (fixed costs eliminated) and the money invested in a more profitable alternative. However, short-run losses may occur during the wait for an expected increase in the selling price. It is hoped that future profits will make up for current losses.

ECONOMIES OF SIZE

Economists and managers are interested in farm size and the relationship between costs and size for a number of reasons. The following are examples of questions being asked which relate to farm size and costs. What is the most profitable farm size? Can larger farms produce food and fiber cheaper? Are large farms more efficient? Will family farms disappear and be replaced by large corporate farms? Will the number of farms continue to decline? The answers to all these questions depend at least in part on what happens to costs and the cost per unit of output as farm size increases.

First, how is farm size measured? Number of livestock, number of acres, number of full-time workers, net worth, total assets, profit, and other factors have all been used to measure size, and all have some advantages and disadvantages. For example, number of acres is a common and convenient measure of farm size but should be used only to compare farm sizes in a limited geographical area where farm type, soil type, and climate are very similar. It is obvious that 100 acres of irrigated vegetables in California is not the same size operation as 100 acres of arid range land in neighboring Arizona or Nevada.

Gross farm income or total revenue is a common measure of farm size. It has the advantage of converting everything into the common denominator of the dollar. This and other measures which in dollar terms are better than any physical measure for measuring and comparing farm size in widely different farming regions.

Size in the Short Run

In the short run, one or more inputs are fixed in amount, with land often being the fixed input. Given this fixed input, there will be a short-run average total cost curve as shown in Figure 3-3. Short-run average cost curves will typically be U-shaped, with the average cost increasing at higher levels of production because the limited fixed input makes additional production more and more difficult and therefore increases average cost per unit of output.

For simplicity, size is measured as the output of a single product in Figure 3-3. The product can be produced at the lowest average cost per unit by producing the quantity $0a$. However, this may not be the profit-maximizing quantity, as profit is maximized at the output level where marginal revenue is equal to marginal cost. Since output price is equal to marginal revenue, a price of P' would maximize profit by producing the quantity $0b$. A higher or lower price would cause output to increase or decrease to correspond with the point where the new price is equal to marginal cost.

Because of a fixed input such as land, output can be increased in the short run only by intensifying production. This means the use of more variable inputs such as fertilizer, chemicals, irrigation water, labor, and machinery time. However, the limited fixed input tends to increase average costs as production is increased past some point and a production limit is eventually reached. Ad-

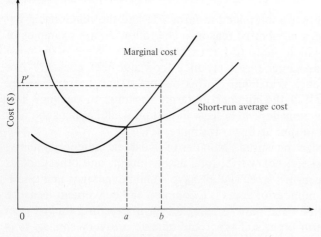

Size (production level)

Figure 3-3 Farm size in short run.

ditional production is possible only by acquiring more of the fixed input, which is a long-run problem.

Size in the Long Run

The economics of farm size is more interesting when discussed in a long-run context. This gives the manager time to adjust all inputs to the level which will result in the desired farm size. One measure of the relationship between output and costs as farm size increases is expressed in the following ratio:

$$\frac{\text{Percent change in costs}}{\text{Percent change in output value}}$$

Both changes are calculated in monetary terms to allow combining the cost of the many inputs and the value of several outputs into one figure. The above ratio can have three possible outcomes called *decreasing costs, constant costs,* or *increasing costs.*

Ratio value	Type of costs
< 1	Decreasing
= 1	Constant
> 1	Increasing

These three possible results are also called, respectively, *increasing returns to size, constant returns to size,* and *decreasing returns to size.* Decreasing costs means increasing returns to size and vice versa. These relationships are shown in Figure 3-4 using a long-run average cost curve which is the average cost per unit of output. When decreasing costs exist, the average cost per unit of output is decreasing, so that the average *profit* per unit of output is increasing. Therefore, increasing returns to size are said to exist. The same line of reasoning

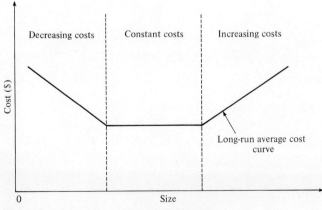

Figure 3-4 Possible size-cost relationships.

explains the relation between constant costs and constant returns and between increasing costs and decreasing returns.

Studies on the economics of size are concerned with identifying which type of costs and returns exist for a given farm type and hence the shape of the long-run average cost curve (LRAC). A short-run average cost curve (SRAC) exists for each and every possible farm size as defined by the amount of the fixed input available. Theoretically an infinite number of SRAC curves exist. Two such curves are shown in Figure 3-5 along with their relation to the LRAC curve. The latter can be thought of as the "envelope curve" containing a point on each of the infinite number of SRAC curves. Any point on the LRAC can be attained by selecting a given SRAC curve with its associated farm size and then operating at the point where it is just tangent to the LRAC curve.

The answers to the questions raised at the beginning of this section depend in full or in part on the shape of the LRAC curve for actual farms and ranches. If it is falling, there is an incentive for farmers to increase the size of their business as average costs are decreasing and profit per unit of output is increasing given fixed output prices. Conversely, if the LRAC curve is rising after some point, as is commonly assumed, there will be little or no incentive to continue increasing farm size, as costs are increasing and profit per unit of output will begin to decrease.

Numerous studies have shown that the long-run average cost curve for farms declines rapidly at first, as shown in Figure 3-5. The LRAC curve then declines more slowly, with studies showing that most of the decline has taken place at a farm size equivalent to what two full-time workers can produce. This result is fairly consistent regardless of farm type. What is less clear is

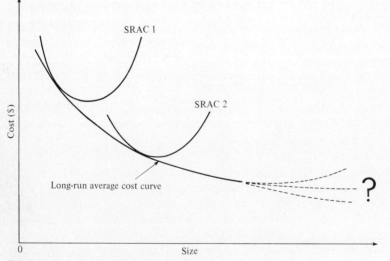

Figure 3-5 Long-run average-cost curve.

whether or not these economies of size continue for even larger and larger farms. In other words, does the LRAC curve continue to decrease because of economies of size, does it become flat, or does it begin to increase because of diseconomies of size?

Economies of Size Economies of size or increasing returns to size exist when the LRAC curve is decreasing. These economies can come from a number of sources, including the spreading of total fixed costs over a larger amount of output. (Remember the shape of the average fixed cost curve.) Full utilization of labor, machinery, and buildings is another factor. These two factors account for much of the initial decrease in the LRAC curve. Other possible economies of size include price discounts for volume purchasing of inputs, possible price advantages when selling large amounts of output, and added advantages of more specialized management. Larger tractors and buildings also tend to cost less per horsepower and per square foot than smaller ones. These factors all combine to exert a downward pressure on the LRAC curve.

Diseconomies of Size Diseconomies of size exist when the LRAC curve is increasing, and this combination discourages further increases in farm size. Economists have long assumed a LRAC curve will eventually begin to rise as business size continues to increase. A lack of sufficient managerial skill to keep a large business running smoothly and efficiently is used to explain the rising LRAC curve. Related to this is the need to hire, train, supervise, and coordinate the activities of a larger labor force, which becomes more difficult as size increases. Another diseconomy of size in agriculture is the dispersion over a larger geographical area as size increases. This increases travel time and the cost of getting to and from work and from field to field. It also makes management and labor supervision more difficult.

Figure 3-5 indicates some uncertainty about the shape of the LRAC curve for larger farm sizes. Both economies and diseconomies of size probably exist for these farm sizes, with their relative strengths determining what happens to the LRAC curve. The studies mentioned previously generally show a rapidly decreasing LRAC curve which then becomes relatively flat over a wide range of sizes. Insufficient data usually prevent arriving at a general conclusion about the shape of the LRAC curve for very large farm sizes. The relatively poor success of some very large farming operations in the United States is cited as evidence of diseconomies of size. However, there are also some very successful large farm and ranch operations.

One example of the initial economies of size is shown in Table 3-3 for cash grain farms in northern Illinois. Machinery investment per acre declines for each successively larger farm size. Labor costs per acre decline continuously, and annual machinery cost per acre declines for all but the largest farm size. The largest farm size group has a nearly $20 per acre cost advantage over the smallest size for the combined machinery and labor cost per acre. Similar results can be found for other farm types and in other states. Unfortunately

**Table 3-3   Machinery and Labor Costs by Farm Size—Northern
Illinois Grain Farms with a Soil Rating 86 to 100 (1976)**

	Farm size (acres)					
	260–339	340–499	500–649	650–799	800–949	>950
Machinery investment per acre ($)	79.00	78.07	76.02	73.59	71.60	71.08
Machinery costs per acre ($)	49.39	46.75	45.93	42.70	41.24	43.16
Labor costs per acre ($)	34.13	26.62	23.36	22.49	22.38	20.73
Total machinery and labor cost ($)	83.52	73.37	69.29	65.19	63.62	63.89

Source: *1976 Summary of Illinois Farm Business Records,* Cooperative Extension Service Circular 1140, University of Illinois.

there are not sufficient data to determine these costs for very large crop farms of several thousand acres or more.

COMPARATIVE ADVANTAGE

Certain crops can be grown in only limited areas because of specific soil and climatic requirements. However, even those crops and livestock which can be raised over a broad geographical area often have production concentrated in one region. For example, why do Iowa farmers specialize in corn and soybean production while Kansas farmers specialize in wheat production? All three crops can be grown in each state. Regional specialization in the production of agricultural commodities and other products is explained by the *principle of comparative advantage.*

While livestock and some crops can be raised over a broad geographical area, the yields, production costs, and profit may be different in each area. The principle of comparative advantage states that *individuals or regions will tend to specialize in the production of those commodities for which their resources give them a relative or comparative advantage.* It is *relative* yields, costs, and profits which are important for this principle.

An illustration of this principle using yields is shown below. Region A has an *absolute advantage* in the production of both crops because of the higher yields. However, Region A must give up 2½ bushels of corn for every bushel of wheat it grows while Region B has to give up only 2 bushels of corn to get a bushel of wheat. Region B has an *absolute disadvantage* in the production of both crops but a relative or *comparative advantage* in the production of wheat, since it gives up less corn for a bushel of wheat than Region A.

	Yield per acre	
	Region A	Region B
Corn	100	60
Wheat	40	30

Wheat farmers in Region B would be willing to give up 0.5 bushel of wheat to get a bushel of corn, and corn farmers in Region A would be willing to take 0.4 bushel or more of wheat for a bushel of corn. Assume Region A specializes in corn production and Region B in wheat production. Farmers in both regions would be willing to trade if 0.4 to 0.5 bushel of wheat could be exchanged for a bushel of corn. Farmers in each region could obtain the product from the other region at less cost than raising it themselves and therefore will tend to specialize in producing the product for which they have the comparative advantage.

Specialization can also make the combined regions better off. Assume there are 100 acres in each region and each plants one-half corn and one-half wheat. Total production is 8,000 bushels of corn and 3,500 bushels of wheat. If Region A specializes in corn and Region B in wheat, total production is 10,000 bushels of corn and 3,000 bushels of wheat. As long as the income from an additional 2,000 bushels of corn is more than the income lost from 500 bushels less wheat, specialization increases the total value of the crops produced. Trade between the regions allows each to obtain the final desired combination of the two products.

SUMMARY

This chapter continued the discussion of economic principles which began in Chapter 2. The equal marginal principle was discussed as the decision rule to use when allocating a limited amount of an input among a number of competing and alternative uses. It was shown that profit will be maximized when the marginal value products of the last unit of input in each alternative use are all equal. A related concept is that of opportunity cost. Inputs often have several alternative uses, and using a unit of input for one alternative means the income from its use in another must be foregone. The income which must be given up is the input's opportunity cost. The proper use of the equal marginal principle and the concept of opportunity cost will maximize the profit obtainable from a limited amount of any input.

An analysis of costs is important for understanding and improving the profitability of a business. The distinction between fixed and variable costs is useful when making short-run decisions to produce or not produce. In the short run, production should take place only if the expected income will cover the variable costs. Otherwise losses will be minimized by not producing. Production will take place in the long run only if all costs, including both fixed and variable, are covered. If all costs are not covered in the long run, the business will eventually go bankrupt or will be receiving less than opportunity cost on the investment in fixed assets.

An understanding of costs is also necessary for analyzing economies of size. The relationship between cost per unit of output and the size of the business determines if there are increasing, decreasing, or constant returns to size. If unit costs decrease as size increases, there are increasing returns to size, and the business can be expected to grow and vice versa. The type of returns which exist for an individual farm will determine in large part the success or failure of expanding business size. If one type of return dominated our nation's farm firms, it would help explain and predict future trends in farm size, number of farms, and the form of business ownership and control.

QUESTIONS FOR REVIEW AND FURTHER THOUGHT

1 Freda Farmer can invest capital in $100 increments and has three alternative uses for the capital, as shown in the following table. The values in the table are the marginal value products for each successive $100 of capital invested.

Capital invested	Fertilizer ($)	Seed ($)	Chemicals ($)
First $100	400	250	350
Second $100	300	200	300
Third $100	250	150	250
Fourth $100	150	105	200
Fifth $100	100	90	150

   a If Freda has an unlimited amount of her own capital available and no other alternative uses for it, how much should she allocate to each alternative?
   b If Freda can borrow all the capital she needs for 1 year at 10 percent interest, how much should she borrow and how should it be used?
   c Assume Freda has only $700 available. How should this limited amount of capital be allocated among the three uses? Does your answer satisfy the equal marginal principle?
   d Assume Freda has only $1,200 available. How should this amount be allocated? What is the total income from using the $1,200 this way? Would a different allocation increase the total income?
2 How would you estimate the opportunity cost for each of the following items? What do you think the opportunity cost would be?
   a Capital invested in land
   b Your labor used in a farm business
   c Your management used in a farm business
   d One hour of tractor time
   e The hour you wasted instead of studying for your next exam
   f Your college education
3 For each of the following indicate if it is a fixed or variable cost and a cash or noncash expense. (Assume short run.)

		Fixed	Variable	Cash	Noncash
a	Gas and oil	___	___	___	___
b	Depreciation	___	___	___	___
c	Property taxes	___	___	___	___
d	Salt and minerals	___	___	___	___
e	Labor hired on an hourly basis	___	___	___	___
f	Labor contracted for 1 year in advance	___	___	___	___
g	Insurance premiums	___	___	___	___
h	Electricity	___	___	___	___

4 Assume Freda Farmer has just purchased a new combine. She has calculated total fixed cost at $6,000 per year and estimates the variable costs will be $5 per acre.
   a What will her average fixed cost per acre be if she combines 1,000 acres? If she combines 800 acres?
   b What is the additional cost of combining an additional acre?
   c Assume Freda plans to use the combine only for custom work on 750 acres. How much should she charge *per acre* to be sure all costs will be covered?
5 Assume Freda's combine cost $40,000 and has a salvage value of $10,000 and that her capital has an opportunity cost of 10 percent. How much interest should be included as part of total fixed cost?
6 Select a typical farm or ranch from your home area. Assume it doubles in size to where it is producing twice as much of each product as before.
   a If total cost also exactly doubles, would there be increasing, decreasing, or constant returns to size? What if total cost increased by only 80 percent?
   b Which individual costs would you expect to exactly double? Which would increase less than 100 percent? Which more than 100 percent?
   c Would you expect a typical farm or ranch in your area to have increasing, decreasing, or constant returns to size? Why?

REFERENCES

Barnard, C. S., and J. S. Nix: *Farm Planning and Control,* Cambridge University Press, Cambridge, 1973, chap. 2.
Doll, John P., and Frank Orazem: *Production Economics: Theory with Applications,* Grid, Inc., Columbus, Ohio, 1978, chaps. 2, 7.
Heady, Earl O.: *Economics of Agricultural Production and Resource Use,* Prentice-Hall, Inc., Englewood Cliffs, N.J., 1952, chaps. 11, 12.
Madden, J. Patrick: *Economies of Size in Farming,* Agricultural Economic Report 107, ERS, U.S. Department of Agriculture, 1967.
Osburn, Donald D., and Kenneth C. Schneeberger: *Modern Agriculture Management,* Reston Publishing Co., Reston, Va., 1978, chaps. 3, 4.

Chapter 4

Enterprise and
Partial Budgeting

CHAPTER OBJECTIVES

   1 To introduce budgeting as another tool for farm planning
   2 To discuss the method, procedures, and problems in developing an enterprise budget
   3 To show how an enterprise budget can be used for break-even analysis, calculating cost of production, and selecting enterprises
   4 To illustrate and discuss the format and procedure for developing a partial budget
   5 To learn how to prepare a partial budget by the use of several examples

Economic principles and budgeting are the primary tools used by a farm manager for planning and decision making. Budgeting can be used to select the most profitable plan from among a number of alternatives and to test the profitability of any proposed change in a plan. It involves testing a new plan on paper before implementing it to be sure it will improve profit. This "pencil farming" can save time and money, improve decision making, and increase profits. Of all the tools and equipment used by a manager, a pencil, paper, and a calculator may well be the most important when properly used for budgeting and planning.

There are several types of budgeting, each of which is adapted to a particular size and type of planning problem. *Whole farm* planning and budgeting and *cash flow* budgeting involve plans for the entire farm or ranch business, and each will be discussed later in a separate chapter. *Enterprise* budgeting and *partial* budgeting are related, as they are used to analyze only a part of the overall business or a small change in the whole farm plan. They are the subject of this chapter.

ENTERPRISE BUDGETS

As discussed in Chapter 2, an enterprise is defined as a single crop or livestock commodity being produced on a farm, and most farms consist of a combination of several enterprises. An enterprise budget is a listing of all estimated income and expenses associated with a specific enterprise to provide an estimate of its profitability. One can be developed for each actual or potential enterprise in a farm plan such as the corn enterprise, wheat enterprise, or a cow/calf enterprise. Each is developed on the basis of a small common unit such as 1 acre for crops or 1 head for livestock. This permits easier comparison of the profit for alternative and competing enterprises. There are several differences between crop and livestock enterprise budgets, and each will be discussed separately in the following sections.

Crop Enterprise Budgets

Enterprise budgets can be organized and presented in several different formats, but they typically contain three sections: income, variable costs, and fixed costs. An enterprise budget for corn production containing these three sections is shown in Table 4-1.

The first step in developing an enterprise budget is to estimate the total production and the expected output price. Both of these values will obviously have a great effect on enterprise profitability, and they should be carefully estimated. The estimated yield should be the average yield expected under normal weather conditions given the soil type and input levels to be used. Input levels must be considered because seeding rates, fertilizer levels, chemical use, and tillage practices all affect yield. Since enterprise budgets are used for forward planning or making future plans, the output price should be the manager's best estimate of the average price expected during the next year or next several years depending on the planning horizon.

Variable costs are estimated next, and some, such as for seed, fertilizer, and chemicals, are relatively easy. The quantities to be used and input prices are generally known or easy to obtain. Other variable costs such as fuel, machinery repairs, and labor are more difficult to estimate, particularly on a per acre basis. These costs depend on machinery type and size and the number of tillage operations to be performed. Records for several years and enterprise analysis, which will be discussed in Chapter 9, are good sources of information along with research and extension bulletins available from state colleges of agriculture.

As shown in Table 4-1, enterprise budgets include a charge for the op-

Table 4-1   Example Enterprise Budget for Corn Production (1 Acre)

Item	Value per acre	
Income:		
120 bushels at $2.30 per bushel		$276.00
Variable costs:		
Seed	$ 12.00	
Fertilizer and lime	34.50	
Chemicals	16.00	
Machinery fuel and repairs	22.50	
Drying expense	12.00	
Hauling	6.00	
Labor at $4 per hour	22.00	
Miscellaneous	4.00	
Interest on variable costs (10% for 6 months)	6.45	
Total variable costs		$135.45
Income above variable costs		$140.55
Fixed costs:		
Machinery depreciation, interest, taxes, and insurance	$ 36.00	
Land charge	100.00	
Total fixed costs		$136.00
Total costs		$271.45
Estimated profit		$ 4.55

portunity cost on capital invested in the variable costs. This charge covers the time period between expenditure of the capital and harvest when the income is or can be received. In this example, an average time period of 6 months is assumed and a 10 percent opportunity cost is charged on the $129 of variable costs for 6 months, which amounts to $6.45. The estimated total variable cost is $135.45, making the income above variable costs equal $140.55.

The fixed costs in a crop enterprise budget are those associated with machinery plus a charge for land use. Machinery fixed costs include those discussed in Chapter 3, but they must be prorated to the specific crop enterprise on a per acre basis. The amount of machinery fixed costs will depend on the size, age, and number of machines used in producing the crop as well as the tillage practices used. These costs are often difficult to estimate unless all machinery work is hired on a custom basis.

The land charge is the opportunity cost of land and represents a return for its use in crop production. Three methods can be used to determine a land charge: (1) an interest opportunity cost based on the current value of the land, (2) the owner's rental income from a typical crop share lease, or (3) a typical cash rent charge. In the first method, the land charge would be the opportunity cost of capital times the current land value. For example, 10 percent times a land value of $1,500 per acre would result in an annual land charge of $150 per acre. The share rental method would include the value of the owner's share of the crop less any crop production expenses paid by the owner.

Most crop enterprise budgets base the land charge on one of the above rental methods for several reasons. First, it is the appropriate charge to use if the land is actually being rented for crop production. Second, when the land being used is owned, the rental income represents the actual short-run opportunity cost. As long as the land is owned, the only feasible alternative to an owner/operator is to rent it to someone else.

Another reason is related to the rapid increase in land values in recent years and the psychology of land ownership. A land charge based on the actual opportunity cost of capital and current land value results in a land charge considerably higher than either of the rental methods. It would also be higher than the current return on an investment in land. This indicates people own land for reasons other than receiving a high current return on their investment. Examples would be personal satisfaction and prestige, pride of ownership, and anticipation of continued inflation in land values.

Interpreting the Enterprise Budget   The enterprise budget for corn production presented in Table 4-1 shows an estimated profit of $4.55 per acre above all costs. However, this may not be the maximum profit possible from an acre of corn. Any enterprise budget represents only one point on a production function. For example, changing the fertilizer level would change its cost, the yield, total income, and therefore the expected profit. Strictly speaking, there is an enterprise budget for every point on a production function; so a budget does not automatically determine the profit-maximizing input levels. This should be done prior to completing the enterprise budget, with the resulting input levels then used to complete the budget.

The estimated profit can be compared against the estimated per acre profit for other crops and used to select the more profitable crops and crop combinations to be grown each year. However, the profit figures must be properly interpreted, as they are the return or profit above *all* costs including opportunity costs on owned inputs.

Review the figures in Table 4-1 again and notice that there is a charge for all purchased inputs as well as an opportunity cost on capital used for variable costs, a $4 an hour charge on all labor whether hired or operator labor, opportunity cost on the investment in machinery, and a land charge. The estimated $4.55 per acre profit is a true return above all costs and might be thought of as a "pure" profit. Viewed another way, any enterprise budget with an estimated profit of zero is not as bad as it might seem at first. All labor required in the enterprise would be earning an hourly rate equal to the budgeted rate, and all required capital would be earning its opportunity cost.

The enterprise budget in Table 4-1 is typical in that there is a charge for all inputs used with one exception; there is no charge for management. Therefore, another interpretation of the estimated profit is to consider it a return to management or payment for the management input. Some budget formats use Return to Management instead of Estimated Profit to label the last time.

Break-even Analysis   Enterprise budgets can be used to perform a break-even analysis for either prices or yields. The formula for calculating the break-even yield is

$$\text{Break-even yield} = \frac{\text{total costs}}{\text{output price}}$$

This is the yield necessary to just cover all costs at a given output price. For the example in Table 4-1 it would be $271.45 ÷ $2.30, or 118.0 bushels per acre. Since the output price is only an estimate of the expected price, the break-even yield can be calculated for a range of possible prices as shown below.

Price per bushel ($)	Break-even yield, bushels
1.90	142.9
2.10	129.3
2.30	118.0
2.50	108.6

The break-even price, or the price necessary to cover all costs at a given yield level, can be found from the equation

$$\text{Break-even price} = \frac{\text{total costs}}{\text{expected yield}}$$

Continuing with the same example, the break-even price would be $271.45 ÷ 120 bushels, or $2.26 per bushel. The break-even price can also be calculated for a range of possible prices as shown below.

Yield, bushels	Break-even price ($)
80	3.39
100	2.71
120	2.26
140	1.94

Since both the yield and output price in an enterprise budget are estimated rather than actual values, the calculation of break-even yields and prices can aid managerial decision making. By studying the various combinations of break-even prices and yields, managers can form their own expectations about the probability of obtaining a price and yield combination which would just cover total costs. Notice that break-even prices and yields can also be calculated based on total variable costs. The results can help make the type of decision discussed in Chapter 3 on whether to produce or not in order to minimize losses in the short run.

Cost of Production Cost of production is a term used to describe the average cost of producing one unit of a given product. It is equivalent to the concept of average total cost discussed in the last chapter, provided that the same costs and yield are used to calculate each. The cost of production concept is becoming important for several reasons, including the setting of price support levels for government farm programs.

The estimated cost of production is found by dividing the total cost per acre by the estimated yield. For the example in Table 4-1, the cost of production for corn would be $271.45 divided by 120 bushels, or an estimated $2.26 per bushel. Notice that the cost of production is the same as the break-even price. As with the break-even price, the cost of production will change not only with changes in the estimated costs but with changes in yield. While cost of production is becoming a widely used concept, any value is only as good as the cost and yield estimates used in the computations. Because of many differences in costs and yields, the actual cost of production for any crop is likely to be different between farms, counties, regions, and states.

Livestock Enterprise Budgets

Budgets for livestock enterprises follow the same general format as crop budgets but are often more difficult to complete. First, there is the problem of accounting for multiple outputs such as calves and cull cows for a beef cow enterprise; milk, calves, and cull cows for a dairy enterprise; and lambs, wool, and cull ewes for a sheep enterprise. A second problem is a proper accounting for the cost of raising or purchasing replacement animals to maintain a breeding herd over time, and a third problem is the valuation of farm-raised feed fed to the animals. The latter problem is particularly difficult in the case of pasture and crop residues, which may have little or no value if not used by livestock.

An example of a budget for a cow/calf enterprise is shown in Table 4-2, and it illustrates the problems mentioned above. This budget is for one beef cow; so it must contain a prorated share of the income from steer calves, heifer calves, and cull cow sales. With an assumed 90 percent calf crop and the 10 percent replacement rate noted in the footnote, an average of 0.45 steer calf, 0.35 heifer calf, and 0.1 cull cow will be sold annually for each cow in the herd. The latter two figures reflect the 10 percent culling rate with 0.1 cull cow sold and 0.1 replacement heifer retained per cow per year. For simplicity, the budget assumes no death loss in the cow herd.

Many of the variable cost items are self-explanatory, but several deserve some explanation. All purchased feed should be included at its estimated cost, but farm-raised feed such as the hay should be valued at market value. This is the opportunity cost of using the hay in the cow/calf enterprise. The charge for pasture maintenance is for items such as fertilizer, seed, and chemicals that are used on the livestock pasture. A prorated charge for repairs to fences, buildings, and equipment used by the cow herd should be included, along with a share of the costs for any machinery used by the enterprise. Interest on the variable costs is included as the last variable cost in the same manner and for

Table 4-2 Example Enterprise Budget for Cow/Calf Production (One Head)*

Item	Value per head	
Income:		
Steer calf (0.45 hd at 450 lbs at 68¢)	$137.70	
Heifer calf (0.35 hd at 420 lbs at 62¢)	91.14	
Cull cow (0.10 hd at 900 lbs at 40¢)	36.00	
Total		$264.84
Variable costs:		
Salt and minerals	$ 2.50	
Purchased supplement	11.50	
Hay	34.00	
Pasture maintenance	16.00	
Veterinary and medicine	6.00	
Repairs—fences, buildings, equipment	5.25	
Machinery expense	4.50	
Hauling and marketing	6.00	
Labor	24.00	
Miscellaneous	5.00	
Interest on variable costs (10% for 6 months)	5.74	
Total variable cost		$120.49
Income above variable cost		$144.35
Fixed costs:		
Land charge	$ 85.00	
Depreciation—bull	5.50	
Depreciation—fences, buildings, equipment	5.20	
Interest on livestock investment	32.50	
Interest on fences, buildings, equipment	8.30	
Total fixed cost		$136.50
Total cost		$256.99
Estimated profit		$ 7.85

*Assumes a 90 percent calf crop, 10 percent of herd replaced each year with raised replacement heifers.

the same reason as in the crop enterprise budget. The variable costs of maintaining the replacement herd should also be prorated on a per cow basis and included in the budget figures.

The fixed costs in the cow/calf budget include a land charge, depreciation on bull and facilities, and opportunity cost interest on the capital investment in livestock and facilities. A land charge can be computed as either a cash rent charge or as an opportunity cost on the value of the land used. In most areas of the country, one beef cow will require several acres of land, and the land charge should include the total number of acres utilized by the cow and her share of the replacement herd.

Depreciation on the bull is the prorated share of the annual decrease in the value of the bull. If replacement cows were being purchased rather than raised, a charge for cow depreciation would need to be included in a similar manner. This annual depreciation accounts for the net cost of purchasing replacement cows. It can be estimated by dividing the difference between the cost of replacements and sale price of cull cows by the number of years the average cow is kept in the herd.

The final fixed costs are interest charges representing the opportunity cost on the capital invested in the cow, a share of the bull and replacement herd, and the equipment and facilities used by the cow herd. This is often a substantial cost because of the relatively large capital investment per cow.

Interpretation and Analysis As with a crop enterprise budget, the estimated profit on a livestock enterprise budget can also be interpreted as a return to management. All inputs other than management have been charged in the budget at their actual cost or opportunity cost.

Any enterprise budget can also be analyzed in terms of cash versus noncash expenses and total costs versus actual cash outlay. If the owner of this cow herd owns all the land and livestock free of any debt, the fixed costs are all noncash depreciation and opportunity costs. For the case where all labor is furnished by the owner, the labor charge also becomes a noncash opportunity cost. Under these conditions the actual cash expenses become less than $100 per cow in the example budget and could be even less if the cost of making hay is less than the market value used in the budget. At the other extreme where all labor is hired and there is a large debt against both land and cattle, only depreciation would be a noncash expense. Depending on the size of the annual debt payments, the total cash requirements for operating expenses, interest, and principal could equal or even exceed the total cost shown in the budget.

Break-even and Cost of Production Break-even prices and yields and the cost of production for a livestock budget with a single product are calculated in the same manner as discussed for the crop budget. For the example in Table 4-2 and other livestock enterprises with multiple products, the calculations may require some trial and error. The problem is one of keeping the proper relationship between the prices or yields for each of the products. One possible set of break-even prices for the example in Table 4-2 which maintains the 6-cent spread between steer and heifer prices is 65.9 cents for steer calves, 59.9 cents for heifer calves, and 39.43 cents for cull cows. Other sets of break-even prices are possible if the price relationships between the products are allowed to vary.

Sources of Data and Prepared Budgets

The value of any enterprise budget depends on the accuracy of the data used. Managers will generally know the amount of variable inputs such as seed, fertilizer, and chemicals they plan to use, and their current prices are readily obtainable. Other input requirements such as feed, machinery needs, and labor requirements are more difficult to estimate.

Several sources of data and information are available to use in enterprise budgeting. Past farm records are an excellent source if available in sufficient detail and for the enterprise being budgeted. Many states publish an annual summary of the average income and expenses for the farms participating in a statewide record-keeping service. These summaries may contain sufficient detail to be a useful source of data for enterprise budgeting. They are available from either the state agricultural college or the extension service.

Research studies conducted by agricultural colleges, the U.S. Department of Agriculture, or agribusiness firms are reported in bulletins, pamphlets, special reports, and farm magazines. Whether obtained from experimental farms or from a survey of actual farms, the information obtained from these studies often includes average yields and input requirements for individual enterprises which can be used for budgeting.

As part of either their agricultural research or extension responsibilities, many state land grant colleges prepare budgets for the more important enterprises in the state and make them available to the public. Preparing a large number of enterprise budgets is a tedious and time-consuming task. To save time and increase accuracy, computers are now being used to calculate and print enterprise budgets. An example of a computerized enterprise budget is shown in Table 4-3. This particular budget was prepared by the U.S. Department of Agriculture utilizing its Firm Enterprise Data System (FEDS). The FEDS system is used to prepare regional enterprise budgets for the more important agricultural commodities in the United States.

The use of a computer does not reduce the data requirements for an enterprise budget, but it does speed up the calculation and printing of a budget plus providing consistency and uniformity. Computer budgets may also contain more detail than those prepared by hand. No computer prepared budget nor any budget prepared by a third party is likely to fit any individual farm situation exactly. They are typically average budgets for a state or local area, and there are differences in yields, input levels, and other management practices from farm to farm. However, these budgets can provide some basic information which a manager can modify as necessary to fit an individual farm.

PARTIAL BUDGETS

A partial budget is used to calculate the expected change in profit for a proposed change in the farm business. It differs from an enterprise budget in that several enterprises might be involved in the change, but a partial budget is not suitable for preparing a plan for the whole farm. Partial budgeting is therefore intermediate in scope between enterprise budgeting and whole farm planning. It is useful to think of partial budgeting as a type of marginal analysis, as it is best adapted to analyzing relatively small changes in the whole farm plan.

A partial budget contains only those income and expense items which will *change* if the proposed modification in the farm plan is implemented. Only the *changes* in income and expenses are included and not the total values. The final result is an estimate of the gain or loss in profit. To make this estimate,

Table 4-3 Example of a Computer Enterprise Budget for Alfalfa Hay

TITLE: ALFALFA HAY - OKLAHOMA - AREA 300

	UNIT	PRICE OR COST/UNIT	QUANTITY	VALUE OR COST PER ACRE	COST PER UNIT OF PRODUCTION
1. GROSS RECEIPTS FROM PRODUCTION:					
HAY	TN.	65.000	3.130	203.45	
TOTAL RECEIPTS				203.45	
2. VARIABLE COSTS:					
PREHARVEST:					
SEED	LBS.	1.300	5.000	6.50	2.08
NITROGEN	LBS.	0.144	10.000	1.44	0.46
PHOSPHATE	LBS.	0.165	60.000	9.90	3.16
INSECTICIDE	APPL	2.200	2.910	6.40	2.05
SEED TREATMENT	ACRE	0.500	0.200	0.10	0.03
TRACTOR FUEL & LUBE	ACRE			1.54	0.49
TRACTOR REPAIRS	ACRE			0.94	0.30
EQUIP REPAIRS	ACRE			0.82	0.26
MACHINERY LABOR	HRS	2.850	0.813	2.32	0.74
INTEREST ON OP. CAP.	DOLS	0.078	8.255	0.64	0.21
TOTAL PREHARVEST				30.60	9.78
HARVEST:					
BALER TWINE-WIRE	TN.	1.220	3.130	3.82	1.22
TRACTOR FUEL & LUBE	ACRE			2.15	0.69
TRACTOR REPAIRS	ACRE			1.36	0.44
EQUIP FUEL & LUBE	ACRE			5.14	1.64
EQUIP REPAIRS	ACRE			9.71	3.10
MACHINERY LABOR	HRS	2.850	6.398	18.23	5.83
INTEREST ON OP. CAP.	DOLS	0.078	9.477	0.74	0.24
TOTAL HARVEST				41.16	13.15
TOTAL VARIABLE COSTS				71.76	22.93
3. INCOME ABOVE VARIABLE COSTS				131.69	42.07
4. OWNERSHIP COSTS (REPLACEMENT, TAXES, INTEREST, INS.)					
TRACTORS				3.92	1.25
MACHINERY & EQUIP				25.99	8.30
TOTAL OWNERSHIP COSTS				29.91	9.56
5. OTHER COSTS					
LAND CHARGE (CASH RENT)				27.25	8.71
GEN FARM OVERHEAD				6.55	2.09
MANAGEMENT CHARGE (10.0% OF TC-LAND)				10.82	3.46
TOTAL OTHER COSTS				44.62	14.26
6. TOTAL OF ABOVE COSTS				146.29	46.74
7. RETURN TO RISK				57.16	18.26

FOOTNOTES: BASED UPON OKLA. EXTENSION BUDGET FOR SOUTHWEST OKLA.   09/21/76
ESTABLISHMENT COSTS PRORATED OVER FIVE YEARS.   FEDS
 01/09/79

Prepared by Firm Enterprise Data System, Commodity Economics Division, ESCS, in Cooperation with Oklahoma State University, Stillwater, Okla. FEDS budgets are prepared for research purposes and are not official U.S. Department of Agriculture estimates of production costs.

a partial budget systematically organizes the answers to four questions relating to the proposed change:

1 What new or additional costs will be incurred?
2 What current income will be lost or reduced?
3 What new or additional income will be received?
4 What current costs will be reduced or eliminated?

The first two questions identify changes which will reduce profit by either increasing costs or reducing income. Similarly, the last two questions identify factors which will increase profit by generating additional income or lowering costs. By comparing the total reduction in profit found by answering the first two questions with the total increase in profit shown by the answers to the last two, the net change in profit can be computed. A positive value indicates the proposed change in the farm plan will be profitable. However, the manager may want to consider additional factors such as additional risk, uncertainty, and capital requirements before implementing the change. A full discussion of risk and uncertainty will be delayed until Chapter 18 in order to concentrate on the form and substance of a partial budget.

A partial budget can be used to analyze a long-run change such as buying or renting an additional 160 acres or a short-run change such as altering the crop rotation for 1 year in response to weather or price changes. Changes in the farm plan or organization adapted to analysis by use of a partial budget are of three general types.

1 *Enterprise Substitution.* This includes a complete or partial substitution of one enterprise for another. Examples would include substituting 80 acres of soybeans for 80 acres of corn, substituting alfalfa for all the current barley production, or replacing the beef cow herd with a stocker steer enterprise.

2 *Input Substitution or Level.* Changes involving the substitution of one input for another or the total amount of input to be used are easily analyzed with a partial budget. Examples would include substituting machinery for labor by purchasing larger machinery, changes in livestock feed rations, owning harvesting equipment instead of hiring a custom operator, and increasing or decreasing fertilizer or chemical usage.

3 *Size or Scale of Operation.* Included in this category would be changes in total size of the farm business or in the size of a single enterprise. Buying or renting additional land, purchasing additional beef cows, or expanding the swine enterprise would be examples.

These three types of changes are not mutually exclusive, as any single proposal might include a combination of two or more.

The Partial Budget Format

A widely used format for partial budgeting is shown in Table 4-4. Other forms with a slightly different organization are also used, but all contain four basic headings to organize the information relating to the four questions presented in the last section.

Additional Costs   A proposed change may cause additional costs because of a new or expanded enterprise requiring the purchase of additional inputs, or a new input will be purchased as a substitute for another. Any additional fixed costs should be included as well as additional variable costs. If the pro-

Table 4-4 Format for Partial Budgeting

Partial budget

Proposed change: _____

Additional costs ($)	Additional income ($)
Reduced income ($)	**Reduced costs ($)**
A. Total annual additional costs and reduced income $ _____	B. Total annual additional income and reduced costs $ _____
	$ _____
Net change in profit (B minus A) $ _____	

posed change requires the purchase of new machinery, buildings, land, or breeding livestock, there will be additional fixed costs. These should be average annual values; so depreciation should be computed using the straight-line method (see Chapter 7). Opportunity cost on any new capital investment should also be included as an additional fixed cost.

Reduced Income   Income may be reduced if the proposed change would eliminate an enterprise, reduce the size of an enterprise, or cause a reduction in yield or production levels. Proper estimation of reduced income requires careful attention to estimating average yields, production levels, or changes in these values as well as output prices.

Additional Income   A proposed change may cause an increase in total farm income if a new enterprise is being added, if an enterprise is being expanded, or if the change will cause yields or production levels to increase. As with all parts of a partial budget only the additional income expected as a result of the proposed change is listed under this section and not the total income. Accurate estimates of output prices and yields are important for completing this section, as they were for estimating reduced income.

Reduced Costs   Both fixed and variable costs may be reduced by the proposed change. The fixed costs of depreciation and interest or opportunity cost on the investment will be reduced if the change results in eliminating or reducing the investment in machinery, equipment, buildings, breeding livestock, or land. In addition, variable costs will be reduced if an enterprise is eliminated or reduced in size or there is some change in a production technique or method which decreases the need for variable inputs.

The reduced costs associated with lower labor requirements must be carefully evaluated. Costs will be reduced only if less total labor is hired and the total cost of labor decreases. When all labor is provided by the manager and full-time employees, the total labor cost will remain the same unless one less employee is needed. Often proposed changes which reduce labor need by several hundred hours per year do not actually reduce labor costs because the full-time labor force is unchanged. However, if the labor released by the proposed change can be profitably used in another enterprise, any additional income generated should be included as additional income in the analysis.

Partial Budgeting Examples

Two examples will illustrate the procedure and uses of partial budgeting. Table 4-5 is a relatively simple partial budget analyzing the profitability of purchasing a combine which would replace the current practice of hiring a custom combine operator to harvest 800 acres of wheat. All values in the budget are average annual costs, and the result is net change in annual profit. Purchase of the combine will increase fixed costs as well as incurring the additional variable costs associated with operating the combine. The additional fixed costs for

Table 4-5 Partial Budget for Owning Combine versus Custom Hiring

Partial budget

Proposed change: Purchasing combine to replace custom hiring (800 acres of wheat)

Additional costs ($)		Additional income ($)	
Fixed costs		None	
Depreciation	5,000		
Interest	1,600		
Taxes	50		
Insurance	50		
Variable costs			
Repairs	800		
Fuel, oil	600		
Additional labor	500		
Reduced income ($)		**Reduced costs ($)**	
None		Custom combining charge — 800 acres @ $10	8,000
A. Total annual additional costs and reduced income	$ 8,600	B. Total annual additional income and reduced costs	$ 8,000
			$ 8,600
Net changes in profit (B minus A)			$ −600

depreciation, interest, taxes, and insurance total $6,700, or the majority of the additional costs. Additional variable costs are combine repairs, fuel and oil, and some additional labor. There should be no reduced income from this change; so the total of additional costs and reduced income is $8,600.

No additional income is shown in this example, although some might be expected if timeliness of harvesting would be improved and field losses reduced. These factors are difficult to estimate and were excluded from the example. The only reduced cost is the elimination of the payment for custom combining, which is $8,000, making the sum of total additional income and reduced costs equal $8,000.

This example shows purchasing the combine instead of hiring a custom operator would reduce annual farm profit by $600. However, there is another alternative the manager may wish to consider. If the combine could also be used for custom work, the partial budget would need to show additional income from this source and additional variable costs, which would increase directly with the number of acres custom harvested. Fixed costs would not change. Assuming variable costs at $4 per acre and a custom charge of $10 per acre, some quick calculations show only 100 acres would need to be custom harvested to make this a break-even decision.

A second and more detailed example of a partial budget is shown in Table 4-6, where the proposed change is the addition of 50 beef cows to an existing herd. However, not enough forage is available and 100 acres currently in grain production will have to be converted to forage production.

There will be additional fixed costs including additional interest on the increased investment in beef cows, depreciation on bulls, and additional property taxes. Herd replacements are assumed to be raised; so there is no depreciation included on the cows. Variable costs will also increase as shown, including an annual charge for fertilizer and maintenance costs on the new 100 acres of pasture. Income from the grain now being produced on the 100 acres will no longer be received, and this reduced income is estimated at $9,600, making the total annual additional costs and reduced income equal $15,750.

Additional income will be received from the sale of cull cows, steer calves, and heifer calves. Several items are important in estimating this income in addition to carefully estimating prices and weights. First, it is unrealistic to assume every cow will wean a calf every year, and this example assumes 46 calves from the 50 cows. Second, this example assumes herd replacements are raised rather than purchased; so six heifer calves must be retained each year to replace the six cull cows which are sold. This is reflected by only 17 heifer calves being sold each year compared with 23 steer calves.

The reduced costs include expenses which will no longer be incurred from planting the 100 acres to grain. No reduction in machinery fixed costs is included, as the machinery complement is assumed to be no different after the proposed change. Labor costs are also assumed to be unaffected by the change; so no additional or reduced costs for labor are included.

Table 4-6   Partial Budget for Adding 50 Beef Cows

Partial budget

Proposed change: Add 50 beef cows and convert 100 acres to forage production

Additional costs ($)		Additional income ($)	
Fixed costs		6 cull cows	2,100
Interest on cow herd	1,800	23 steer calves	
Bull depreciation	300	450 lbs. @ 65¢	6,728
Taxes	100	17 heifer calves	
Variable costs		420 lbs. @ 60¢	4,284
Veterinary and health	200		
Supplemental feed	750		
Hay	1,200		
Hauling	200		
Misc.	100		
Pasture fertilizer and maintenance	1,500		
Reduced income ($)		Reduced costs ($)	
Grain production		Fertilizer	1,500
2,400 bu. @ $4.00	9,600	Seed	400
		Herbicide	300
		Machinery expense	700

A. Total annual additional costs and reduced income	$ 15,750	B. Total annual additional income and reduced costs	$ 16,012
			$ 15,750

Net change in profit (B minus A) $ +262

The total additional income and reduced costs are $16,012, or $262 more than the total additional costs and reduced income, indicating the proposed change would cause a small increase in farm profit. However, an increase this small could easily become negative with rather small changes in the assumed prices and yields. This points out the importance of accurately estimating these values. Another factor to be considered in the final decision is the additional capital investment required for the beef cows and additional bulls. Even though opportunity cost on this capital is included in the budget, there may be other side effects. Borrowing and debt repayment capacities may be affected, and for a farm with very little capital, the amount of capital available for use in the other enterprises may become limited.

SUMMARY

Both enterprise and partial budgeting are important tools for farm planning. Enterprise budgets are a summary of income and expenses for a small unit such as 1 acre for a crop or 1 head for a livestock enterprise. All costs, including both fixed and variable, are part of an enterprise budget whose purpose is to estimate the profit from a single unit of the enterprise. An enterprise budget can be used to calculate the cost of production, break-even prices and yields and to make decisions about enterprises and enterprise combinations to be included in either short-run or long-run farm plans.

Partial budgets are designed to analyze the profitability of proposed changes in the operation of a farm where the change is relatively small. Only the changes in costs and income are included in a partial budget, and the total of additional costs and reduced income is compared with the total of additional income and reduced costs to find the estimated change in profit. Partial budgeting can be a useful and powerful tool for analyzing the many small or marginal changes in farm plans which a manager may wish to consider.

QUESTIONS FOR REVIEW AND FURTHER THOUGHT

1 Name the four types of budgeting useful in farm planning.
2 Why is budgeting often called forward planning?
3 Discuss how a set of crop enterprise budgets can be used by a manager to select the crops to be grown during the coming year.
4 Will all partial budgets contain some fixed costs? Why or why not?
5 Should the economic principles for determining profit-maximizing input levels be applied before or after completing an enterprise budget? Why?
6 Outline how you would use a partial budget to determine the profitability of participating in a government farm program requiring 10 percent of your cropland be left idle in exchange for a lump-sum payment.

REFERENCES

Krenz, Ronald D.: "The USDA Firm Enterprise Data System: Capabilities and Applications," *Southern Journal of Agricultural Economics,* vol. 7, no. 1, pp. 33–38, July 1975.

Luening, Robert A.: "Partial Budgeting," *Journal of the American Society of Farm Managers and Rural Appraisers,* vol. 38, no. 1, pp. 33–38, April 1974.

Osburn, Donald D., and Kenneth C. Schneeberger: *Modern Agriculture Management,* Reston Publishing Co., Reston, Va., 1978, chaps. 9, 11.

Ott, Gene: *Easier Decisions with Partial Budgeting,* New Mexico Cooperative Extension Service Circular 452, 1973.

Chapter 5

Whole Farm Planning and Budgeting

CHAPTER OBJECTIVES

1 To present whole farm planning and budgeting as a technique for developing the profit-maximizing farm plan

2 To explore the differences between whole farm planning and budgeting and other types of budgeting

3 To outline the need for and procedure for taking a resource inventory

4 To learn the steps and procedures to follow in developing a whole farm plan

5 To illustrate whole farm planning by means of an example

6 To explain the procedure for using the farm plan to organize a total farm budget

7 To introduce the use of linear programming as a whole farm planning tool

Every farmer has a "plan," no matter how vague, ill conceived, or poorly organized it may be. Having no plan implies a completely random and haphazard crop-planting and livestock-raising system. Few if any farmers operate in this manner, yet they may have great difficulty describing their plan and the method used to formulate it. Even where a whole farm plan exists, it may only be in the farmer's mind and not fully developed on paper complete with a total farm budget. Systematic planning and budgeting on a whole farm basis can be another powerful tool for increasing farm profit.

DEFINITION AND DESCRIPTION

As the name implies, a whole farm plan is an outline or scheme for the organization of the resources available on a given farm. It may be in sufficient detail to include operational details such as fertilizer, seed, and chemical application rates and actual feed rations for livestock. When the expected costs and returns for the plan are organized into a whole farm budget, the combined result is a detailed *physical and financial plan for the organization and operation of the total farm or ranch business*.

Enterprise and partial budgeting were discussed in the last chapter and are useful for comparing and analyzing alternatives where the proposed change affects only a small part of the total business. Both can be used to assist in the development of a whole farm plan and are particularly useful for making minor adjustments or "fine tuning" a whole farm plan. However, the procedure for working out a whole farm plan and budget is different from that for the other types of budgets. The total procedure can be divided into two parts to simplify the presentation. In practice, managers will often work on both parts simultaneously.

The two parts of the procedure are: (1) developing the whole farm plan and (2) using the plan to complete a whole farm budget. Part 1 includes taking an inventory of the available resources and organizing the resources into a plan which best meets the owner's goals and objectives. Figure 5-1 shows these steps in the first two blocks. Part 2 of the procedure includes estimating the total costs and returns for the whole farm plan and organizing them into a whole farm budget. These are the last two steps in Figure 5-1.

Given the usual goal of profit maximization, the objective of whole farm planning and budgeting is to find the most profitable organization of the available resources and estimate the potential profit. There may be many alternative ways to combine the resources, and the objective of planning is to systematically eliminate the less profitable while working toward the plan with the greatest profit. The profit for the final plan is summarized in the whole farm budget which can be compared with the profit from the current or alternative plans.

Whole farm planning and budgeting, like the other types of budgeting, is a technique for forward planning. The end product provides a plan for future action complete with the expected income, expenses, and profit. It is similar to an architect's blueprints for a new building in that it provides a plan for the manager to follow to arrive at the desired goal. Whole farm plans and budgets, like building blueprints, are very individualized and different for every situation. Only if you wanted to build the exact same building or had two identical farms would you expect to use the exact same plans. Different goals and resource availability make whole farm planning a very individualized process.

A whole farm plan and budget should be completed upon taking over the operation of a new farm business. Some blueprint or plan is needed to combine the available resources into a production and financial system which best meets

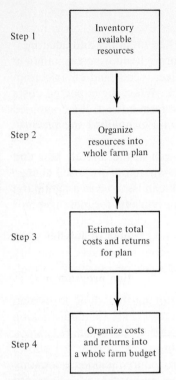

Step 1 — Inventory available resources

Step 2 — Organize resources into whole farm plan

Step 3 — Estimate total costs and returns for plan

Step 4 — Organize costs and returns into a whole farm budget

Figure 5-1   Procedure for developing a whole farm plan and budget.

the goals and objectives. It may be even better to develop the plan before acquiring the new business to determine if there is any plan capable of showing a profit. A new plan may also be needed whenever a major change is planned for an existing farm business. Partial budgeting can handle small changes, but a major change which affects several enterprises may require a new whole farm plan and budget to compare adequately the profitability of the proposed change with the current plan. Finally, existing farm plans should be reviewed on a periodic basis. Changes in prices, technology, and resource availability can quickly outdate a plan.

THE RESOURCE INVENTORY

The development of a whole farm plan is directly dependent upon an accurate inventory of available resources. These resources provide the means for production and profit, but as several are likely to be limited, they also place an upper bound on how much production and profit are possible. The type and quality of resources available determine which enterprises can be considered in the whole farm plan and which can automatically be eliminated because a necessary resource is not available.

Whole farm planning is a short-run planning procedure, which means one or more resources will be available in a limited and fixed amount. It is important that the upper bound on these fixed resources be carefully and accurately identified. As will be shown later, the fixed resources become a key factor in the development of the whole farm plan.

Land

The land resource should receive top priority when completing the resource inventory, as it is generally the most valuable resource, will often be one of the fixed resources, and will greatly influence the type and number of enterprises to be considered. Land is also a complex resource with many characteristics to be identified and listed for later reference. The following are some of the important items to be included in the land inventory.

1 Total number of acres available, including the number of acres in cropland, pasture, timber, and wasteland.

2 The soil types including such factors as slope, texture, and depth.

3 Current soil fertility levels and needs. A soil testing program may be needed as part of the inventory.

4 The existing irrigation system and water supply or the potential for developing an irrigation system.

5 Surface and subsoil drainage problems and possible corrective measures.

6 Existing soil conservation practices and structures including any current and future needs for improvement.

7 Existing and potential pest and weed problems which might affect enterprise selection and crop yields.

8 Climatic factors including annual rainfall, growing season, etc.

This is also a good time to draw up a field map for the farm showing field sizes, field layout, fences, drainageways and ditches, tile lines, and other physical features. This map can provide the basis for planning changes in field sizes and shapes along with changes in the drainage system. If available, the cropping history of each field, including crop grown, yield, fertilizers, and chemicals used, can be recorded on a copy of the field map. This information is very useful for developing a crop program where crop rotation is desirable and herbicide carry-over may be a problem with some crops.

Buildings

The building inventory should include a listing of all buildings along with their size, capacity, and potential uses. Livestock enterprises and crop storage may be severely limited in both number and size by the buildings available. Feed-handling equipment, grain storage, water supply, and arrangement and size of livestock pens all affect the livestock enterprises and should be noted in the inventory.

Information obtained from the building inventory can be used to draw a map of the farmstead. Future building construction and additions to livestock pens and facilities can be planned with this farmstead map to improve farmstead appearance and the efficiency of handling grain and livestock.

Labor

The labor resource should be analyzed for both quantity and quality. Quantity can be measured in days, weeks, or months of labor available from the operator, family members, and hired labor. A very detailed whole farm plan may require information on the seasonal distribution of labor to prevent including enterprises with seasonal labor requirements which exceed available labor during certain times of the year. The availability and cost of additional full-time or part-time labor should be noted in the inventory, as the final farm plan might profitably use additional labor if it is available.

Labor quality is more difficult to measure, but any special skills, training, and experience which would affect the possible success and profit of certain enterprises should be noted. If no one in the labor force has any training or experience in raising hogs, for example, the planner should be cautious about including a swine enterprise in the whole farm plan and would want to adjust expected production levels downward because of the inexperience. Conversely, labor with skills and experience in dairying might give the dairy enterprise a certain advantage over others.

Machinery

Machinery may also be a fixed resource, particularly in the short run, and the number, size, and capacity of the available machinery should be included in the inventory. Special attention should be given to any specialized, single-purpose machines. The capacity limit of a very specialized machine such as a cotton picker will often determine the maximum size of the enterprise where it is needed.

Capital

Capital in the form of land, machinery, and buildings will already be included in the inventory. This should be considered fixed capital, as it cannot be easily released from these investments for alternative uses except in the long run. The capital inventory should concentrate on identifying the capital available for additional investment and for purchasing the variable inputs needed by the potential enterprises. Both the owner's own capital and an estimate of the amount which can be borrowed should be included. This total represents the actual upper limit on capital available for developing the whole farm plan.

Management

The last part of a resource inventory is an assessment of the management available for the business. Like labor, management may have special skills, training, experience, strengths, and weaknesses which need to be considered when selecting enterprises for the whole farm plan. If the manager has no training or experience with a certain enterprise and personally dislikes it, that enterprise is likely to be inefficient and unprofitable. However, managers can be trained and management abilities can and do change over time; so profitable enterprises should not be eliminated solely on the basis of the manager's inexperience.

THE PLANNING PROCEDURE

Before beginning with the development of the whole farm plan, it is important that the owner's and/or manager's goals and objectives be clearly identified. They guide, direct, and focus the decision making and provide a means for comparing and selecting the better and finally the best of the alternative plans. Without a well-defined goal or goals, there is no way to choose the "best" alternative, and the planning procedure will be an aimless and frustrating experience at best. Where more than one person is involved, goals may often be in conflict, such as might happen in a father-son partnership. The father might be satisfied with the farm organization he has developed over time while the son is likely to be more interested in growth, expansion, changing enterprises, and adopting new technology. These goal conflicts need to be carefully identified and resolved before a whole farm plan is developed. Profit maximization will be the assumed goal throughout the remainder of this chapter, but the reader should remember other goals are possible and could result in a different whole farm plan.

The development of a short-run plan can be divided into three steps: (1) identifying possible enterprises and related technical coefficients, (2) estimating gross margins or income above variable costs for each enterprise, and (3) developing the plan itself. Each of these steps is described in the following sections. This discussion will be followed by an example to clarify and illustrate each step.

Identifying Enterprises and Technical Coefficients

Based on the resource inventory, certain crop and livestock enterprises will be feasible alternatives. Those requiring a resource which is not available can be automatically eliminated from consideration. However, care should be taken to include all possible enterprises to avoid missing one with profit potential. Custom and tradition should not be allowed to restrict the list of potential enterprises, only the resource limitations.

Each enterprise should be defined on some small unit such as 1 acre for crops and 1 head for livestock. The resource requirements per unit of each enterprise or the technical coefficients must be estimated. For example, the technical coefficients for an acre of corn might be 1 acre of land, 4 hours of labor, 3.5 hours of tractor time, and $85 of operating capital, while one beef cow might require 4 acres of pasture, 5 hours of labor, and $100 of operating capital. These technical coefficients or resource requirements become very important in determining the maximum size of enterprises and the final enterprise combination.

Estimating Gross Margins

Expenses such as property taxes, depreciation, insurance, and opportunity cost on investments are fixed in the short run and will not change regardless of the enterprise combination included in the whole farm plan. These fixed costs can be set aside temporarily, as eliminating them from the planning process will not affect the final plan and simplifies calculations. However, they will be needed later to complete the total budget.

The next step is to estimate the *gross margin* or the income above variable costs for each enterprise to be considered in the farm plan. A gross margin is estimated for a single unit of each enterprise and is the difference between total income and total variable costs. Another way of viewing gross margin is to consider it the enterprise's contribution to fixed costs and profit after the variable costs have been paid. Calculating gross margins requires the manager's best estimate of yields or production levels for each enterprise and expected prices for the output. Since total income per unit of the enterprise is equal to output price times yield or production, these estimates directly affect the estimated gross margin.

The calculation of total variable cost requires a list of each variable input needed, the amount required, and the price of each. Input levels should be determined only after considering the economic principles of Chapter 2 relating to optimum input levels. Yields should be estimated in conjunction with input levels to be sure they are consistent with the input levels selected.

Developing the Whole Farm Plan

All information necessary to organize a whole farm plan is now ready for use. Developing a whole farm plan can be a long and tedious project requiring the comparison of many alternative plans unless a systematic procedure is used. That systematic procedure, and the key to whole farm planning, is identifying the most limiting resource and selecting those enterprises with the greatest return or gross margin per unit of this resource.

The return per unit of limiting resource is found by dividing the gross margin by the number of resource units needed, ignoring the cost of any other resources needed.

$$\text{Return per unit of resource} = \frac{\text{gross margin}}{\text{units of resource required}}$$

For example, if the corn enterprise has a gross margin of $100 per acre and requires 1 acre of land and 4 hours of labor, the return is $100 per acre of land and $25 per hour of labor. Once these same returns have been calculated for all enterprises, they become the keys for systematically developing the profit-maximizing whole farm plan.

Land will generally be a limiting resource, and it provides a good starting point if the most limiting resource cannot be identified. Another rule of thumb used by experienced planners is to plan the cropping program first, add livestock enterprises to the limit of any remaining resources, and then look for changes in the cropping program which will free resources and increase profit by allowing additional livestock.

The planning procedure can be summarized in the following steps, assuming land is the most limiting resource. At some point in the planning procedure, a resource other than land may become more limiting, and the emphasis shifts to identifying enterprises with the greatest return per unit of this resource.

1   Select the crop enterprise which has the greatest return per acre of land. Introduce it into the plan up to the limit imposed by land or some other resource. The need for crop rotation and/or soil conservation will often limit the acres of this crop to something less than the total acres available.

2   Select the crop with the next greatest return per acre of land and introduce it into the plan up to the limit of the remaining land or some other restriction. Repeat this step until all the land is used or until another resource is exhausted.

3   If another resource is exhausted before land, find the crop not in the plan with the greatest return per unit of this resource. Substitute it for the enterprise in the plan with the lowest return per unit of this resource until a limit is reached. Continue this process until this resource or land is exhausted.

4   The above step may need to be repeated if a third resource is found to be exhausted before all the land is used.

5   Once the crop plan has been determined, check to be sure there are no other substitutions which will increase the total gross margin from all crop enterprises and that no resource limits have been exceeded.

6   Identify any unused resources which can be used for livestock enterprises and the one which appears to be most limiting.

7   Select the livestock enterprise with the greatest return per unit of this limiting resource and add it to the plan until this or another resource is exhausted.

8   Continue as in steps 2 and 3 above until no additions or substitutions in the livestock plan will increase total gross margin.

9   Check the crop plan for changes which would free some of an exhausted resource to increase the size of a livestock enterprise. Profitable substitutions can be identified by comparing the return per unit of the exhausted resource. A simple partial budget is also very useful for checking the profitability of such substitutions.

10   Check the final plan for accuracy, making sure none of the resource limits have been exceeded.

While the above procedure will eliminate the less profitable enterprises, it does not guarantee the most profitable plan has been found. Particularly when both crop and livestock enterprises are included, step 9 may have many possible changes to budget out, and the most profitable can be overlooked.

One method of checking the final plan is to repeat the entire procedure starting with the assumption that some resource other than land is the most limiting. This gives a different direction to the procedure and may point out an alternative not considered in the first plan. If no important alternative has been overlooked, the second plan should be identical to or should very closely resemble the first.

With profit maximization as the assumed goal, it may seem strange that the procedure outlined above maximizes gross margin rather than profit. However, it assumes a short-run situation where fixed costs are constant regardless of the farm plan selected. Any positive gross margin represents a contribution toward paying those fixed costs with any remaining gross margin accumulating as profit. Therefore, maximizing gross margin is equivalent to maximizing profit (or minimizing loss) in the short run where fixed costs are constant.

A large planning problem with many fixed resources and/or many alternatives becomes very difficult to solve by hand calculation methods. Experienced planners can solve problems with three or four limited resources and possibly eight to ten enterprise alternatives. Even a problem of this size might take considerable time to identify and compare all the potential profit-maximizing enterprise combinations. For large planning problems, a computer can be used to save time and increase the accuracy of the planning process. One such procedure will be discussed at the end of the chapter.

EXAMPLE OF WHOLE FARM PLANNING

The procedure used in whole farm planning is best learned by working through an example. A relatively small problem is used in this section to simplify the discussion and concentrate on the planning procedure itself. Once the planning procedure is mastered, it becomes relatively easy to move on to larger and larger problems.

Resource Inventory

Table 5-1 contains the resource inventory for the example farm. The land resource has been divided into three types: Class A cropland which can be planted entirely in row crops (cotton and milo), Class B cropland which is limited to 50 percent row crops, and land which is in permanent pasture. In addition to land, the only other resource with an effective limit is labor, which has a maximum of 2,000 hours. Capital and machinery are both available in adequate amounts, and the few buildings available serve mostly to limit the number of livestock enterprises which can be considered.

Identifying Enterprises and Resource Requirements

Potential crop and livestock enterprises are identified and listed in Table 5-2. Any enterprise which is obviously unprofitable or which requires a resource which is not available should be eliminated. However, if there is any question about an enterprise's profitability, it should be considered. The interaction of

Table 5-1 Resource Inventory for Example Farm

Resource	Amount and comments
Class A cropland	400 acres (adapted to continuous row crop production)
Class B cropland	200 acres (conservation needs limit row crops to 50% of total)
Pasture	200 acres
Buildings	Only hay shed and cattle shed are available
Labor	2,000 hrs available annually
Capital	Adequate for any farm plan
Machinery	Adequate for any potential crop plan but all harvesting to be custom hired
Management	Owner/manager appears capable and has experience with crops and beef cattle
Other limitations	Selling hay not permitted. Any hay produced must be fed on farm

the various resource requirements will sometimes cause one of the less profitable enterprises to be included in the final plan.

As shown in Table 5-2, the example farm has three potential crop enterprises on Class A cropland, three on Class B cropland, and two livestock enterprises. The livestock enterprises are limited to forage-intensive beef enterprises because of the few buildings available. Resource requirements per unit of each enterprise are also shown in Table 5-2. For example, 1 acre of cotton on Class A land requires 1 acre of Class A cropland, 4 hours of labor, and $115 of operating capital. Even though operating capital is not limited in this example, it is included for illustration.

Estimating Gross Margins

Table 5-3 contains the estimated gross margins for the eight potential enterprises to be considered in the whole farm plan. Detailed breakdowns on the components of total variable costs have been omitted to save space but should be done on a separate worksheet for use in estimating the gross margins. The accuracy of the whole farm plan depends heavily upon the estimated gross margins. Careful attention should be paid to estimating yields, output prices, input levels, and input prices.

Developing the Whole Farm Plan

It is not readily apparent whether land or labor will be the most limiting resource; so land is selected to provide a starting point. The cropping program will be developed first and in two steps, one for each type of cropland. Following the rule of selecting the enterprise with the greatest return per unit of the fixed resource, note that cotton has the greatest return per acre of Class A cropland. Therefore, it is included in the plan up to the maximum allowed,

Table 5-2 Potential Enterprises and Resource Requirements

| Resource | Crops per acre | | | | | | Livestock per head | |
| | Class A cropland | | | Class B cropland | | | | |
	Cotton*	Milo	Wheat	Milo	Wheat	Hay†	Beef cows	Stocker steers
Class A cropland (acres)	1	1	1					
Class B cropland (acres)				1	1	1		
Pasture (acres)							4	2
Labor (hrs)	4	3	2	3	2	1	3	1.5
Operating capital ($)	115	60	30	60	30	40	120	320
Hay (tons)							2	

*Limited to one-half of the Class A cropland for crop rotation needs.
† Will be custom harvested and baled, since no haying equipment is available.

Table 5-3   Estimating Gross Margins

Enterprise	Yield	Price ($)	Total income ($)	Total variable costs ($)	Gross margin ($)
Class A cropland:					
Cotton (acre)	450 lbs	0.60	270	115	155
Milo (acre)	45 cwt	4.00	180	60	120
Wheat (acre)	40 bu	3.00	120	30	90
Class B cropland:					
Milo (acre)	35 cwt	4.00	140	60	80
Wheat (acre)	30 bu	3.00	90	30	60
Hay (acre)	2 tons			40	−40*
Livestock:					
Beef cows (head)			250	120	130
Stocker steers (head)			400	320	80

*Hay is not sold directly; so producing it shows a negative gross margin. Income from hay production is received indirectly from producing and selling beef.

which is 200 acres because of crop rotation requirements (Footnote to Table 5-2). Milo has the next greatest return per acre of Class A cropland, and 200 acres are added to the plan, which is the limit on the remaining Class A cropland.

Moving to Class B cropland, milo has the greatest return per acre. However, milo is a row crop, which limits it to one-half of this land type, or 100 acres. The remaining 100 acres of Class B cropland is placed in wheat, since it has the next greatest return per acre. This completes the crop plan, which was done without considering any livestock enterprises.

At this point the crop plan should be summarized for later use and to be sure the land and labor restrictions have not been exceeded. This summary will be called Plan 1 and can take the following form:

Enterprise	Cropland Class A	Cropland Class B	Labor required (hrs)	Total gross margin ($)
Cotton	200		800	31,000
Milo	200		600	24,000
Milo		100	300	8,000
Wheat		100	200	6,000
Total	400	200	1,900	69,000

The summary confirms that neither the land nor the labor restriction has been exceeded and shows a total gross margin of $69,000. This will be used to compare the profitability of Plan 1 with new alternatives.

A review of the resource inventory and the above summary shows 200 acres of pasture and 100 hours of labor are the only resources remaining which can be used for adding livestock enterprises. The two livestock enterprises have the following returns per unit of pasture and labor:

	Returns per Unit of Limited Resource ($)	
	Pasture	Labor
Beef cows	32.50	43.33
Stocker steers	40.00	53.33

Since stocker steers have the greatest return per unit of each resource, they appear to be the more profitable livestock enterprise.

Pasture limits the stockers to 100 head (200 acres ÷ 2 acres per head), but the remaining 100 hours of labor permits only 66.6 head (100 hours ÷ 1.5 hours per head). Our alternative Plan 2 can be summarized as follows:

Total gross margin from crops ($)	69,000
Total gross margin from steers for 66.6 head ($)	5,328
Total ($)	74,328

This is an improvement over Plan 1 but uses only 133.2 acres of pasture, leaving 66.8 acres unused. Labor has now become the most limiting resource, and attention must now be given to those enterprises with the greatest return per hour of labor.

It is now obvious that expanding the stocker steer enterprise to utilize all the pasture will require a substitution in the crop plan, which will release some labor. This should also be a profitable substitution, as the steers have a greater return per hour of labor than most crops. Milo on Class B cropland has the smallest return per hour of labor ($26.67), and substituting wheat for milo will reduce the labor requirements for crops. The additional 33.4 head of stocker steers needed to utilize the pasture completely will require 33.4 × 1.5 hours = 50 hours of additional labor, which can be obtained from substituting 50 acres of wheat for 50 acres of milo on the Class B cropland. This change gives us alternative Plan 3 summarized below:

	Cropland (acres)		Pasture	Labor	Total gross
Enterprise	Class A	Class B	(acres)	(hrs)	margin ($)
Cotton	200			800	31,000
Milo	200			600	24,000
Milo		50		150	4,000
Wheat		150		300	9,000
Stocker steers					
(100 head)			200	150	8,000
Totals	400	200	200	2,000	76,000

Plan 3 does not exceed any of the resource limits and increases the total gross margin by $1,672 over Plan 2.

By systematically following the rules and procedures for whole farm planning, we have arrived at Plan 3, which gives every indication of being the profit-maximizing plan. However, beef cows were never considered as part of any plan, and substituting them for stocker steers is another alternative. If a plan including beef cows shows less total gross margin, it will help verify Plan 3 as the profit-maximizing plan. Our manager may also prefer beef cows over stocker steers and would like to know how much they would lower profit if included in the whole farm plan.

Complete utilization of the pasture requires 50 beef cows, which in turn will need 100 tons of hay (refer to Table 5-2). The hay can be produced on 50 acres of Class B cropland and should be substituted for wheat, as it has the lowest return per acre. However, this substitution results in 50 hours of excess labor, which can then be used to substitute 50 acres of milo for another 50 acres of wheat on Class B cropland. This additional substitution is profitable because milo has a higher return per acre and the additional labor is now available. Alternative Plan 4 can be summarized as follows:

Enterprise	Cropland (acres)		Pasture (acres)	Labor (hrs)	Total gross margin ($)
	Class A	Class B			
Cotton	200			800	31,000
Milo	200			600	24,000
Milo		100		300	8,000
Wheat		50		100	3,000
Hay		50		50	(2,000)
Beef cows (50 head)			200	150	6,500
Totals	400	200	200	2,000	70,500

The result shows that the procedure used to select stocker steers over beef cows in Plan 3 actually gave us the profit-maximizing whole farm plan. Plan 4 has $5,500 less total gross margin than Plan 3. Given that stocker steers have a greater return per acre of pasture and per hour of labor, the results in Plan 4 should not be surprising. Properly used, the basic planning rule of selecting those enterprises with the greatest return per unit of limited resource in a step-by-step manner will result in the profit-maximizing plan. In this example, Plan 3 is that plan.

Profit-maximizing Plan 3 completely utilizes all of each available resource, which will not happen in all problems. The planner should not be surprised if one or two resources are not completely exhausted in the final plan. This indicates these resources, while fixed in amount, are not actually limiting. Some other resource is so limiting it prevents total use of all resources in the profit-maximizing whole farm plan.

THE WHOLE FARM BUDGET

The whole farm plan itself does not provide full information and details on sources and amounts of income, types and amount of expenses, and the total expected profit for the farm business using the plan. Fixed costs were ignored during the planning process but need to be included in any estimate of farm profit. A whole farm budget is needed to provide additional details and the final estimate of farm profit.

Preparing the Budget

A whole farm budget is a summary of the expected income, expenses, and profit for a given farm plan. It can be developed in sufficient detail to include estimates of total input requirements for crop production, livestock feed requirements, capital needed, and other information to implement the whole farm plan properly. Forms for organizing and recording these details are often available in farm record books or in leaflets and pamphlets available through the local extension service office. Use of such forms will save time and improve the accuracy of the budget estimates.

Much of the information needed to complete the budget will already have been gathered during the development of the whole farm plan. Table 5-4 is an example of a whole farm budget based on the whole farm plan completed earlier in this chapter. Total farm income is calculated for each of the enterprises included in this plan and totals $150,500. The next step is to estimate the variable costs by type or category such as seed, feed, fertilizer, and repairs. Many of these variable costs will be the same as those used to estimate the gross margins needed in the planning procedure. The total for each variable cost can be found by calculating the total for each enterprise and then summing across the enterprises.

Notice that the income above variable expenses in Table 5-4 is $76,000, which is the same as the total gross margin for Plan 3 which was used to develop the total budget. This will always be true *provided* all variable costs were included in the calculation of enterprise gross margins, which was assumed here for illustrative purposes. In actual practice, variable expenses such as building repairs, auto and pickup expenses, utilities, and other farm overhead expenses are very difficult to allocate to specific enterprises and are affected very little by the final enterprise combination. If these and similar expenses were not included in the calculation of gross margins, they must be included in the total budget, which will make income above total variable expenses less than the total gross margin in the whole farm plan.

The last section of Table 5-4 contains the fixed expenses, which were omitted from the calculation of enterprise gross margins. They are fixed in the short run and do not change for different enterprise combinations; so their omission did not affect the selection of a profit-maximizing plan. However, fixed expenses do affect farm profit and must be included in the whole farm budget. Expenses such as depreciation, property taxes, and interest are often a major portion of the total expenses.

Table 5-4 Example of a Whole Farm Budget Showing Projected Income, Expenses, and Profit

Income:
Cotton	$54,000	
Milo......................................	43,000	
Wheat	13,500	
Stocker steers	40,000	
Total income	$150,500	$150,500

Variable expenses:
Fertilizer	$11,900	
Seed	3,600	
Chemicals	7,900	
Fuel, oil, grease	4,050	
Machinery repairs..........................	2,650	
Feed purchased	1,600	
Feeder livestock purchased	29,000	
Other livestock expenses	1,100	
Custom machine hire	10,250	
Miscellaneous	2,450	
Total variable expenses	$74,500	

Income above variable expenses	$76,000	

Fixed expenses:
Property taxes	$ 2,600	
Insurance	1,250	
Interest on debt...........................	22,000	
Machinery depreciation	7,200	
Building depreciation	3,200	
Total fixed expenses	$36,250	
Total variable expenses	74,500	
Total expenses		$110,750
Net farm income (profit)		$ 39,750

The budget in Table 5-4 shows an estimated profit or net farm income of $39,750 if the price and yield estimates are actually realized. Changes in any of these factors will obviously affect the actual profit received from operating the farm under this plan. The estimated profit also needs to be carefully interpreted. No opportunity cost has been charged for the owner's capital invested in land, buildings, and machinery or for the owner's labor and management. Including these opportunity costs as additional expenses will further reduce the net farm income. A discussion of these opportunity costs will be deferred until Chapter 8.

Using the Budget

In addition to providing an estimate of net farm income, a whole farm budget has several other potential uses.

1 It provides a basis for comparing alternative plans for profitability. This can be particularly useful when planning for growth and expansion.

2   The cash expenses in the budget provide an estimate of the operating capital the business will need during the year.

3   Much of the information needed to complete the cash flow budget has already been gathered and organized in the whole farm budget. (Cash flow budgeting will be discussed in the next chapter.)

4   A detailed whole farm budget showing the estimated profit can be used to help establish credit and borrow the necessary operating capital.

5   The worksheets used to prepare the budget contain estimates of total input requirements. Orders for inputs such as fertilizer, seed, chemicals, and feed can be placed using this information.

The whole farm budget can also be used as part of a system for monitoring and controlling the business during the year. Although the control function of management will not be fully discussed until Part 3, one budgetary control method using the whole farm budget will be illustrated here. A form such as the one shown in Table 5-5 provides an organized way to compare the budgeted cash income and expenses with the actual amounts.

The estimated cash income and expenses from the whole farm budget are entered in the first column. Budgeted vs. actual comparisons can be made at any time during the year or at the end of the year. If made quarterly, for example, that portion of the estimated income and expenses expected between January 1 and March 31 is entered in the second column, and actual income and expenses during that same time period are entered in the third column. This permits a quick comparison of the budgeted and actual values.

This comparison is a means of monitoring and controlling cash expenses throughout the year. Expenses which are exceeding budgeted amounts are quickly identified, and action can be taken to find and correct the causes. The actual results at the end of the year can be used to make adjustments in the budgeted values for next year and to improve the accuracy of future planning and budgeting efforts.

LINEAR PROGRAMMING

A large whole farm planning problem with many fixed resources and potential enterprises is very difficult to solve using hand calculation methods. Linear programming is a mathematical technique which can be used to solve large whole farm planning problems on a computer. Problems with 50 or more resource restrictions and 100 or more potential enterprises can be solved in several minutes or less on a modern computer. Accuracy is improved, and the linear programming procedure guarantees the "best" plan will be found provided the data are correct.

In mathematical terms, linear programming is a procedure for maximizing or minimizing a linear objective function subject to linear restraints. The objective of whole farm planning is maximization of total gross margin or income above variable costs (the objective function), and the restraints are the amounts

Table 5-5   Budgetary Control Form Using Whole Farm Budget

		Annual Budget	Budget to Date	Actual to Date
INCOME	**CASH INCOME**			
	1. Crops			
	2. Feeder Livestock and Livestock Products			
	3. Government Payments			
	4.			
	5. TOTAL OPERATING RECEIPTS			
	INCOME FROM SALE CAPITAL ITEMS			
	6. Breeding Livestock			
	7. Machinery and Equipment			
	8.			
	9. TOTAL CAPITAL SALES			
	10. *TOTAL INCOME (5+9)*			
EXPENSE	**CASH EXPENSES**			
	11. Hired Labor			
	12. Fertilizers and Lime			
	13. Spray Materials and Chemicals			
	14. Seed and Treatment			
	15. Taxes—Real and Personal			
	16. Insurance			
	17. Interest			
	18. Auto (farm share)			
	19. Fuel and Oil			
	20. Machinery or Custom Hire			
	21. Freight and Trucking			
	22. Machinery Repairs			
	23. Other Repairs			
	24. Utilities (farm share)			
	25. Rent and Leases			
	26. Livestock Expenses			
	27. Purchased Feeds			
	28. Purchased Feeder Stock			
	29.			
	30.			
	31. TOTAL OPERATING EXPENSES			
	CAPITAL EXPENDITURES			
	32. Breeding Stock			
	33. Machinery and Equipment			
	34. Buildings, Fences, Tile, Etc.			
	35.			
	36. TOTAL CAPITAL EXPENDITURES			
	37. *TOTAL EXPENSES (31+36)*			
SUMMARY	38. Family and Living Expenses (include inc. tax)			
	39. Repayment Other Loans			
	40. Accumulated Borrowings			
	41.			

of the fixed resources. Linear programming requires exactly the same type of information needed for the earlier farm planning example. The resource inventory must be completed, potential crop and livestock enterprises identified, the resource requirements per unit of each enterprise listed, and the gross margins estimated.

Since linear programming can quickly solve large problems, considerable detail can be included in the resource restrictions and in the number of enterprises to be considered. For example, the labor resource is often defined on a monthly basis instead of annually, resulting in 12 labor restrictions instead of one. Limits on operating capital can be defined in a similar manner, and the land resource can be divided into a number of different soil types. Several enterprises can be defined for each crop or type of livestock with different levels or combinations of resources.

The procedure for solving a linear programming problem organized to find the profit-maximizing whole farm plan requires too much space and too many computations to be included here. However, the basic logic can be illustrated in graphic form for a small problem involving two enterprises and three limited resources. The necessary information is shown in Table 5-6 for the corn and soybean enterprises with land, labor, and operating capital as the limited resources. Gross margins and the resource requirements per unit of each enterprise (called technical coefficients in linear programming) are also shown.

The resource limits and technical coefficients are used to graph the possible enterprise combinations as shown in Figure 5-2. Land limits corn to 120 ÷ 1 = 120 acres and soybeans to 120 ÷ 1 = 120 acres. These points are found on the graph and connected with a straight line. Any point on the line AA' is a possible combination of corn and soybeans given only the land restriction. Labor restricts corn to a maximum of 500 ÷ 5 = 100 acres and soybeans to 500 ÷ 3 = 166.7 acres, and these points on the graph are connected by the line BB'. In a similar manner the line CC' connects the maximum corn acres (150) permitted by the operating capital restriction with the maximum soybean acres (187.5). Any point on the line BB' is a possible combination of corn and soybeans permitted by the labor restriction, and line CC' identifies the possible combinations based only on the operating capital restriction.

A careful study of Figure 5-2 shows corn is limited to a maximum of 100 acres by the labor restriction and soybeans to 120 acres by the land restriction. For combinations of corn and soybeans along line segment BD, labor is the limiting resource. Along line segment DA' land is limiting the combinations of corn and soybeans that can be grown. Therefore, the line BDA' and points below it and to the left represent the only possible combinations of corn and soybeans permitted by the resource limits. The line BDA' is actually a seg-

Table 5-6   Information for Linear Programming Example

		Resource requirements (per acre)	
Resource	Limit	Corn	Soybeans
Land (acres)	120	1	1
Labor (hrs)	500	5	3
Operating capital ($)	15,000	100	80
Gross margin ($)		120	95

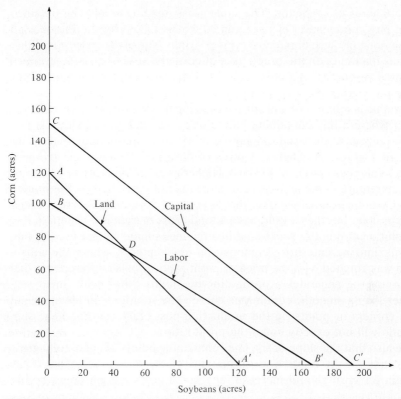

Figure 5-2 Graphical illustration of resource restrictions in linear programming problem.

mented production-possibility curve similar to those for competitive enterprises discussed in Chapter 2.

In this example, operating capital is not a limiting resource. It is fixed in amount, but the $15,000 is more than sufficient for any combination of corn and soybeans permitted by the land and labor resources.

The next step is to find the profit-maximizing combination of corn and soybeans given that many combinations are possible. This can be done graphically using lines containing points of equal total gross margin and the production-possibility curve BDA'. For example, a total gross margin of $9,600 can be obtained by growing 80 acres of corn (80 acres times the gross margin of $120 per acre). Alternatively, the same gross margin can be obtained by growing 101.05 acres of soybeans ($9,600 divided by the soybean gross margin of $95 per acre). A straight line between these two points on the graph contains every combination of corn and soybean acreage which will generate a $9,600 gross margin. However, there are many possible combinations of corn and soybeans above and to the right of the $9,600 line, any of which would increase the total gross margin.

A total gross margin of $14,400 can be obtained by planting 120 acres of corn or 151.6 acres of soybeans. The same gross margin can also be obtained by planting any combination of corn and soybeans falling on the line labeled $14,400, but none of these combinations is possible. The production-possibility curve defines the limits on the production of corn and soybeans as determined by the limited resources. All points on the $14,400 line lie above and to the right of the production-possibility curve.

The graphical solution to a profit-maximizing linear programming problem is the point where a line containing points of equal total gross margin is just touching or tangent to the production-possibility curve on its upper side. This is point D in Figure 5-3, where 70 acres of corn and 50 acres of soybeans generates a total gross margin of $13,150. Higher gross margins are not possible because they require combinations of enterprises not permitted by the limited resources. Combinations other than the 70 acres of corn and 50 acres of soybeans are possible, but they would have a total gross margin less than $13,150.

The solution at point D was found in a manner similar to that used to find the profit-maximizing enterprise combination in Chapter 2, where the substitution ratio was equated with the price or profit ratio. A basic difference is that linear programming generates a production-possibility curve with linear segments rather than a smooth, continuous curve. The solution will always be at one of the corners or points on the production-possibility curve; so the substitution ratio will not exactly equal the profit ratio.

Notice also that the slope of the lines containing points of equal total gross margin depends on the relative gross margins of the two enterprises. If the gross margin for corn should increase, any given gross margin could be ob-

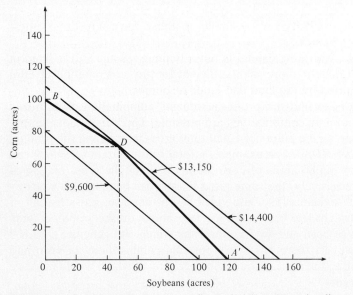

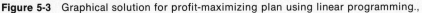

Figure 5-3 Graphical solution for profit-maximizing plan using linear programming.,

tained from fewer acres of corn, and the slope of the lines would become flatter. It is possible that the profit-maximizing solution would be at point *B* if the slope changed enough. Conversely, if the soybean gross margin increased, the slope of the lines would increase, and *A'* could become the solution. Any profit-maximizing solution can also be changed by increasing or decreasing the amount of a limited resource, as this changes the shape of the production-possibility curve.

SUMMARY

Whole farm planning and budgeting is another of the planning tools needed by a farm manager. Partial and enterprise budgeting cannot be used to develop a plan for an entire farm or ranch, but each can be used in whole farm planning. The data contained in enterprise budgets can be used directly or modified for use in calculating the enterprise gross margins needed for whole farm planning. Partial budgeting is useful for checking the profitability of each possible substitution of enterprises as the planning procedure progresses.

Whole farm planning starts with an inventory of the resources available. These resources determine which enterprises are possible, and the limits on resource availability play a role in determining the combination of enterprises which will maximize profit and the limits on profit. The systematic planning procedure works from the principle of selecting enterprises with the greatest return per unit of the most limiting resource in arriving at the profit-maximizing plan.

A whole farm budget utilizes this plan to calculate expected income, expenses, and profit. This step is necessary because the enterprise gross margins used in planning do not contain all the farm expenses. Fixed costs were excluded, and there may be additional variable costs, particularly general overhead costs. The completed whole farm budget is an organized presentation of the sources and amounts of income and expenses along with the expected profit.

Large farm planning problems with many resources and enterprises can be solved using a computer and a mathematical technique called linear programming. The same basic data are required for linear programming as for hand-calculated planning methods, but a greater volume of data can be used because of the speed and capacity of a computer.

QUESTIONS FOR REVIEW AND FURTHER THOUGHT

1 How does a whole farm plan and budget differ from a partial budget and an enterprise budget?
2 Why is a resource inventory needed for whole farm planning?
3 Why is land such an important resource in whole farm planning?
4 Why can fixed costs be ignored when developing the whole farm plan but must be included in the whole farm budget?

5 How would you relate the concept of opportunity costs to the planning principle of selecting enterprises with the greatest return per unit of the most fixed resource?

6 Whole farm planning and budgeting has been criticized for being too time-consuming and for requiring too much information which is often only "best estimates" and subject to change. How would you counter these arguments?

7 Use the planning procedures in this chapter to find the profit-maximizing whole farm plan using the following information:

Resource	Resource limit	Resource requirements per acre	
		Cotton	Grain sorghum
Land (acres)	400	1	1
Capital ($)	28,000	100	40
Labor (hrs)	3,000	10	6
Gross margin ($)		100	80

8 Check your answer to the above question by solving the same problem using a piece of graph paper and the linear programming technique.

REFERENCES

Barnard, C. S., and J. S. Nix: *Farm Planning and Control,* Cambridge University Press, Cambridge, 1973, chaps. 13, 14, 15.

Boutwell, J. L., and E. W. McCoy: *Simplified Programming as a Farm Management Tool,* Alabama Agricultural Experiment Station, Circular 232, 1977.

Doll, John P., and Frank Orazem: *Production Economics: Theory with Applications,* Grid, Inc., Columbus, Ohio, 1978, chap. 9.

Osburn, Donald D., and Kenneth C. Schnccbcrgcr: *Modern Agriculture Management,* Reston Publishing Co., Reston, Va., 1978, chaps. 10, 12, 13.

Scott, John T., Jr.: *The Basics of Linear Programming and Their Use in Farm Management,* AER-3-70, Department of Agricultural Economics, University of Illinois, 1970.

Thomas, Kenneth, R. N. Weigle, and Richard Hawkins: *Where Do I Want to Be?* North Central Regional Extension Publication 34-3, 1973.

Chapter 6

Cash Flow
Budgeting

CHAPTER OBJECTIVES

1 To identify cash flow budgeting as another tool for use in forward planning

2 To learn the nature of the entries on a cash flow budget and why certain items are or are not included

3 To illustrate the procedure for completing a cash flow budget by the use of a cash flow form and an example

4 To discuss the advantages and potential uses of cash flow budgeting

A cash flow budget is another tool which has important applications in the forward planning activities for a farm business. It is the next logical step after a whole farm plan and budget are completed and serves to complete the entire planning and budgeting process. However, a cash flow budget should be completed at least once a year whether or not a whole farm plan is developed or revised. This means a cash flow budget will generally be completed more frequently than a whole farm plan and budget.

CHARACTERISTICS OF A CASH FLOW BUDGET

A cash flow budget is a summary of the cash inflows and cash outflows for a business over a given time period. It is rapidly becoming one of the most important budgeting and financial management tools given the large amounts of capital required on commercial farms and ranches today. As a forward planning tool, its primary use is to estimate future borrowing needs and the loan repayment capacity for the business.

Cash flows into the business from many sources throughout the year and flows out to pay business expenses and to meet other cash requirements. These flows are shown diagrammatically in Figure 6-1 assuming all cash moves through a business checking account. The objective of cash flow budgeting is to measure these flows for a given period of time such as 1 year. Two features make a cash flow budget substantially different from a whole farm budget. First, a cash flow budget measures all *cash* flows but does not include any noncash income or noncash expenses. Cash inflows would include income from the sale of capital items and proceeds from new loans, for example, but not inventory increases. Principal payments on loans and cost of new capital assets would be included as cash outflows but not depreciation or inventory decreases. The emphasis is on *cash* flows, all cash flows regardless of the source or use.

The second difference between a whole farm budget and a cash flow budget is the latter's concern with the timing of income and expenses. In other words, a cash flow budget also includes "when" the income and expenses will occur as well as the "what" and "how much." To show this timing of cash flows properly, a cash flow budget is typically done on a quarterly or monthly basis. Because farming is a very seasonal business, most farm cash flow budgets are done on a monthly basis to permit a more detailed analysis of the relationship between time and cash flows.

It should also be emphasized that a cash flow budget does not replace any other type of budget or any of the records to be discussed in Part 3. It fills other needs and is used for different purposes. However, we will see shortly that much of the information needed for a cash flow budget can be found in the whole farm budget and in other types of budgets and records.

Actual versus Projected Cash Flows

Because it is a forward planning tool, a cash flow budget contains estimates or projections for a future time period such as next year. However, a record of cash flows for last year can be developed from the year's records to give some insight into the past financial management of the business. This record of actual or historic cash flows has two other potential uses.

Many financial managers keep a record of actual cash flows on a monthly basis to compare with the figures in the projected cash flow budget. This running comparison helps to verify the accuracy of the projected cash flows and identifies the need to adjust borrowing and loan repayment plans if the actual figures deviate too far from projected figures. The other use for historic cash flows is in making estimates for next year's cash flow budget. Beginning with the totals and timing of cash flows in the past, it is relatively easy to make any adjustments needed to project future cash flows. It also prevents some important items from being overlooked.

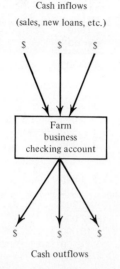

Cash inflows

(sales, new loans, etc.)

Cash outflows

(expenses, debt payments, taxes, etc.)

Figure 6-1 Measuring cash flows.

Structure of a Cash Flow Budget

The structure and format of a cash flow budget is shown in Table 6-1 in a simplified and condensed form. Only two time periods are shown, but once the basic procedure is understood it can be extended to other time periods. In the first time period, there is $3,000 of cash inflow, including the beginning cash balance. Total cash outflow is $14,000, leaving a projected cash balance of −$11,000. This will require borrowing $11,500 to permit a $500 minimum ending cash balance.

The total cash inflow during the second period is estimated at $18,000, which leaves a projected cash balance of $16,000 after subtracting the total cash outflow of $2,000. This large cash balance permits paying off the debt incurred in the first period, which is estimated at $11,700 when interest is included. The final result is an estimated $4,300 cash balance at the end of the second period. Following this same procedure for all subsequent time periods traces out the projected pattern of borrowing needs and debt repayment potential as well as the timing for both.

A CASH FLOW BUDGETING FORM

Printed forms for completing a cash flow budget are available from many sources, including lending agencies and the agricultural extension service in many states. Some managers prefer to develop their own using a large sheet of paper with the necessary lines and columns. Table 6-2 is an example of a form which can be used for cash flow budgeting. To save space, only the

Table 6-1   Simplified Cash Flow Budget

		Time period 1	Time period 2
1.	Beginning Cash Balance	$1,000	$ 500
	Cash Inflow:		
2.	Farm product sales	$2,000	$12,000
3.	Capital sales	0	5,000
4.	Miscellaneous cash income	0	500
5.	Total Cash Inflow	$3,000	$18,000
	Cash Outflow:		
6.	Farm operating expenses..............	$ 3,500	$ 1,800
7.	Capital purchases	10,000	0
8.	Miscellaneous expenses	500	200
9.	Total cash outflow	$14,000	$ 2,000
10.	Cash balance (line 5 − line 9)	−11,000	16,000
11.	Borrowed funds needed	$11,500	0
12.	Loan repayments (principal and interest)	0	11,700
13.	Ending cash balance	500	4,300
	(line 10 + line 11 − line 12)		
14.	Debt outstanding	$11,500	$ 0

headings and the first three columns are shown. Other forms may differ somewhat in organization, headings, and details, but all are designed to give the
same end result.

The first 13 lines of the form permit the recording of all cash inflows
projected from both farm and nonfarm sources. Since nonfarm income and
expenses will both affect the cash available for farm business use, it is standard
practice to include these items in the budget even though they are not directly
related to the farm business. Each type of income is recorded as the total
amount expected for the year in the Total column, and this amount is then
listed under the month or divided between the months when it will be received.
This is the *timing* part of a cash flow budget.

Cash farm operating expenses are listed from line 14 through line 34, with
the total on line 35. As with all entries on a cash flow budget, the projected
total for each expense item is put in the Total column, and this amount is then
prorated to the month or months when the expense will actually be paid. The
sum of total expenses for the individual months should always be compared
with the sum of the Total column to check for errors in dividing and prorating
the total.

Several other potential requirements for cash outflows are shown on lines
36 through 49. Capital expenditures for machinery and equipment, breeding
livestock, land, and buildings require a cash outflow. The full purchase price
for any projected capital expenditures should be recorded even though borrowing will be necessary to make the purchase. One purpose of the budget is

to estimate the amount of such borrowing. Family living expenses, income taxes, social security payments, and other nonfarm cash expenses should be entered on lines 39 to 43. Care should be taken to include all personal expenses such as automobile expenses and insurance premiums as part of the family living expenses.

Lines 44 to 49 are used to enter the scheduled principal and interest payments on debt incurred in past years. Payment dates and amounts on loans such as the farm mortgage, intermediate loans on machinery and breeding livestock, and any remaining short-term loans should be known or easily calculated for the coming year. Only scheduled payments on *old* debts are entered in this section, as payments on any *new* borrowing during the coming year are entered in a later section.

Total cash outflows for the year and for each individual month are entered on line 50 by adding lines 35 through 49. Next, the total estimated cash available at the end of each month is calculated by subtracting line 50 from line 13, and it is entered on line 51. If the total cash outflow is greater than the total cash inflow, the cash available will be negative, and some new borrowing will have to be arranged to bring the ending cash balance above zero. This new borrowing is entered on lines 52 to 54 according to the type of loan. The amount of new borrowing is added to the cash available on line 51 to find the ending cash balance for the month.

If the cash available on line 51 is greater than zero, the total cash inflow for the month is projected to be greater than total cash outflow. This amount can be used to pay off part or all of any *new* short-term debt incurred earlier in the year, with the appropriate amount of principal and interest entered on lines 56 and 57. These amounts should be adjusted to permit a positive ending cash balance, which is found by subtracting line 58 from line 51. The ending cash balance for this month is entered as the beginning cash balance for the next month, and the entire process is repeated for another month.

The last section of the form (lines 60 to 63) is not a direct part of cash flow budgeting but is useful to complete at the same time. It is a summary of each type of debt outstanding at the end of each month. For each type, the amount outstanding at the end of any month will be equal to the amount outstanding at the end of the previous month plus any new debt of this type minus any payments made during the month. Lines 60 to 62 should be added and the total debt outstanding entered on line 63. When the budget is completed, this figure shows the pattern of debt levels and changes throughout the annual production cycle. Because of the cyclical nature of agricultural production, income, and expenses, this pattern will often repeat itself each year.

EXAMPLE OF A CASH FLOW BUDGET

A completed cash flow budget is shown in Table 6-3. To assist further in the understanding of how to proceed with completing such a budget, the steps will be reviewed and several special calculations pointed out. The first estimates needed are the beginning cash balance on January 1 and all sources and

Table 6-2 Form for Cash Flow Budget

Name _____   Year _____

		Total	January	February	
1	BEGINNING CASH BALANCE				
	Operating Receipts:				
2	Grain and feed				
3	Feeder livestock				
4	Livestock products				
5	Other				
6					
	Capital Receipts:				
7	Breeding livestock				
8	Machinery and equipment				
9	Other				
	Non-farm Income:				
10	Wages and salary				
11	Investments				
12	Other				
13	TOTAL CASH INFLOW (add lines 1–12)				
	Operating Expenses:				
14	Seed				
15	Fertilizer and lime				
16	Chemicals				
17	Other crop expenses				
18	Gas, oil, lubricants				
19	Hired labor				
20	Machine hire				
21	Feed and grain				
22	Feeder livestock				
23	Livestock expenses				
24	Repairs — machinery				
25	Repairs — buildings and improvements				
26	Cash rent				
27	Supplies				
28	Property taxes				
29	Insurance				
30	Utilities				
31	Auto and pickup (farm share)				
32	Other farm expenses				
33					

amounts of cash inflows for the year. These amounts are entered in the Total column and again under the month or months when the income is actually expected. This example shows an estimated total cash inflow for the year of $256,900 including the beginning cash balance of $2,500. Notice the total cash inflow for months other than January cannot be determined until later when the beginning cash balance is known. The ending cash balance for each month must be calculated, and this value becomes the beginning cash balance for the next month.

		Total	January	February	
34					
35	Total Cash Operating Expenses				
	Capital Expenditures:				
36	Machinery and equipment				
37	Breeding livestock				
38					
	Other Expenditures:				
39	Family living expenses				
40	Income tax and social security				
41	Other non-farm expenses				
42					
43					
	Scheduled Debt Payments:				
44	Short-term　– principal				
45	– interest				
46	Intermediate　– principal				
47	– interest				
48	Long-term　– principal				
49	– interest				
50	TOTAL CASH OUTFLOW (add lines 35–49)				
51	CASH AVAILABLE (line 13–line 50)				
	New Borrowing				
52	Short-term				
53	Intermediate				
54	Long-term				
55	Total New Borrowing (add lines 52–54)				
	Payments on New Short-term Debt:				
56	Principal				
57	Interest				
58	Total Debt Payments (line 56 + line 57)				
59	ENDING CASH BALANCE (51 + 55 – 58)				
	Summary of Debt Outstanding:				
60	Short-term				
61	Intermediate				
62	Long-term				
63	TOTAL DEBT OUTSTANDING				

The next step is to estimate total cash operating expenses by type, placing each figure in the Total column. Each total expense estimate is then prorated to the appropriate month(s) and the total expenses for each month entered on line 35. The same procedure is followed for capital expenditures, family living expenses, income taxes, and social security payments. Another important requirement for cash is the scheduled principal and interest payments on debt outstanding at the beginning of the year. These amounts are shown on lines 44 to 49. Total cash outflow, found by summing lines 35 to 49, is $245,500 in the

Table 6-3 Example of a Cash Flow Budget

Name I. M. Farmer

CASH FLOW BUDGET

Year 1980

#		Total	Jan	Feb	March	April	May	June	July	Aug	Sept	Oct	Nov	Dec
1	BEGINNING CASH BALANCE	2,500	2,500	20,650	19,250	900	450	550	500	450	1,050	500	39,650	52,850
	Operating Receipts:													
2	Grain and feed	160,000	20,000	20,000								60,000	60,000	
3	Feeder livestock	82,000								82,000				
4	Livestock products													
5	Other	1,200									1,200			
6														
	Capital Receipts:													
7	Breeding livestock	3,800								3,800				
8	Machinery and equipment													
9														
	Non-farm Income:													
10	Wages and salary	7,200	600	600	600	600	600	600	600	600	600	600	600	600
11	Investments	200	200											
12														
13	TOTAL CASH INFLOW (add lines 1–12)	256,900	23,300	41,250	19,850	1,500	1,050	1,150	1,100	86,850	2,850	61,100	100,250	53,450
	Operating Expenses:													
14	Seed	5,800			5,800									
15	Fertilizer and lime	26,000			8,000	10,000							8,000	
16	Chemicals	4,000			4,000									
17	Other crop expenses	2,600										2,600		
18	Gas, oil, lubricants	3,000					1,500							1,500
19	Hired labor	6,000			500	1,500	1,500	500				1,000	1,000	
20	Machine hire	800						400			400			
21	Feed and grain	4,000		800		800		800		800				800
22	Feeder livestock	36,000											36,000	
23	Livestock expenses	7,500	1,000	500	500		500	1,000	500	500	500	500	1,000	1,000
24	Repairs – machinery	3,600	500	500	500		600				500	1,000		
25	Repairs – buildings & improvements	1,800									1,800			
26	Cash rent	1,000												
27	Supplies	1,000		250			250			250			250	
28	Property taxes	3,400			1,700							1,700		
29	Insurance	700		700										
30	Utilities	600	50	50	50	50	50	50	50	50	50	50	50	50
31	Auto and pickup (farm share)	1,200	100	100	100	100	100	100	100	100	100	100	100	100
32	Other farm expenses	500		100		100	100	100	100					
33														
34														

		Total	Jan	Feb	March	April	May	June	July	Aug	Sept	Oct	Nov	Dec
35	Total Cash Operating Expenses	108,500	1,650	3,000	21,150	14,050	4,500	2,950	650	1,800	2,850	6,050	46,400	3,450
	Capital Expenditures:													
36	Machinery and equipment	60,000			60,000									
37	Breeding livestock	1,000						1,000						
38														
	Other Expenditures:													
39	Family living expenses	12,000	1,000	1,000	1,000	1,000	1,000	1,000	1,000	1,000	1,000	1,000	1,000	1,000
40	Income tax and social security	4,800			4,800									
41	Other non-farm expenses													
42														
43														
	Scheduled Debt Payments:													
44	Short-term – principal	0												
45	– interest	0												
46	Intermediate – principal	20,000						20,000						
47	– interest	3,200						3,200						
48	Long-term – principal	12,000		6,000						6,000				
49	– interest	24,000		12,000						12,000				
50	TOTAL CASH OUTFLOW (add lines 35-49)	245,500	2,650	22,000	86,950	15,050	5,500	28,150	1,650	20,800	3,850	7,050	47,400	4,450
51	CASH AVAILABLE (line 13-line 50)	11,400	20,650	19,250	(67,100)	(13,550)	(4,450)	(27,000)	(550)	66,050	(1,000)	54,050	52,850	49,000
	New Borrowing													
52	Short-term	77,000			28,000	14,000	5,000	27,500	1,000		1,500			
53	Intermediate	40,000			40,000									
54	Long-term	0												
55	Total New Borrowing (add lines 52-54)	117,000			68,000	14,000	5,000	27,500	1,000		1,500			
	Payments on New Short-term Debt:													
56	Principal	77,000								63,000		14,000		
57	Interest	2,400								2,000		400		
58	Total Debt Payments (line 56 + line 57)	79,400								65,000		14,400		
59	ENDING CASH BALANCE (51 + 55 – 58)	49,000	20,650	19,250	900	450	550	500	450	1,050	500	39,650	52,850	49,000
	Summary of Debt Outstanding:													
60	Short-term	0			28,000	42,000	47,000	74,500	75,500	12,500	14,000			
61	Intermediate	40,000	40,000	40,000	80,000	80,000	80,000	60,000	60,000	60,000	60,000	60,000	60,000	60,000
62	Long-term	300,000	300,000	294,000	294,000	294,000	294,000	294,000	294,000	288,000	288,000	288,000	288,000	288,000
63	TOTAL DEBT OUTSTANDING	340,000	340,000	334,000	402,000	416,000	421,000	428,500	429,500	360,500	362,000	348,000	348,000	348,000

example. All the above steps should be completed before any of the calculations on lines 51 to 63 are attempted.

Beginning with the month of January, note that total cash inflow is $23,300 and total cash outflow is $2,650, leaving $20,650 of cash available at the end of January (line 51). There is no need to borrow any money in January, and there are no new loans that can be paid off. Therefore, lines 52 to 58 are all zero and the $20,650 becomes the ending cash balance on line 59. Lines 60 to 63 (short column on far left) indicate $40,000 intermediate debt and $300,000 long-term debt on January 1, and there are no changes in the balances during the month. These figures are transferred to the January column, showing $340,000 of total debt outstanding at the end of January.

The next step is to transfer the January ending cash balance of $20,650 to the beginning cash balance for February. Calculations for February are similar to those for January with one exception. There is a $6,000 principal payment on the long-term loan, which reduces its balance to $294,000 as shown on line 62, and the total debt outstanding is reduced to $334,000.

February's ending cash balance of $19,250 is transferred to the beginning balance for March where the first new borrowing occurs. Cash outflow exceeds cash inflow by $67,100 in March, requiring the borrowing of $68,000 to cover this amount and leave a small ending balance of $900. New machinery will be purchased in March at a cost of $60,000; so a *new* intermediate loan of $40,000 is included as part of the new borrowing, and the remaining $28,000 is shown as a *new* short-term loan. After the appropriate adjustments in the loan balances on lines 60 and 61, March concludes with $402,000 of debt outstanding.

This example shows additional new borrowing will also be needed in April, May, June, July, and September, and payments can be made in August when the feeder livestock are sold and in October when some crop income is received. Repayments are handled in the following manner, using August as the example. A total of $66,050 in cash (line 51) is available for repaying new debt incurred earlier in the year. All this cannot be used for principal payments, as there will be some interest due and a positive ending balance is needed. A principal payment of $63,000 plus $2,000 interest on this amount will leave an ending balance of $1,050. The short-term debt outstanding must be reduced by the $63,000 and the long-term debt by the $6,000 principal payment (line 48). Total debt outstanding at the end of August is $360,500.

The principal repaid in August assumes the oldest of the new short-term borrowing was repaid first. It included the $28,000 borrowed in March, the $14,000 borrowed in April, the $5,000 borrowed in May, and $16,000 of the June borrowing for a total of $63,000. The interest rate was assumed to be 10 percent and the interest due was calculated as below using the equation interest = principal × rate × time.

March borrowing:	$28,000 × 10% × 5/12 of a year =	$1,166
April borrowing:	14,000 × 10% × 4/12 of a year =	466
May borrowing:	5,000 × 10% × 3/12 of a year =	125

June borrowing: $\underline{16{,}000} \times 10\% \times 2/12$ of a year = $\underline{266}$
Totals: $\$63{,}000$ $\$2{,}023$

For convenience, the interest was rounded to $2,000 in Table 6-3.

Sufficient cash was available in October to repay all remaining new short-term debt consisting of $11,500 left from June borrowing, the $1,000 borrowed in July, and the $1,500 borrowed in September. Interest due was calculated as above and rounded to $400 for convenience.

Large cash balances are projected for October, November, and December after all new short-term debt has been repaid. However, the budget shows that new borrowing will peak in July with $75,500 of new short-term debt and $40,000 of new intermediate debt for the new machinery. With the repayment capacity exhibited in this cash flow budget, a borrower should have no trouble obtaining necessary funds from a lender.

The large cash balances toward the end of the year suggest several alternatives which should be considered. First, arrangements might be made to invest this money for several months rather than have it sit idle in a checking account. Any interest earned would be additional income. Second, this excess cash could be used to make early payments on the intermediate or long-term loans to reduce the interest charges. A third alternative relates to the $40,000 new intermediate loan used to purchase machinery in March. If this amount was included as part of the new short-term borrowing instead of a new intermediate loan, it could have been paid off by November. This alternative would reduce the ending intermediate debt to $20,000, the total debt outstanding at year-end to $308,000, and the ending cash balance to slightly less than $9,000 after paying interest on the additional $40,000 of short-term debt.

This last alternative would require paying for all the new machinery in the year of purchase and would add considerable risk to the operation. If prices and yields were below expectations, there might not be sufficient cash available to repay all the new short-term debt. For this reason, using short-term debt to finance the purchase of long-lived items such as machinery and buildings is not recommended. A better practice would be to obtain a longer loan and then make additional loan payments in years when extra cash is available.

USES FOR A CASH FLOW BUDGET

The primary use of a cash flow budget is to project the timing and amount of new borrowing the business will need during the year and the timing and amount of loan repayments. Discussion in the last paragraph suggests there may be other ways a cash flow budget can be used to improve the financial management of the business. Other uses and advantages are:

1 A borrowing and debt repayment plan can be developed which fits an individual farm business. The budget can prevent borrowing too much money too soon and shows how repaying debts as quickly as possible will save interest.

2   A cash flow budget may suggest ways to rearrange purchases and scheduled debt repayments to minimize borrowing. For example, capital expenditures and insurance premiums might be moved to months where a large cash inflow is expected.

3   A cash flow budget combines both business and personal financial affairs into one complete plan.

4   A bank or other lending agency is better able to offer financial advice and spot potential weaknesses or strengths in the business based on a completed cash flow budget.

5   With planning ahead and knowing adequate cash will be available and when it will be available, discounts on input purchases can be obtained by making a prompt cash payment.

6   A cash flow budget can also have a payoff in tax planning by pointing out the income tax effects of the timing of purchases, sales, and capital expenditures.

7   A cash flow budget can help spot an imbalance between short, intermediate, and long-term credit and suggest ways to improve the situation. For example, too much short-term debt relative to long-term debt can create cash flow problems.

Other uses and advantages of a cash flow budget could be listed depending on the individual financial situation. The alert manager will find many ways to improve the planning and financial management of a business through the use of a cash flow budget.

While there are many ways to use a cash flow budget, it should *not* be used for some purposes. A common mistake is to project business profit or net income based on the cash flow estimates. This cannot be done because several noncash items which affect profit are not included in a cash flow budget. Depreciation and changes in inventory values are examples. Cash outflows such as principal payments on loans, capital expenditures, and family living expenses are also included in a cash flow budget but do not affect profit. Chapter 8 will discuss in detail the income and expenses which directly affect profit. After reading Chapter 8, the reader may wish to compare the differences between a cash flow budget and an income statement.

SUMMARY

A cash flow budget is a summary of all cash inflows and outflows for a future time period and is another method of forward planning. It includes all cash flows regardless of type, source, or use, including both farm and personal finances. Cash flow budgets are typically done on a monthly basis for a farm to show the timing of the cash inflows and outflows. This information can be used in a number of ways, the most important being the planning of borrowing needs and debt repayment capacity and the timing of both.

QUESTIONS FOR REVIEW AND FURTHER THOUGHT

1 Why is machinery depreciation not included in a cash flow budget?
2 Identify four sources of cash inflows which are not included on a whole farm budget. Why are they included on the cash flow budget?
3 Identify four cash outflow items which are not included on a whole farm budget. Why are they included on a cash flow budget?
4 What distinguishes a cash flow budget from the other types of budgets?
5 Why are cash inflows from nonfarm sources and outflows for family living expenses included on a farm cash flow budget?

REFERENCES

Barry, Peter J., John A. Hopkin, and C. B. Baker: *Financial Management in Agriculture*, 2d ed., Interstate Printers and Publishers, Inc., Danville, Ill., 1979, chap. 6.
Frey, Thomas L., and Danny A. Klinefelter: *Coordinated Financial Statements for Agriculture*, Agri Finance, Skokie, Ill., 1978.
Penson, John B., Jr., and David A. Lins: *Agricultural Finance: An Introduction to Micro and Macro Concepts*, Prentice-Hall, Inc., Englewood Cliffs, N.J., 1980, chap. 2.

Part 3
CONTROL

HIGHLIGHTS

Control is the second primary function of management. Plans should not be developed, implemented, and then ignored. Whatever the plan, the business needs to be watched, monitored, and directed. Are the goals being attained? Is the plan actually being followed? How far are the actual results deviating from the planned results? What corrections need to be made? The answers to these questions require a system of control.

Control panels on modern aircraft contain many dials and gauges to monitor speed, altitude, direction, fuel supply, oil pressure, etc. Their purpose is to identify malfunctions and provide information needed by the pilot to keep the airplane on course. A control system for a farm business performs many of the same functions. It permits the manager to check and monitor progress, identify problems which may require adjustments in the farm plan, and measure how far the actual results are deviating from the goals and objectives. Control can be defined as the measurement and correction of performance to make sure plans are being followed and objectives are being attained.

Control consists of two related tasks: (1) recording information and (2) analyzing this information to identify problems and the corrective action to be taken. The monitoring and analysis of the business is a continuous process so that problems can be identified and corrected as quickly as possible. In practice, much of the analysis in a farm business is done at the end of a year when full information from one complete production cycle is available.

Planning and control are discussed in two separate parts in this book, but a plan is necessary for control and, since both are continuous functions, the manager will often be performing both at the same time. The plan provides the standards, goals, and procedures to be attained or followed and control monitors progress related to each of these. Without a plan there are no established goals or standards, no way of measuring deviations, and little to help the manager make corrections or changes in the plan.

Planning and control are related in another way, even though planning looks forward and control utilizes information on past results or historical information. The information recorded and analyses performed as part of the control function provide important data for the planning function. Therefore, there is a continual flow of information from the control system which can be used to correct and alter plans. This feedback from the control system to the planning function is an important part of a complete management system.

Part 3 contains Chapters 7 through 10, with Chapter 7 covering the balance sheet and its analysis. Chapter 8 describes the income statement and its analysis. The balance sheet and income statement along with their proper analysis provide a minimum control system. Additional methods for control and analysis of an entire farm business are outlined in Chapter 9. Part 3 concludes with Chapter 10, which discusses supplemental or additional records useful in performing the control function.

Chapter 7

The Balance Sheet
and Its Analysis

CHAPTER OBJECTIVES

1 To introduce the balance sheet as one of the financial summaries needed to organize a control system

2 To show how a complete inventory is taken and valued as the first step in completing a balance sheet

3 To note three depreciation methods which can be used to value depreciable assets on a cost less depreciation basis

4 To analyze the three classes of assets and liabilities which are used to construct a balance sheet

5 To define net worth as owner's equity or the owner's investment in the business

6 To illustrate how to analyze a balance sheet through the use of an example and several financial ratios

Two basic parts of a complete set of farm records are a *balance sheet* and an *income statement*. Both are financial statements, but they serve different purposes. The balance sheet summarizes the financial condition of the business *at a point in time* while the income statement summarizes the financial transactions (revenue and expenses) which occurred *over a period of time*. Since every revenue and expense affects the financial condition of the business, the balance sheet is continually changing. That is why the point in time concept must be emphasized in discussing the balance sheet.

This chapter will discuss the balance sheet, and the following chapter will discuss the income statement. However, both of these financial statements require some basic information about the type, number, and value of items owned by the business. Obtaining this information requires taking an inventory of business property.

TAKING INVENTORY

A complete inventory is a listing of all physical and financial items owned by the business. It includes both *personal property* such as livestock, machinery, grain, stocks, and bank balances and *real property* such as land and buildings. If no records exist, taking an inventory would be the first step in organizing a complete set of farm records. To be useful in a record-keeping system, the inventory must be in dollar values. Therefore, taking an inventory consists of two parts, the physical count and valuation.

The Physical Count

The physical part of an inventory consists of listing and describing each piece of property. Physical units such as bushels, tons, head, and pounds are used to record the quantities of each type of property. It may be necessary to measure a grain bin or hay shed and convert the cubic feet into bushels or bales or tons. Obviously the physical count will be easier if some record or count was made at the time the bin, shed, or pen was filled.

Since the final objective of an inventory is the dollar value of all items owned, the physical count should be as accurate as possible. Estimating the weights of feeder livestock can be particularly troublesome, as it is often impractical or impossible to weigh them. Yet price and total value are dependent on their weight. Experience and good judgment are important here, as they are in all areas when performing the physical count part of the inventory.

Inventory Valuation

The physical quantities of property owned must be converted into dollar values to complete the balance sheet and income statement. This valuation process can be completed using one of several methods to place a value on each type of property. The choice of valuation method will depend on the type of property and use to be made of the inventory. Whichever method is used, the accounting concepts of "conservatism" and "consistency" in valuation should be kept in mind. Conservatism cautions against placing too high a value on any item, while consistency stresses using the same valuation method or methods over time. Use of these concepts makes financial statements directly comparable from year to year and prevents an overly optimistic view of the firm's financial condition.

Net Market Price   This valuation method places a value on an inventory item equal to its current market price (price times quantity inventoried). Any marketing charges such as transportation, selling commissions, and fees are subtracted to find the net market price. This method can be used for many types of property but works particularly well for items which could or will be sold in a relatively short period of time as a normal part of the business activities and for which current market prices are easily obtainable. Examples would be hay, grain, feeder livestock, stocks, and bonds.

Cost   Items which have been purchased can be valued at their original cost. This method works well for items which have been purchased recently and for which cost records are still available. Feed, fertilizer, supplies, and purchased feeder livestock can be valued at their original cost, and land can also have its value determined this way. Items such as buildings and machinery which normally lose value or depreciate over time should not be valued with this method. Livestock and crops which have been raised cannot be valued with this method, as there is no purchase price to use.

Lower of Cost or Market   This valuation method requires valuing an item at both its net market price and its cost and then using whichever value is lower. This is a conservative method, as it minimizes the chance of placing too high a value on any item. Using this method, property which is increasing in value because of inflation will have a value equal to its original cost. Valuing such property at cost eliminates any increase in inventory value over time caused solely by inflation or a general increase in prices. When prices have decreased since the item was purchased, this method results in a valuation at net market value.

Farm Production Cost   Items produced on the farm and still on hand when the inventory is taken can be valued at their farm production cost. This cost is equal to the actual cost of producing the item but should not include profit or any opportunity costs associated with the production. Grain, hay, silage, and raised livestock can be valued by this method if good cost of production records are available. Established but immature crops growing in a field at inventory time are generally valued by this method, with the value set equal to the actual production expenses to date. It is not appropriate to value a growing crop using the expected yield and price because poor weather, a hailstorm, or lower prices could drastically change the value before harvest and final sale. This procedure is an example of conservatism and the point in time concept of a balance sheet.

Cost Less Depreciation   Property which provides services to a business over a period of years but loses value over time because of age, use, or obsolescence should be valued at the original cost less depreciation. Examples would be machinery, buildings, fences and purchased breeding livestock. Each year the item's value is reduced by the amount of depreciation for that year. Therefore, the value in the current time period is equal to the original cost less the total accumulated depreciation from purchase date to date of inventory. This value is referred to as the item's *book value*.

Depreciation is also a business expense and can be viewed as such from two different but related viewpoints. First, it represents a loss in value because the item is used in the business to produce income. Second, it is an accounting procedure to spread the original cost over the item's useful life. It is not appropriate or correct to deduct the full purchase price as an expense in the year of purchase, as the item will be used to generate income for many years. Instead, the purchase price less salvage value is allocated or "spread" over time through the business expense called depreciation.

Before the three methods for estimating annual depreciation are discussed, several additional terms need to be introduced. *Useful life* is the expected number of years the item will be used in the business. It may be the age at which the item will be completely worn out if the manager expects to own it that long, or it may be a shorter period if it will be sold before then. The key to determining a useful life is the number of years the manager *expects* to own the item and is therefore an estimate and subject to error. Another estimate is *salvage value* or terminal value, which is the item's value at the end of its assigned useful life. Salvage value may be zero if the item will be owned until completely worn out and will have no junk or scrap value at that time. A positive salvage value should be assigned to an item if it will have some value as scrap or will be sold before it is completely worn out. In the latter case, the salvage value should be its estimated market value at the end of its assigned useful life. In general, the shorter the useful life the higher the salvage value.

Straight Line   The straight-line method of calculating depreciation is the most widely used and the easiest to use. Annual depreciation is computed from the equation

$$\text{Annual depreciation} = \frac{\text{cost} - \text{salvage value}}{\text{useful life}}$$

and is the same for each year. Straight-line depreciation can be computed from an alternate method using the equation

$$\text{Annual depreciation} = (\text{cost} - \text{salvage value}) \times R$$

where R is the annual percentage depreciation rate found by dividing 100 percent by the useful life (100 percent $\div$ useful life).

For example, assume the purchase of a machine for \$10,000 which is assigned a \$2,000 salvage value and a 10-year useful life. The annual depreciation using the first equation would be

$$\frac{\$10,000 - \$2,000}{10 \text{ years}} = \$800$$

Using the second equation, the percentage rate would be 100 percent ÷ 10, or 10 percent, and the annual depreciation is

$$(\$10,000 - \$2,000) \times 10\% = \$800$$

The result is the same for either procedure, and the total depreciation over 10 years would be $800 × 10 years = $8,000, reducing the machine's book value to its salvage value of $2,000.

Double Declining Balance   Several types of declining balance depreciation are possible, but the most common is double declining balance. The "double" comes from using a depreciation rate which is double or twice the straight-line rate. This rate is allowed on some types of property when calculating depreciation for income tax purposes. Annual depreciation can be computed from the equation

$$\text{Annual depreciation} = \left(\begin{array}{c} \text{book value at} \\ \text{beginning of year} \end{array} \right) \times R$$

where R is equal to two times the straight-line percentage rate. The percentage rate remains constant each year, but it is multiplied by the book value, which declines each year by an amount equal to the previous year's depreciation. Notice also that the percentage rate is multiplied by each year's book value and *not* cost minus salvage value as with the straight-line method.

Using the previous example, the double declining balance rate would be 2 times 10 percent, or 20 percent, and the annual depreciation would be computed in the following manner:

Year 1: $10,000 × 20% = $2,000
Year 2: $ 8,000 × 20% = $1,600
Year 3: $ 6,400 × 20% = $1,280

Year 7: $ 2,622 × 20% = $ 524
Year 8: $ 2,098 × 20% = $ 420 (but this amount would reduce the book value below the $2,000 salvage value; so only $98 of depreciation can be taken)
Year 9 and 10:   No remaining depreciation

This example is not unusual, as double declining balance will often result in the total allowable depreciation being taken before the end of the useful life and depreciation must stop when the book value equals salvage value. Notice also that the declining balance method will never reduce the book value to zero. With a zero salvage value it is necessary to switch to straight-line depreciation at some point to get all the allowable depreciation or to take all remaining depreciation in the last year.

Sum-of-the-Year's Digits   The annual depreciation using the sum-of-the-year's digits method is computed from the equation

$$\text{Annual depreciation} = (\text{cost} - \text{salvage value}) \times \frac{RL}{SOYD}$$

where RL   = remaining years of useful life as of the beginning of the year for which depreciation is being computed

SOYD   = sum of all the numbers from 1 through the estimated useful life. For example, for a 5-year useful life SOYD would be $1 + 2 + 3 + 4 + 5 = 15$ and would be 55 for a 10-year useful life[1]

Continuing with the same example used in the previous sections, the SOYD would be 55 (the sum of the numbers 1 through 10). The annual depreciation would be computed in the following manner:

Year   1: $(\$10,000 - \$2,000) \times \dfrac{10}{55} = \$1,454.55$

Year   2: $(\$10,000 - \$2,000) \times \dfrac{9}{55} = \$1,309.09$

Year   3: $(\$10,000 - \$2,000) \times \dfrac{8}{55} = \$1,163.64$

. . . . .
. . . . .
. . . . .

Year 10: $(10,000 - \$2,000) \times \dfrac{1}{55} = \$145.45$

Notice the annual depreciation is highest in the first year and declines by a constant amount each year thereafter.

Comparing Depreciation Methods   Figure 7-1 graphs the annual depreciation for each depreciation method based on a $10,000 machine with a $2,000 salvage value and a 10-year life. The annual depreciation over time is considerably different for each method. Double declining balance and sum-of-the-year's digits have a higher annual depreciation in the early years than straight-line, with the reverse being true in the later years. For this reason, double declining balance and sum-of-the-year's digits are referred to as "fast" or

[1]A quick way to find the sum-of-the-year's digits (SOYD) is from the equation $\dfrac{(n)(n+1)}{2}$, where n is the useful life.

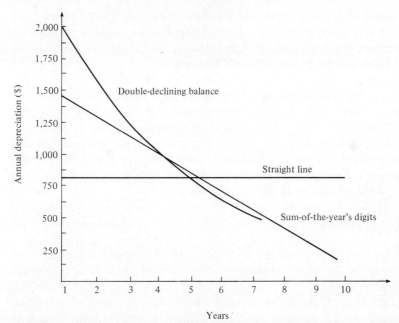

Figure 7-1 Comparison of annual depreciation for three depreciation methods.

"accelerated" depreciation methods, with double declining balance being the "fastest" method.

It is also important to note that the choice of depreciation method does not change the total depreciation taken or allowable over the useful life. In the example used, there is only $8,000 of depreciation regardless of the method selected. The depreciation methods affect only the pattern or distribution of depreciation over time. A final choice of the most appropriate method will depend on the type of property, the use to be made of the resulting book value, and income tax considerations. For example, the actual market value of automobiles, tractors, and other motorized machinery tends to decline most rapidly during the first few years of life and more slowly in the later years. If it is important for depreciation on these items to approximate their actual decline in value, one of the "fast" depreciation methods should be used. For property such as fences and buildings which have little or no market value and provide a rather uniform flow of services to the business over time, straight-line depreciation would be appropriate.

Items purchased during the year should have the first year's depreciation prorated according to the length of time the item was actually owned. For example, a tractor purchased on April 1 would be eligible for 9/12 of a full year's depreciation the first year and a pickup purchased on October 1 would get 3/12 of a year's depreciation the first year. Any time a partial year's depreciation is taken the first year, there will be only a partial year's depreciation remaining in the last year of the item's useful life.

Depreciation is also an important tax management tool, and income tax considerations will often affect the choice of depreciation method, useful life, and salvage value. Discussion of these and other factors related to depreciation and income taxes will be postponed until Chapter 17.

Summary of Valuation Methods   The valuation method or methods to use will depend not only on the type of property but also on the final use of the inventory values. Consistency in the valuation methods selected is important. Valuation can be done on a "cost" basis using primarily the cost and cost less depreciation methods or on a "market" basis using the net market value method whenever possible. These two procedures will be discussed in more detail during the explanation of the balance sheet.

THE BALANCE SHEET

One use of the complete inventory and valuation of property is to construct a *balance sheet* or *net worth statement*. The balance sheet is a systematic organization of everything "owned" and "owed" by a business or individual at a given point in time. Anything of value owned by a business or individual is more properly called an *asset*, and any obligation or debt owed someone else is referred to as a *liability*. Therefore, accountants refer to a balance sheet as a listing of assets and liabilities concluding with an estimate of *net worth* or *owner's equity*, which is the difference between total assets and total liabilities.

A balance sheet can be completed any time during the year, but the usual time is at the end of the accounting period. On farms and ranches this will generally be December 31. This procedure allows a single balance sheet to be both an end of the year and beginning of the year statement for the adjoining years. For purposes of comparison, it is necessary to have a balance sheet available for the beginning and ending of each year, as farm profit is generally computed annually for a calendar year.

The primary use of a balance sheet is to measure the financial strength and position of the business. Several measures of financial strength and position can be obtained from a balance sheet:

1   *Solvency,* which measures whether total assets are greater than total liabilities. If not, the business is insolvent or technically bankrupt.
2   *Liquidity,* which measures the ability to generate cash needed to meet cash obligations without seriously disrupting the production activities of the business.
3   *Net worth or owner's equity,* which is the amount of money remaining for the owner of the business after liquidating the business and paying all liabilities.

Each of these measures will be analyzed later in this chapter.

A general format for a balance sheet is shown in Table 7-1. An important characteristic is that total assets must exactly equal total liabilities *plus* net

Table 7-1   General Format of a Balance Sheet

Assets		Liabilities	
Current assets	$XXX	Current liabilities	$XXX
Intermediate assets	XXX	Intermediate liabilities	XXX
Fixed assets	XXX	Long-term liabilities	XXX
		Total liabilities	$XXX
		Net worth	XXX
Total assets	$XXX	Total liabilities and net worth	$XXX

worth, making the bottom-line values on both sides of a balance sheet equal to each other. Hence the name "balance" sheet.

Assets

The purpose of the inventory discussed earlier in the chapter was to identify and value the assets for inclusion on the balance sheet. An asset can have value for one or both of two reasons. First, it can be sold to generate cash, or second, it can be used to produce other goods which can be sold to provide cash income at some future time. Goods which have already been produced such as grain and feeder livestock can be sold quickly and easily without disrupting future production activities and are called *liquid assets*. Assets such as machinery, breeding livestock, and land are owned primarily to produce future income. Selling them to generate cash to meet current obligations would affect the firm's ability to produce future income; so they are less liquid or are illiquid. These assets are also more difficult to sell quickly and easily at their full market value.

Assets are traditionally divided into three categories on a farm balance sheet. This division is based on liquidity and useful life. Those assets which have the shorter useful lives and are the most liquid are listed first with land, the most illiquid asset and the one with the longest life, listed last.

Current Assets   The more liquid assets are listed in the current asset category. They will be either used up or sold in the next year as a normal part of business activities, and their sale will not disrupt future production activities. Cash on hand and checking account and savings account balances are current assets, as these are the most liquid of all assets. Other current assets include readily marketable stocks and bonds, accounts or notes receivable which represent money owed to the business because of loans granted or services rendered, feed, grain, supplies on hand, and feeder livestock or livestock held primarily for sale. The cash value of life insurance, any prepaid expenses, and the value of growing crops would also be included.

Intermediate Assets   As the name implies, these assets are intermediate in liquidity and useful life. They have a useful life greater than 1 year but generally less than 7 to 10 years and are less liquid than current assets, as their sale affects the future income potential of the business. The most important intermediate assets on a farm balance sheet are machinery, equipment, and breeding livestock. Most intermediate assets are characterized by being depreciable. They are not purchased for resale in a relatively short period but to be used over time to produce other salable products.

Fixed Assets   Real estate or land and permanent buildings is the most important fixed asset on farms and ranches. Fixed assets are the least liquid of all assets; they have a useful life greater than 10 years, and their sale would seriously affect the ongoing nature of a business. For example, if all the owned land and buildings were sold, the business might be totally eliminated.

Liabilities

A liability is an obligation or debt owed to someone else. It represents an outsider's claim against one or more business assets. As with the assets, liabilities are divided into three categories, with time or the length of the loan being the primary difference between categories. Another relationship between the grouping of assets and liabilities is that a loan in any liability category will generally have been obtained to finance the production or purchase of an asset in the corresponding asset category.

Current Liabilities   Current liabilities are those financial obligations which will become due and payable within 1 year from the date of the balance sheet. Included in this category would be accounts payable at farm supply stores for goods and services received but not yet paid for and the full amount of principal on any short-term loans or notes payable. Short-term loans are those requiring complete repayment of the principal in 1 year or less.

Intermediate and long-term loans typically require annual or semiannual payments of principal and interest. The next year's principal payments on these loans are listed as a current liability, as they represent cash obligations falling due within the next year. Interest on all three types of loans should also be included as a current liability. However, interest due is a function of time and accumulates or accrues day by day. Normal accounting procedure is to include only that interest which would be due if the loan was paid off on the date of the balance sheet. In other words, the interest shown would include only the interest which has accrued since the date of the loan or the last loan payment, whichever is later. This is another example of the point in time concept of a balance sheet.

Intermediate Liabilities   These liabilities represent loans where repayment is extended over at least 2 years and up to as long as 7 to 10 years. They would typically have some principal and interest due each year. Most intermediate liabilities will be loans for the purchase of machinery, breeding livestock, or other intermediate assets. The current year's principal payment and accrued interest would be listed as a current liability, with the remaining loan balance included as an intermediate liability. Care must be taken to subtract the principal payment included in current liabilities from the remaining loan balance to avoid double counting.

Long-term Liabilities Loans for the purchase of real estate or where land and buildings provide the collateral for the loan would be listed as long-term liabilities. They will be in the form of a farm mortgage loan or land purchase contract, and the repayment period will generally be from 10 to 40 years. As with intermediate liabilities, any principal due within the next year plus accrued interest would be listed as a current liability. Only the loan balance remaining after this payment would be entered as a long-term liability.

Net Worth

Net worth represents the amount of money left for the owner of the business should all assets be sold and all liabilities paid on the date of the balance sheet. It is found by subtracting total liabilities from total assets and is therefore the "balancing" amount which causes total assets to be exactly equal to total liabilities plus net worth. In other words, net worth is the owner's current investment or equity in the business and is properly listed as a liability as it is money due the owner upon liquidation of the business. Another name for net worth is *owner's equity*.

Net worth will change if there is a change in an asset's value, a gift or inheritance is received, or an asset is sold for more or less than its book value on the balance sheet. Increases in net worth more commonly result from using the assets to produce crops and livestock, and the profit from this production is used in turn to purchase new assets and/or reduce liabilities. However, this process requires time, and one of the reasons for comparing a balance sheet for the beginning of the year with one for the end of the year is to study the effects of the year's production on net worth and composition of assets and liabilities.

However, changes in the composition of assets and liabilities may not cause a change in net worth. For example, if $10,000 in cash is used to purchase a new machine, net worth does not change. Current assets have been reduced by $10,000, but intermediate assets have increased by $10,000 and net worth is unchanged. If the $10,000 is used to pay principal on a loan, assets will decrease by $10,000, but so will liabilities, and net worth is still the same. Borrowing $10,000 to purchase a machine of the same value also leaves net worth unchanged, as both total assets and total liabilities increase by $10,000.

These examples illustrate an important concept. Business net worth changes only when the owner puts additional personal capital into the business (increasing net worth) or withdraws capital as might be done to meet family living expenses (reducing net worth) or when the business generates a profit (increasing net worth) or shows a loss (reducing net worth). Many business transactions only change the mix or composition of assets and liabilities but do not affect net worth.

Balance Sheet Example

A balance sheet can be constructed just for the farm business itself, for the family or household listing only personal and nonbusiness assets and liabilities, or for a combination of both. While it is preferable for business assets and liabilities to be listed separately from those which are personal in nature, farm and ranch balance sheets often contain both. One reason is the joint use of some assets such as an automobile, and another is a lender's desire to see the total financial condition of both the individual and the business. The balance sheet for I. M. Farmer shown in Table 7-2 concentrates on business assets and liabilities.

A balance sheet can be constructed on either a cost or a market basis. The cost basis balance sheet has assets valued at original cost and cost less depreciation for depreciable assets. This results in a very conservative estimate of the firm's financial condition, particularly during periods of inflation. A market basis balance sheet has assets valued at net market price and is a more accurate estimate of the firm's actual financial condition at a given point in time. The method to use will depend primarily on the purpose of the balance sheet, although both sets of values can be recorded simultaneously by using two columns on the same balance sheet. The cost basis is more useful for measuring financial progress over time without considering or including the effects of inflation on asset values. A balance sheet on a market basis may present a more accurate and useful set of values when applying for a loan.

The example in Table 7-2 contains the typical entries on a farm or ranch balance sheet. It is on a cost basis, although assets such as grain, hay, and feeder cattle are listed at net market value. Current assets are at market value because many have not been purchased, so no cost values are available and others represent readily marketable assets. Machinery, equipment, and buildings are valued at cost less accumulated depreciation and land at original cost. Beef cows could be valued at cost less depreciation if they were purchased or at market value if they have been raised.

Current liabilities include an account payable, a loan on the feeder cattle, accrued property taxes payable, and interest accrued as of December 31, 19XX, on all loans. Principal payments due during the next 12 months on the intermediate and long-term loans are also shown as current liabilities. There are intermediate loans outstanding on machinery and the beef cows, and the balances shown are after the principal payments shown as current liabilities. The only long-term liability is a mortgage on the land and the loan balance shown is again the amount that remains due after the following year's payment.

As of December 31, 19XX, I. M. Farmer has total assets of $602,500 and total liabilities of $284,500, and the difference or net worth amounts to $318,000. These are all substantial amounts, but the balance sheet requires further analysis to determine the financial condition of this farm business.

Table 7-2   Balance Sheet for I. M. Farmer (as of December 31, 19XX)

Assets

Current assets:

Cash on hand	$ 400	
Checking account balance	3,300	
Savings account	5,000	
Cash value of life insurance	800	
Grain (10,000 bu of corn)	24,000	
Hay (100 tons)	3,000	
Feeder cattle (110 head)	48,000	
Miscellaneous supplies	2,000	
Total current assets		$86,500

Intermediate assets:

Machinery and equipment	$ 72,000	
Beef cows (50 head)	20,000	
Total intermediate assets		$92,000

Fixed assets:
Real estate:

Land (320 acres)	$384,000	
Buildings and improvements	40,000	
Total fixed assets		$424,000
Total assets		$602,500

Liabilities

Current liabilities:

Account payable (J & J Farm Supply)	$ 1,400	
Accrued taxes payable	800	
Operating loan (feeder cattle)	26,000	

Accrued interest on loans:

Operating loan	$ 700	
Intermediate loans	1,600	
Long-term loan	10,000	

Principal payment on intermediate and long-term loans
due within 12 months:

Intermediate loans	$ 12,000	
Long-term loans	20,000	
Total current liabilities		$72,500

Intermediate liabilities:

Machinery loan	$ 22,000	
Beef cow loan	10,000	
Total intermediate liabilities		$32,000

Long-term liabilities:

Farm mortgage		180,000
Total long-term liabilities		180,000
Total liabilities		$284,500
Net worth		$318,000
Total liabilities and net worth		$602,500

RATIO ANALYSIS

A balance sheet is often analyzed using ratios to obtain measures of the financial position and strength of the business. Ratios are used because they provide a standard unit of measurement and permit comparison over time and between firms of different sizes. A large firm and a small firm would have substantial differences in the dollar values on their balance sheets, but the same ratio value would indicate the same relative degree of financial strength for each firm.

It is also easier to use ratios rather than dollar values to establish goals or standards. The actual ratios can be compared against goals or standards to perform the control function of management, and deviations from these goals are easily observed. In addition, many lending institutions use ratio analysis from balance sheet information to monitor the financial progress of their customers.

Net Capital Ratio

The net capital ratio is a measure of the overall financial strength and solvency of the business. It is computed from the equation

$$\text{Net capital ratio} = \frac{\text{total assets}}{\text{total liabilities}}$$

For the balance sheet in Table 7-2, I. M. Farmer's net capital ratio would be

$$\frac{\$602,500}{\$284,500} = 2.12$$

for the cost basis valuation used in this example. Since the net capital ratio measures solvency, a ratio computed from a market basis balance sheet may be more appropriate, particularly if there is any question about solvency. During inflationary periods market values will generally be higher than cost basis values for assets such as land and machinery.

A net capital ratio of 1 indicates total liabilities are just equal to total assets and implies net worth is zero. Insolvency exists if the net capital ratio is less than 1 because, should the business be liquidated and the assets sold, there would not be sufficient cash to pay all the liabilities. Therefore, 1 is the minimum net capital ratio for a business if it is to remain solvent, but this is certainly not a safe ratio. There is no room for error, and only a slight decrease in asset values would make the business technically insolvent.

A safe or acceptable net capital ratio depends on the type of business and the type of assets in the balance sheet. Two is often considered a safe ratio, but change over time may be as important as the actual value. A net capital ratio which has been increasing from year to year, particularly when computed from a cost basis balance sheet, indicates the business is making financial progress. Using a market basis balance sheet, the net capital ratio may be increasing over time only because of increasing market values for land and other assets. In this case, financial progress is a result of inflation rather than production and financial decisions made by the manager.

Debt/Equity Ratio

Another measure of solvency is the debt/equity ratio, or leverage ratio, which shows the relationship of owned capital to borrowed capital. This ratio is computed from the equation

$$\text{Debt/equity ratio} = \frac{\text{total liabilities}}{\text{net worth}}$$

I. M. Farmer would have a debt/equity ratio of

$$\frac{\$284,500}{\$318,000} = 0.89$$

This ratio is interpreted differently than the others in that a smaller value indicates a stronger financial position. The smaller the value the larger net worth or equity is relative to total liabilities. Notice that a debt/equity ratio of 1 indicates the owner is providing 50 percent of the capital and 50 percent of the capital is borrowed, and the ratio is exactly equivalent to a net capital ratio of 2.

Current Ratio

The current ratio is a measure of the liquidity of the business and shows the relationship between current assets and current liabilities. It is computed from the equation

$$\text{Current ratio} = \frac{\text{current assets}}{\text{current liabilities}}$$

Again using the I. M. Farmer example, the current ratio for the balance sheet shown in Table 7-2 would be

$$\frac{\$86,500}{\$72,500} = 1.19$$

Current assets are items which will be used up in production or sold within the next year, and current liabilities are all cash obligations due within the next year. Therefore, the current ratio is a measure of the ability to generate cash within the next year to meet cash payments on debts and other current liabilities. This ratio is important to consider because a business may be solvent as measured by the net capital ratio but still have difficulty generating the cash needed to meet current liabilities.

A current ratio equal to 1 means current liabilities are just equal to current assets. Higher ratios would be preferred, and a ratio less than 1 indicates a potential liquidity problem. In the latter case, additional borrowing against intermediate or long-term assets or the sale of some of these assets may be required during the next year to obtain the needed cash.

Working Capital Ratio

The working capital ratio is an intermediate measure of both liquidity and solvency. It is computed from the equation

$$\text{Working capital ratio} = \frac{\text{current assets} + \text{intermediate assets}}{\text{current liabilities} + \text{intermediate liabilities}}$$

In I. M. Farmer's situation the working capital ratio would be

$$\frac{\$86,500 + \$92,000}{\$72,500 + \$32,000} = 1.71$$

This ratio measures whether the value of all current and intermediate assets exceeds the total of current and intermediate liabilities. Hence it measures potential liquidity over several years as opposed to 1 year as well as measuring business solvency ignoring fixed assets and long-term liabilities. Many farms have a major portion of their net worth in land; so this ratio becomes important in determining if the business can meet cash obligations over the next several years without additional borrowing against the land.

The four ratios discussed above are commonly used for analyzing a balance sheet. Other ratios, including the "quick" or "acid test" ratio and ratios measuring the structure and composition of assets and liabilities, are sometimes used for additional analyses. Explanation of these ratios can be found in many financial management texts and in several of the references listed at the end of this chapter.

SUMMARY

The balance sheet is a basic financial statement necessary for implementing a monitoring and control system for the farm business. It is a systematic listing of the assets and liabilities of the business at a given point in time. An inventory of the physical and financial assets owned is required to complete the balance sheet, and each asset must be valued before it is entered on the balance sheet. Valuation of assets on a balance sheet can be on either a cost basis or a market basis.

A complete balance sheet shows the structure and composition of both assets and liabilities. Net worth or owner's equity is found by subtracting total liabilities from total assets and represents the owner's contribution of capital to the business. Ratio analysis can be used to measure the degree of solvency and liquidity exhibited by the business. These ratios become part of a complete system for monitoring and controlling the financial affairs of the business.

QUESTIONS FOR REVIEW AND FURTHER THOUGHT

1 Why is double declining balance depreciation referred to as a "fast" depreciation method?

2 What are the advantages and disadvantages of each valuation method? For each method list some assets which might properly be valued by this method and several for which it would be inappropriate.

3 Assume a new tractor is purchased on January 1 for $40,000 and is assigned a salvage value of $8,000 and an 8-year useful life. What would the annual depreciation be for the first 2 years under each depreciation method?

	Year 1	Year 2
Straight line	_____	_____
Double declining balance	_____	_____
Sum-of-the-year's digits	_____	_____

4 In the problem above, what would the tractor's book value be at the end of the second year under each depreciation method?

5 True or false. If the net capital ratio increases, the debt/equity ratio decreases. Why or why not?

6 Use your knowledge of a balance sheet and ratio analysis to complete the following abbreviated balance sheet. The net capital ratio = 4, the current ratio = 2, and the working ratio = 3.

Assets		Liabilities	
Total current assets	$40,000	Total current liabilities	20,000
Total intermediate assets	80,000	Total intermediate liabilities	$20,000
Total fixed assets	280,000	Total long-term liabilities	60,000
		Total liabilities	100,000
		Net worth	300,000
Total assets	400,000	Total liabilities and net worth	$400,000

7 Assume you are an agricultural loan officer for a bank and Betty Beefraiser requests a loan based on the balance sheet shown below. Conduct a ratio analysis and give your reasons for granting or denying an additional loan. What is the weakest part of this balance sheet?

	Assets		**Liabilities**	
Current assets	$ 40,000		Current liabilities	$ 60,000
Intermediate assets	$ 50,000		Intermediate liabilities	$ 10,000
Fixed assets	$200,000		Long-term liabilities	$ 40,000
			Total liabilities	$110,000
			Net worth	$180,000
Total assets	$290,000		Total liabilities + net worth	$290,000

REFERENCES

Barry, Peter J., John A. Hopkin, and C. B. Baker: *Financial Management in Agriculture,* 2d ed., The Interstate Printers and Publishers, Inc., Danville, Ill., 1979, chaps. 6, 7.

Duft, Ken D.: *Financial Ratio Analysis,* Washington Cooperative Extension Service, 1972.

Frey, Thomas L., and Danny A. Klinefelter: *Coordinated Financial Statements for Agriculture,* Agri Finance, Skokie, Ill., 1978.

James, Sydney C., and Everett Stoneberg: *Farm Accounting and Business Analysis,* Iowa State University Press, Ames, Iowa, 1974, chap. 4.

Penson, John B., Jr., and David A. Lins: *Agricultural Finance: An Introduction to Micro and Macro Concepts,* Prentice-Hall, Inc., Englewood Cliffs, N.J., 1980, chaps. 2, 3.

Chapter 8

The Income Statement
and Its Analysis

CHAPTER OBJECTIVES

1   To define and discuss the purpose and use of an income statement
2   To explain the different sources and types of income and expenses to be included in an income statement
3   To understand the different parts of an income statement and how one is constructed
4   To show how farm profit or net farm income is computed from an income statement
5   To analyze farm profitability by calculating returns to labor, management, capital, and equity

The *income statement* is a summary of income and expenses over a given time period and is the second type of financial statement needed for the control function. It is sometimes called an *operating statement* or *profit and loss statement*, and its primary purpose is to compute profit for a given time period. In other words, an income statement is used to answer the question: Did the farm or ranch business make a profit and, if so, how much? Some income statements may also include nonfarm income and therefore show the total annual net income for the farm family.

The period of time covered by an income statement is called the *accounting period*. Many large corporations prepare an income statement quarterly as

well as annually. For most farm and ranch businesses, an annual income statement covering a January 1 to December 31 time period is both adequate and
convenient, although other time periods can be used. The calendar year is a
common accounting period for farms and ranches. It covers a complete production cycle for most agricultural enterprises, and the end of the year is
generally a slow period in the business and production activities.

The balance sheet and income statement are two different yet related
records of the firm's business activities. A balance sheet is a record of financial
position at a given point in time, and an income statement is a summary of
income and expenses over a period of time. This relationship is shown in
Figure 8-1. For an accounting period of a calendar year, a balance sheet can
be prepared at the end of each year which will also serve as the balance sheet
for the beginning of the following year. However, comparing the beginning and
ending balance sheets does not permit a direct calculation of profit for the year.
This is the job of the income statement prepared for the accounting period.

Even though the balance sheet and income statement contain different
information, they are both financial statements for the same business. It seems
only logical that there be some relationship or connection between the two
even though they serve different purposes. Discussion of this relationship will
be delayed until later in the chapter after a full presentation of the components
and construction of the income statement.

IDENTIFYING INCOME AND EXPENSES

The definition of an income statement implies all income and expenses associated with the business must be identified and recorded so they can be summarized at the end of the accounting period. Farm record books are available
from many sources and provide a convenient and organized system for recording income and expenses. However, the problem of identifying the correct
income and expenses to be recorded for inclusion on the income statement
still remains, as there are several types of both.

Income

Income can be received in two forms, cash and noncash. Cash income is easily
identified as payments received from selling commodities produced on the farm
and from other farm-related income such as custom work performed for others
and government farm payments. In addition, noncash income can be received
in the form of goods and services. It seems only logical that payment in the
form of grain or livestock for custom work performed for a neighbor should
somehow be counted as income just as a cash payment for the same work
would be. Another source of noncash income on farms and ranches is the
value of farm-raised products consumed by the farm household. The fact that
these products, such as a steer butchered for family use, are no longer available
to be sold for cash reduces and therefore distorts the actual farm income. An

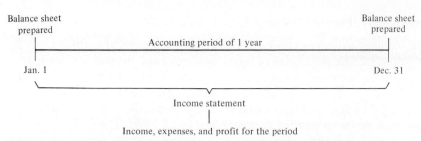

Figure 8-1 Relationship between balance sheet and income statement.

accurate measure of total farm income requires that the value of these products be included as income.

There is another important source of noncash income. A basic accounting principle requires that income be recognized and counted in the same accounting period as the expenses which were incurred in its production. What if the expenses to produce a crop were incurred and paid in one year but the resulting crop was put into storage and not sold until after the end of the current accounting period? The income statement would show the expenses but no cash income even though a crop was produced. In other words, the income generated by these expenses would not be included in the same accounting period. Some technique is needed to reconcile income with related expenses in the same accounting period. Without some adjustment, the net income for the accounting period will be badly distorted.

The solution to this problem is to include changes in inventory value on the income statement. In the above example, the value of the crop inventory at the end of the accounting period would be included as income to match it with its related expenses in the same accounting period. This increase in inventory value is a noncash income but represents products to be sold and converted into cash during some later accounting period. At that time, cash income would be recorded but also an offsetting decrease in inventory value. Therefore, the income statement includes inventory increases as noncash income while inventory decreases are shown as a noncash reduction in income.

The above discussion illustrates one of the differences between a *cash basis* income statement and an *accrual basis* income statement. Using the cash basis, the income statement includes only the cash income which has been received during the accounting period, and changes in inventory values are ignored. An accrual basis income statement recognizes income when it is earned irrespective of when the cash payment is received. Inventory is considered earned income under the accrual basis. Another example of the difference between cash and accrual basis would be the treatment of income from custom work performed in December with the payment received in January of the next year. The accrual basis would count the income in the year the work was performed even though no cash was received while the cash basis would not count this income until the following year when the cash payment was actually received.

Expenses

As with income, expenses can be either cash or noncash in nature. Cash expenses would include purchases of feed, fertilizer, seed, market livestock, fuel, etc. These items are easily identified from entries in a record book and require little explanation. Noncash expenses include depreciation on machinery, equipment, buildings, and purchased breeding livestock. There is no annual cash payment made to pay for depreciation, as an asset is used up over time to produce other products. However, this decline in value represents an expense to the business and must be included on the income statement.

The justification for including depreciation as an expense can be presented another way. An income statement does not include entries for the cost of new capital assets such as tractors, buildings, and fences purchased during the year. Including their cost would distort profit for the year in which they were purchased, as these capital assets will be used in production for many years. Instead, part of the purchase cost is included as a depreciation expense each year of its useful life. This prorates the purchase price over the asset's useful and productive life and serves to satisfy the accounting principle of matching expenses to related income in the same accounting period.

In addition to a record of income, expenses, and inventory values, a depreciation schedule is needed to supply information for completion of the income statement. A depreciation schedule such as the one in Table 8-1 should be used to record annual depreciation and maintain the book value of depreciable assets. Total depreciation for each year can be found by adding the values in the depreciation column. The total value (on a cost less depreciation basis) for the assets is the total of the book value column.

Expenses are also handled differently under the cash and accrual forms of accounting. The cash basis recognizes expenses only in the accounting period in which they are paid, which might be a different period from the one in which they were incurred. Expenses are recognized in the accounting period in which they were incurred under accrual accounting. Consider some feed or fertilizer purchased in December of one year but not paid for until January of the next year. Using the accrual basis, this would be an expense in the year the feed or fertilizer was ordered and received, but with the cash basis it would not be counted as an expense until the following year when it was actually paid for.

THE INCOME STATEMENT

Completing an income statement for a farm or ranch presents the same problem faced with the balance sheet: Should the income statement be only for the farm business or include both farm and nonfarm income? Since the primary purpose of an income statement is to determine business profit, only farm income and expenses will be included in the following example. However, the importance and role of any nonfarm income will be discussed later in a discussion of the relationship between the two types of financial statements.

Table 8-1 Depreciation Schedule

Item	Date purchased	Cost or basis	Salvage value	Life	Depreciation method	19__ Depreciation	19__ Book value	19__ Depreciation	19__ Book value	19__ Depreciation	19__ Book value	19__ Depreciation	19__ Book value

An example of an income statement with typical entries for a farm or ranch business is shown in Table 8-2. Several of the entries could be broken down into more detail if necessary, but this format will provide sufficient information for most uses. Each part of the income statement will be discussed in the following sections.

Cash Farm Income

The normal production activities of the farm business generate most of the cash farm income. Cash receipts from the sale of grain, hay, livestock, livestock products such as milk and wool, custom work performed for others, government payments, and other cash income are recorded in this section of the income statement. The gross receipts should be entered as cash farm income, and any selling expenses such as hauling or selling commissions should be included as an expense in the next section of the income statement.

Any gain or loss from the sale of capital assets such as purchased breeding livestock, machinery, and equipment is also entered as a cash farm income. This entry is the difference between the asset's selling price and its book value. If the selling price is greater than book value, there is a gain to be included as additional income. There may be a gain because too much depreciation was taken in the past. A loss occurs when the selling price is less than book value. This indicates too little depreciation was taken in past years or the asset was overvalued in the inventory, and this loss is deducted from current income.

Cash Farm Expenses

Two categories of cash farm expenses are shown in Table 8-2. Variable cash expenses include fertilizer, seed, feed, purchases of market or feeder livestock, hired labor, and cost of other inputs needed if production takes place. The fixed cash expenses include property taxes, insurance, and interest or those expenses which would still exist if no production took place. Notice that depreciation is not included as it is a noncash fixed cost.

The cost of any new capital assets such as machinery, purchased breeding livestock, buildings, and fences is not included as a cash farm expense, as these assets will be used in the business for more than 1 year. The cost of newly purchased depreciable assets is recovered over time as an annual depreciation expense (the total amount recovered will be the difference between cost and salvage value). It is not correct to expense the full purchase price in the year of purchase, as this will greatly distort the year's profit and does not correctly match the income produced by the asset over time with the cost of the services it provides.

It is also incorrect to include principal payments on loans as a cash farm expense. Interest paid on the loans is a business expense, but principal payments can be viewed as returning borrowed property and therefore not affecting profit. Rent and interest are similar in that each is a payment or expense required for the use of someone else's property.

Table 8-2 Income Statement for I. M. Farmer for Year Ending December 31, 19XX

Cash farm income:		
Grain and hay sold	134,500	
Market livestock sold	62,100	
Raised breeding livestock sold	2,400	
Livestock product sales	0	
Custom work	0	
Government program payments	3,200	
Other cash income	750	
Gain or loss on sale of capital assets		
Machinery and equipment	− 1,750	
Purchased breeding livestock	1,400	
Total cash Income		$202,600
Cash farm expenses:		
Variable cash expenses:		
Crop expenses	46,500	
Livestock expenses	6,000	
Feed purchased	8,400	
Market livestock purchased	36,000	
Gasoline, fuel, and oil	3,100	
Labor hired	8,600	
Utilities	1,500	
Repairs and maintenance	3,800	
Miscellaneous	850	
Other cash expenses	400	
Fixed cash expenses:		
Property taxes	2,700	
Insurance	1,800	
Interest on debt	28,000	
Total cash expenses		$147,650
Net cash farm income		$ 54,950
Noncash adjustments to income:		
Depreciation:		
Machinery and equipment	5,200	
Buildings and improvements	2,200	
Purchased breeding livestock	650	
Total depreciation		−$8,050
Inventory changes:		
Crops	+8,200	
Market livestock	−9,600	
Raised breeding livestock	+800	
Supplies	−2,600	
Net inventory change		−$3,200
Value of products consumed in home:		+400
Net farm income		$44,100

Net Cash Farm Income

Net cash farm income is simply the difference between total cash income and total cash expenses. It is often interpreted as profit for the year, but this is an erroneous conclusion. There has been no adjustment for noncash items such as depreciation or inventory changes, and both adjustments can be large. Net cash income is more properly interpreted as the net cash flow from the production activities of the farm business adjusted for any gain or loss from the sale of capital assets. The latter item may vary widely from year to year depending on whether or not any capital assets are sold. These gains or losses should always be identified separately so cash income from the operation of the business over time can be fairly compared.

Noncash Adjustments to Income

The final section of the income statement includes all noncash adjustments to income. Depreciation is a noncash expense, and this adjustment will always be a negative entry reducing the year's profit. The total depreciation for machinery and equipment, purchased breeding livestock, buildings, and other improvements can be found by summing the annual depreciation for the individual items shown on the depreciation schedule.

The second major noncash adjustment to income is the net change in inventory value. Only those assets grown or raised on the farm, those purchased for resale, and supplies such as feed and fertilizer are included. Capital assets such as machinery, buildings, and purchased breeding livestock are not included, as any change in their value has already been accounted for by the depreciation expense. Raised breeding livestock, although a capital asset, are included in these inventory changes, as they were not purchased and cannot be depreciated. However, care must be taken to adjust the inventory values properly for both market and breeding livestock when replacement animals are transferred from one classification to the other.

The final noncash adjustment to income is the value of products consumed in the home. To reflect farm profit for the year accurately, the value of these products should be included as income in lieu of the cash income which would have been received had they been sold. These products can be valued conservatively at their cost of production or perhaps more appropriately at their net market price at the time of consumption. An alternative procedure which is used on farm income tax returns is to reduce farm expenses by an amount equal to the cost of raising or producing these products.

Net Farm Income

Net farm income is obtained by adjusting net cash farm income for total depreciation, net inventory changes, and value of products consumed in the home. This is the only true measure of profit for the accounting period, as net cash farm income does not include the above adjustments, which can be quite large.

Net farm income is the profit from the year's operation and represents the return to the owner for personal labor, management, and equity capital used in the farm or ranch business. Whether or not this is a satisfactory or adequate return to these factors will be analyzed in the next section.

ANALYSIS OF NET FARM INCOME

Before analyzing net farm income, we should note the distinction between profit and profitability. Profit is a dollar value which is found by calculating net farm income. Profitability is concerned with the size of this profit *relative to* the size of the business or the value of the resources used to produce the profit. A business may show a positive profit but have a poor profitability rating if this profit is small relative to the size of the business. For example, two farms with the same net farm income are not equally profitable if one used twice as much capital as the other. This section will analyze profitability relative to the total capital invested in the business and the return provided to the owner's labor, management, and equity capital.

Return to Capital

The *return to capital* or the *return on investment* is a measure of profitability based on a ratio obtained by dividing the return to total capital by total farm assets.[1] It is normally expressed as a percentage to allow easy comparison with returns from other investments. The equation is

$$\text{Rate of return to capital } (\%) = \frac{\text{return to total capital}}{\text{total farm assets}} \times 100$$

Return to capital is the dollar return to both debt and equity capital, so net farm income must be adjusted. The interest on debt capital was deducted as an expense in calculating net farm income. This interest must be added back to net farm income before the return to capital is computed. In other words, we calculate what net farm income would have been if no borrowed capital had been used in the business and then proceed to compute return to all capital. The calculations for the I. M. Farmer example in Table 8-2 would be

Net farm income	$44,100
Plus interest paid	28,000
Equals adjusted net farm income	$72,100

Further adjustments are necessary, as adjusted net farm income still includes the return to the owner's labor and management as well as the return

---

[1] If information is available on the value of total farm assets at both the beginning and the end of the year, accuracy is improved by using the average of the two values. This is particularly important if there has been a significant change in total asset value during the year.

to all capital. Therefore, a return to owner's labor and management must be subtracted from adjusted net farm income to find the actual return to capital in dollars. This is done by estimating the opportunity cost of the labor and management. Assuming the opportunity cost is $10,000 for I. M. Farmer's labor and $5,000 for management, the calculations would be

Adjusted net farm income	$72,100
Less opportunity cost of labor	−10,000
Less opportunity cost of management	−5,000
Equals return to capital	$57,100

The final step is to convert this dollar return to capital into a percentage of the total capital invested in the business using the equation above. For I. M. Farmer the calculation of the rate of return to capital would be

$$\frac{\$57,100}{\$602,500} = 0.095 \times 100 = 9.5\%$$

The result indicates I. M. Farmer's rather substantial net farm income is slightly more modest when expressed in relation to the total capital used in the business.

Several things should be noted in the calculations of return to capital or return on investment. First, the opportunity costs for labor and management are estimates, and changing them affects the final results. Increasing or decreasing would either lower or raise the return to capital, respectively. Second, net farm income included only farm income, while the total assets on I. M. Farmer's balance sheet included assets such as stocks, bonds, and savings accounts, which may be personal assets. They will generally be a small part of total assets, but accuracy is improved by subtracting any personal assets and dividing the return to total capital by the value of only the farm assets.

Return to Labor and Management

Another measure of profitability is the portion of net farm income which remains to pay the owner for personal labor and management after capital is paid a return equal to its opportunity cost. The procedure is similar to that used for return to capital except the return to labor and management is expressed in dollars and not a ratio or percentage. The return to labor and management is equal to

Adjusted net farm income
Less opportunity cost on total capital
Equals return to labor and management

If the opportunity cost of I. M. Farmer's capital is 10 percent, the opportunity cost on total capital is $602,500 × 10 percent, or $60,250. Therefore, I. M. Farmer's labor and management earned $72,100 − $60,250, or $11,850, after assigning total capital a return equal to its opportunity cost. In this example, it is obvious that either capital, labor, or management did not receive a return quite equal to its opportunity cost.

Return to Labor   The return to labor and management can be used to compute a return to labor alone. Since the opportunity cost of total capital has already been subtracted from adjusted net farm income, the only remaining step is to subtract the opportunity cost of management.

Return to labor and management	$11,850
Less opportunity cost of management	−5,000
Equals return to labor	$ 6,850

This is further confirmation that, in this example, net farm income was not sufficient to provide labor, management, and capital a return at least equal to their opportunity cost.

Return to Management   Management is often considered the residual claimant to net farm income, as its opportunity cost is difficult to estimate. The return to management can be found by subtracting the opportunity cost of labor from the return to labor and management.

Return to labor and management	$11,850
Less opportunity cost of labor	−10,000
Equals return to management	$ 1,850

This is again less than the assumed opportunity cost of management.

Return to Equity

Perhaps the most important measure of profitability is return to equity. The return to capital was a return to both debt and equity capital, and a business owner may be more interested in the return to personal or equity capital invested in the business. It is this capital which would be available for alternative investments should the business be liquidated, and it is useful to compare its return with returns from alternative investments.

The calculation of return to equity begins directly with net farm income, as no adjustment is needed for any interest expense. Interest is the payment or return to borrowed capital, which must properly be deducted as an expense before the return to equity is computed. This has been done when computing net farm income. However, the opportunity cost of labor and management must be subtracted to find the dollar return to equity. Continuing with the same example, the dollar return to equity would be

Net farm income $44,100
Less opportunity cost of own labor   − 10,000
Less opportunity cost of management   −5,000
Equals return to equity $29,100

The rate of return to equity is computed from the following equation:

$$\text{Rate of return to equity (\%)} = \frac{\text{return to equity}}{\text{net worth or owner's equity}} \times 100$$

It is expressed as a ratio or as a percentage of owner's equity. In the I. M. Farmer example, return to equity would be

$$\frac{\$29,100}{\$318,000} = 0.092 \times 100 = 9.2\%$$

In this example, the return to equity is very close to the return to total capital or return on investment, but this will not always be true. It can be either greater or less than the return to total capital, depending on its relationship to the average interest rate paid on debt capital. If the return to total capital is greater than the interest rate on debt capital, debt capital was earning an average return greater than its average cost which is the interest rate. This "profit" accrues to equity capital, making its return greater than the average return to total capital. Conversely, if the return to total capital is less than the interest rate on borrowed capital, the return to equity will be less than the return to total capital.

In analyzing the returns to capital and equity, it is important to remember they are *average* returns. Similarly, converting the return to labor into a return per hour results in an *average* return per hour of owner's labor. These average returns provide little information about the marginal returns which are needed for determining the profit-maximizing input levels. It is important that these average returns not be used in place of marginal returns, as the latter will be less than average returns whenever diminishing returns exist.

CHANGE IN OWNER'S EQUITY

After net farm income is calculated, several questions may come to mind. What was this income used for? Where is this money now? How did the year's operation and the resulting net farm income affect assets, liabilities, and net worth? The answers to all these questions are related and illustrate the relationship between the income statement and balance sheets for the beginning and end of the year.

The year's profit or net farm income must end up in one of four uses: family living expenses, payment of income and social security taxes, increases in farm and nonfarm assets, or principal payments on debts which reduce liabilities. These potential uses for net farm income are shown in Figure 8-2.

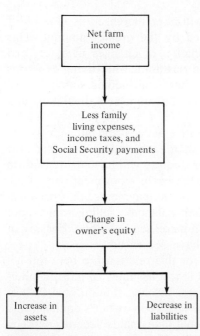

Figure 8-2 Distribution of net farm income.

Beginning with net farm income, cash withdrawals from the business to pay for family living expenses and income and social security taxes reduce the amount available for other uses. Accounting for the remainder of net farm income is not quite so obvious but is important for an understanding of the relationship between the income statement and the balance sheet.

For simplicity, assume total liabilities were exactly the same at the end of the year as at the beginning. In this case, the net farm income remaining after family living expenses and taxes were paid must have gone to increase assets. There must be an increase in one or more of the assets such as cash, bank balances, or inventory values. New purchases might also have increased machinery or land values. How much did owner's equity increase during the year? It increased by an amount equal to the increase in asset value, which must be equal to the net farm income remaining after family living expenses and taxes are paid.

Now take the opposite situation and assume the total asset value was the same at the end of the year as at the beginning. The net farm income after living expenses and taxes were paid must have been used for principal payments on debts, which would reduce liabilities. Since net worth or owner's equity increases by reducing liabilities as well as by increasing assets, it will again have increased by the same amount as before.

It would be unusual for either total assets or total liabilities to be the same at the end of the year as at the beginning. Both are likely to be different, and it is the net change which is of interest. If both assets and liabilities increased but assets increased more, owner's equity will have increased as it would if both decreased but total liabilities decreased by the greater amount. This change in owner's equity, from any combination of changes in assets and liabilities, will just equal the net farm income remaining after living expenses and taxes have been deducted. The balance sheet and income statement are therefore related by the effect net farm income has on assets, liabilities, and owner's equity.

The discussion so far has assumed positive values and an increase in owner's equity. If net farm income is less than cash withdrawals from the business for living expenses and taxes, owner's equity will have decreased. In this case, money had to be withdrawn from the business to meet part of the cash requirements for family living expenses and tax payments. This cash had to come from reducing cash on hand or bank balances, selling some other assets, or borrowing additional money, which increased liabilities. For any of these or a combination, owner's equity will have decreased.

Several qualifications need to be made for this relationship between net farm income and change in owner's equity. First, it assumes no gifts or inheritances were received and there was no nonfarm income. If additional cash or property was received from these sources, the change in owner's equity would increase by an equal amount less any additional taxes paid. Second, depreciable property on the balance sheet such as machinery and equipment, purchased breeding livestock, and buildings must be valued at cost less depreciation and not market value. With this valuation method, the decline in their value between the beginning and ending balance sheets is exactly equal to the depreciation expense on the income statement. The final assumption is that land and other nondepreciable assets such as stocks and bonds are valued at cost.

If land and stocks were valued at market and increased in value during the year, this unrealized gain would increase owner's equity. However, this increase was not a result of the year's production activities and is therefore not included in net farm income but is on the balance sheet. Whenever market valuation is used for these assets, any unrealized gains (or loss) must be included to account properly for the change in owner's equity.

The income statement in combination with balance sheets for the beginning and end of the accounting period provides considerable information for exercising the control function of management. This financial information will identify an earnings or profitability problem, but the source of the problem is not always obvious. Additional information based on some physical and economic efficiency factors is required, and this will be the subject of the next chapter.

SUMMARY

The income statement is a summary of income and expenses for an accounting period and is used to find profit or net farm income. It contains cash income and expenses as well as noncash items such as depreciation and inventory changes to compute net farm income properly. This value is the return to the owner's personal labor, management, and equity capital. Net farm income can be used to compute returns to capital, labor, management, and equity to determine if it is adequate to provide a fair and acceptable return to these resources.

Net farm income is used for family living expenses, payment of income and social security taxes, increases in assets, or decreases in liabilities. The amount left after living expenses and taxes must have been used for some combination of increasing assets or decreasing liabilities and will be equal to the change in owner's equity during the accounting period.

QUESTIONS FOR REVIEW AND FURTHER THOUGHT

1 Why is net inventory change included on an income statement? What effect does an increase in inventory value have on net farm income? A decrease?
2 What is the difference between net cash farm income and net farm income? Which is the better measure of farm profit?
3 As a farm owner which would you rather see higher, rate of return to total capital or rate of return to equity? Why?
4 Can net farm income be determined by comparing beginning and ending balance sheets for an accounting period? Why or why not?
5 Use the following information to compute values for each of the items listed below.

Net farm income	$34,600	Opportunity cost of labor	$8,000
Ending net worth	$206,000	Opportunity cost of	
Total assets	$308,000	management	$3,000
Interest paid during year	$7,500	Opportunity cost of capital	10%
		Family living expenses	$10,500
		Income taxes paid	$3,400

    a Rate of return to total capital _____%
    b Return to labor and management $_____
    c Rate of return to equity _____%
    d Change in owner's equity or net worth $_____
    e Beginning net worth $_____

REFERENCES

Barry, Peter J., John A. Hopkin, and C. B. Baker: *Financial Management in Agriculture*, 2d ed., The Interstate Printers and Publishers, Danville, Ill., 1979, chaps. 6, 7.

Frey, Thomas L., and Danny A. Klinefelter: *Coordinated Financial Statements for Agriculture*, Agri Finance, Skokie, Ill., 1978.

Henderson, Philip A., and Thomas L. Frey: *Your Income Statement*, EC 71-848, Nebraska Cooperative Extension Service, 1971.

Penson, John B., Jr., and David A. Lins: *Agricultural Finance: An Introduction to Micro and Macro Concepts*, Prentice-Hall, Inc., Englewood Cliffs, N.J., 1980, chaps. 2, 3.

Chapter 9

Whole Farm
Business Analysis

CHAPTER OBJECTIVES

1 To point out the need for conducting an analysis of the whole farm business

2 To suggest the need for standards of comparison to use in the analysis of the whole farm business

3 To review measures which can be used to analyze the financial condition and profitability of the business

4 To identify some measures which can be used to analyze business size and efficiency

5 To explore the use of enterprise analysis as a means of identifying strengths and weaknesses in a business

6 To outline a procedure for troubleshooting or locating problem areas through record analysis

Farm management specialists have always been interested in the reasons behind the observed differences in net farm income on farms of the same type and size. The observation and study of these differences and research to identify the causes began in the early 1900s and marked the beginning of the farm management profession. Differences in "management" is a common explanation for the different net farm incomes, but this is too easy and not very satisfactory. Unless the actual differences in management can be identified, there can be no specific recommendations for improving net farm income on the farms with "poor" management.

The differences in net farm income or profitability of similar farms can be expressed in several ways. Table 9-1 shows some observed differences in the returns to labor and management per cow on a sample of Washington dairy farms. Similar differences can be found in every state for every farm type. Notice that high production does not ensure profitability, as shown in Table 9-1. The return to labor and management per cow was −$212 for the lowest dairy farm in the high-production group while the highest farm in the low-production group had a positive return of $225. Several questions are begging for an answer. Why the differences? What causes them? What can be done to improve return to labor and management on the less profitable farms? Differences in goals and available resources may be partial answers. However, complete answers can be found only by performing a whole farm business analysis.

Farm records are often poorly kept and incomplete and are seldom used to their full potential in whole farm analysis. Keeping a good set of records is both time-consuming and costly. It is easy to let this task slide or do it in a slipshod manner if there is no identifiable end result. This end result, or the final payoff from keeping a good set of records, comes when they are used to analyze the whole business with an eye toward making improvements. The "payoff" for the time spent keeping and analyzing records comes in the form of better business management and therefore higher profits in the future.

TYPES OF ANALYSIS

A whole farm analysis can be completed using several types of analyses each of which concentrates on a specific aspect of the business. When done in a step-by-step manner, the procedure first identifies any problems and then proceeds to isolate the causes to permit the formulation of specific recommendations for improvement.

This chapter will divide a whole farm analysis into five areas of concentration, as follows:

Table 9-1   Returns to Labor and Management per Dairy Cow by Level of Productivity

Milk production per cow (lbs)	Returns to labor and management per cow ($)		
	Average	High	Low
Over 16,000	121	318	−212
14,000 − 15,999	−23	261	−226
12,000 − 13,999	−104	−14	−470
Under 12,000	−134	225	−735

Source: Gayle S. Willett, "How to Analyze the Dairy Farm Business," E.M. 4368, Washington State University Cooperative Extension Service, July 1978.

1 *Financial.* A financial analysis concentrates on the capital position of the business including solvency, liquidity, and changes in net worth.

2 *Profitability.* Income and profitability problems are identified by calculating net farm income, rate of return to capital and equity, and returns to labor and managment.

3 *Farm Size.* Several measures can be used to analyze and compare farm size as a potential cause of low-income problems.

4 *Efficiency.* Profitability or income problems can often be traced to poor efficiency in one or more areas of the business. Both economic and physical efficiency measures will be used to identify problem areas.

5 *Enterprise.* The final step is to conduct an enterprise analysis to estimate the relative profitability of each enterprise. Low-income problems are often the result of low or negative profits in one or more enterprises which offset good profits in others and lower net farm income.

STANDARDS OF COMPARISON

The remainder of this chapter will use various measures and ratios to illustrate the procedure for a whole farm analysis. Once a measure or ratio is calculated, the problem becomes one of evaluating the result. Is the value good, bad, or indifferent? Compared with what? Can it be improved? These questions emphasize the need for some standards against which the measures and ratios can be compared and evaluated. Unfortunately a single set of standards cannot be presented for all farms because satisfactory measures of performance will vary by type and size of farm.

Several types of standards can be used to compare and evaluate the various measures and ratios for a given farm.

1 *Budgeted Objectives.* If the primary purpose of a whole farm analysis is for control and monitoring purposes, budgeted goals and objectives provide a good standard of comparison. When results fall short of any budgeted objective, it quickly identifies an area needing additional managerial effort.

2. *Historical Records.* After a whole farm analysis has been completed for several years, the results for the past years provide another standard of comparison. In particular, any trend toward improvement or weakness in the measures and ratios can be easily identified. However, historical records are less useful for determining appropriate or minimum standards.

3 *Other Farm Records.* The results from a whole farm analysis on another farm or group of farms of the same size and type provide another set of standards to use for comparison. However, care must be taken to compare a given farm only against other farms of the same size and type.

Two or more of the above standards can be used together. Even if budgeted or other farm records are used, a historical comparison should be used to identify changes and trends. One of the major advantages of participating in an organized record-keeping service such as those available through lending agencies, private firms, or the agricultural extension service in many states is the annual summary provided for all farms using the service. These summaries often contain averages and ranges of the analysis measures for all farms and/ or by farm size and type. When such results are available, they provide an excellent set of standards for comparison.

FINANCIAL MEASURES

The balance sheet is the source of data for calculating the measures related to the financial or capital position of the business. These financial measures or ratios were presented in Chapter 7 but will be reviewed briefly in this section to show how they fit into a whole farm analysis. The financial portion of the analysis is designed to measure the solvency and liquidity of the business, note changes in net worth, and identify weaknesses in the structure or mix of the various types of assets and liabilities.

It is convenient to record the established goal or standard along with historical values on a form such as that shown in Table 9-2. This permits a quick and easy comparison of current values against both the standard and the historical values to identify any trends which have developed. Table 9-2 contains the more important financial measures to be included in the analysis.

Net Capital Ratio The net capital ratio measures business solvency and is calculated by dividing total assets by total liabilities:

$$\text{Net capital ratio} = \frac{\text{total assets}}{\text{total liabilities}}$$

Larger values are preferred to smaller ones, as they indicate a better chance of maintaining the solvency of the business should it ever be faced with a period of adverse economic conditions. However, high net capital ratios must be carefully analyzed. They may indicate a manager's reluctance or failure to incur debt to take advantage of profitable investment opportunities. In this case, the high ratio would be at the expense of a potentially higher net farm income.

Table 9-2   Analyzing the Financial Condition of the Business

Item	Budgeted goal or standard	Year 19__	19__	19__
1. Net capital ratio	_____	_____	_____	_____
2. Debt/equity ratio	_____	_____	_____	_____
3. Current capital ratio	_____	_____	_____	_____
4. Net worth	_____	_____	_____	_____
5. Change in net worth	_____	_____	_____	_____

Debt/Equity Ratio   This is another measure of business solvency and is found by dividing total liabilities by owner's equity or net worth:

$$\text{Debt/equity ratio} = \frac{\text{total liabilities}}{\text{owner's equity}}$$

Smaller debt/equity ratios are preferred to larger ones, which is just opposite of the net capital ratio. However, unusually small ratios must be carefully analyzed for the same reason as discussed above for high net capital ratios.

Current Ratio   The current ratio is a measure of business liquidity, or the ability to meet short-term financial obligations from current assets. It is calculated by dividing current assets by current liabilities:

$$\text{Current ratio} = \frac{\text{current assets}}{\text{current liabilities}}$$

It should be greater than 1. A current ratio less than 1 indicates the business may be facing a liquidity problem.

Change in Net Worth   The ultimate measure of financial progress for a business is a net worth which is increasing over time. This is an indication of business growth, additional capital investment, and a greater borrowing capacity. As discussed in Chapter 7, net worth should be increasing without the benefit of inflation and its effect on the value of assets such as land. This requires a balance sheet prepared on a cost rather than a market basis so that any increase in net worth is a result of the production activities during the accounting period and not inflation in asset values. However, increasing asset values can have substantial impact on net worth, and some managers may wish to compute change in net worth on both a cost and a market basis.

MEASURES OF PROFITABILITY

A business which is both solvent and liquid as shown by a financial analysis is not necessarily a profitable business. Profitability is determined by analyzing the income statement as was done in the last chapter. Several measures of profitability were discussed, and they are shown in Table 9-3, which is a form for recording and comparing them over time. Each will be briefly discussed again as it relates to a whole farm analysis.

Net Farm Income   The measure of profit for the farm business is net farm income. One method for establishing a goal for net farm income is to estimate the income the owner's labor, management, and capital could earn in nonfarm uses. In other words, the total opportunity cost for these factors of production becomes the goal or standard for net farm income. In any year the income

Table 9-3 Measures of Farm Profitability

Item	Budgeted goal or standard	Year 19__	19__	19__
1. Net farm income ($)	_____	_____	_____	_____
2. Return to labor and management ($)	_____	_____	_____	_____
3. Return to management ($)	_____	_____	_____	_____
4. Rate of return to capital (%)	_____	_____	_____	_____
5. Rate of return to equity (%)	_____	_____	_____	_____

statement shows a lower net farm income, one or more of these factors did not earn its opportunity cost. Another goal would be an income level to be reached at some time in the future such as at the end of 5 years. Progress toward this goal could be measured over time.

Return to Labor and Management This is one of the more common measures of profitability and is often included as a summary statistic in studies of farm income and profitability. Annual summaries for organized record-keeping groups typically include this figure calculated in the same manner as shown in the previous chapter. The goal or standard for return to labor and management should be an amount at least as great as the opportunity cost on the owner's labor and management in a nonfarm occupation.

Return to Management As shown in the previous chapter, the return to management is that portion of adjusted net farm income remaining after the opportunity cost of labor and capital is subtracted. It represents the residual return to the owner for the management input and as such will be highly variable, as prices and yields vary from year to year. Negative returns to management are common, but the goal should be a positive value to provide some compensation for the owner's management input.

Rate of Return to Capital The rate of return to capital is adjusted net farm income less the opportunity cost of labor and management and is expressed as a percentage of the total capital used in the business. It is also called the return on investment. The minimum standard or goal for the rate of return to capital should approximate the interest rate on borrowed capital. Higher rates of return to capital are desirable but are difficult to achieve if land is valued at current market value when the total capital used is estimated. Historical rates of return to farmland based on current market value have generally been in the 3 to 6 percent range.

Rate of Return to Equity This measure is perhaps more important to the business owner than rate of return to capital. It indicates the percentage return to the owner's personal or equity capital, and there are two possible goals for this measure of profitability. First, it should be greater than rate of return to capital if any borrowed money is used in the business. As explained in the last chapter, this indicates the average return on borrowed capital was greater than the interest rate paid for its use. A rate of return to equity which is less than the rate of return to capital indicates just the opposite, or that the borrowed capital was not paying for itself on the average. The second goal for rate of return to equity can be some specific percentage rate set at least equal to and preferably higher than the goal assigned to rate of return to capital.

General Comments   There are two criticisms of the procedure used to calculate returns to labor, management, capital, and equity. The first is the somewhat arbitrary nature of assigning the opportunity costs used in the calculations. There are no fixed rules to use, and individuals may have different opinions about the appropriate values to use. Obviously the calculated return to any factor will change if different opportunity costs are used for the others. The second criticism is that these values are the *average* return to the factor and not the *marginal* return. For example, the rate of return to capital is the average rate of return on all capital invested in the business and not the marginal return on the last dollar invested. The marginal returns would be much more useful for planning purposes.

Both these criticisms are valid, but they should not prevent the use of these measures of profitability. If the opportunity costs are carefully estimated, are used consistently from year to year, and the average nature of the result is kept in mind, these measures provide a satisfactory means of historical and between-farm comparison of profitability. They are, however, not as useful for making marginal changes in the organization and operation of the farm business.

The measures of profitability included in Table 9-3 can be used only to identify the existence of a problem. If the income or profitability falls short of the goal or standard, a problem exists, but these measures provide little insight into the cause or source of the problem. Further analysis is needed to identify the cause of the problem and suggest the corrective action needed. The next three sections proceed with a more in-depth analysis of the farm business to pinpoint the source of an income problem.

MEASURES OF SIZE

An income or profitability problem can exist in any single year owing to poor weather with low crop yields or to low product prices. If the problem persists in years with average or better prices and yields, it can generally be traced to either insufficient farm size or inefficient operation in one or more areas. The first step is to analyze farm size to determine if it is large enough to generate an adequate net farm income under the most efficient methods of operation. Historically, net farm income has been highly correlated with farm size and a low income may be due entirely to a farm which is too small.

Several of the more common measures of farm size are shown in Table 9-4. Each has its own advantages and disadvantages, and no single measure is entirely satisfactory for all farm types.

Value of Farm Production   One measure of farm size is the volume or amount of production which has taken place during the year. The *value of farm production*, or *gross profit*, as it is sometimes called, measures the volume of production in dollar terms because physical units of different products cannot be added to get a meaningful value. It is calculated as follows:

Total cash receipts
plus Inventory increases
minus Inventory decreases
minus Livestock purchases
minus Feed purchases
equals Value of farm production

The result is the dollar value of all agricultural production which has taken place on the farm during the year after adjusting for inventory changes. Livestock and feed purchases are deducted, as they represent agricultural products which were produced by some other farmer or rancher. If the farm under analysis can purchase livestock and feed and increase their total value through livestock feeding, this increase will be credited to it by these calculations.

Value of farm production has the advantage of combining many different farm products into one measure of size which, because of the common dollar denominator, allows comparison between different types of farms. It has two disadvantages, the first being it is affected by output prices. This will cause two years with the same physical production to have a different value of farm production if product prices are different. A second disadvantage is that the

Table 9-4   Measures of Farm Size

Item	Budgeted goal or standard	Year 19__	19__	19__
1. Value of farm production	_____	_____	_____	_____
2. Total capital invested	_____	_____	_____	_____
3. Total acres controlled	_____	_____	_____	_____
Owned	_____	_____	_____	_____
Rented	_____	_____	_____	_____
4. Livestock numbers	_____	_____	_____	_____
Beef	_____	_____	_____	_____
Dairy	_____	_____	_____	_____
Swine	_____	_____	_____	_____
5. Total labor used	_____	_____	_____	_____

value of farm production is not a pure measure of size but is also affected by efficiency of production. In other words, two farms of exactly the same size based on some other measure could have different values of farm production because of differences in managerial efficiency and not because of differences in farm size.

Total Capital Invested   Another measure of size is the total capital invested in land, buildings, machinery, and livestock. With all values in dollar terms, this measure allows an easy comparison of farm size across different farm types, but it also has two disadvantages. The current dollar value of the various assets must be fairly and accurately estimated, and farms with a disproportionately large investment in labor-saving items such as big machinery and confinement livestock buildings will have their "size" overestimated.

Total Acres Controlled   The number of acres controlled is a common measure of farm size, and it can be subdivided into acres owned and acres rented. While this is a common measure of size, it is not a particularly good measure for comparing different types of farms. A California farm with 200 acres of irrigated vegetables is obviously not the same-size operation as 200 acres of dryland wheat in western Kansas or a 200-acre cattle feedlot in Texas. Number of acres is best used for comparing the size of crop farms of the same general type in an area with similar soil types.

Livestock Numbers   It is common to speak of a 200-cow ranch or a 100-cow dairy or a 100-sow hog farm. These measures of size can be useful but only for comparing size among farms with the same class of livestock. For example, comparing 50,000 laying hens with 100 beef cows sheds little light on comparable farm sizes.

Total Labor Used   Labor is a resource common to all farms regardless of type. Terms such as one-person or two-person farms are frequently used to describe farm size. A full-time worker equivalent can be calculated by summing the months of labor provided by operator, family, and hired labor and dividing the result by 12. For example, if the operator worked 12 months, family members provided 4 months of labor, and 5 months of labor was hired, the full-time worker equivalent would be 21 months divided by 12, or 1.75 years of labor. This measure of size is affected by the amount of labor-saving technology used and should therefore be carefully interpreted when comparing farm size.

EFFICIENCY MEASURES

If the measures of size indicate the farm is large enough to provide a better net farm income, the next step is to analyze the efficiency of the operation. Efficiency measures can be broken down into two types, economic and physical. There are a large number of potential measures of each type, and only the more useful and/or more common will be discussed here.

Measures of Economic Efficiency

These measures differ from the physical measures primarily because they are either dollar values or some rate or percentage relating to capital use. All measures of economic efficiency must be carefully interpreted and used. They are average values and as such provide little information on marginal values and the effect small changes would have on overall profit. Several have the characteristic that a value which is either too low or too high indicates a problem. These require a careful evaluation against values for similar farms to determine if a problem exists. The measures to be discussed are shown in Table 9-5.

Rate of Capital Turnover This measure is an indication of how efficiently capital is being used in production. It is found by dividing the value of farm production by the total capital used in the business. For example, a rate of

Table 9-5   Measures of Economic Efficiency

Item	Budgeted goal or standard	Year 19__	19__	19__
Capital efficiency:				
1. Rate of capital turnover	_____	_____	_____	_____
2. Capital per person	_____	_____	_____	_____
Livestock efficiency:				
3. Returns per $100 of feed fed	_____	_____	_____	_____
4. Feed cost per 100 lbs of gain (or milk)	_____	_____	_____	_____
Crop efficiency:				
5. Crop value per tillable acre	_____	_____	_____	_____
6. Net crop income per tillable acre	_____	_____	_____	_____
Machinery efficiency:				
7. Machinery investment per tillable acre	_____	_____	_____	_____
8. Machinery cost per tillable acre	_____	_____	_____	_____
Labor efficiency:				
9. Value of farm production per person	_____	_____	_____	_____
10. Net farm income per person	_____	_____	_____	_____

capital turnover equal to 0.3 or 30 percent indicates the value of farm production is equal to 30 percent of the total capital invested in the business. This value means it would take 3⅓ years to produce agricultural products with a value equal to the total capital investment. Higher rates of return mean it takes fewer years to produce products with a value equal to the capital investment and the rate of capital turnover will vary by farm type. Dairy, hog, and poultry farms will have the higher rates, beef cow farms will tend to be among the lower, and crop farms will have intermediate values. Therefore, the rate of capital turnover should be compared only between farms of the same general type.

Capital per Person   Dividing the total capital used in the business by the full-time worker equivalent gives the capital investment per person employed in the farm business. This is a measure of capital use relative to labor use and will vary by farm type and by the amount of labor-saving technology used. The capital per person can be too high, indicating too much capital investment relative to the labor being used. It may also be too low and cause poor labor efficiency if too little capital is invested in labor-saving equipment and buildings. This is another measure which should be compared only with values for farms of a similar size and type.

Return per $100 of Feed Fed   This is a common measure of efficiency in livestock production. It is calculated by dividing the livestock increase for the year by the total value of all feed fed during the year and multiplying the result by 100. Annual livestock increase is equal to:

Total livestock cash income
minus Value of livestock purchased
minus Livestock inventory decrease
plus Livestock inventory increase
equals Annual livestock increase

This is used in the following equation to calculate the return per $100 of feed fed.

$$\text{Return per \$100 of feed fed} = \frac{\text{annual livestock increase}}{\text{value of feed fed}} \times 100$$

A return per $100 of feed fed equal to $100 indicates the livestock just paid for the feed consumed with no income to pay for other expenses.

The return per $100 of feed fed should be greater than $100 and will vary by livestock enterprise, as shown in the following table.

Livestock enterprise	Return per $100 of feed fed (15-year average, 1963–1977)
Beef cow	$133
Dairy	183
Feeder cattle	123
Sheep	125
Feeder pigs	137
Hogs (farrow to finish)	169
Poultry	149

Source: 1977 Summary of Illinois Farm Business Records, University of Illinois Cooperative Extension Service Circular 1162, 1978.

Livestock enterprises whose total cost of production includes a higher proportion of nonfeed costs require a higher return per $100 of feed fed to cover these nonfeed costs. As shown above, enterprises such as dairy, hogs, and poultry with higher building and labor costs have the higher returns. Because of these differences, the return per $100 of feed fed should be calculated for each individual livestock enterprise and compared only with values for the same enterprise.

Feed Cost per 100 Pounds of Gain The feed cost per 100 pounds of gain (or per 100 pounds of milk for a dairy enterprise) should also be computed separately for each livestock enterprise. It is found by dividing the total feed cost for the enterprise by the total pounds of production and multiplying the result by 100. The total pounds of production for the year should be adjusted for pounds purchased and any inventory changes. This measure is affected by both feed and livestock prices, and values should be compared only against those for the same type of livestock.

Crop Value per Tillable Acre This value measures the intensity of crop production and whether or not the higher-value crops are included in the crop plan. It is calculated by dividing the total value of all crops produced during the year by the number of tillable or rotated acres. Higher values are generally preferred, but they can be too high. Using variable inputs beyond the point where marginal value product is equal to marginal input cost can result in a high crop value per tillable acre but can actually reduce profit per acre.

Net Crop Income per Tillable Acre This is a better measure than the one above but is more difficult to calculate. It requires identifying all crop-related costs and subtracting them from total crop value before dividing by the number of tillable acres. Expenses such as depreciation and other fixed costs may be difficult to allocate properly between crop and livestock production.

Machinery Investment per Tillable Acre Dividing the current value of all machinery and equipment by the number of tillable acres provides a measure of machinery efficiency. This is another measure which should be compared only with values for farms of the same type and size. The additional machinery needed for livestock will make the machinery investment per tillable acre higher on livestock farms than on crop farms, and larger farms tend to have lower investments per acre because of economies of size.

This is another measure which can be either too high or too low. A high value indicates there may be an excessive machinery investment and machinery fixed costs can be seriously affecting net farm income. Low values may indicate the machinery is too old and unreliable or too small for the acres being farmed and may explain poor yields. There is an important interaction between machinery investment, labor requirements, timeliness of field operations, and the amount of custom work hired. These factors should all be evaluated together.

Machinery Cost per Tillable Acre   This measure differs from the one above in that the total of all annual costs related to machinery is divided by the number of tillable acres. The total annual machinery costs include all fixed and variable costs plus the cost of custom work hired. For the same reasons discussed above, this measure will vary by type and size of farm and can be either too high or too low.

Value of Farm Production per Person   This is a measure of labor efficiency and is calculated by dividing the value of farm production by the number of full-time worker equivalents. Higher values are preferred but may be caused by a higher than average capital investment per person.

Net Farm Income per Person   Dividing net farm income by the number of full-time worker equivalents gives the net farm income per person employed, which is another measure of labor efficiency. If the value of farm production per person is high but the net farm income per person is low, labor efficiency is good but a cost problem exists. The efficient use of labor in producing agricultural products is being offset by excessive machinery or other costs, which is causing the low net farm income per person.

Measures of Physical Efficiency

There are many different types of physical efficiency measures, particularly for livestock enterprises. As with the measures of economic efficiency, they are average values and must be interpreted as such. An average value should not be used in place of a marginal value when determining the profit-maximizing input or output level.

A sample of physical efficiency measures is shown in Table 9-6. These are some commonly used measures, with higher values generally preferred to lower. However, the economic principles for determining the profit-maximizing input and output levels should always be kept in mind when analyzing physical measures related to input use and output levels. It may be that high

Table 9-6 Examples of Physical Efficiency Measures

Item	Budgeted goal or standard	Year 19__	19__	19__
Crops:				
1. Crop yield	_____	_____	_____	_____
Livestock:				
2. Average daily gain	_____	_____	_____	_____
3. Feed per pound of gain	_____	_____	_____	_____
4. Calving percent	_____	_____	_____	_____
5. Pigs weaned per litter	_____	_____	_____	_____
6. Milk production per cow	_____	_____	_____	_____
7. Eggs per hen	_____	_____	_____	_____

values are a result of using too much input and producing at a level which is beyond the profit-maximizing quantity. In other words, physical efficiency measures can be too high in relation to the profit-maximizing values. This is not a common occurrence but should be considered when analyzing unusually high values.

There are many physical efficiency measures which can be used to analyze an individual livestock enterprise. They are too many to list here for all livestock enterprises, but an example for a dairy enterprise is shown in Table 9-7. Similar measures can be developed for each livestock enterprise on the farm.

Notice that the measures in Table 9-7 are designed to analyze four general areas of the dairy enterprise. The first two relate to physical production in terms of average milk production per cow and average butterfat content. Items 3 and 4 analyze input levels using grain, as it is a major input in milk production. Labor productivity in the dairy enterprise is measured by items 5 and 6. The final three items relate to general herd management practices which affect productivity and profit. These four general areas of analysis can be used to develop similar measures for other livestock enterprises.

ENTERPRISE ANALYSIS

Enterprise analysis or *cost accounting* is another procedure used to identify strengths and weaknesses in the farm business. A profitability analysis on a whole farm basis may indicate a problem, but the source of the problem is often difficult to find if there are many enterprises. Several enterprises may be highly profitable and several others unprofitable or only marginally profitable. Enterprise analysis can identify the less profitable enterprises so that some type of corrective action can be taken.

Table 9-7 Physical Efficiency Measures for a Dairy Enterprise

Item	Budgeted goal or standard	Year 19___	19___	19___
1. Average milk production per cow (lbs)	_____	_____	_____	_____
2. Butterfat content (%)	_____	_____	_____	_____
3. Grain fed per cow (lbs)	_____	_____	_____	_____
4. Grain per 100 lbs of milk (lbs)	_____	_____	_____	_____
5. Cows per full-time worker equivalent	_____	_____	_____	_____
6. Milk production per full-time worker equivalent (cwt)	_____	_____	_____	_____
7. Cows in milk (%)	_____	_____	_____	_____
8. Average calving interval (days)	_____	_____	_____	_____
9. Herd turnover (%)	_____	_____	_____	_____

An enterprise analysis consists of identifying and then allocating all income and expenses to the individual enterprise which generated the income and incurred the expense. The end result is similar to an income statement for each enterprise showing the profit for each after adjusting for opportunity costs on owned inputs and operator labor. If the enterprise analysis is done on a per acre or per head basis, the end result is much like an enterprise budget. The difference is that the latter is based on projected figures for a future period while enterprise analysis uses actual data for the past year.

An enterprise analysis has two additional uses. The data gathered during the analysis are extremely useful in developing enterprise budgets for future years. They can also be used to calculate the actual cost of production, which can be useful in marketing decisions.

Crop Enterprise Analysis

An example of an enterprise analysis for soybeans is contained in Table 9-8. Values are shown both for the whole farm and on a per acre basis. The first step is to calculate the total income, which must include any change in inventory value for soybeans to determine the total income accurately. For crops which are also used for livestock feed, the value of any amounts already fed must be included in the total income as well as any inventory change.

Variable costs are estimated next. The total cost of items such as seed, fertilizer, and chemicals is relatively easy to find in farm records or to estimate based on the quantities actually used. Other costs such as gas, oil, machinery

Table 9-8 Example of Enterprise Analysis for Soybeans

	Farm total	Per acre
Soybean production (200 acres)	6,800 bu	34.0 bu
Income:	$40,800	$204.00
Variable costs:		
Seed	$2,400	$12.00
Fertilizer	1,500	7.50
Chemicals	2,000	10.00
Gas, oil	1,200	6.00
Machinery repairs	1,600	8.00
Labor	3,000	15.00
Interest on variable costs (10% for 6 months)	585	2.93
Fixed costs:		
Machinery fixed costs	4,800	24.00
Other farm fixed costs	1,000	5.00
Land charge including property taxes	19,000	95.00
Total costs	$37,085	$185.43
Profit	$3,715	$18.57
Average cost per bushel	$5.45	$5.45

repairs, and labor are more difficult. The problem is to allocate the total farm expenditure for these items fairly among all enterprises. Without detailed records on machinery and labor use by enterprise, some estimation will be necessary.

The usual procedure is to avoid the problem of allocating the actual farm interest expense among enterprises. This is done by including a charge for interest on variable costs, much as was done on the enterprise budgets. If the same policy is followed for all enterprises, their profitability can be fairly compared.

Fixed costs are the most difficult to estimate. A fair and equitable allocation of machinery depreciation, interest on the machinery investment, insurance expense, building depreciation, and other farm overhead expenses must be done if the enterprises are to be accurately compared for profitability. Several procedures are possible, but each requires either extensive records or some estimation.

1 Per Acre The total machinery fixed costs and other farm overhead costs can be divided equally among the total acres in the farm. This procedure underestimates machinery fixed costs for those crops requiring above average machinery use and vice versa.

2 Gross Income The fixed costs can be allocated among the various enterprises based on their proportion of enterprise gross income to total gross income. For example, if the gross income from soybeans is 25 percent of total gross farm income, 25 percent of the total fixed costs would be allocated to soybean production.

3 *Actual Use* When detailed records are available, they can be used to allocate some types of fixed costs. For example, if records on hours of machinery use by crop enterprise have been kept, the fixed cost per hour of actual use can be used to allocate the fixed costs back to each enterprise. This procedure works well for machinery fixed costs but is less useful for other types of fixed costs.

The example in Table 9-8 indicates the soybean enterprise had a total profit above all costs of $3,715, or $18.57 per acre. These values can be compared against similar values for other crop enterprises to determine which are contributing the most to overall farm profit. If any crop shows a consistent loss for several years, action should be taken either to improve its profitability or to shift resources to the production of some other more profitable crop.

Livestock Enterprise Analysis

An enterprise analysis of livestock enterprises is conducted in the same manner as for a crop enterprise. However, several special problems should be noted. Inventory changes are likely to be more important in determining income for a livestock enterprise and should be carefully estimated to avoid biasing the results. Another problem is how to handle farm-raised feed fed to livestock. The amount of grain, hay, and silage fed must be known or estimated and then valued. This feed should be valued at the average market price for the year or the actual price received for any feed sold. Hay and silage are especially difficult to value and pasture and crop residue grazing even more difficult. Pasture can be valued using either the opportunity cost on the land itself or the income which could have been received from renting the pasture to someone else. Crop residue often has little or no opportunity cost, as it has little use if not grazed by livestock. Its value is often ignored in a livestock enterprise analysis or entered at a very low value.

Fixed costs and farm overhead expenses are always difficult to allocate and may be even more so for livestock enterprises. Depreciation, interest, taxes, repairs and insurance on buildings, fences, wells, water systems, feeders, machinery, and other equipment used in livestock production are examples. The problem is less difficult if these items are used by only one type of livestock, but it quickly multiplies if their use is shared by several types. These allocation problems are not insurmountable, but the procedure used may affect the accuracy of the enterprise analysis.

DIAGNOSING A FARM PROFITABILITY PROBLEM

This chapter has concentrated on the procedures and measures used to conduct a complete analysis of the farm business. A complete analysis is time-consuming, and many of the measures will have satisfactory values. If there is a need to identify and isolate the cause of a profitability problem quickly, a number of steps can be eliminated by a systematic procedure. A diagnostic procedure is needed such as those used by doctors to identify the cause of a medical problem. It will systematically analyze symptoms and eliminate some possibilities while working toward identifying the source of a problem. Such a procedure minimizes the number of tests or measures to be conducted.

A diagnostic procedure or troubleshooting guide for identifying the source of profitability problems in a farm business is illustrated in Figure 9-1. It assumes a profitability problem exists and uses value of farm production as the starting point. If this value is low, farm size may be the problem. The farm may be too small to produce the level of production needed for an adequate profit, and farm size should be increased or off-farm employment considered as a way to increase family income.

If the farm size appears adequate to produce an acceptable level of income, the low value of farm production may be due to poor physical efficiency in crop and livestock production. Low physical efficiency measures indicate a need to improve management practices to obtain more production from the available resources. Satisfactory physical efficiency measures for the current enterprises may mean the wrong enterprises are in the current farm plan. Enterprise analysis and enterprise budgeting can be used to identify the more profitable enterprises, and a new whole farm plan should be developed.

If the original evaluation of the value of farm production indicates it is high enough to provide a satisfactory net farm income, the profitability problem will generally be caused by excessive costs. This requires following the diagnostic procedure in the right-hand side of Figure 9-1. The fixed costs such as machinery and building depreciation, interest, and general farm overhead costs should be carefully evaluated. If they are high relative to the farm size and value of production, steps should be taken to reduce those which will have little or no effect on the level of production. Reducing fixed costs may be difficult and require some time, but all current and new investments and their related fixed costs should be carefully scrutinized.

If the fixed and overhead costs appear satisfactory, the next step is an analysis of variable costs. The economic efficiency measures will help isolate a cost problem in the area of livestock production or crop production or in the use of inputs such as machinery, labor, or capital. Poor values for one of these measures indicate too much of some input is being used and/or poor purchasing practices have resulted in unnecessarily high prices paid for purchased inputs. If the economic efficiency measures are satisfactory, one remaining explanation of the poor profit is poor marketing practices. The average selling price for the commodities may be below the season average price, causing both a low profit and a lower value of farm production.

The above procedure should allow a manager to isolate and identify the cause of a profitability problem quickly. Another procedure would be to evaluate just those measures which show the greatest variation between low- and

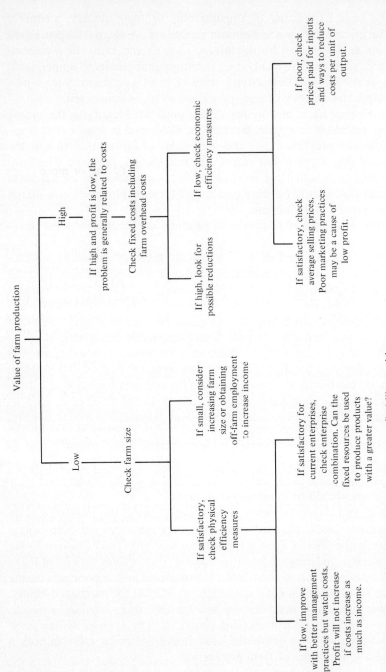

Figure 9-1 Procedure for diagnosing a farm profitability problem.

high-income farms. For example, James and Stoneberg state that around 75 percent of the income difference between farms can be accounted for in the following five measures.[1]

1 Crop value per tillable acre
2 Livestock return per $100 of feed fed
3 Value of farm production per person
4 Value of farm production per $100 of expense
5 Machinery cost per tillable acre

An evaluation of these five measures may quickly identify one or more areas in need of a more in-depth analysis.

SUMMARY

A whole farm analysis is much like a complete medical examination. It should be conducted periodically and whenever a symptom exists which indicates the business is not functioning as it should. The whole farm analysis can be broken down into several parts beginning with the financial analysis. This concentrates on the balance sheet to determine business solvency and liquidity. The next part uses several measures to analyze profitability in terms of net farm income and returns to labor, management, capital, and equity.

If a profitability problem is found, the analysis proceeds toward identifying the cause. The first step is a look at farm size to see if there is at least the potential for an adequate profit or if the farm size is too small. From here the analysis proceeds through various measures relating to economic and physical efficiency in the areas of crop and livestock production and the use of machinery, labor, capital, and other inputs. Finally, enterprise analysis can be used to identify the less profitable enterprises so they can be reduced in size or eliminated and replaced by more profitable enterprises, thereby increasing profit.

The various measures calculated during a whole farm analysis also have another use. They provide a detailed system of monitoring the farm business over time as part of the control function of management. As such, they should be used to identify and isolate a problem before it begins to have a serious impact on business profit.

QUESTIONS FOR REVIEW AND FURTHER THOUGHT

1 Why and when should the whole farm business be analyzed?
2 What types of standards or values can be used to compare and evaluate efficiency measures for an individual farm? Discuss some advantages and disadvantages of each.

[1]Sydney C. James and Everett Stoneberg, *Farm Accounting and Business Analysis*, Iowa State University Press, Ames, Iowa, 1974, p. 136.

3 Can a farm have satisfactory measures of financial condition but a poor profit? Why?
4 What is the difference between "value of farm production" and "net farm income"?
5 What is the purpose of enterprise analysis? What is the most difficult part of enterprise analysis?
6 Use the following data to calculate the efficiency measures listed below:

Net farm income $28,000   Value of farm production $90,000
Tillable acres 620   Annual machinery expenses $26,000
Total asset value $300,000   Full-time worker equivalent 1.75
Machinery value $54,000

  a Rate of capital turnover _____
  b Capital investment per person _____
  c Machinery investment per tillable acre _____
  d Machinery cost per tillable acre _____
  e Value of farm production per person _____
  f Net farm income per person _____

REFERENCES

Castle, Emery N., Manning H. Becker, and Frederick J. Smith: *Farm Business Management*, 2d ed., The Macmillan Company, New York, 1972, chap. 4.

Herbst, J. H.: *Farm Management Principles, Budgets, Plans,* 4th ed. Stipes Publishing Co., Champaign, Ill., 1976, chap. 11.

James, Sydney C., and Everett Stoneberg: *Farm Accounting and Business Analysis*, Iowa State University Press, Ames, Iowa, 1974, chaps. 7, 8.

Willett, Gayle S.: *How to Analyze the Dairy Farm Business*, E.M. 4368, Washington State University Cooperative Extension Service, 1978.

Chapter 10

Other Useful
Records

CHAPTER OBJECTIVES

   1   To discuss the need for supplemental records as a source of physical data for use in farm planning, budgeting, and analysis
   2   To illustrate forms which can be used to record production, input use, and inventory changes for crops
   3   To present forms which can be used to record production, inventory changes, feed use, and breeding data for livestock enterprises
   4   To show how detailed records can be kept on the use and cost of machinery and labor

A great deal of information is required for farm planning and budgeting, for whole farm analysis, and for enterprise analysis. Much of the information is not directly available in the financial records of the business, and additional records can be very useful. These records provide the physical and cost data necessary in planning, budgeting, and analysis as well as simplifying the process of taking a physical inventory.

There is always the problem of how much detail to include in the record-keeping process. The law of diminishing returns undoubtedly applies to keeping records, and the manager should carefully weigh the added cost of additional records against the added returns. Most farms and ranches could benefit from keeping and using additional recorded information, but there is a limit.

The opportunity cost on the time spent recording information is an important factor to be considered. Above all, these additional records are valuable only if they are used and used in a way which increases farm efficiency and profit.

GENERAL FARM RECORDS

There are several items which form a record of the physical features of any given farm. Their primary use is in planning, and they should be filed in a convenient place as part of the permanent records or file on each farm. They will need to be referred to from time to time and particularly when developing a whole farm plan.

Aerial Photograph An aerial photograph of a farm can be obtained for a small fee through the local county office of the Agricultural Stabilization and Conservation Service. Figure 10-1 is an example of an aerial photograph in an area which is predominately cropland.

The physical characteristics of a farm are relatively easy to identify on an aerial photograph. Locations of fields, fences, drainageways, lanes, woodlots, and farmsteads are clearly shown and can be used to draw a farm map to scale. This map can be used for planning changes in field sizes and arrangement, drainage systems, and other changes in the physical layout of the farm which will improve productivity and efficiency. Instruments are also available to measure field sizes directly from an aerial photograph.

An aerial photograph can also be used to assist in identifying soil types when developing a soil map. Subtle differences in the shading on the photograph often indicate a change from one soil type to another, and the changes can be properly located relative to some physical characteristic of the farm as shown on the photograph. Soil scientists often develop a soil map directly on an aerial photograph as an aid in identifying soil types and the boundary between different types.

Soil Map Every farmer or rancher should be familiar with the types and characteristics of soils in the local area. Crop yield potential, conservation measures, drainage problems, and fertility requirements are all a function of soil type. Therefore, a soil map for the farm along with a knowledge of the soil characteristics greatly aids farm planning and budgeting. It is also useful for planning field arrangements in an attempt to get nearly uniform soil types within each field. This greatly simplifies the planning of fertilization and conservation practices on a field-by-field basis.

County soil maps are often available through the Soil Conservation Service. However, the scale may be too small to provide much detail on an individual farm. Personnel from the county Soil Conservation Service office will prepare a soil map for an individual farm as part of the services they provide in preparing a farm conservation plan. An example of a completed soil map is shown in Figure 10-2. Special training in soils and soil classification is necessary to prepare an accurate soil map.

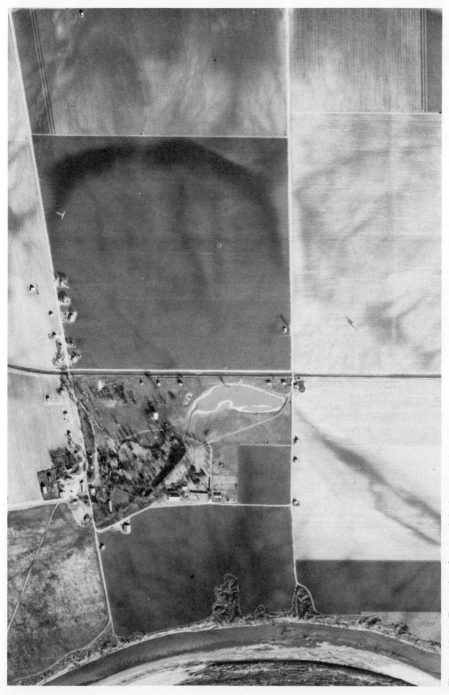

Figure 10-1 Example of an aerial photograph.

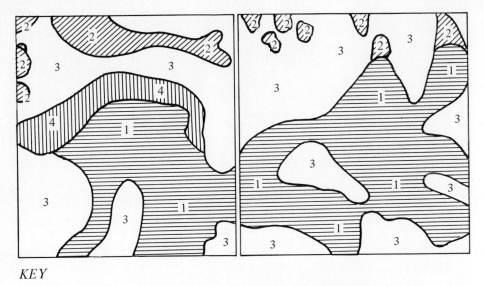

KEY

1 Brookston silty clay loam   3 Fincastle silt loam

2 Cope silt loam   4 Russell silt loam

Figure 10-2 Illustration of a soil map.

Farm Maps Farm or field maps have a variety of uses and are simply a scale drawing of the farm showing the important physical features and field arrangements. An accurate farm map can be obtained by tracing an aerial photograph including fence lines, streams and drainageways, field boundaries, and farmstead location. An example of a farm map is shown in Figure 10-3.

Managers use farm maps for two basic purposes. The first is as a worksheet to sketch in proposed changes in fence lines, field boundaries, and drainageways. This allows several alternatives to be compared on paper before the change is selected which will result in the most efficient field arrangement. The second use of farm or field maps is to plan and record cropping programs. Plans for the coming year in terms of the crop to be grown, seeding rate and variety, fertilizer level, and herbicide to be used can be entered on each field on the map and used by employees during the planting season. In the same manner, the actual plan including yield and problems such as drainage and weed infestations can be noted on the map for each field and filed for future reference.

Farmstead Map An accurate scale map of the farmstead can be valuable when planning new buildings, changing or adding to existing livestock pens, and extending utilities. If the location of existing underground utilities such as water and sewer lines and electrical cables is known, they should be included on the map. This can save many hours of digging in an attempt to locate these

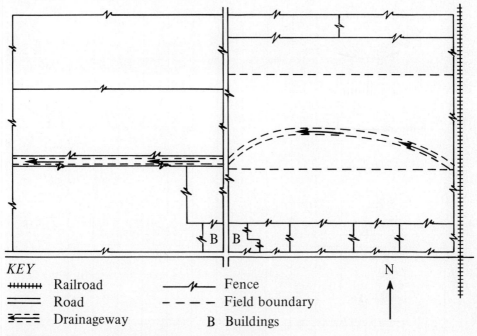

KEY

┼┼┼┼┼┼ Railroad	──┼──	Fence
══════ Road	── ── ──	Field boundary
⇌═══ Drainageway	B	Buildings

N ↑

Figure 10-3 Farm map including field arrangement.

lines in later years and prevent inadvertently breaking one of these lines when doing other ditching or underground work.

CROP RECORDS

Supplemental crop records are primarily of two types, inventory records and detailed field records. Each will be discussed below.

Crop Inventory A running inventory on a monthly basis permits a manager to organize and manage crop sales, purchases, and livestock feed requirements to assure sufficient amounts will be available for livestock feed and for carry-over into the next year. It also permits a quick and easy method of taking a crop inventory whenever one is needed for completing a balance sheet or income statement. Several different forms can be used, and one example is shown in Table 10-1. A separate form is required for each type of grain or forage.

Each month begins with the beginning inventory, with farm production and purchases during the month added to this amount. This total is entered in the total available column. Quantities used for livestock feed, for seed, or sold during the month are subtracted from the total available to arrive at the ending inventory, and the process is repeated for the following month. It is often useful for later analyses to indicate which type of livestock consumed the feed.

Table 10-1   Monthly Crop Inventory

Crop _____   Year _____

Month	Beginning inventory	Production	Purchases	Total available	Livestock feed	Farm seed	Sales	Ending inventory
January								
February								
March								
April								
May								
June								
July								
August								
September								
October								
November								
December								

While some estimation will undoubtedly be necessary, a few simple notations on production and usage will provide satisfactory accuracy for this running inventory. A complete inventory at the end of each year can be used to correct any inaccuracies which have crept into the figures during the year.

Field Records   Detailed field records have several important uses, including enterprise analysis on the basis of individual fields. Many managers have developed their own form for recording and maintaining this information, and an example of such a form is shown in Table 10-2. The heading contains spaces for entering the year, crop grown, field number, acres in the field, and several lines for recording weather information, effectiveness of chemicals, weed and insect problems, etc.

Information on seed variety and rates, fertilizer applications, and chemicals used can be recorded on the main part of the form. A record of chemical use is becoming very important as regulations concerning their application continue to increase. This information can also be used to plan next year's crop for each field to prevent inadvertent crop damage from herbicide carryover from one year to the next.

Table 10-2 also includes space to record the machine operations performed on the field along with the cost or hours of machinery time. If recorded in hours, this information can be used to estimate the machinery cost for the field at a later time after computing machinery cost on an hourly basis.

One objective of maintaining complete field records is to estimate profit on a field and per acre basis. Space is provided on the bottom of the form to calculate this information. The result is similar to enterprise analysis except that it is for an individual field rather than the total for all fields producing the same crop. This permits analysis on a field-by-field basis and provides more information for identifying problems and adjusting input levels based on the characteristics of an individual field.

LIVESTOCK RECORDS

Three types of livestock records will be illustrated in this section. Others are possible, including detailed input and cost records on each pen or lot of livestock, much like the field records for crop production.

Livestock Inventory   A monthly livestock inventory on a form such as the one in Table 10-3 provides a convenient way to record the number of animals purchased, produced, sold, or transferred and any deaths. It also saves time when a livestock inventory is needed for completing a balance sheet or income statement or for some other purpose.

The form in Table 10-3 begins with both the number and value of the livestock on hand at the beginning of each month and ends with the same items. Additions or deletions from the inventory are recorded by number of head, including the number transferred from one class of livestock to another.

Table 10-2 Form for Maintaining Field Records on Crop Production

Year _____   Crop _____

Field No. _____   Acres _____

Comments: _____

Date	Seed		Fertilizer		Chemicals		Machinery operations	
	Variety	Rate	Analysis	Rate	Type	Rate	Type	Cost or Hours

Total Production _____   Total Crop Value _____   Field Profit _____

Per Acre Yield _____   Total Costs _____   Profit Per Acre _____

Table 10-3 Monthly Livestock Inventory

Year _____ Type _____ Lot or Pen No. _____

Month	Beginning inventory		Purchased (No.)	Produced (No.)	Sold (No.)	Deaths (No.)	Transferred (No.)		Ending inventory	
	No.	Value					In	Out	No.	Value
January										
February										
March										
April										
May										
June										
July										
August										
September										
October										
November										
December										

The latter columns can be used when transferring replacement heifers and gilts from the inventory of market livestock to the breeding livestock inventory.

The form used to maintain the livestock inventory could be expanded to include weights and value for each of the columns. This would provide additional information but would require more space and a longer form.

Feed Records An analysis of the individual livestock enterprises or even an analysis of the profitability of the combined livestock enterprises requires feed records. Without them, it is impossible to calculate accurately profit for each livestock enterprise, returns per $100 of feed fed, or other measures of efficiency.

A feed record can be kept on a form such as the one shown in Table 10-4. It is designed to record feed fed to livestock on a monthly basis, but the same type of form can be used on a daily or weekly basis. Space is provided for three types of grain, three types of commercial feed, hay and silage, and two types of pasture. For feedlot livestock, the pasture columns can be eliminated to provide space for more types of the other feeds.

Special care must be taken to account for farm-raised feed fed to livestock and to price it at market value. It may be desirable to record the feed fed on both a quantity and a value basis each month. Particularly where large amounts of feed are purchased during the year at different prices, recording the feed value monthly eliminates the need to estimate an average annual price at the end of the year when calculating the total value of all feed fed.

Breeding Records The third general type of supplemental livestock record is a breeding record. Breeding records will be required for a purebred livestock operation, and they aid in the analysis and improvement of a commercial breeding herd. Several types of forms can be used for breeding records, and one type suitable for a beef cow herd is shown in Table 10-5. Most breeding records also include space to record some production and performance information to aid in culling decisions and selection of herd replacements.

The form in Table 10-5 includes spaces for recording breeding dates, sires, due dates, and actual calving dates. Limited space is available for performance data on the calf. Additional spaces could be added for other measures of cow performance such as cow weight, adjusted weaning weight, weaning index, and overall cow efficiency. This additional information can be used by the manager to form the basis for culling cows and selecting replacement heifers from the better cows.

MACHINERY RECORDS

There are two general types of machinery records. The first is a cost record to permit the calculation of machinery costs for individual machines and the second is a record of scheduled repair and maintenance. Table 10-6 is a ma-

Table 10-4 Livestock Feed Record

Kind of Livestock or Pen No. _____ Year _____

Month	No. of animals	Grain		Commercial feed		Forage		Pasture
		Corn (bu.)				Hay	Silage	
January								
February								
March								
April								
May								
June								
July								
August								
September								
October								
November								
December								
Totals								
Price								
Total value								

Table 10-5 Beef Cow Breeding and Performance Record

Cow number _____

Birth date or year acquired _____

Breed _____

Purchased or raised _____

Year	Date bred	Sire	Date due	Calving date	Calf information			Remarks
					Sex	Birth weight	Wean weight	

Medical and health notes: _____

Table 10-6 Farm Machinery Record

Item _____ Identification no. _____

Year _____ Date purchased _____

Month or date	Hours of use	Fuel		Oil and lubricant		Repairs and maintenance	
		Gallons	Cost	Qty.	Cost	Cost (including labor)	Description
Totals							

Property taxes _____ Total fixed cost _____

Insurance _____ Total variable cost _____

Depreciation _____ Total cost _____

Interest _____

Average fixed costs per hour _____

Average variable cost per hour _____

Average total cost per hour _____

chinery record form which emphasizes cost information, but it also contains space for recording all repair and maintenance activities.

Entries on this form can be made daily or weekly for nonpowered machines which receive little use during the year. For machines which require fuel and daily servicing and receive heavy use, many managers employ another procedure. Each machine carries a form to record daily fuel and oil consumption and minor repairs. These forms are collected weekly or monthly, and the totals for each item are entered on a form such as the one in Table 10-6. This procedure minimizes the entries on this permanent record while still providing the necessary information.

The bottom of the form contains spaces for recording the fixed costs as well as the total variable costs from the form itself. This information can be used to calculate the machine's cost per hour, which in turn provides some important information for enterprise budgeting and analysis.

LABOR RECORDS

Payroll records are an important type of labor record for farms with hired labor. These must be kept to meet government requirements regarding the withholding and reporting of social security and income taxes and certain other requirements. While necessary and important, payroll records will not be discussed here. Instead, the emphasis will be on a record designed to improve whole farm analysis.

Determining labor requirements for enterprise budgeting and labor allocation for enterprise analysis are two difficult problems without some record of labor utilization. Table 10-7 is one type of form some managers have found useful. Hours of labor used by crop and livestock enterprises can be recorded on a weekly or monthly basis to form a permanent record of labor utilization by enterprise. Actual labor spent operating machinery should be recorded in the appropriate enterprise column, but space is provided to also record labor spent on machinery repairs and maintenance. This labor should be allocated to machinery costs.

The final column can be used to record labor used for general farm overhead which is not directly related to any enterprise. Examples would be labor for building and fence repairs and time spent marketing products and purchasing supplies. While not directly applicable to any single enterprise this labor is nevertheless necessary and for budgeting or analysis purposes should be charged or allocated back against the various enterprises using one of the methods discussed in the last chapter.

SUMMARY

In addition to the balance sheet, record of receipts and expenses, depreciation schedule, and income statement, which are basic and necessary records, many additional records aid and simplify whole farm planning, budgeting, analysis,

Table 10-7   Record of Labor Utilization (Hours)

Month or week	Crop enterprises				Livestock enterprises				Machinery repairs	Farm overhead
Cost per hour										
Total cost										

and the control function. However, there is a limit on the number of records that should be kept because of the time required and their cost.

This chapter presented several types of supplemental or additional records which are useful and can be kept with a minimum of effort. The secret to keeping supplemental records is to use the simplest form which contains the necessary information and to collect and record information on a daily or weekly basis in an organized and efficient manner. The time required should be minimized and some use made of the information collected. If the collected information is not used, it is very easy to become discouraged and let record maintenance receive low or last priority for use of the manager's time.

QUESTIONS FOR REVIEW AND FURTHER THOUGHT

1 Explain diminishing returns as applied to keeping supplemental records.
2 Why are machinery and labor records useful for enterprise budgeting and analysis?
3 Suggest additional or supplemental records that might be kept on a specific enterprise to provide complete information for enterprise analysis.
4 Develop your own form for keeping a complete field record or machinery record for cost analysis. Which items are absolutely necessary and which might be eliminated? Can the form be simplified?

REFERENCES

Barnard, C. S., and J. S. Nix: *Farm Planning and Control*, Cambridge University Press, Cambridge, 1973, chap. 18.
James, Sydney C., and Everett Stoneberg: *Farm Accounting and Business Analysis*, Iowa State University Press, Ames, 1974, chap. 6.

Part 4
IMPLEMENTATION
ACQUIRING AND MANAGING RESOURCES

HIGHLIGHTS

Implementation is another of the three basic functions of management. The effort put into developing a good plan or making the best possible decision is wasted if no further action is taken. A plan must be implemented or some action taken before there will be any results approaching those planned for or desired.

Implementing a plan is often a two-step procedure. First, the necessary resources must be acquired. This may involve purchasing or leasing additional resources or a reorganization of resources currently owned. Second, these resources must be managed over time as they are being used. The time necessary for agricultural production to take place requires most plans to be implemented step by step over time and the resources to be properly managed and organized throughout this time period.

This part begins with a chapter on the forms of business organization. A farm or ranch business may be legally organized as a sole proprietorship, partnership, or corporation. Each has certain characteristics which may affect how a plan is implemented and how resources are acquired and managed. Selecting the form of business organization may be the first decision made after choosing farming or ranching as a career.

The remaining chapters in this part discuss the acquisition and management of the more important resources needed for agricultural production. Chapters 12 and 13 explore the use of capital and credit and the procedures which can be used to evaluate alternative capital investments. The control and use of land is discussed in Chapter 14, which emphasizes that land can be controlled and used by either purchasing or leasing. Labor use and the management of hired labor are the subjects presented in Chapter 15. Part Four concludes with Chapter 16, which discusses the importance of machinery management, as machinery represents both a large investment and a large annual expense on most farms.

Chapter 11

Forms of
Business Organization

CHAPTER OBJECTIVES

    1 To identify the sole proprietorship, partnership, and corporation as the three primary forms of business organization
    2 To discuss the organization and characteristics of each form of business organization
    3 To analyze the advantages and disadvantages of each form of business organization
    4 To show how income taxes may be affected by the form of business organization
    5 To summarize the factors to be considered when selecting a form of business organization

Any business, including a farm or ranch business, may be legally organized in a number of ways to produce goods and services. The legal form of business organization used has both short-run and long-run implications for the firm. Unfortunately, many people give little thought to the form of business organization when they begin farming or ranching. While it is generally possible to change during the life of the business, a little thought and legal advice at the beginning may save time, trouble, and expense at a later date.
    The three basic forms of business organization are: (1) *sole proprietorship (or individual proprietorship)*, (2) *partnership*, and (3) *corporation*. There are

different legal and organizational characteristics, advantages, disadvantages, and income tax regulations for each form. Most farms and ranches are organized as sole proprietorships, but there are reasons to investigate the other forms. The proper choice may depend upon whether the business is just getting started, is well established and going through its growing phase, or is at the stage where the owner is nearing retirement.

Many farmers operating as sole proprietors have become interested in the other business forms in recent years. The increase in farm sizes, larger capital requirements, and an increased awareness of estate taxes and estate transfer problems in general have stimulated the interest. All these factors are important in choosing a form of business organization. In addition, personal goals are important, and a final choice should be made only after a complete analysis of all possible long-run effects on the business and the individuals involved.

THE SOLE PROPRIETORSHIP

The sole proprietorship is the most common form of business organization. Many small businesses are organized as sole proprietorships, as are nearly 90 percent of our nation's farms and ranches, according to the 1974 Census of Agriculture. A sole proprietorship is easy to form and easy to operate, which accounts for much of its popularity.

Organization and Characteristics

In a sole proprietorship, the owner or sole proprietor owns and manages the business, assumes all the risks, and receives all the profits (or losses). Its distinguishing characteristic is the single owner, who acquires and organizes the necessary resources, provides the management, and is solely responsible for the success or failure of the business as well as all business debts. Perhaps the sole proprietorship should be more accurately called a family proprietorship on many farms and ranches, as husband, wife, and children may all be involved in providing labor and management. However, until arrangements are made to share these responsibilities legally, debts and/or profits fall primarily on one individual, and a sole proprietorship exists.

A sole proprietorship is established simply by starting the business as such. No legal requirements, permits, or licenses are required unless the business is to perform certain functions. Sales tax permits, health inspections, and other types of permits and licenses may be required, depending on the type of business to be done, but they would also be required for any of the other forms of business ownership.

A sole proprietorship is not limited in size by either the amount of inputs which can be used or the amount of products produced. The business can be as large or small as the owner desires, with the maximum size limited only by the owner's ability to acquire and manage the necessary resources. There can be any number of employees, additional management may be hired, and property may even be co-owned with others. A sole proprietorship does not necessarily need to own any assets, and one could exist even though all land and machinery are leased. In this last situation, a business still exists to produce agricultural products, but the sole proprietor simply owns few if any assets.

Advantages

The advantages of a sole proprietorship are related to its simplicity and the freedom the owner has in operating the business. No one needs to be consulted when a management decision is made, and the owner is free to organize and operate the business in any legal manner. All business profits belong to the owner who is sole proprietor. However, the same is true for any losses incurred.

A sole proprietorship is also flexible. The owner as the sole decision maker can quickly make decisions regarding investments, purchases, sales, enterprise combinations, input levels, etc., based solely on his or her best judgment. Assets can be quickly purchased or sold, money borrowed, or the business even liquidated if necessary without consulting anyone. All these transactions may be accomplished with a minimum of time, effort, and legal complications.

Disadvantages

The management freedom inherent in a sole proprietorship includes both responsibilities and disadvantages. Owners of sole proprietorships are personally liable for any legal difficulties and debts related to the business. Creditors have the legal right to attach not only the assets of the business but the personal assets of the owner in fulfillment of any unpaid financial obligations. This feature of a sole proprietorship can be an important disadvantage for a large, heavily financed business where the owner has substantial personal and non-farm assets. Business failure can result in these assets being acquired by creditors to pay the debts of the sole proprietorship.

The size of a sole proprietorship is limited by the capital available to the single owner. If only a small amount is available, the business may be too small to realize any economies of size, making it difficult to compete with larger and more efficient farms. At the other extreme, the management abilities and time of the single owner may be insufficient for a large business, causing management inefficiencies. Thus, a large sole proprietorship may need to hire additional management personnel.

Another disadvantage of a sole proprietorship is poor business continuity. It is difficult to bring sons or daughters (or their spouses) into the business on any basis other than as an employee. Death of the owner also terminates the business, which means it may have to be liquidated or reorganized under new ownership. This liquidation or reorganization can be time-consuming and costly, resulting in a smaller inheritance and/or smaller income for the heirs during the transition period.

Income Taxes

The owner of a business organized as a sole proprietorship pays income taxes on any business profit at the same tax rates in effect for individuals. Business profits are added to other taxable income earned by the individual to determine the total taxable income. Individual marginal income tax rates established by the Revenue Act of 1978 range from 14 to 70 percent.

Any capital gains resulting from the business transactions of a sole proprietorship are also taxed at the same rates applicable to individuals. However, the Revenue Act of 1978 allows 60 percent of individual capital gains to be *excluded* from taxable income. Total taxable income is then all business and nonbusiness ordinary income plus 40 percent of all capital gain income from both business and nonbusiness sources.

PARTNERSHIPS

A partnership is an association of two or more persons who share the ownership of a business to be carried on for profit. Partnerships can be organized to last for a very brief time or for a long duration depending on the desires of the partners and the type of business to be conducted. If two or more persons associate to make a profit on a short-term basis for a single transaction, the arrangement is often called a *joint venture*. A joint venture is subject to the same legal rights and restrictions as a long-term partnership.

Two types of partnerships are recognized in most states. The *general partnership* is the most common, but the *limited partnership* is used for some situations. Both types have the same characteristics with one exception. The limited partnership must have at least one general partner and any number of limited partners. An important difference is that limited partners cannot participate in the management of the partnership business and their financial liability for partnership debts and obligations is limited to their actual investment in the partnership. The liability of general partners will be discussed later.

Limited partnerships are most often used for businesses such as land speculation and cattle feeding ventures. Most farm and ranch operating partnerships are general partnerships. For this reason, the discussion in the remainder of this section will assume a general partnership unless otherwise indicated.

Organization and Characteristics

A partnership is formed simply by two or more persons agreeing to join together to conduct a business for profit. Oral partnership agreements are legal in most states but are not recommended. Important points can be overlooked, and fading memories over time on the details in an oral agreement can later create friction between the partners. Problems can also be encountered when filing the partnership income tax return.

A written partnership agreement is of particular importance if the profits are not to be divided equally. The courts and the Uniform Partnership Act, which is a set of regulations enacted by most states to govern the operation of partnerships, assumes a 50-50 partnership in everything including management decisions unless there is a written agreement specifying a different arrangement. For any situation not covered in the written agreement, the regulations in the Uniform Partnership Act will apply.

A written partnership agreement should cover all points in the establishment and operation of the partnership. Putting the agreement in writing does not mean the partners do not trust each other. It is simply good business, a way to prevent future problems, and will ensure that the partners have carefully considered all points before entering the partnership. The written agreement should cover the following points, although others may need to be included:

1 *Management.* Who is responsible for management decisions and how will they be made?

2 *Share of Profit and Losses.* The method and proportion of profit and losses going to each partner should be carefully described, particularly if there is not an equal division.

3 *Property Ownership and Contribution.* This section should contain a listing of the property each partner will contribute to the partnership and how it will be owned.

4 *Records.* Records are important for the division of profits and for maintaining an inventory of assets and their ownership. Who will keep what records should be part of the agreement.

5 *Taxation.* Related to records is the need to keep a detailed account of the tax basis of property owned and controlled by the partnership and the preparation of the partnership information tax return.

6 *Termination.* The agreement should contain the date the partnership will be terminated if it is known or can be determined.

7 *Dissolution.* The termination of the partnership on either a voluntary or involuntary basis requires a division of partnership assets. The method for making this division should be described to prevent disagreements and an unfair division.

There are many possible patterns and variations in partnership arrangements. However, the partnership form of business organization has three basic characteristics:

1 A sharing of the business profits and losses

2 Shared control of property with possible shared ownership of some property

3 Shared management of the business

The exact sharing arrangement for each of these characteristics is flexible and should be outlined in the partnership agreement.

Partners may contribute land, capital, labor, management, and other assets to the partnership. Profits are generally divided in proportion to the value of the assets, labor, and management contributed to the business; i.e., if each of the two partners contribute one-half of the assets, labor, and management, they share the profits on a 50-50 basis. However, the profits may be shared on any basis agreeable to the partners regardless of their contributions.

Property may be owned by the partnership, or the partners may retain ownership of their individual property but allow it to be used by the partnership. Individual ownership still allows every partner access to and control of the asset for partnership use. When the partnership itself owns property, any partner may sell or dispose of any asset without the consent and permission of the other partners. This aspect of a partnership suggests individual ownership may be desirable in some cases particularly as it does not affect its use by the partnership.

A partnership can be terminated in a number of ways. The partnership agreement may specify a termination date. If not, a partnership will terminate upon the death of a partner, the incapacitation of a partner, bankruptcy, or by agreement between the partners. Termination upon the death of a partner can be prevented by provisions in the written agreement allowing the deceased partner's share to pass to the estate and hence to the legal heirs.

In addition to the three basic characteristics mentioned above, others are used to determine whether or not a particular business arrangement is legally a partnership. They are:

1   Joint ownership of assets
2   Operation under a firm name
3   A joint bank account
4   A single set of business records
5   Management participation by all parties
6   Sharing of profits and losses

Joint ownership of property does not by itself imply a partnership. However, a business arrangement with all or most of these characteristics may be a legal partnership even though a partnership was not intended. These characteristics should be kept in mind for landlord-tenant arrangements, for example. An unintentional partnership can be created by a leasing arrangement based on shares unless steps are taken to prevent it.

In the final analysis a partnership is a close relationship, both legal and personal, between two or more persons. There needs to be a complete understanding and complete trust between the partners if the business is to succeed. Personal characteristics and compatibility are very important, as personal conflicts over relatively small matters probably terminate more partnerships than any other reason. Each partner must believe the partnership will be more advantageous than operating alone. If the final agreement is not fair and equitable to each partner, there will be a temptation to remove the contributed capital, labor, and management to some other business to the detriment of the partnership.

Advantages

The primary advantages of a partnership over a sole proprietorship are in the areas of capital and management. Pooling the capital of the partners allows a larger business, which can be more efficient than two or more smaller businesses. It may also increase the amount of credit available, allowing further increases in business size. Total management is also increased by pooling the management capabilities of the partners. Management efforts can be divided, with each partner specializing in the management of one area of the business, which can increase overall management efficiency.

A partnership is relatively easy to form and to dissolve and is cheaper to form than a corporation. It may require more records than a sole proprietorship, but fewer are required than for a corporation. While each partner may lose some individual freedom in making management decisions, a carefully drawn written agreement can maintain some of this freedom.

A partnership is a flexible form of business organization where many types of arrangements can be accommodated and included in a written agreement. This makes it suitable for situations such as a parent desiring to bring children and/or their spouses into the business. The children may contribute only labor to the partnership initially, but the partnership agreement can be modified over time to allow for their increasing contributions of management and capital.

Disadvantages

The unlimited liability of each partner is an important disadvantage of a partnership. A partner cannot be held personally responsible for the personal debts of the other partners. However, each partner can be held personally and individually responsible for any lawsuits and financial obligations arising from the operation of the partnership. If the partnership does not have sufficient assets to cover its legal financial obligations, creditors can bring suit against all partners individually to collect any money due them. In other words, a partner's personal assets can be claimed by a creditor to pay partnership debts.

This takes on a special significance considering that any partner, acting individually, can act for the partnership in legal and financial transactions. For this reason if for no other, it is important to know and trust your partners and to have the management decision-making procedure included in the partnership agreement. Too many partners and/or an unstructured management system can easily create problems. The primary feature of a limited partnership is that it places unlimited liability on the general partner but limits the liability of the limited partners to only the capital they have actually contributed to the partnership.

Similar to a sole proprietorship, a partnership has the disadvantage of poor business continuity. It can be unexpectedly terminated by the death of one partner (unless the partnership agreement provides for continuity) or a disagreement among the partners. The dissolution of any business is generally time-consuming and costly, particularly when it is caused by the death of a close friend and partner or by a disagreement resulting in bad feelings among the partners. The required sharing of management decision making and the loss of some personal freedom in a partnership are always potential sources of conflict between the partners.

Income Taxes

A partnership does not directly pay any income taxes. Instead it files an information income tax return reporting the income and expenses for the partnership. Any income tax payable is paid by each of the individual partners based on their respective share of the partnership income as stated in the partnership agreement.

In a 50-50 partnership between two persons, for example, each would report one-half of the partnership income, capital gains, expenses, depreciation, losses, etc. These would be included with any other income the partner may have to determine the total income tax liability. Partnership income is therefore taxed at individual tax rates, with the exact rate depending on the amount of partnership income and the amount of other income earned by the partner/taxpayer.

CORPORATION

A corporation is a separate legal entity which must be formed and operated in accordance with the laws of the state in which it is organized. It is a legal "person" separate and apart from the corporation owners and management. This separation of the business entity from its owners distinguishes a corporation from the other forms of business organization. As a separate business entity or legal "person," a corporation can own property, borrow money, enter into contracts, sue, and be sued. It has most of the basic rights and duties of an individual.

Two types of corporate structures are recognized by the Internal Revenue Service. The first is the regular corporation, which is also called a Subchapter C corporation, referring to that part of the Internal Revenue Code which covers this type. The second type of corporate structure is the Subchapter S corporation, sometimes referred to as a tax-option corporation. Both types have many of the same characteristics, and the differences between them will be pointed out in the following sections.

Organization and Characteristics

The state laws affecting the formation and operation of a corporation vary somewhat from state to state. In addition, several states have laws preventing a corporation from engaging in farming or ranching or place special restrictions on farm and ranch corporations. For this and other reasons, competent legal advice should be sought before attempting to form a corporation.

While state laws do vary, there are some basic steps that will generally apply to forming a corporation. These are:

1 The incorporators file a preliminary application with the appropriate state official. This may include reserving a corporation name.
2 The incorporators draft a preincorporation agreement outlining the major rights and duties of the parties after the corporation is formed.

3 The Articles of Incorporation are prepared and filed with the proper state office.

4 The incorporators turn property and/or cash over to the corporation in exchange for shares of stock representing their ownership share of the corporation.

5 The shareholders meet to organize the business and elect directors.

6 The directors meet to elect officers, adopt any bylaws that may be necessary, and begin business in the name of the corporation.

These steps identify the three groups of individuals involved in a corporation as shareholders, directors, and officers. The shareholders own the corporation and provide much of its capital. Stock certificates are issued to the shareholders for property transferred to the corporation or in exchange for cash. As owners, the shareholders have the right to direct the affairs of the corporation, which is done through the elected directors and at annual meetings. Each shareholder has one vote for each share of voting stock owned. Therefore, any shareholder with 51 percent or more of the outstanding voting stock has effective control over the business affairs of the corporation.

The directors are elected by the shareholders at each annual meeting and hold office for the following year. They are responsible to the shareholders for the management of the business. The number of directors is normally fixed by the Articles of Incorporation. Meetings of the directors are held to conduct the business affairs of the corporation and to set broad management policy to be carried out by the officers.

The officers of a corporation are elected by the board of directors and may be removed by them. They are responsible for the day-to-day operation of the business within the guidelines established by the board. The officers' authority flows from the board of directors, to whom they are ultimately responsible. A corporation president may sign certain contracts, borrow money, and perform other duties without board approval but will normally need board approval before committing the corporation to large financial transactions or performing certain other acts.

The number of shareholders may be as few as one in some states, and three is the minimum number in several states. In many small family farm corporations, the shareholders, directors, and officers are all the same individuals. To an outsider, the business may appear to be operated little differently from a sole proprietorship or partnership. Even the directors' meetings may be held informally around a kitchen table, but a set of minutes should be kept on each meeting.

The above discussion applies to both Subchapter C and Subchapter S corporations. However, there are certain restrictions on the formation of a Subchapter S corporation. The more important restrictions are:

1 There must be no more than 15 shareholders (a husband and wife are considered one shareholder even though they both own stock).

2 There can be only one class of stock outstanding.

3 All shareholders must be either an individual, estate, grantor trust, or voting trust.
4 All shareholders must consent to this form of incorporation.

There are also certain limitations on the types and amounts of income that can be received from specified sources and still maintain the Subchapter S status for income taxation. The taxation of a Subchapter S corporation will be covered in a later section. Selecting the form of corporate organization should be done only after giving careful thought to the possible consequences both short-run and long-run.

Advantages

Farm and ranch corporations, though still small in number, have increased rapidly in the last 10 to 15 years. The majority are classified as family farm corporations with a relatively small number of shareholders all related by blood or marriage. This increased interest in farm corporations has resulted from better research and publicity about their operation and advantages.

Corporations provide limited liability for the shareholder/owners. They are legally responsible only to the extent of the capital they have invested. Personal assets of the shareholders cannot be attached by creditors to meet the financial obligations of the corporation. This advantage may be negated in some cases where a corporation officer is required to personally cosign a note for corporation borrowing. In this case, the officer can be held personally responsible for the debt if the corporation cannot meet its responsibilities.

A corporation, like a partnership, provides a means for several individuals to pool their resources and management. The resulting business, with a larger size and the possibility of specialized management, can provide greater efficiency than two or more smaller businesses. Credit may also be easier to obtain because of the business continuity embodied in a corporation. The business is not terminated by the death of a shareholder, as the shares simply pass to the heirs and the business continues. However, a plan for management continuity should exist by having more than one person involved in management and capable of taking over complete management. Otherwise the death of a principal shareholder who may also be president and responsible for all management decisions will disrupt the business during the transition to new management.

A corporation provides a convenient way to divide business ownership and to transfer ownership. Shares of stock can be easily purchased, sold, or given as gifts without actually transferring title to specific parcels of land or other assets. Transferring shares does not disrupt or reduce the size of the business and is a convenient way for a retiring farmer to transfer part of the business to the next generation while maintaining an ongoing business.

There can be income tax advantages to incorporation depending on the size of business, how it is organized, and the income level of the shareholders. No general statement can be made, and the income tax consequences of incorporation should be carefully investigated before a corporation is formed. One general advantage is the tax deductibility of certain fringe benefits provided to the shareholder/employees. Premiums for health, accident, and life insurance provided for employees are a tax-deductible expense for the corporation, as may be certain other fringe benefits. These would not be tax deductible with the other forms of business organization.

Disadvantages

Corporations are more costly to form than sole proprietorships and partnerships and have some annual costs the others do not. Certain legal fees are necessary when organizing a corporation, and legal advice will be needed on a continuing basis to ensure compliance with various state regulations. An accountant may also be needed during the formation period and throughout the life of the corporation to handle tax-related matters. Most states require various fees when filing the Articles of Incorporation and have some type of annual fee or tax on corporations which are not assessed on the other forms of business organization.

    Doing business as a corporation requires additional records and "red tape." Shareholder and directors' meetings must be held, minutes kept of directors' meetings, and annual reports filed with the state. However, if forming a corporation results in better business and financial records being kept, this might be viewed as an advantage rather than a disadvantage because of better business efficiency.

Income Taxes

A Subchapter C corporation is a separate taxpaying entity, and corporations are subject to different tax rates than individuals. Corporate tax rates have been changed from time to time, and the Revenue Act of 1978 set them as follows:

Taxable Income ($)	Marginal Tax Rate (%)
Up to 25,000	17
25,001–50,000	20
50,001–75,000	30
75,001–100,000	40
Over 100,000	46

Special tax rates also apply to corporate long-term capital gains, which are taxed at a flat rate of 28 percent based on the Revenue Act of 1978. This is a higher rate than would apply to most individuals and may be a disadvantage of incorporation if substantial capital gain income is expected.

    Another disadvantage of a Subchapter C corporation is the potential "double taxation" of income. After the corporation pays tax on its taxable income, any after-tax income which is distributed to the shareholders as dividends is also taxable income to the shareholders at the applicable individual rates. Many small farm corporations avoid this double taxation by distributing most of the corporation income to the shareholders as wages, salary, and bonuses. These items are tax deductible for the corporation but taxable income to the shareholders/employees. Any wages and salaries paid must be for bona fide work performed for the corporation and not just a means to avoid the double taxation. The combined employee and employer social security tax on these salaries is higher than for self-employed individuals, which can be another disadvantage of the corporate form of business organization.

Subchapter S or "tax-option" corporations do not pay income tax themselves but are taxed like a partnership. The corporation files an information tax return, but the shareholders actually pay any tax due. Shareholders report a pro rata share of the corporation income, expenses, and capital gains according to the proportion of the total outstanding stock they own. This income is included with the shareholder's other income, and tax is paid based on the applicable individual rates. The income tax treatment of a Subchapter S corporation avoids the double-taxation problem of a Subchapter C corporation, making it a popular choice for many farm corporations that qualify for the Subchapter S treatment.

This is only a partial treatment of the income tax regulations applicable to corporations. There are other regulations pertaining to corporations which may affect some farm and ranch corporations. These should be reviewed with a qualified tax consultant before the corporate form of business organization is selected.

OTHER CONSIDERATIONS IN SELECTING A BUSINESS ORGANIZATION

Table 11-1 summarizes the important features of each of the three forms of business organization. The advantages and disadvantages of each feature should be carefully evaluated before a form of business organization is selected. There are additional factors to be considered in the selection. Estate planning and inheritance taxes may be affected by the form of business organization chosen. The importance of estate planning is becoming widely recognized as even moderate-sized farms represent a large estate and heirs face large inheritance taxes because of increasing land values. Many farmers are discovering that a change in business organization may be desirable as a way to meet their estate transfer plans and minimize inheritance taxes.

Related to estate planning may be the need or desire to bring children and/ or their spouses into the farm business. A partnership or corporation is often advantageous for this purpose and with proper planning can provide for business continuity as well as income for a retiring farmer and/or a surviving spouse. Some farmers have found that combinations of business organizations fit their plans. They may have one form of business organization which only owns land and another which actually operates the farming business. For example, the land may be owned by a corporation for ease of transfer to heirs

Table 11-1 Comparison of Forms of Farm Business Organization

Category	Sole proprietor	Partnership	Corporation
Ownership	Single individual	Two or more individuals	A separate legal entity which is separate from shareholders (but made up of individual stockholders)
Life of business	Terminates on death	Agreed term or terminates at death of a partner	Forever or fixed number of years; in case of death, stock passes by will or inheritance
Liability	Proprietor is liable	Each partner liable for all partnership obligations	Shareholders not liable for corporate obligations; in some cases individual stockholders may be asked to sign corporation notes
Source of capital	Personal investments, loans	Partnership contributions, loans	Shareholders' stock, sale of stock and loans
Management decisions	Proprietor	Agreement of partners	Shareholders elect directors who manage business
Income taxes	Tax on income of individual and related tax laws	Each partner pays his or her own income tax based on share of partnership income and related tax laws; partnership does file IRS Information Report	Regular corporation: Corporations file a tax return and pay income tax; salaries to shareholders and employees are deductible; tax rate is from 17 to 46%; shareholders taxed on dividends received Tax-option corporation: Shareholders report their share of income, operating loss, and long-term capital gain; IRS Information Report filed by corporation

both on and off the farm, with the land leased to a father-son partnership engaged in the actual business of raising crops and livestock.

SUMMARY

This chapter serves as an introduction to Part 4, which is concerned with acquiring and managing the resources necessary to implement a farm or ranch production plan. Before the resources to implement the plan are actually acquired, a form of business organization must be selected in beginning a new business. The selection should also be reviewed from time to time as the business grows and the owner approaches retirement.

A farm or ranch business can be organized as a sole proprietorship, a partnership, or a corporation of either the Subchapter C or Subchapter S type. There are advantages and disadvantages to each form of business organization, with their relative importance depending on the size of the business, desires of the owner, and many other factors. Some of the more important factors to be considered are continuity of the business, owner liability, sources and amount of capital, size, management, income taxes, and estate planning.

QUESTIONS FOR REVIEW AND FURTHER THOUGHT

1 What form of business organization would you choose if you were just beginning a small farming operation? What advantages would this form have for you? What disadvantages?
2 What form(s) of business organization might be preferable if you had just graduated from college and were joining your parents in the operation and management of an existing farm? What advantages and disadvantages would there be to you? To your parents?
3 Why might a partnership or corporation have more and better records than many sole proprietorships?
4 Look up the marginal tax rates for an individual (try Chapter 17) and compare them with the corporate tax rates shown in this chapter. Would a sole proprietor (individual) or a corporation pay more taxes on a taxable income of $10,000? On $25,000? On $50,000?
5 Explain the differences between a Subchapter C and Subchapter S corporation. Can 30 individuals form a Subchapter S corporation?
6 Explain the importance of a written partnership agreement. What should be included in a partnership agreement?
7 Does a two-person partnership have to be 50-50? Can it be a 30-70 or a 70-30 partnership? How should the division of profits be determined?

REFERENCES

Brock, Richard A., Eddy L. LaDue, and Robert S. Smith: *Preincorporation Considerations for the Farm Firm,* Department of Agricultural Economics, A.E. Res. 76-28, Cornell University, Ithaca, N.Y., 1976.

Harl, Neil E., and John C. O'Byrne: *The Farm Corporation,* North Central Regional Publication 11, April 1979, revised.

Hepp, Ralph E., and Myron Kelsey: *General Partnership for Agricultural Producers,* Michigan Cooperative Extension Service, Extension Bulletin E-731, East Lansing, Mich., 1972.

Krausz, N. G. P.: *Corporations in the Farm Business,* Illinois Cooperative Extension Service Circular 797, Champaign, Ill., 1972.

Levi, Donald R.: *Agricultural Law,* 3d ed., Lucas Brothers Pub., Columbia, Mo., 1977.

Levi, Donald R., Tom E. Prater, and James I. Mallett: *Incorporating the Texas Family Farm or Ranch Business,* Texas Agricultural Extension Service, MP-1158, College Station, Tex., 1975.

Levi, Donald R., Tom E. Prater, and James I. Mallett: *Organizing the Texas Family Farm or Ranch Business as a Partnership,* Texas Agricultural Extension Service, MP-1159, College Station, Tex., 1975.

Thomas, Kenneth H., and Michael D. Boehlje: *Farm Business Arrangements: Which One for You?* North Central Regional Publication 50, 1976.

Chapter 12

Capital and
the Use of Credit

CHAPTER OBJECTIVES

    1 To explain the importance of capital use in agriculture and the difference between capital and credit
    2 To illustrate the use of economic principles to determine the optimal use of capital
    3 To present the terminology used to classify different types of loans by use, length, collateral, and repayment schedule
    4 To outline the procedures and principles which are important for establishing and developing credit
    5 To learn the different methods of calculating the annual percentage rate of interest

Capital can be defined in narrow terms or very broadly. Many people think of capital as only cash, balances in checking and savings accounts, and other types of liquid savings. This is the narrow definition of capital, which is not widely used, particularly in economics. Agricultural economists define capital in much broader terms to also include money invested in livestock, machinery, and buildings. Land can also be included in a definition of capital, although it is often considered separately.

    With land included in the broad definition of capital, it is easy to see that capital is extremely important in agricultural production. Whether measured in total or on a per farm basis the capital requirements have been increasing. One of the characteristics of farming and ranching is the large capital investment per worker. Agriculture has one of the larger capital investments per worker of any major industry in the United States.

Figure 12-1 shows the capital investment in agriculture as well as the changes that have been taking place. Asset value has been increasing as investments in machinery and livestock have increased. Land has been a major factor in the increase, not because of more acres being used for agricultural production but because of the steady increase in land values. This has been particularly true since about 1972.

The capital investment *per farm* shows the same pattern as in Figure 12-1, including the rapid rise since 1972. Capital investment per farm was estimated at over $300,000 in 1979. This is only an average figure and includes many small farms and part-time farmers. Many larger commercial farms and ranches would have a capital investment between $500,000 and $1,000,000, with some having even larger investments. Land accounts for most of the investment, but livestock and machinery are also important. The size of capital investment per farm emphasizes the need for and importance of acquiring and managing large amounts of capital in order to compete in today's modern agriculture.

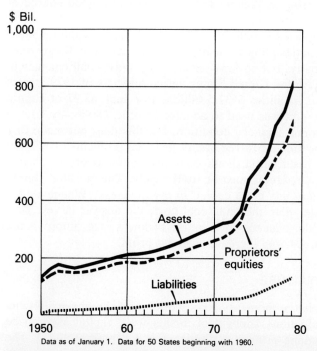

Data as of January 1. Data for 50 States beginning with 1960.

Figure 12-1 Capital investment in United States agriculture. (*Economic, Statistical and Cooperative Service, U.S. Department of Agriculture.*)

Credit is related to the study of capital acquisition and use. People often make a statement such as "I'm going to the bank to get some credit." This statement is not really correct, as *credit is defined as the capacity or ability to borrow money*. This definition places credit in the possession of an individual or business and not with a bank or other lending agency. The above statement really means "I'm going to the bank to exchange some of my credit for the use of some of the bank's money." Borrowing money is really the exchange of a borrower's credit for use of the lender's money with a promise to return the money and pay interest for its use. Thought of in these terms, borrowing money is little different from renting an asset such as land. In both cases rent (or interest) is paid for the use of another person's property with an agreement to return the property in good condition at the end of a specified period of time.

Credit, or the ability to borrow money, is a valuable possession or asset even though it does not show up on a balance sheet. The ability to borrow money is valuable, as it allows an individual to use borrowed money to help start a business, grow, expand, and make additional profit. Whenever credit is used, a debt or liability is created, and the original credit is reduced by the amount of money borrowed. Farmers and ranchers have used their credit in increasing amounts in recent years as the total capital requirements have increased because of inflation and larger farm sizes. The credit they have available has also been increasing as higher land values create a good source of credit and collateral for landowners.

Figure 12-2 shows the use of credit by United States farmers and ranchers in terms of the total debt outstanding at the beginning of each year. Borrowings have been increasing rapidly, but so have assets, with only small changes in the overall net capital ratio for United States agriculture. As of 1979, assets totaled $820.2 billion and liabilities $137.5 billion. For each $5.97 of capital invested in agriculture, credit was used to acquire $1 of it. Obviously United States agriculture is in sound financial condition, but this does not mean that each and every farmer or rancher is free of any financial problems.

Not only is credit an asset, but it should be used as other assets are used—to increase profit. However, credit must be used wisely. The question should always be: Can I *profitably* use more capital in my business? Whenever the additional return is greater than the additional cost, the answer is yes. Borrowed money can provide a means to increase business size, improve the efficiency of other resources, and increase business profit.

ECONOMICS OF CAPITAL USE

Broadly defined, capital is the monetary representation of the physical inputs used in agricultural production. Thought of in this way, capital use can be analyzed using the economic principles discussed in Chapters 2 and 3. The basic economic questions to be answered are: (1) how much total capital to use and (2) how limited capital should be allocated among its many potential uses.

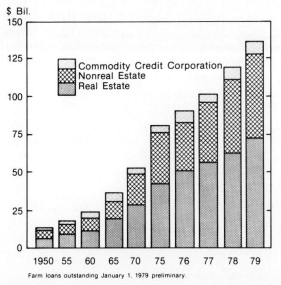

Farm loans outstanding January 1. 1979 preliminary.

Figure 12-2 Total farm debt by type. (*Economic, Statistical and Cooperative Service, U.S. Department of Agriculture.*)

Total Capital Use

When capital is not limited, the problem is one of determining the total amount of capital to use. This would be the situation when the manager has all the capital that can be profitably used in the business or has sufficient credit to borrow that amount. In Chapter 2 the question of how much input to use was answered by finding the input level where marginal value product (MVP) was equal to marginal input cost (MIC). The same principle can be applied to the use of capital.

Figure 12-3 is a graphic presentation of MVP and MIC where MVP is declining as occurs whenever diminishing marginal returns exist. Marginal input cost is equal to the additional dollar of capital plus the interest that must be paid to use it. Therefore, MIC is equal to $1 + i$, where i is the rate of interest. In this example, profit will be maximized by using the amount of capital represented by a, where MVP is equal to MIC.

The second graph in Figure 12-3 illustrates a common situation when capital is being borrowed. It assumes that capital equal to the amount $0b$ can be borrowed from one source and/or for one purpose at an interest rate equal to i. Once this amount is borrowed, additional money must be borrowed from a different source or for a different use, and the interest rate is higher. The amount bc can be borrowed but at a higher interest rate equal to i'. In a similar manner capital greater than the amount $0c$ can be borrowed but only at an even higher interest rate equal to i''. This might be the higher rate typically charged for installment loans used to finance machinery purchases through a dealer or finance company.

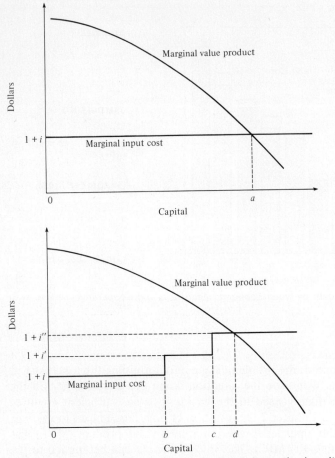

Figure 12-3 Using marginal principles to determine optimal capital use.

In this example MIC increases in a stepwise manner at each point where one source of borrowed capital is exhausted and any additional borrowing must be at a higher interest rate. Profit is still maximized where MVP is equal to MIC, which occurs when the amount of capital equal to $0d$ is used. Notice this is less than the amount $0a$ in the first graph even though the MVP curve is the same. The higher MIC reduces the amount of capital used.

Application of the principle shown in Figure 12-3 differs slightly depending on whether the capital is owned or borrowed. If the capital is owned, no interest will be paid, but the capital will have an opportunity cost equal to the return in its best alternative use outside the farm business. In this case i should be thought of as the opportunity cost, and capital should be invested in the farm business only as long as the additional return is greater than the opportunity cost. Once the point of equality is reached (MVP $= 1 + i$), any remaining capital should be invested in the alternative use in order to maximize profit from the available capital. If the capital is being borrowed, i would be the rate of interest on borrowed funds, and additional borrowing would be profitable as long as the MVP is greater than $1 + i$.

Figure 12-3 has been discussed in terms of the total capital invested in the business. The same principle applies to each individual use of capital. It should be used up to the point where MVP is equal to MIC in each and every possible use. This will also result in MVP being equal to MIC for the total amount of capital being used in the business.

Allocation of Limited Capital

Many businesses will not have sufficient capital of their own and may not be able to borrow enough to reach the point where MVP is equal to MIC for the total capital being used. In other words, capital is limited to something less than the amount which will allow total profit maximization. The problem now becomes one of allocating capital between the alternative uses to maximize profit given the limited amount available. This can be accomplished for any limited input by using the equal marginal principle, which was discussed in Chapter 3.

Use of the equal marginal principle results in capital being allocated between alternative uses in such a way that the marginal value product of the last dollar is equal in all uses. This principle is often difficult to apply in an actual farm situation for a number of reasons. First, there may be insufficient information available to calculate the marginal value products accurately. Second, several alternative uses may require fairly large lump-sum investments of an all-or-nothing nature. This makes it difficult to equate the marginal value products for these alternatives with others where capital can be invested dollar by dollar.

Difficulties encountered in applying the equal marginal principle should not discourage its use when capital is limited. Whenever capital can be reallocated to make the marginal value products more nearly equal, profit will be increased. The principle of opportunity cost can also be useful in the allocation process. Each successive increment of capital should be invested where its return is greatest so its opportunity cost does not exceed its expected marginal value product from the proposed use.

Anyone taking on the management of an existing business should be alert for ways to reallocate the existing capital. Even if no additional capital is available for investment, there are often opportunities for shifting capital between uses to equate more nearly its marginal value products. As always, it is the marginal changes that are important. If the marginal increase in profit from a reallocation to another use is greater than the marginal decrease in profit from its original use, the reallocation will show a net increase in profit.

Capital Rationing

Studies often show farmers and ranchers do not use capital up to the point where marginal value product is equal to marginal input cost. In Figure 12-3 this would mean less than 0a capital being used in the upper figure and less than 0d in the lower figure. There may be a number of explanations for these observations, which can be classified as either *external* capital rationing or *internal* capital rationing.

External capital rationing exists where the farmer or rancher desires to borrow additional money to equate MVP and MIC more nearly but is prevented from doing so by factors external to or outside the business. This external factor is typically the lending agency which refuses to lend additional funds because it feels the borrower's credit has been exhausted and/or too much risk is associated with additional lending.

Internal capital rationing exists when additional money can be borrowed but the manager makes a conscious management decision to borrow less than the amount necessary to equate MVP and MIC. This decision is typically made because the perceived risk and uncertainty associated with additional borrowed capital is greater than the borrower wishes to be exposed to. A more detailed explanation of the effects of risk and uncertainty on management decision making in the use of capital will be postponed until Chapter 18.

Leverage and the Use of Credit

The combination of equity capital and borrowed capital permits a larger business and more profit than would be possible from using only equity capital. Using borrowed capital to supplement and extend the use of equity capital is called *leverage*. The degree or amount of leverage is measured by the debt/equity ratio, and leverage increases with increases in this ratio. A debt/equity ratio of 1 indicates that one-half of the total capital used in the business is borrowed and one-half is equity capital. As the percentage of borrowed or debt capital increases, the debt/equity ratio increases, indicating greater leverage.

The use of borrowed capital can increase business profit as well as the return to equity capital. However, the converse is also true if the business is not profitable enough to have a return to total capital greater than the interest rate on borrowed capital. Table 12-1 illustrates both situations.

Table 12-1   The Effect of Leverage on Return to Equity (8% Interest Paid on Borrowed Capital)

Average return on total capital (%)	Debt/equity ratio			
	0	0.5	1.0	2.0
	Return to equity (%)			
15	15	18.5	22.0	29.0
10	10	11.0	12.0	14.0
5	5	3.5	2.0	−1.0
2	2	−1.0	−4.0	−10.0

When the return to total capital is greater than the interest rate on borrowed capital, a higher leverage will increase the return to equity. For example, assume the return to all capital is 15 percent, $10,000 is borrowed at 8 percent interest and there is $10,000 of equity capital for a debt/equity ratio of 1. The borrowed capital earns a return of $1,500 but costs $800, leaving a "profit" of $700. Adding this amount to the $1,500 earned by the equity capital results in a 22 percent return to equity. Increasing the leverage or debt/equity ratio results in an even higher return to equity, as shown in Table 12-1. Obviously profitable businesses are tempted to increase their leverage to increase not only profit but the return to equity capital.

However, there is another side to the coin. If the return to total capital is less than the interest rate on borrowed capital, return to equity is adversely affected by increased leverage, as shown in the last two lines of Table 12-1. In this case the borrowed capital does not earn enough income to pay the interest. Part of the income from equity capital must be used to pay the interest, which makes the return to equity less than the return to all capital. A combination of high leverage and a low return to total capital may require the use of equity capital to pay part of the interest. When this happens, the return to equity is negative.

Principle of Increasing Risk

The example in the last section contained only positive rates of return to total capital, but in some cases equity capital had to be used to pay part of the interest on borrowed capital. Higher leverage has an even greater impact if the return on total capital happens to be negative. Low returns and high leverage combine to confirm the *principle of increasing risk,* which states that *as the debt/equity ratio or leverage increases, the borrower has a greater risk of losing equity capital.*

The principle of increasing risk is illustrated in the bottom two lines of Table 12-1, and Table 12-2 contains a more extreme example where the return to total capital is assumed to be a *minus* 10 percent. When a business loss equal to 10 percent of the total capital is added to the interest on borrowed capital, the total loss increases rapidly as leverage increases. Equity capital must bear the brunt of its own loss, the loss on borrowed capital plus the interest on borrowed capital. The result is a rapidly increasing loss of equity capital as leverage increases. By comparing Tables 12-1 and 12-2 it can be seen that increased leverage causes the loss of equity to increase faster with a negative 10 percent return than it increases the return to equity with a positive 10 percent return to total capital.

Leverage and the principle of increasing risk emphasize two of the most important rules in the use of credit. First, money should not be borrowed unless the expected return is greater than the interest rate on the borrowed money. Second, because the expected return cannot be known with certainty, the amount of leverage used should be carefully controlled to avoid large losses of equity capital. Leverage should always be thought of as a two-edged sword.

Table 12-2   Illustration of the Principle of Increasing Risk

	Debt/equity ratio			
	0	0.5	1.0	2.0
Equity capital ($)	50,000	50,000	50,000	50,000
Borrowed capital ($)	0	25,000	50,000	100,000
Total capital ($)	50,000	75,000	100,000	150,000
Business loss with a −10% return on total capital ($)	5,000	7,500	10,000	15,000
Cost of borrowed capital at 8% ($)	0	2,000	4,000	8,000
Total loss ($)	5,000	9,500	14,000	23,000
Equity lost (%)	10	19	28	46

It can be used to increase the return to equity substantially under favorable conditions. It can also result in large losses of equity when the realized returns turn out to be very low or negative.

TYPES OF LOANS

There are many different types of agricultural loans, and several systems can be used to classify or describe them. Any classification system describing the different types of loans introduces a certain amount of terminology used by lenders. A prospective borrower needs to be familiar with this terminology to improve communication with lenders. Loans can be described or classified by length, use, security, and repayment schedule.

Length

Classifying loans by time or length of the loan is widely used. This system was used in preparing the balance sheet in Chapter 7. Three time classifications are commonly used in agricultural lending.

Short-Term Loans   Short-term loans include those with the full amount borrowed due within the next 12 months and would include loans for a period of 90 days, 6 months, or 1 year, for example. Money borrowed for the purchase of fertilizer, seed, feeder livestock, and feed would normally be a short-term loan, with repayment due within a year or less when the crops are harvested and sold or when the feeder livestock are sold. Short-term loans may also be called *production or operating loans,* as they are used to purchase inputs needed to operate through the current production cycle.

Intermediate-Term Loans   When the length of the loan is over 1 year but less than 7 to 10 years, it is classified as an intermediate loan. Many intermediate loans are for a term of 3 to 5 years. Some payment may be due each year, but the borrower has several years to complete repaying the loan. These loans are often used to provide money for the purchase of machinery, breeding and dairy livestock, and some buildings. A short-term loan is not appropriate for the purchase of these assets, as they last for more than 1 year and cannot be expected to pay for themselves in a short time.

Long-Term Loans   A loan with a term of 10 years or longer would be classified as a long-term loan. Assets with a long or indefinite life such as land and buildings are purchased with funds from a long-term loan. Loans for the purchase of land may be for a term of 20 to 40 years, for example. Annual or semiannual payments are normally required throughout the term of the loan.

Use

The use or purpose of the loan is another common system of classification. Three categories are used in this system, which is used in many studies of credit use.

Real Estate Loans   This category includes loans for the purchase of real estate such as land and buildings or where these assets serve as security for the loan. Real estate loans are typically long-term loans.

Non–Real Estate Loans   All business loans other than real estate loans are included in this category, which would include both short-term and intermediate-term loans. Loans in this category may also be referred to as production or operating loans.

Personal Loans   These are nonbusiness loans used to purchase personal assets such as homes, automobiles, and appliances. Even though they are nonbusiness loans, most lenders want them included on borrowers' farm balance sheets to get a complete picture of their financial condition.

Security

The security for a loan refers to the asset or assets pledged or mortgaged to the lender to ensure loan repayment. If the borrower is unable to make the necessary principal and interest payments on the loan, the lender has the legal right to take possession of the mortgaged assets. These assets are typically sold by the lender and the proceeds used to pay off the loan. Assets which are pledged or mortgaged as security are called loan *collateral*.

Secured Loans   With secured loans, some asset is mortgaged to provide collateral for the loan. Lenders obviously favor secured loans, as it gives them greater assurance that the loan will be repaid. Land and buildings provide collateral for real estate or long-term loans, and machinery, equipment, and breeding livestock are used as collateral for intermediate-term loans.

Unsecured Loans   A borrower with good credit and a history of prompt loan repayment may be able to borrow some money with only "a promise to repay" or without pledging any specific collateral. This would be an unsecured loan, which is also called a *signature loan,* as the borrower's signature is the only security provided the lender. Some short-term loans may be unsecured, although it is possible to mortgage feeder livestock and growing crops to provide security.

Repayment

Loans can also be classified according to the repayment plan or schedule. There are many types and variations of repayment plans coming into use as lenders try to fit repayment to the borrower's ability to repay. However, there are two basic types of repayment schedules.

Single Payment   A single-payment loan has all the principal payable in one lump sum when the loan is due. Short-term or operating loans are of this type. Some intermediate-term loans may require only annual interest payments, with the total principal due at the end of the loan. Single-payment loans obviously require good cash flow planning to ensure that sufficient cash will be available when the loan is due.

Amortized   An amortized loan is one which has periodic interest and principal payments. Installment loans with monthly payments would be a type of amortized loan. Amortization is often used for intermediate- and long-term loans, and there are two types, the *equal principal payment* and the *equal total payment.*

An amortized loan with equal principal payments has the same amount of principal due on each payment date plus interest on the unpaid balance. For example, a 20-year loan of $100,000 would have annual principal payments of $5,000 (or $2,500 on a semiannual basis) plus interest on the unpaid balance. Since the loan balance decreases with each principal payment, the interest payments are decreasing. Therefore, the first payment on an amortized loan with equal principal payments will be the largest total payment of principal plus interest. Each successive payment will be smaller because less interest is due.

Borrowers often find the first loan payment the most difficult to make, as a new or expanded business may take some time to generate its maximum potential cash flow. This is a disadvantage of the equal principal payment amortized loan, which has the largest payment the first year. For this reason, many long-term real estate loans have an amortized repayment schedule with equal *total* payments. This type of amortization results in smaller principal payments in the early years but larger principal payments toward the end. A large portion of the total loan payment is interest in the early years, but the interest decreases and the principal increases with each payment, making the last payment mostly principal.

A table of amortization factors is needed to calculate the total loan payment for an amortized loan with equal total payments.[1] The annual payment will depend on the interest rate and the length of the loan, and mathematicians have computed the amortization factors for various combinations of these factors. Calculating the annual payment using the appropriate amortization factor will result in the loan being paid off in the specified time with interest paid only on the unpaid loan balance. The amortization factor for a 20-year loan at 8 percent interest is 0.1019, and this factor is multiplied by the amount of the loan to find the total annual payment. For example, a loan of $100,000 would have an annual payment of $10,190.

A comparison of the total annual payments plus their interest and principal components is shown in Figure 12-4 for each type of amortization. Each graph assumes a 10-year, $100,000 loan at 8 percent interest. Amortization with an equal annual principal payment would require a total payment of $18,000 the first year declining to $10,800 in the tenth and final year. The principal payment is always $10,000, but the interest declines each year, causing the total payment to decline.

[1]See Appendix Table 1.

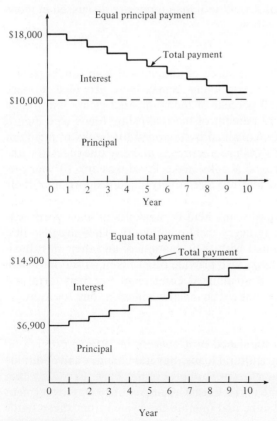

Figure 12-4   Loan repayment under two types of amortization.

Amortization with an equal total payment results in an annual payment of $14,900. (The amortization factor is 0.1490.) While the total payment remains the same, the interest and principal change each year. Principal is $6,900 and interest $8,000 the first year, with the principal increasing and interest decreasing until they are approximately $13,800 and $1,100, respectively, in the tenth year. The equal total payment method results in a smaller total loan payment in the first 4 years but a larger payment in the last 6 years. Any advantage of the lower initial payments is at least partially offset by more total interest being paid over the life of the loan, since the principal is being reduced at a slower rate.

SOURCES OF LOAN FUNDS

Farmers and ranchers can and do borrow money from a number of different sources. Some lending agencies specialize in certain types of loans and some provide other financial services in addition to lending money. The more important sources of funds for both real estate and non–real estate loans are shown in Figure 12-5. Included in this figure is the relative importance of each expressed as a percentage of the total real estate or non–real estate debt held by each source. These sources of agricultural loan funds are discussed in more detail in the remainder of this section.

Commercial Banks

Commercial banks are an important source of agricultural loan funds, particularly for short- and intermediate-term loans. Banks have provided farmers and ranchers with about 40 to 50 percent of their non–real estate loan funds in recent years but only about 12 percent of the real estate loans (see Figure 12-5). This difference is partially explained by the need for banks to maintain liquidity to meet their customer's cash requirements and any unexpected withdrawal of deposits. For this reason, banks make few loans for 10 years or longer and will limit these longer loans to a relatively small proportion of their total loan portfolio.

The large share of agricultural loans held by banks is at least partly explained by their location in nearly every rural community. They are also in a position to become well acquainted with their customers and their past business activities and vice versa. Banks also provide other financial services such as checking and savings accounts, making it convenient for their farm and ranch customers to take care of all their financial business at one location.

Farm Credit System

The Farm Credit System was established by Congress in 1916 to provide an additional source of funds for agricultural loans. Several changes and additions were made at various times. The current structure of the Farm Credit System became effective with the passage of the Farm Credit Act of 1933. Government funds were used initially to organize and operate the system, but these funds

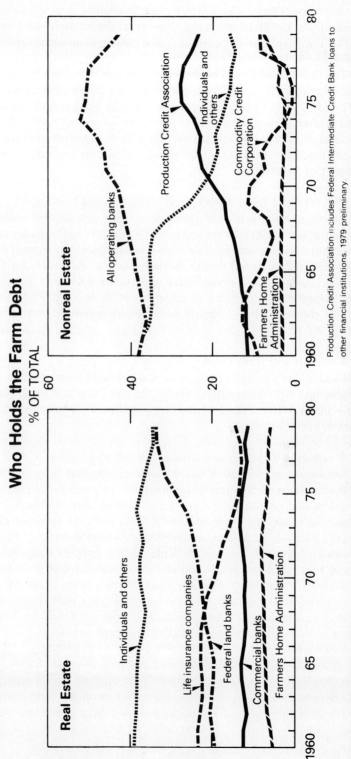

Figure 12-5 Sources of agricultural loan funds and the relative importance of each. (*Economic, Statistical and Cooperative Service, U.S. Department of Agriculture.*)

have all been repaid. The Farm Credit System is now a cooperative wholly owned by its member/borrowers. However, the system is supervised and audited by the Farm Credit Administration, which is an independent government agency.

The Farm Credit System obtains loan funds by selling bonds in the national money markets. Proceeds from bond sales are channeled through district Federal Land Banks, Federal Intermediate Credit Banks, and Banks for Cooperatives located across the country. There are 12 district banks of each type plus a Central Bank for Cooperatives. They in turn either make direct loans or provide funds for local associations, which then initiate and supervise loans to farmers and ranchers.

Federal Land Bank Associations   The Federal Land Bank part of the system provides long-term real estate loans through local Federal Land Bank Associations (FLBAs). There are over 500 FLBAs nationwide, and many have one or more branch offices. The FLBA is a cooperative owned by its member/borrowers and governed by the elected board of directors. Each district Federal Land Bank is also a cooperative with the FLBAs in its district as members. Farmers and ranchers become members of their local FLBA by purchasing stock at the time they obtain a loan. Each member with money borrowed through the FLBA has one vote in its business affairs regardless of the size of the loan.

Federal Land Banks make only real estate loans which range from 5 to 40 years in length. The loan funds may not necessarily be used to purchase land or buildings, but real estate provides the loan security or collateral for these loans. Federal Land Banks have approximately 30 percent of the farm real estate debt outstanding.

Production Credit Associations   Local Production Credit Associations (PCAs) are organized much like FLBAs except that they specialize in short- and intermediate-term loans to qualified farmers and ranchers. There are over 400 PCAs nationwide, and many have several branch offices. Although they are another branch of the Farm Credit System, PCAs maintain offices separate from the FLBAs. Borrowers become members of their local PCA by purchasing stock at the time a loan is made, which entitles them to one vote. An elected board of directors directs the business affairs of each local PCA.

Funds for the short- and intermediate-term loans made by the local PCA are received from a district Federal Intermediate Credit Bank. PCA loans can be for a maximum of 7 years and have accounted for 25 to 30 percent of the farm non–real estate debt outstanding in recent years.

Life Insurance Companies

Some life insurance companies place part of their investment funds in long-term farm real estate loans. Their participation in the farm loan market tends to vary over time depending on the rate of return in alternative investments.

Life insurance companies also tend to favor larger loans as a way to minimize their administrative costs per dollar loaned. They typically have about 15 percent of the farm real estate debt outstanding.

Farmers Home Administration

The Farmers Home Administration (FmHA) is an agency of the U.S. Department of Agriculture with county offices in most of the predominantly agricultural counties. This agency is authorized to make farm ownership and operating loans in addition to several other types of loans for rural development purposes. It also has authority to make emergency loans to qualified farmers and ranchers in officially declared disaster areas. These are temporary loans with the money used to restore normal operations after a natural disaster such as flood or drought.

To be eligible for FmHA farm loans the borrower must operate a family-size farm or ranch, receive a substantial portion of total family income from farming or ranching, and be unable to obtain adequate loan funds from other lending institutions. The last requirement does not mean FmHA borrowers are poor credit risks. Many are beginning farmers who simply do not have sufficient equity to borrow the necessary capital from other sources. As soon as FmHA borrowers have improved their financial condition to the point where funds can be obtained from another source, they must switch to another lender.

Farmers Home Administration loans are made from funds appropriated by Congress and carry a lower interest rate than loans from other sources. Funds available for FmHA loans vary from year to year depending on the size of the congressional appropriation. Farmers Home Administration loans account for approximately 3 percent of non–real estate debt outstanding and 6 to 7 percent of the real estate debt outstanding.

Individuals

Individuals are an important source of funds for agricultural loans. Included in this category would be loans from friends, parents, and other relatives. More flexible terms and interest rates may account for the substantial use of individuals as a source of loan funds. They have provided a little over one-third of the real estate debt outstanding in recent years.

The relatively large proportion of real estate debt owed to individuals comes mostly from seller-financed land sales, which often have income tax benefits for the seller. Many land sales are being made utilizing a land purchase contract where the seller provides the financing and the buyer makes periodic loan payments direct to the seller. This differs from a cash sale where the buyer borrows from a commercial lender, pays the seller cash for the full purchase price, and then makes periodic payments to the commercial lender.

Merchants and Dealers

This source of agricultural loan funds includes accounts payable at farm supply stores and farm equipment and machinery purchases where the dealer finances the sale through an installment sales contract. Many farm supply stores allow customers 30, 60, or 90 days to pay their accounts before any interest is charged, and may finance a purchase for a longer period with interest. This policy is essentially a loan, and the total balances in these accounts can be large at certain times of the year. Farm equipment dealers and automobile dealers also provide loans by financing purchases themselves or through an affiliated finance company.

Other Sources

Farmers and ranchers can also obtain loan funds for some purposes from several other government agencies. The Small Business Administration can make some agricultural loans and also has an emergency loan program for farmers in designated disaster areas. Loans specifically for the construction of grain storage facilities are available from the U.S. Department of Agriculture Agricultural Stabilization and Conservation Service. This agency can also assist in obtaining a Commodity Credit Corporation price support loan if the farmer is eligible based on participation in the current government farm program.

ESTABLISHING AND DEVELOPING CREDIT

Credit was defined as the ability to borrow money and therefore an asset belonging to the business or individual. As such it needs to be established and developed in a manner which increases its quantity and quality. Credit can be thought of as something to be organized, packaged, and merchandised much like a new brand of toothpaste or soap powder. While credit is not actually sold, it is useful to think of it in these terms to emphasize what can be done to increase one's credit. A borrower should be aware of the need to demonstrate and communicate credit worthiness to lenders.

When trying to establish or develop credit it is useful to look at it from the lender's viewpoint. What does a lender consider when making a decision on a loan application? Why can one person borrow more money than another? Why are interest rates and repayment plans different? Many factors go into making loan decisions, but most can be included in one of the following categories:

1 Personal character
2 Management ability
3 Financial position and progress over time
4 Repayment capacity
5 Purpose of the loan
6 Collateral

When using these factors as a guide for establishing and developing credit, a prospective borrower should remember that lenders want to make loans. That is their business. However, they are in business to make a profit and are therefore looking for profitable loans which will be repaid.

Personal Character   Honesty, integrity, judgment, reputation, and other personal characteristics of the loan applicant are considered by lenders. Credit can be quickly lost by being untruthful and dishonest in business dealings and slow in making loan payments or meeting other financial obligations. If the lender is not acquainted with the borrower, character references will usually be asked for and checked. To maintain a good credit record, borrowers should promptly inform lenders of any change in their financial condition which might affect loan repayment. An honest and open relationship with lenders is necessary to maintain credit.

Management Ability   A lender must try to evaluate a borrower's management ability. Established farmers and ranchers will be evaluated on their past record, but beginners must be judged only on their background, education, and training. A lender is interested in the applicant's decision-making ability and the efficiency and productivity of the applicant's business. These factors affect profitability and therefore the ability to repay a loan. Lenders often rate poor management ability as the number-one reason for borrowers getting into financial difficulty and therefore place heavy emphasis on this factor.

Financial Position   Accurate, well-prepared balance sheets and income statements are needed to document the current financial position of the business and its income level. Lenders can learn much about a business from these records, and financial progress over time can be as important as the current financial position. Both factors reflect the applicant's management ability, business profitability, growth, and repayment capacity. Complete and detailed records included with a loan application will do much to ensure a favorable response.

Repayment Capacity   Loans cannot be repaid if the business is not profitable. However, just having a profitable business is not sufficient. There must be enough profit to meet family living expenses and income tax payments as well as the interest and principal payments on loans. Repayment capacity is best measured by the cash flow generated by the business. A cash flow budget projected for one or more years will indicate potential repayment problems and should be completed before borrowing large amounts and establishing rigid repayment schedules. Too often money is borrowed for an obviously profitable business only to find cash flow in the early years is not sufficient to make interest and principal payments. A longer loan or a more flexible repayment schedule may solve the problem if it is identified in time.

Purpose of the Loan   Money can be borrowed for many purposes, and borrowers as well as lenders should identify the more profitable alternatives.

Additional capital should be used for these purposes, remembering that profitability affects repayment capacity. Loans for family living expenses should receive low priority, as they do not increase profit and repayment must come from business profits.

Lenders may view short-term and long-term loans somewhat differently. Short-term loans have a rapid turnover and are repaid out of current-year earnings, while long-term loans may have repayment problems caused by uncertain future events. Loans which are either *self-liquidating* or *asset-generating* may also influence a lender's decision. Self-liquidating loans are for items such as fertilizer, seed, and feeder livestock where the loan can be repaid in a short time from the sale of crops or livestock. Asset-generating loans are those used to purchase new tangible assets which provide additional collateral. Examples would be loans providing funds for the purchase of land or machinery.

Collateral   Land, livestock, machinery, grain in storage, and growing crops can all be used as loan collateral. The amount and type of collateral available may be important factors in a loan request. Loans should not be made or requested unless repayment can be projected from farm income. However, lenders may still ask for collateral to support a loan request. If the unexpected happens and the loan is in default, it may be the lender's only means of recovering the loan funds.

These six factors which a lender considers when reviewing a loan application can also be used by an individual to improve and increase the amount of credit available. Prospective borrowers should place themselves in the lender's position and review their situation in each of the six areas. If a weakness is found, credit may be increased by making the necessary improvements. However, it is not enough just to have credit. To obtain a loan against that credit it must be recognized by the lenders. This requires good communication with lenders with good information to support the loan request.

COST OF BORROWING

Interest can be thought of as the "rent" paid for the use of borrowed money. The total "rent" or interest paid will increase if the interest rate increases or if the money is "rented" for a longer period of time. Table 12-3 shows the total amount of interest paid for various combinations of interest rates and length of loan. Both factors have an important effect on the total interest paid. For loans at 8 percent interest or more and over 15 to 20 years in length, the total interest paid will be greater than the original amount borrowed.

The annual payment on an amortized loan can be decreased by obtaining a longer loan. For the example in Table 12-3 at the 8 percent interest rate, annual payments would be $2,500 for a 5-year loan, $1,490 for a 10-year loan, and $1,020 for a 20-year loan. Borrowers should be aware of the relationships

**Table 12-3   Total Interest Paid on a $10,000 Amortized
Loan with Equal Annual Total Payments**

Interest Rate (%)	Length of loan (years)			
	1	5	10	20
6	$ 600	$1,850	$3,600	$ 7,400
8	800	2,500	4,900	10,400
10	1,000	3,200	6,300	13,400

between interest rate, length of loan, annual payments, and total interest cost. Repayment capacity can be estimated by cash flow budgeting and the length of the loan adjusted accordingly. The most flexible situation would be the longest loan possible, but one with early payments permitted. This would minimize the required annual payments, but additional payments could be made in good years to minimize the total interest paid.

Calculating Interest Rate

Interest can be a major expense for a farm or ranch business with a heavy debt. Borrowers are often advised to "shop around" for the best combination of interest rate and loan terms or repayment schedule. However, lenders use several different methods of charging interest which can make it difficult to determine the best "deal." A standard or basic interest rate must be calculated for each possible loan source to provide a basis for comparison.

The true or actual annual interest rate is called the *effective rate* or the *annual percentage rate*. Whenever a loan is available from several sources with different stated interest rates and repayment plans, they should be compared on the basis of their annual percentage rate.[2] Other loan charges such as closing costs, "points," service charges, and any required insurance should also be considered as part of the loan cost.

Simple Interest   Simple interest is used to describe the interest rate on a loan with a single payment. For example, if $10,000 is borrowed for 1 year at 8 percent interest, the single payment would be $10,800 including the $800 interest. The simple interest rate of 8 percent is also the annual percentage rate. Most simple interest, single-payment loans are for 1 year or less. If for less than a year, interest would be computed for only the actual time the money was borrowed.

Interest on the Unpaid Balance   The amortized loans discussed earlier have interest charged only on the unpaid balance. As the principal is repaid the interest payments decline as the loan balance declines. In the example

[2]The Truth in Lending Act passed by the U.S. Congress requires the annual percentage rate to be stated in the loan agreement. However, a borrower should understand how it is calculated.

above, assume the repayment was $5,000 in 6 months and the remaining $5,000 at the end of the year. The interest calculations would be as follows:

$10,000 at 8% for ½ year = $400
$ 5,000 at 8% for ½ year = $200
Total interest = $600

Notice that interest is paid only on the unpaid loan balance and then only for the length of time that amount was still borrowed. The total interest is less than in the previous example, as only $5,000 was still outstanding for the last half of the year. Loans amortized over a longer period would have interest calculated in the same manner. When interest is paid only on the unpaid balance, the stated interest rate is the same as the annual percentage rate.

Discount Interest   Some loans may require the interest to be paid in advance or at the time the loan is obtained. In practice, the lender deducts the interest from the loan proceeds, with the borrower receiving something less than the amount actually borrowed. A discount loan of $1,000 for 1 year at 8 percent interest would have $80 interest deducted. The borrower would receive $920 but must repay the full $1,000.

The stated interest rate on a discount loan is not the same as the annual percentage rate. In the above example, interest is paid on $1,000 but the borrower has the use of only $920. The result is $80 interest paid for the use of $920, making the annual percentage rate higher than the stated rate. A formula for calculating the annual percentage rate on discounted loans is

$$R = \frac{d}{L - d} \times 100$$

where R = annual percentage rate
d = discount or amount of interest paid
L = original amount borrowed and to be repaid

Applying this formula to the example above results in an annual percentage rate of 8.7 percent for this loan (80/920 × 100 = 8.7 percent). A similar formula giving the same answer is

$$R = \frac{i}{1 - i} \times 100$$

where i is equal to the stated interest rate. Both formulas apply only to single-payment loans.

Add-On Interest   Installment loans used to finance the purchase of automobiles, machinery, household furniture, or appliances typically use add-on interest. An example will best illustrate this type of interest. Assume $5,000 is needed to finance the purchase of an automobile, the stated interest rate is 8 percent, and the loan will be repaid in 36 equal monthly payments. The monthly payments would be computed as follows:

1 Interest calculation: $5,000 × 8% × 3 years = $1,200 (the finance charges)
2 Interest added to amount of loan: $5,000 + $1,200 = $6,200 (the total amount to be repaid)
3 Calculation of monthly payment: $6,200/36 payments = $172.22

Notice that interest is charged on the full amount of the loan for all 3 years as if there would be no principal payment until the end of 3 years. However, some principal is being repaid with every monthly payment; so interest is being paid on more than the unpaid balance.

This procedure results in an annual percentage rate which can be much higher than the stated rate depending upon the length of the loan and the repayment schedule. A number of formulas are available which can be used to estimate the annual percentage rate on installment loans using add-on interest. One of the easiest to use is the Stelson equation

$$R = \frac{2C}{L(P + A)} \times 100$$

where R = annual percentage rate
C = total interest cost or finance charges
L = length of the loan in years
P = beginning principal of the loan
A = amount of each periodic payment

In this equation the periodic payments need not be monthly but might be quarterly or semiannually. For the example above, the approximate annual percentage rate would be

$$\frac{2 \times \$1,200}{3(\$5,000 + \$172.22)} \times 100 = 15.47\%$$

Borrowers are often advised, and wisely so, to check several sources for an installment loan. There can be a variety of quoted or stated interest rates and different finance charges of other types. All loans should be compared on the basis of their annual percentage rate. Credit card purchases typically have an interest charge of 1½ percent per month or an annual percentage rate of 18 percent. This rate may decrease if the account balance is above a certain amount.

SUMMARY

Capital was broadly defined to include money invested in machinery, livestock, buildings, and other assets as well as cash and bank account balances. Credit was defined as the ability to borrow money. These two factors play an important role on a modern commercial farm or ranch as large amounts of each are necessary. Today's managers must be skilled in acquiring, organizing, and using capital whether it is equity capital or borrowed capital. The economic principles discussed in Chapters 2 and 3 can be used to determine how much total capital can be profitably used or how to allocate limited capital between alternative uses.

Agricultural loans are available from a number of sources including commercial banks, Farmers Home Administration, Federal Land Banks, Production Credit Associations, life insurance companies, individuals, and other sources. Some specialize in certain types of loans, but all are interested in the quality and quantity of credit a prospective borrower possesses. Borrowers should work at improving their credit by maintaining good personal character, improving management skills, demonstrating adequate financial progress and repayment capacity, and providing sufficient collateral.

Interest rates, loan terms, and repayment schedules can vary from lender to lender and by loan type. Borrowers should shop for loans just as they do for purchased inputs by comparing the annual percentage rate of interest. A small savings on a large loan can accumulate into a substantial reduction in the total interest paid over the life of a long-term loan.

QUESTIONS FOR REVIEW AND FURTHER THOUGHT

1   Explain how the terms credit, debt, liability, and loan are related. How are they different?
2   Identify the different sources of agricultural loans in your home town or home county. Which type(s) of loans does each specialize in or prefer? You might interview several lending institutions to learn more about their lending policies and procedures.
3   What are the advantages and disadvantages of a 20-year loan vs. a 10-year loan of the same amount and with the same interest rate?
4   What is the difference between short-term, intermediate-term, and long-term loans? List the type of assets which might be collateral for each.
5   Assume you are about to begin farming and will need additional capital. What information and material would you need to provide a lender to improve your chances of getting a loan?
6   What is the annual percentage rate on an installment loan of $2,000 with 24 monthly payments of $97? On a $500 loan with 12 monthly payments of $45.75?
7   Define the following terms:
    a   Secured loan
    b   Add-on interest
    c   Amortized loan

    d Real estate loan

    e Collateral

8 Assume a $200,000 loan for 30 years at 8 percent interest and annual payments. How much principal and interest would be in the first payment if the loan is amortized with equal principal payments? If it is amortized with equal total payments? How would these figures change for the second payment in each case? (Use Appendix Table 1 to find the amortization factor for the equal total payment case.)

REFERENCES

Barry, Peter J., John A. Hopkin, and C. B. Baker: *Financial Management in Agriculture,* 2d ed., The Interstate Printers and Publishers, Danville, Ill., 1979, chaps. 2, 3.

Hardy, W. E.: *The Cost of Money—A Look at Interest Rates and Government Regulations,* Alabama Agricultural Experiment Station Bulletin 482, Auburn University, 1976.

Penson, John B., Jr., and David A. Lins: *Agricultural Finance: An Introduction to Micro and Macro Concepts,* Prentice-Hall, Inc., Englewood Cliffs, N.J., 1980, chaps. 19–22.

Osburn, Donald D., and Kenneth C. Schneeberger: *Modern Agriculture Management,* Reston Publishing Co., Reston, Va., 1978, chaps. 15, 16.

Schneeberger, Kenneth C., and Donald D. Osburn: *Financial Planning in Agriculture,* The Interstate Printers and Publishers, Danville, Ill., 1977.

Chapter 13

Investment Analysis

CHAPTER OBJECTIVES

    1 To note the time value of money and its use in decision making and investment analysis
    2 To illustrate the process of compounding or determining the future value of a sum of money
    3 To illustrate the process of discounting or determining the present value of a sum of money
    4 To show how to analyze different investments using the methods of payback period, simple rate of return, net present value, and internal rate of return
    5 To learn how to apply these methods to different types of investment alternatives
    6 To compare the advantages and disadvantages of each method

Capital can be invested in two general types of investments. The first is annual operating inputs such as feed, seed, fertilizer, and fuel, and the second is capital assets such as land, machinery, buildings, and breeding stock. Different procedures must be used to analyze each type because of differences in the timing of expenses and the associated returns. Both the expenses and returns from investing in an operating input occur within one production cycle of a year or less. Investing in a capital asset means the expense occurs in one time period and the resulting returns in a number of later time periods.

The marginal principles used to find the profit-maximizing level or allocation of annual operating inputs were discussed in Chapters 2 and 3. There was no need to bring time into the discussion, as both the expense and return were assumed to fall within the same year or production cycle. The situation is different for capital investments where the expense and returns are in different time periods and the returns may be received over many years. Alternative and competing investments may have different returns for different lengths of time. A proper analysis of these investments requires the recognition of the time value of money and how it can be used to compare and determine the profitability of capital investments.

THE TIME VALUE OF MONEY

Time is money. This and similar statements recognize that a dollar today is worth more than a dollar at some future date. Why? There are two answers to this question, the first being that a dollar received today can be invested to earn interest and therefore increase to a dollar *plus* the interest on the future date. This is the investment explanation for the time value of money, but it can also be explained from the viewpoint of consumption. If the dollar was to be spent for consumer goods such as a new TV set, stereo, or automobile, most people would prefer the dollar now rather than later. This would allow a more immediate enjoyment of the item rather than having to wait until later to make the purchase.

Both the investment and consumption explanations of the time value of money are important. However, this chapter will focus on the investment aspect as this is more important in business and for a manager who must choose the more profitable investments from among a number of alternatives. The time value of money can be discussed in terms of either the *future value* of a present lump-sum amount or stream of payments over time, or the *present value* of a future lump-sum amount or a stream of income. Both are discussed in the next sections along with examples and applications of their use.

Future Value

The future value of money refers to the value of an investment at a specified date in the future. This concept assumes the investment will earn interest which is reinvested at the end of each time period to also earn interest. In other words, the future value includes the original investment, the interest it earns, and interest on the accumulated interest. The procedure for determining future values is called *compounding,* and it can be applied to a one-time lump-sum investment or to an investment which takes place periodically over time. Each case will be analyzed separately.

Future Value of a Present Sum   Assume you have just invested $100 in a savings account which earns 6 percent interest compounded annually and you would like to know the future value of this sum after 3 years. The following table illustrates how you might perform the necessary calculations:

Year	Amount ($)	Interest rate (%)	Interest earned ($)
1	100.00	6	6.00
2	106.00	6	6.36
3	112.36	6	6.74

Future value at end of year 3: $112.36 + $6.74 = $119.10

Notice the assumption that all interest earned is allowed to accumulate in the account so that it also earns interest for the remaining years. In this example, a present sum of $100 has a future value of $119.10 when invested at 6 percent interest for 3 years. Interest is compounded, or compound interest is being used, when accumulated interest also earns future interest.

Allowing the accumulated interest to also earn interest is an integral part of the compounding procedure to find a future value. If the interest had been withdrawn, only $100 would have earned interest each year. A total of $18 in interest would have been withdrawn compared with the $19.10 of earned interest in the example.

The above procedure for finding a future value can become very tedious if the investment is for a long period of time. Fortunately the calculations can be simplified by using the mathematical equation

$$FV = P(1 + i)^n$$

where FV is the future value, P is the present sum, i is the interest rate, and n is the number of years. Applied to the example above, the calculations would be

$$FV = \$100(1 + 0.06)^3$$
$$= \$100(1.191)$$
$$= \$119.10$$

giving the same future value as before.

This equation can be quickly and easily applied using a calculator which will raise numbers to a power. Without such an aid, the equation can be difficult to use, particularly when n is large. To simplify the calculation of future values, tables have been developed giving values of $(1 + i)^n$ for different combinations of i and n. Appendix Table 2 is a future value table, and the reader should become familiar with its use. Any future value can be found by multiplying the present sum by the factor from the table corresponding to the appropriate interest rate and length of the investment. The value for 6 percent and 3 years is 1.191, which when multiplied by the $100 in our example, gives a future value of $119.10 as before.

An interesting and useful rule of thumb is provided by the *Rule of 72*. The approximate time it takes for an investment to double can be found by dividing 72 by the compound interest rate. For example, an investment at 6 percent interest would double in approximately 12 years. (Notice the table value is 2.012.) At 8 percent interest a present sum would double in approximately 9 years (table value of 1.999).

The concept of future value can be useful in a number of ways. For example, what is the future value of $1,000 deposited in a savings account at 5 percent interest for 10 years? The table value is 1.629, which gives a future value of $1,629. Another use is estimating future land values. If land values are expected to increase at an annual compound rate of 6 percent, what will land currently valued at $1,000 per acre be worth 5 years from now? The table value is 1.338, providing an estimated future value of $1,338 per acre.

Future Value of an Investment Stream   The concept of future value or compounding can also be applied to an investment which takes place periodically or is a stream of investments over time. Suppose $1,000 is deposited at the end of each year in a savings account which pays 6 percent interest. What is the future value of this investment at the end of 3 years? It can be calculated in the following manner:

$$
\begin{aligned}
\text{First } \$1,000 &= 1,000(1 + 0.06)^2 = & 1,123.60 \\
\text{Second } \$1,000 &= 1,000(1 + 0.06)^1 = & 1,060.00 \\
\text{Third } \$1,000 &= 1,000(1 + 0.06)^0 = & \underline{1,000.00} \\
\text{Future value} &= & \$3,183.60
\end{aligned}
$$

Since the money is deposited at the end of each year, the first $1,000 earns interest for only 2 years, the second $1,000 earns interest for 1 year, and the third $1,000 earns no interest, as the future value is being measured at the end of 3 years. The total interest earned is $183.60.

A stream of payments over time is called an *annuity*. The future value of an annuity can be found using the above procedure, but an annuity over a long period of time requires many calculations. An easier method is to use the equation

$$
FV = P \frac{(1 + i)^n - 1}{i}
$$

where FV is the future value, P is the annual year-end investment (assumed equal each year), and the other symbols are as previously defined. It is even easier to use table values such as those in Appendix Table 3 which cover a wide range of interest rates and years. Continuing with the same example, the table value for 6 percent interest and 3 years is 3.184. Multiplying this factor by the annual investment or annuity of $1,000 confirms the previous future value of $3,183.60 with a little rounding error.

The equation and table values assume the annual annuity is always the same amount. If the amounts vary, the procedure illustrated in the calculations above can be used to find the future value.

Present Value

The concept of present value refers to the current value of a sum of money to be received in the future. Present values are found using a process called *discounting,* meaning the future sum is discounted back to the present to find its current or present value. This discounting is done because a sum to be received in the future is worth somewhat less now because of the time difference assuming a positive interest rate. A present value can be interpreted as the sum of money which would have to be invested now at a given rate of interest to equal the future sum on the same date.

Compounding and discounting are reverse or opposite procedures, as shown in Figure 13-1. A present sum is compounded to find its future value and a future sum is discounted to find its present value. These reciprocal relationships will become more apparent in the following discussion.

Present Value of a Future Sum   The present value of a future sum depends on the interest rate and the length of time before the payment is received. Higher interest rates and longer time periods will reduce the present value. The equation for finding the present value of a single payment in the future is

$$PV = \frac{P}{(1 + i)^n} \quad \text{or} \quad P\,\frac{1}{(1 + i)^n}$$

where P is the future sum, PV the present value, i the interest rate, and n the number of years.

This equation can be used to find the present value of $1,000 to be received in 5 years using an interest rate of 8 percent. The calculations would be

$$PV = 1,000\,\frac{1}{(1 + 0.08)^5}$$
$$= 1,000(0.681)$$
$$= \$681$$

A payment of $1,000 to be received in 5 years has a present value of $681 at 8 percent interest. Stated differently, $681 invested for 5 years at 8 percent compound interest would have a future value of $1,000, which illustrates the reciprocal relationship between compounding and discounting. A more practical interpretation is that an investor should not pay more than $681 for an investment which will return $1,000 in 5 years if there are other alternatives

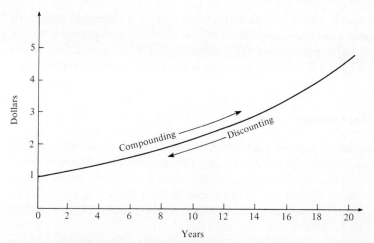

Figure 13-1 Relationship between compounding and discounting ($1 at 8 percent interest).

which will pay 8 percent interest or more. Investment analysis makes heavy use of present values, as will be seen later in this chapter.

Tables are also available to assist in calculating present values as shown in Appendix Table 4. The factor for the appropriate interest rate and number of years is multiplied by the future sum to obtain the present value.

Present Value of a Stream of Income The present value of a stream of payments received annually can also be calculated. Suppose an annuity of $1,000 will be received at the end of each year for 3 years and the interest rate is 8 percent. The present value of this income stream or annuity can be found using values from Appendix Table 4.

Year	Amount ($)	Present value factor	Present value ($)
1	1,000	0.926	926
2	1,000	0.857	857
3	1,000	0.794	794
		Total	2,577

A present value of $2,577 represents the maximum an investor should pay for an investment which will return $1,000 at the end of each year for 3 years if an 8 percent return is desired. Higher interest rates will reduce the present value and vice versa.

The mathematical equation for finding the present value of an annuity or stream of constant annual payments is

$$PV = P \frac{1 - (1 + i)^{-n}}{i}$$

As before, it is much easier to use table values such as those in Appendix Table 5 which only need to be multiplied by the equal annual payment to find the present value. The table value for 8 percent and 3 years is 2.577, which can be multiplied by the $1,000 in the example above to find the present value of $2,577.

INVESTMENT ANALYSIS

Investment analysis, or *capital budgeting,* is the process of determining the profitability of an investment or comparing the profitability of two or more alternative investments. A thorough analysis of an investment requires four pieces of information: (1) the net cash revenues from the investment, (2) its cost, (3) the terminal or salvage value of the investment, and (4) the interest or discount rate to be used.

Net cash revenues or cash flows must be estimated for each year in the life of the investment. The cash receipts minus the cash expenses equals the additional net cash revenue resulting from the proposed investment. Depreciation is not included as an expense because it is a noncash expense and is accounted for by the difference between cost and terminal value. Any interest payments from financing the investment are also omitted from the calculation of net cash revenue because the several methods of analysis are estimates of the rate of return before any interest payments.

The cost of the investment should be the actual total expenditure for its purchase and not the list price or just the down payment if it is being financed. Of the four types of information required for investment analysis, this will generally be the easiest to obtain. The terminal value will often need to be estimated and may be set equal to the salvage value for a depreciable asset. For a nondepreciable asset such as land, the terminal value should be the estimated market value of the asset at the time the investment is terminated.

The opportunity cost of capital is an important consideration when selecting the appropriate discount or interest rate. However, this value is seldom known with any degree of accuracy, and several alternatives exist. The first is to use the current interest rate paid on savings accounts. This is the minimum opportunity cost of capital, and the discount rate should be at least this value. A second alternative is to use a discount rate equal to the current interest rate on borrowed money. This alternative would be preferred to the first when the investment will be financed with borrowed money. The third alternative would be the minimum rate of return acceptable or desired by the investor. Several possible adjustments to the discount rate are discussed later in this chapter.

An example of the information needed for investment analysis is contained in Table 13-1. For simplicity the terminal values were assumed to be zero. Whenever terminal values exist, they should be added to the net cash revenue for the last year, as they represent an additional cash receipt. The information for the two potential investments in Table 13-1 will be used to illustrate four

Table 13-1   Net Cash Revenues for Two $10,000 Investments (No Terminal Value)

Year	Net cash revenues ($) Investment A	Investment B
1	3,000	1,000
2	3,000	2,000
3	3,000	3,000
4	3,000	4,000
5	3,000	6,000
Total	15,000	16,000
Average return	3,000	3,200
Less annual depreciation	2,000	2,000
Net revenue	1,000	1,200

methods of analyzing and comparing investments. They are: (1) the payback period, (2) the simple rate of return, (3) net present value, and (4) internal rate of return.

Payback Period

The payback period is the number of years it would take for an investment to return its original cost through the net cash revenue it generates. If the net cash revenues are constant each year, the payback period can be calculated from the equation

$$P = \frac{I}{E}$$

where P is the payback period in years, I is the amount of the investment, and E is the expected annual net cash revenue. For example, investment A in Table 13-1 would have a payback period of 3⅓ years. When the annual net cash revenues are not equal, they should be summed year by year to find the year where the total is equal to the amount of the investment. For investment B in Table 13-1, the payback period would be 4 years.

The payback method can be used to rank investments according to payback period as was done above. Limited capital can be invested first in the highest ranked investment and then on down the list until the investment capital is exhausted. Another application is to establish a maximum payback period and reject all investments with a longer payback. For example, a manager may select a 4-year payback and invest only in alternatives with a payback of 4 years or less.

The payback method is easy to use and quickly identifies the investments with the most immediate cash returns. However, it also has several serious disadvantages. This method ignores any cash flows occurring after the end of the payback period and the timing of cash flows during the payback period. Selecting investment A using this method ignores the higher returns from investment B in years 4 and 5 as well as its greater total return. Notice also that the payback method is not really a measure of profitability. For these reasons, it can easily lead to poor investment decisions and is not the best method of investment analysis.

Simple Rate of Return

The simple rate of return expresses the average annual net revenue as a percentage of the investment. Net revenue is found by subtracting the average annual depreciation from the average net cash revenue. The simple rate of return is calculated from the equation

$$\text{Rate of return} = \frac{\text{average annual net revenue}}{\text{cost of the investment}} \times 100$$

Applying the equation to the example in Table 13-1 gives the following results:

$$\text{Investment A:} \frac{\$1,000}{\$10,000} \times 100 = 10\%$$

$$\text{Investment B:} \frac{\$1,200}{\$10,000} \times 100 = 12\%$$

This method would rank investment B higher than A, which is different from the payback method. The simple rate of return method is better than the payback because it considers an investment's earnings over its entire life. However, it uses average annual earnings, which fails to consider the size and timing of annual earnings and can cause errors in selecting investments. For example, investment A would have the same 10 percent rate of return if it had no net cash revenue the first 4 years and $15,000 in year 5, as the average return is still $3,000 per year. However, a consideration of the time value of money would show these to be greatly different investments. Because of this shortcoming, the simple rate of return is not generally recommended.

Net Present Value

A serious shortcoming of the payback and simple rate of return methods was their failure to account properly for the time value of money. For this reason, the net present value method is a preferred method because it does consider the time value of the entire stream of cash flows over the life of the investment. It is also called the *discounted cash flow method*.

Net present value of an investment is the sum of the present values for each year's net cash flow (or net cash revenue) less the initial cost of the investment. The equation for finding the present value of an investment is

$$NPV = \frac{P_1}{(1+i)^1} + \frac{P_2}{(1+i)^2} + \ldots + \frac{P_n}{(1+i)^n} - C$$

where NPV is net present value, P_1 is the net cash flow in year 1, i is the discount rate, and C is the initial cost of the investment. An example of calculating net present values using an 8 percent discount rate is shown in Table 13-2. The present value factors are table values from Appendix Table 4.

Investments with a positive net present value would be accepted using this procedure, those with a negative net present value would be rejected, and a zero value would make the investor indifferent. The rationale behind accepting investments with a positive net present value can be explained two ways. First, it means the actual rate of return on the investment is greater than the discount rate used in the calculations. In other words, the return is greater than the opportunity cost of capital if that was used as the discount rate. A second explanation is that the investor can afford to pay more for the investment and still achieve a rate of return equal to the discount rate used in calculating the net present value. In Table 13-2, an investor could pay up to $11,979 for investment A and $12,048 for investment B and still receive an 8 percent return on invested capital. This method assumes the annual cash flows can also be reinvested to earn a rate of return equal to the discount rate being used.

Both investments in Table 13-2 show a positive net present value using an 8 percent discount rate. In any determination of a present value, the selection of the discount rate affects the result. The net present values in Table 13-2 would be lower if a higher discount rate was used and vice versa. At some

Table 13-2 Net Present Value Calculations for Two Investments of $10,000 (8 % Discount Rate and No Terminal Values)

	Investment A			Investment B		
Year	Net cash flow ($) ×	Present value factor =	Present value($)	Net cash flow ($) ×	Present value factor =	Present value ($)
1	3,000	0.926	2,778	1,000	0.926	926
2	3,000	0.857	2,571	2,000	0.857	1,714
3	3,000	0.794	2,382	3,000	0.794	2,382
4	3,000	0.735	2,205	4,000	0.735	2,940
5	3,000	0.681	2,043	6,000	0.681	4,086
		Total	11,979		Total	12,048
		Less cost	10,000		Less cost	10,000
		Net present value	1,979		Net present value	2,048

higher discount rate the net present values would be zero, and they would become negative at an even higher rate.

Internal Rate of Return

The time value of money is also reflected in another method of analyzing investments, the internal rate of return (IRR). It provides some information not available directly from the present value method. Both our investment examples had a positive net present value using the 8 percent discount rate. But what is the actual rate of return on these investments?

The actual rate of return on an investment with proper accounting for the time value of money is the internal rate of return, which is also called the *marginal efficiency of capital* or the *yield on the investment*. It is that discount rate which makes the present value of the net revenue flows just equal to zero. The equation for finding IRR is

$$NPV = \frac{P_1}{(1 + i)^1} + \frac{P_2}{(1 + i)^2} + \ldots + \frac{P}{(1 + i)^n} - C$$

where *NPV* is set equal to zero and the equation is solved for *i*, the discount rate.[1] A moment's reflection will show this to be a difficult equation to solve.

In the absence of a computer or a sophisticated calculator, the IRR must be found through trial and error with some approximation. The procedure is shown in Table 13-3 for investment A. The relatively high net present value using the 8 percent discount rate indicates the return may be considerably higher; so 14 percent is arbitrarily chosen for the first estimation of IRR. The calculations show a positive net present value of $296, indicating the IRR is still higher. A 16 percent discount rate is used next, resulting in a net present value of *minus* $178. Whenever the net present value is negative, the actual IRR is less than the discount rate used. The determination of IRR could continue using a 15 or 15½ percent discount rate, or linear interpolation would estimate it at approximately 15.2 percent.[2]

The internal rate of return method can be used several ways in investment analysis. Any investment with an IRR greater than the opportunity cost of capital would be profitable investment. However, some investors select an arbitrary cutoff value such as 10, 12, or 15 percent and invest only in those projects with a higher IRR. Unlike the net present value method, the IRR can be used to rank investments which have different initial costs and lives. This is an important consideration when investment capital is limited, as only those investments with the higher returns should be undertaken.

In addition to the rather difficult calculations involved, there is another potential limitation on the use of IRR. It implicitly assumes the annual net

[1]Since NPV is set equal to zero, this equation is often rearranged with *C* to the left of the equal sign to make the present value of the net revenue flows equal to the cost of the investment.

[2]The actual IRR is 15.24 percent for investment A and 13.76 percent for investment B, making A preferred over B using the internal rate of return method.

Table 13-3 Estimation of Internal Rate of Return for Investment A

Year	Net cash revenues ($)	14% Factor	14% Present value ($)	16% Factor	16% Present value ($)
1	3,000	0.877	2,631	0.862	2,586
2	3,000	0.769	2,307	0.743	2,229
3	3,000	0.675	2,025	0.641	1,923
4	3,000	0.592	1,776	0.552	1,656
5	3,000	0.519	1,557	0.476	1,428
		Totals	10,296		9,822
		Less cost	10,000		10,000
		Net present value	296		−178

returns or cash flows from the investment can be reinvested to earn a return equal to the IRR. If the IRR is fairly high, this may not be possible, causing the IRR method to overestimate the actual rate of return.

OTHER FACTORS IN INVESTMENT ANALYSIS

The discussion has so far presented only the basic procedures and methods used for investment analysis. Several additional factors must be included in a thorough analysis of any investment or when comparing alternative investments.

Cash Flow Analysis

The net present value and internal rate of return methods are measures of profitability over the entire life of the investment. However, investments identified as profitable may have years of negative cash flows depending on the pattern of net cash revenues over time and the method of financing. This potential problem is illustrated in Table 13-4 for the example investments A and B. The data assume that each investment is totally financed with a $10,000 loan at 8 percent interest repaid over 5 years with equal principal payments.

Table 13-4 Cash Flow Analysis of Investments A and B

Year	Investment A ($) Net cash revenue	Investment A ($) Debt payment*	Investment A ($) Difference	Investment B ($) Net cash revenue	Investment B ($) Debt payment*	Investment B ($) Difference
1	3,000	2,800	200	1,000	2,800	−1,800
2	3,000	2,640	360	2,000	2,640	− 640
3	3,000	2,480	520	3,000	2,480	520
4	3,000	2,320	680	4,000	2,320	1,680
5	3,000	2,160	840	6,000	2,160	3,840

*Assumes a $10,000 loan at 8 percent interest with equal principal payments over 5 years.

Investment A shows a positive cash flow for each year as the net cash revenue is greater than debt payments. However, investment B has lower net cash revenues the first 2 years, which cause negative cash flows. Both investments had positive net present values using an 8 percent discount rate, and investment B actually had a slightly higher value. However, it is not unusual to find profitable investments which have negative cash flows in the early years if the net cash revenues are low and the investment requires a large amount of borrowed capital.

If a project such as investment B is undertaken, something must be done to make up for the negative cash flows. There are several possibilities which can be used individually or in combination. First, some equity capital can be used for part or all of the investment to reduce the size of the loan and annual debt payments. Second, the payment schedule for the loan may be adjusted to make the debt payments more nearly equal to the net cash revenues. Smaller payments or interest payments only the first few years would be possibilities.

If neither of these methods is feasible, the cash deficits will have to be made up by excess cash available from other parts of the business. This will require a cash flow analysis of the entire business to assure cash will be available in sufficient amounts at the proper times to meet the deficits from the investment.

Income Taxes

The examples used in this chapter to illustrate the four methods of investment analysis did not consider the effects of income taxes on the net cash revenues. Taxes were omitted to simplify the introduction and discussion of investment analysis. However, investments are better analyzed using *after-tax* net cash revenues and after-tax discount rates for two reasons. First, income taxes can substantially change the net cash revenues depending on the investor's tax bracket and the type of investment. Second, since different investments may have different effects on income taxes, they cannot be fairly compared except on an after-tax basis. The after-tax discount rate or opportunity cost should also be used to put everything on an after-tax basis.

Income taxes will reduce the net cash revenues, but there may be other tax savings from certain types of investments. For example, depreciation was not included in calculating net cash revenues because it is a noncash expense. However, depreciation is a tax-deductible expense, which reduces taxable income and therefore income taxes. The tax savings resulting from any additional depreciation generated by the investment should be added to the net cash revenues. Some investments will also reduce income taxes because they are eligible for investment tax credit and additional first-year depreciation. The reader is referred to Chapter 17 for a more detailed discussion of how these factors affect income taxes.

Inflation

Inflation or a general increase in price levels over time can seriously affect investment analysis, particularly during periods of rapid inflation. Future income and expenses associated with the investment will be increasing, perhaps at different rates, and therefore will change the expected annual net revenues over the life of the investment. Terminal values may also increase with inflation and need to be adjusted accordingly.

Inflation also affects the choice of an appropriate discount rate. Discounting or calculating present values reflect the idea that a dollar to be received in the future is worth less than a dollar today because today's dollar can be invested and earn additional income over time. During inflationary periods, a future dollar is worth even less because it will purchase fewer goods and services. For example, when prices are increasing at the rate of 10 percent per year, it will take $1.10 a year from now to purchase the same amount of goods and services as $1 will purchase today.

This discussion implies the discount rate should be higher during inflationary periods than during periods of stable prices. Higher discount rates tend to favor investments with the more immediate net revenues over those with net revenues further into the future. Predicting inflation and making the appropriate adjustments to the discount rate, net revenues, and terminal values are not easy tasks, and no general recommendations are possible. However, the manager should always be aware of the effects inflation has on investment analysis and use good judgment in adjusting the information being used.

Risk and Uncertainty

There is some risk and uncertainty associated with every investment, but the degree or amount can vary widely between investments. Uncertainty about future prices, yields, technology, inflation rates, etc., affects the estimates of net cash revenues and terminal values. These estimates become more difficult for investments with longer lives, as more distant events are more difficult to predict. A complete discussion of the techniques which can be used to analyze investments in a risk environment would take a chapter or more. Only one method will be presented here, adjusting the discount rate.

There are two ways of adjusting the discount rate to account for risk. The first is to group the possible investments by degree of risk such as low, moderate, and high risk and then use different discount rates for each group. For example, 8 percent might be used for investments in the low-risk group, 10 percent for those in the moderate group, and 12 percent for the high group. The higher discount rates used for the higher-risk investments mean some profitable investments may be rejected. However, they also provide a margin for error in estimating the net cash revenues under risk. If an investment is accepted at the higher discount rate, it may still earn an acceptable rate of return even if the net cash revenues should be lower than those estimated.

As an alternative to the above procedure, the discount rate can be adjusted for each year of the investment's life instead of using a constant rate. For example, the discount rate for computing net present values might be increased by one-quarter or one-half of 1 percent each year. The more distant and therefore more uncertain net cash revenues would be discounted at successively higher rates in recognition of the greater uncertainty associated with them.

The problem with both these methods is the lack of guidelines in selecting the appropriate discount rates. They can be determined only by using the judgment and experience of the manager and may well vary between individuals who perceive different degrees of risk in the same investments. It should also be pointed out that risk and uncertainty do not invalidate the basic concepts and procedures in investment analysis; they only make their use more difficult.

SUMMARY

Money has a time value because of the interest or rate of return it can earn over time. The future value of a present sum of money is greater because of the interest the present sum can earn over time. Future values are found through a process called compounding as a compound interest rate is used. The present value of a sum of money to be received in the future is smaller than the future sum because money invested today at compound interest will grow into the larger future sum. Discounting is the process of finding present values for sums to be received in the future.

Investments are commonly analyzed by one or more of four methods: payback, simple rate of return, net present value, and internal rate of return. The first two are easy to use but have the disadvantage of not incorporating the time value of money. This may cause errors in selecting or ranking alternative investments, and they are not recommended. The net present value method is widely recommended, as it properly accounts for the time value of money. Any investment with a positive net present value is profitable, as the rate of return is higher than the discount rate being used. The internal rate of return method also considers the time value of money but is more difficult to use than net present value. It requires estimation of the actual rate of return, which can be difficult without a computer or advanced business calculator.

All four methods of investment analysis require estimation of net cash revenues over the life of the investment. Terminal values are also needed, and the net present value method requires selecting a discount rate. All values should be on an after-tax basis in a practical application of these methods. The discount rate may also need to be adjusted for uncertainty and inflation. A final step in analyzing any investment should be a cash flow budget, particularly when the investment is financed with borrowed capital.

QUESTIONS FOR REVIEW AND FURTHER THOUGHT

1 Put the concepts of future value and present value into your own words. How would you explain these concepts to someone hearing about them for the first time?
2 Explain the relationship between compounding and discounting.
3 Assume someone wishes to have $10,000 ten years from now as a college education fund for a child.
   a How much money would have to be invested now at 6 percent compound interest? At 8 percent?

b How much would have to be invested annually at 6 percent compound interest? At 8 percent?

4 If land is currently worth $1,500 per acre and is expected to increase in value at a rate of 5 percent annually, what will it be worth in 5 years? In 10 years? In 20 years?

5 If you require an 8 percent rate of return, how much could you afford to pay for an acre of land which has annual net cash revenues of $60 and an expected selling price of $2,500 per acre in 10 years?

6 Suppose someone offers you the choice of receiving $1,000 now or $2,000 in 10 years and the opportunity cost of capital is 10 percent. Which option would you choose? What if the opportunity cost of your capital was only 6 percent?

7 Calculate the net present values for the investments in Table 13-2 using a 10 percent discount rate. Which investment would be preferred now? How would you explain the change?

8 Assume you have only $20,000 to invest and must choose between the two investments below. Analyze each using all four methods discussed in this chapter and an 8 percent opportunity cost for capital. Which investment would you select? Why?

	Investment A ($)	Investment B ($)
Initial cost	20,000	20,000
Net cash revenues:		
Year 1	6,000	5,000
Year 2	6,000	5,000
Year 3	6,000	5,000
Year 4	6,000	5,000
Year 5	6,000	5,000
Terminal value	0	8,000

REFERENCES

Alpin, Richard D., George L. Casler, and Cheryl P. Francis: *Capital Investment Analysis Using Discounted Cash Flows,* Grid, Inc., Columbus, Ohio, 1977.

Barnard, C. S., and J. S. Nix: *Farm Planning and Control,* Cambridge University Press, Cambridge, 1973, chap. 3.

Barry, Peter J., John A. Hopkin, and C. B. Baker: *Financial Management in Agriculture,* 2d ed., The Interstate Printers and Publishers, Danville, Ill., 1979, chaps. 10, 11.

Penson, John B., Jr., and David A. Lins: *Agriculture Finance: An Introduction to Micro and Macro Concepts,* Prentice-Hall, Inc., Englewood Cliffs, N.J., 1980, chap. 5.

Van Horne, James C.: *Fundamentals of Financial Management,* Prentice-Hall, Inc., Englewood Cliffs, N.J., 1977.

Chapter 14

Land—
Control and Use

CHAPTER OBJECTIVES

1   To explore the economics of land use and management including the unique characteristics of land which affect its use and management
2   To outline the advantages and disadvantages of landownership
3   To outline the advantages and disadvantages of leasing land
4   To discuss factors important in land purchase decisions including land valuation and the legal aspects of a purchase
5   To summarize the characteristics of cash, crop share, and livestock share leasing arrangements
6   To compare the advantages and disadvantages of each type of leasing arrangement
7   To demonstrate a method for determining equitable share lease arrangements which will maintain efficient production

Agriculture uses large land areas, which distinguishes it from many other types of industries. Land is the basic resource which supports the production of all agricultural commodities including livestock, which depend on land to produce the forage and grain they consume.

Land is the most valuable asset in the balance sheet of United States agriculture, and its value has been increasing at a rapid rate. The index of land values in the top part of Figure 14-1 shows the steady rise in land values since about 1940. There was a spectacular increase in the 1970s, with land values increasing by approximately 250 percent. The bottom part of Figure 14-1 indicates that land values have increased nearly every year with the exception of the 1920s and early 1930s.

A number of factors have contributed to the steady rise in land values. Profit per acre has been increasing, which allows land prices to increase while providing the same rate of return for landowners. Crop yields have increased through many technological advances, and prices have trended upward. Land prices have also kept pace with or exceeded the rate of inflation in the United States, making landownership a good hedge against inflation. Nonfarm inves-

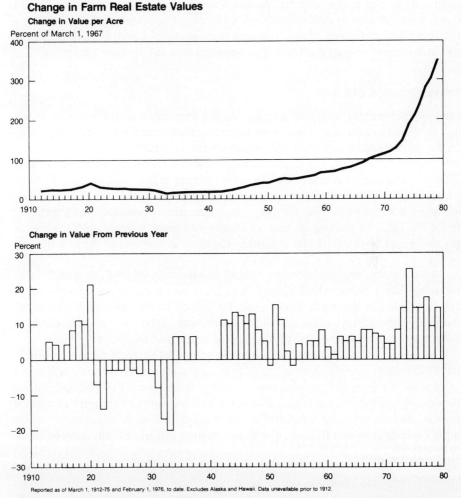

Figure 14-1 Changes in United States land values, 1912–1979. (*Economic, Statistical and Cooperative Service, U.S. Department of Agriculture.*)

tors have recognized this and have entered the land market, helping to bid up and maintain land prices.

While nonfarm investors have been important purchasers of land in some areas, the large majority of land buyers are still other farmers and ranchers. Pressures to expand the size of their operation to take advantage of large-scale technologies have forced many active farmers and ranchers into the land market. They recognize the economies of size they can achieve with a large operation, the opportunity for greater profits, and the effect of increasing land values on their net worth.

THE ECONOMICS OF LAND USE AND MANAGEMENT

Land is unique in many respects, having a number of characteristics not found in other agricultural or nonagricultural resources. These characteristics greatly influence the economics of land use and management. Land is such an important and unique resource that land economics is a subdivision of agricultural economics.

Characteristics of Land

Land is a permanent resource which does not depreciate or wear out provided soil fertility is maintained and appropriate conservation measures are used. Proper management not only will maintain the inherent productivity of land but can also improve it. Land is productive in its native state, producing stands of timber and native grasses, but the management efforts of landowners have greatly improved the productive capacity of many types of land. This has been accomplished through land clearing, drainage, good conservation practices, irrigation, the introduction of new and improved plant species, and the use of limestone and fertilizer. Land use often changes as a result of these improvements.

Area, space, and location are also characteristics of land, and each farm has a legal description which identifies its particular location, size, and shape. Land as space is immobile and cannot be moved to be combined with other resources. Machinery, seed, fertilizer, water, etc., must be moved to the land to be combined with it in the production of crops and livestock.

Not only is land a unique resource in general but each farm or specific parcel of land is unique. Any piece of land larger than several acres will often contain two or more distinct soil types, each with its own set of characteristics. Topography, different soil types, climatic features, and the existence of natural hazards such as flooding, wind and water erosion, and rock outcrops are other factors which combine to make the land resource different from farm to farm.

Planning Land Use

The different land resource on each farm explains why one of the first steps in whole farm planning is a complete inventory of the land including soil types and production potential. Without this inventory, the most profitable farm plan cannot be developed. The potential livestock and crop enterprises, yields, fertility requirements, and conservation practices are directly related to the nature of the land resources available.

Whole farm planning was approached from the standpoint of maximizing the return to the most fixed resource. The fixed nature of land in the short run makes it the center of most planning efforts. It is the fixed resource which often determines the position and shape of the production possibility curves as well as playing a role in explaining the existence of the different types of enterprise relationships.

The principle of comparative advantage can often be explained by regional differences in land productivity which determine land use. However, the most profitable land use is also a function of relative commodity prices and technology, which can change, bringing about changes in land use. Cotton production has tended to move westward out of the southeastern states to be replaced by pasture and livestock production. Soybeans have become the second most important crop in the Midwest and Mississippi Delta region. The development of irrigation has transformed former livestock grazing areas into important crop production regions with interesting side effects. Irrigation greatly increased the supply of grain available in the Southern Plains region of Texas and Oklahoma, which encouraged the development of large-scale cattle feeding operations. All these changes can be traced to changes in relative prices, new technology, and other economic factors.

Economics of Conservation

Land conservation may be defined as the use of those practices which will maximize the present value of the long-run returns from land use. This definition does not prevent land from being used but does require the use of those conservation practices which will maintain soil productivity over time rather than "mining the soil" in the short run. Conservation is often caught in the middle of a conflict between short-run and long-run profit maximization.

Most conservation practices require some cash expenditures, and they may also reduce crop yields temporarily as soil and cropping patterns are disturbed. This short-run reduction in profit may be necessary to achieve higher profits in the future and prevent a possible long-run decline in profits if no conservation practices are used. Figure 14-2 illustrates the possible income flows with and without a certain level of conservation. As conservation practices are a form of investment, the net present value method discussed in the previous chapter can be used to determine the profitability of a particular practice.

The opportunity cost of capital and the planning horizon of the landowner become very important in the adoption of conservation practices. Higher discount rates reduce the present value of the larger future incomes resulting from conservation, and shorter planning horizons also discourage conservation. In

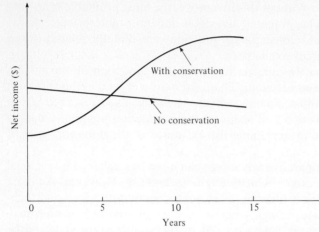

Figure 14-2 Hypothetical illustration of income flows over time with and without conservation.

Figure 14-2, a farmer with a 5-year planning horizon is not likely to adopt the conservation practice, as the net present value of the income flow would be less than that with no conservation. In this example, it may take a planning horizon of 15 years or more before the net present value of the income flow with conservation exceeds that from no conservation.

A high opportunity cost of capital, short planning horizons, and limited capital combine to explain why many landowners are reluctant to adopt conservation practices with high capital requirements and long payoff periods. However, society also has an interest in conservation in order to maintain and expand our nation's long-run food production potential. Societal planning horizons are typically longer than those for an individual farmer, with society wanting more conservation practices than farmers are willing and able to adopt. In recognition of this and the limited capital position of many farmers, society has devised means to encourage more conservation practices. Technical assistance is available at no cost through local offices of the Soil Conservation Service. Financial assistance to pay for part of the costs of certain conservation practices has been available through the Agricultural Conservation Program and the Great Plains Conservation Program.

Legislation at both the federal and state levels now requires minimum levels of conservation in some situations, and these requirements may increase over time. Society's concern with siltation of streams and lakes and the fertilizer and pesticide residues carried into them by silt and water has resulted in regulations restricting soil and water movement. Environmental Protection Agency regulations restricting the runoff from cattle feedlots are an example. As more and more of these regulations are enacted, future conservation efforts may increasingly become a matter of selecting the least-cost combination of conservation practices to meet their requirements and standards.

LAND CONTROL—OWN OR LEASE?

How much land to acquire and how to acquire it are two extremely important decisions to be made by a beginning farmer. Errors made at this point may plague the business for many years. Too little land may mean a business which is too small to utilize other resources fully, restricting profit to low levels. At the other extreme, too much land may require borrowing a large amount of money, cause serious cash flow problems, and stretch a beginning farmer's management capacity. Either situation can result in business failure.

Land acquisition should be thought of in terms of control and not just ownership. Control can be achieved by either ownership or leasing. Many farmers are finding a combination of ownership and leasing to be desirable, particularly when capital is limited. They often own some land and buildings to have a permanent "home base" and then lease land in the neighborhood to attain the desired business size. These are the farmers identified as part owners in Figure 14-3, which shows this type of farm organization increasing in importance relative to both full owners and tenants who own none of the land they farm.

As with many economic decisions there can be no general recommendation about the amount of land that should be owned and how much should be leased. There are advantages and disadvantages to both methods of controlling land. Capital availability, personal preferences and goals, and the amount of land for sale or lease in the area are some of the more important decision factors.

Landownership

Landownership is an important goal for some individuals regardless of the economics involved in this choice. A certain amount of pride, satisfaction, and

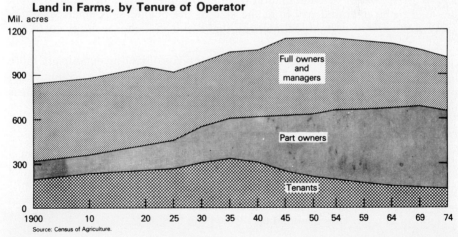

Figure 14-3 Distribution of United States farmland among full owners, part owners, and tenants. (*Economic, Statistical and Cooperative Service, U.S. Department of Agriculture.*)

prestige is derived from owning land. It also provides a tangible estate to pass on to one's heirs, which can be another important personal goal.

Landownership also has the following advantages:

1 *Security of Tenure.* Landownership eliminates the uncertainty of losing a lease and having the size of the business reduced unexpectedly.

2 *Loan Collateral.* Accumulated equity in land provides an excellent source of collateral when borrowing money. Increasing land values have provided substantial equity for landowners in recent years.

3 *Management Independence and Freedom.* Landowners are free to make their own decisions about enterprise combinations, conservation measures, fertilizer levels, etc., without consulting with a landlord.

4 *Hedge against Inflation.* Land has provided an excellent hedge against inflation as land values have tended to equal or exceed the inflation rate.

Ownership of all land controlled by the business can have some disadvantages. These disadvantages are primarily related to the capital position of the business. Possible disadvantages are:

1 *Cash Flow.* A large debt load associated with landownership can create serious cash flow problems. The cash earnings may not be sufficient to meet the required principal and interest payments as well as the other cash obligations of the business.

2 *Lower Return on Capital.* Where capital is limited, there may be alternative uses with a higher return than investment in land. Limited capital often has a higher return when invested in machinery, livestock, and annual operating inputs such as fertilizer, seed, and feed.

3 *Lower Working Capital.* This disadvantage is related to the one above. A heavy debt load on land may restrict the amount of working capital available, severely limiting enterprise selection, input levels, and profit.

4 *Size Limits.* A combination of limited capital and a desire to own all the land to be operated will limit the size of the business. A small size may prevent the use of certain technologies and result in higher average costs.

As can be seen from this list, the disadvantages of landownership are more likely to affect the beginning farmer with limited capital. With the accumulation of capital and borrowing capacity over time, they may become less and less important.

Leasing Land

The beginning farmer or rancher is often advised to lease land. This advice assumes limited capital, and therefore leasing is a means of obtaining control over a larger number of acres. Where land is available for lease, controlling land through leasing will generally provide the greatest return to a limited amount of capital. Other advantages of leasing land are:

1 *More Working Capital.* When capital is not tied up in land purchases,

more is available to purchase machinery, livestock, and annual operating inputs.

2 *Additional Management.* A beginning farmer may be short of management skills. Management assistance can be provided by a knowledgeable landlord or agent.

3 *More Flexible Size.* Lease contracts may be for only 1 year or at most several years. Year-to-year changes in business size can be easily accomplished by giving up old leases or leasing additional land.

4 *More Flexible Financial Obligations.* Lease payments are more flexible than mortgage payments which are fixed for a long period. Share rent will vary with crop yields and prices. Cash rents are less flexible but can be negotiated each time the lease is renewed taking into account current economic conditions.

Leasing land also has disadvantages which take on a special significance when all land is controlled via leasing and none is owned. These disadvantages are:

1 *Uncertainty.* Given the short term of most lease contracts, the danger always exists that all or part of the land being farmed can be lost with fairly short notice. This possibility discourages some good farming practices, may result in a rapid and substantial decrease in business size, and contributes to a general feeling of uncertainty about the future of the business.

2 *Poor Facilities.* Some landlords are reluctant to invest money in buildings and other improvements when the land is rented on a crop share or cash rent basis. Housing, livestock facilities, and machinery storage space may be less than desirable.

3 *Slow Equity Accumulation.* Without landownership equity can be accumulated only in machinery, livestock, or cash savings. In periods of rising land values, landownership can generate substantial equity and increase the owner's borrowing capacity.

A review of the advantages and disadvantages for landownership and leasing reveals no clear recommendation for either method of acquiring control over land. Control is still the important factor, as income can be obtained from either owned or leased land. In the final analysis, the proper combination of owned and leased land is the one providing enough land to use fully the available labor, machinery, and working capital given individual capital limitations and personal preferences.

BUYING LAND

The purchase of a farm or ranch is an important decision often involving large sums of money. A land purchase will have long-run effects on the entire financial structure of the business including increased cash flow requirements to finance the purchase. The first step in a land purchase decision should be a determination of its value.

While income potential is an important determinant of land value, many other factors contribute to value. The following are examples of some of these factors:

1 *Soil, Topography, and Climate.* These factors combine to determine the crop and livestock yield potential and therefore the expected income stream.

2 *Neighborhood.* A farm located in an area of well-managed, well-kept farms has a special attraction which increases its value and vice versa.

3 *Location.* Location with respect to schools, churches, towns, paved roads, and farm input suppliers will affect value. A prospective purchaser who plans to live on the farm will pay particular attention to the community and services provided in the general area.

4 *Buildings and Improvements.* The number, size, condition, and usefulness of buildings, fences, and other land improvements will affect value. A neat, attractive farmstead with a modern house can add many dollars to a farm's value.

5 *Size.* Small farms may sell for a higher price per acre than large farms. A smaller total purchase price puts smaller farms within the financial reach of a larger number of buyers. Several neighboring farmers may also consider the purchase of a small farm a good way to increase the size of their business and help bid up the price.

6 *Markets.* Proximity to a number of markets will reduce transportation costs and increase competition for the farm's products.

7 *Financing.* The method and terms of the financing arrangements related to the purchase will affect value. Land may be sold with a land purchase contract where the seller provides the financing. The terms of a contract may include a smaller down payment and/or a lower interest rate than conventional mortgage financing, which will increase the amount a buyer is willing to pay for a given piece of land.

A thorough inspection of the property should be conducted to identify problem areas which might reduce its value. Buildings should be inspected for structural soundness and soil types properly identified. Drainage and erosion problems, sand and gravel areas, rock outcroppings, and other soil hazards should be noted and yield expectations adjusted accordingly. There is also a tendency to overvalue poorer land, as the asking price may make it appear to be a bargain. If the land is basically productive but has been abused and the fertility level allowed to decline, good management practices may restore its productivity. This type of land may occasionally be found at a bargain price. Land with a naturally low fertility level and/or many natural hazards must be carefully evaluated to determine its value.

Figure 14-4 illustrates the latter problem. The production function for the poor soil shows a lower response from any input level than the production function for the good soil. Maximum yield potential is also lower for the poor soil, but even with this lower yield some costs will be nearly the same for both soils. For example, labor and machinery costs for the primary tillage operations

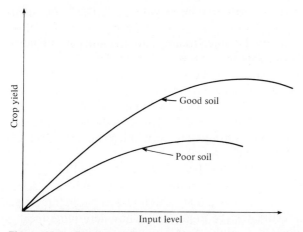

Figure 14-4 Production functions for two soils with different native fertility.

will be nearly the same for both soils, and some other costs may be little different. With many costs nearly the same and a lower yield, the poor soil will have a smaller net income stream over time. The difference in the income streams must be carefully evaluated to find the relative values of the two soil types.

Land Appraisal

An appraisal is a systematic process which leads to an estimate of value for a given piece of real estate. There are business firms which provide appraisal services for a fee. They provide their clients with a detailed analysis of the factors which determine the value of the property and conclude the report with an estimate of current value. Only a brief outline of the appraisal process will be discussed here.

Two basic methods are used to determine the value of income-producing property such as land, the *market data method* and the *income capitalization method*. The market data method compares the characteristics of land which was sold recently with the land being appraised. Sale prices for the comparable land sales are used to estimate value for the subject property after adjusting for differences in factors such as soil types, productivity, location, size, buildings, and time of sale.

The income capitalization method uses present value procedures to estimate the value of the future income stream from the land. This method requires an estimate of the expected annual net income stream and the selection of the appropriate discount rate. Value is estimated using the equation $V = P/i$, where P is the average annual net income from the land, i is the discount rate, or capitalization rate, as it is called in appraisal, and V is the estimated land value. This equation is a variation of the one for calculating the present value of an annuity which was discussed in Chapter 13. The difference is that the above equation assumes the annuity or net income stream from the land will be received in perpetuity.

The first step in estimating the income stream is an inventory of the farm's physical production resources. This inventory is used to determine the most likely cropping program and yields over the long run with estimates of long-run prices then used to determine total income. The results of such a procedure are shown in the top portion of Table 14-1 for a hypothetical 160-acre farm. It has 150 tillable acres after deducting for roads, lanes, waterways, etc. The long-run crop plan is estimated to be 100 acres of corn and 50 acres of soybeans generating an annual gross income of $38,900.

The next step in what is actually the development of a total budget is to estimate the annual expenses associated with the crop plan. These are shown in the next part of Table 14-1 and total $22,800, which makes net income equal to $16,100. Yield and price estimates are important. They determine total income and therefore strongly influence the final estimate of net income. Both

Table 14-1 Estimated Annual Income and Expenses for Appraisal Purposes (Hypothetical 160-Acre Farm with 150 Tillable Acres)

	Acres	Yield (bu.)	Price	Income
Income:				
Corn	100	110	$2.50	$27,500
Soybeans	50	38	$6.00	$11,400
Total income				$38,900
Expenses:				
Fertilizer			$6,000	
Seed			1,200	
Chemicals			900	
Trucking			400	
Insurance			200	
Labor			2,500	
Machinery:				
Fixed costs			3,800	
Variable costs			3,200	
Property taxes			1,800	
Repairs and maintenance			800	
Depreciation—buildings, fences, etc.			2,000	
Total expenses				$22,800
Annual net income				$16,100

Capitalization of income

Capitalization rate		Total value	Per acre
8% ($16,100 ÷ 0.08)	=	$201,250	$1,257.81
6% ($16,100 ÷ 0.06)	=	$268,333	$1,677.08
4% ($16,100 ÷ 0.04)	=	$402,500	$2,515.63

items must be accurately estimated to arrive at an accurate estimate of value. County yield averages and farm yields assigned by the local Agricultural Stabilization and Conservation Service office for government farm programs are useful starting places for yield estimates. Prices should reflect the appraiser's best estimate of long-run prices after a careful review of past price levels.

The final steps in the income capitalization method are to select the capitalization rate and calculate the estimated land value. This process is shown in the bottom portion of Table 14-1 for three different capitalization rates. The effect of capitalization rate on value is readily apparent, and the appropriate rate must be carefully selected. A rate equal to the mortgage interest rate on farm loans will typically result in an estimated value below the selling price for similar farms in the area. Landowners have historically been willing to accept a current rate of return on land which is lower than other investments in anticipation of continued inflation in land prices.

Current appraisal practice is to estimate the average rate of return to land investment in the general area for similar farms at recent sale prices. Using this rate in the capitalization procedure will give a value which is comparable with the recent selling prices for farms. This procedure often results in a capitalization rate of 3 to 6 percent which is the range of historical rates of return to farmland based on current market values. Higher capitalization rates cannot be justified unless the resulting value is somehow adjusted to reflect current market values.

Cash Flow Analysis

A cash flow analysis should be performed on any prospective land purchase. It is not a method for determining land value but, for a given purchase price, will show if there will be sufficient cash flow to meet the annual operating expense as well as the interest and principal payments on any loan. Table 14-2 is a simplified cash flow analysis on the purchase of the example 160-acre farm for $2,000 per acre, or a total of $320,000.

Table 14-2   Cash Flow Analysis on Purchase of 160-Acre Farm at $2,000 per Acre*

	Year 1	Year 2	Year 3	Year 4	Year 5
Cash operating income ($)	38,900	38,900	38,900	38,900	38,900
Cash operating expenses ($)	17,760	17,760	17,760	17,760	17,760
Annual loan payment ($):					
Principal	6,400	6,400	6,400	6,400	6,400
Interest	17,280	16,704	16,128	15,552	14,976
Total cash outflow ($)	41,440	40,864	40,288	39,712	39,136
Net cash flow ($)	−2,540	−1,964	−1,388	−812	−236

*Assumes a down payment of $128,000 with the balance financed by a 30-year loan of $192,000 at 9 percent interest with equal principal payments made annually.

The analysis assumes a 40 percent down payment ($128,000) and a 30-year loan of $192,000 with 9 percent interest and equal annual principal payments. Annual income and expenses are based on the figures in Table 14-1, with 20 percent of the machinery fixed costs estimated to be cash expenses. Depreciation is a noncash expense and therefore is not included. For simplicity, no costs are included for machinery replacement nor are any effects the purchase might have on income taxes.

For the first 5 years, the cash operating income is not enough to meet cash operating expenses and the required principal and interest payments. Because of the declining interest payment each year, net cash flow should become positive in the sixth year of ownership. In the meantime, the cash flow deficits in the first 5 years must be met with cash available from other sources. Any excess cash available from other land being farmed, off-farm employment, or other sources will be needed to make loan payments if this land is purchased. The cash flow problem would be magnified if the down payment were smaller, the interest rate higher, or the loan for a shorter period.

The situation shown in Table 14-2 is typical of land purchases in recent years. Land prices have been bid up to a point where negative cash flows from a land purchase are the rule rather than the exception. Earnings will seldom be sufficient to meet both operating expenses and debt repayment. Several things would reduce the cash flow deficit including a lower purchase price, a lower interest rate, or a longer term on the loan. An amortized loan with equal total payments would also help reduce the cash outflow the first few years. Obviously a cash flow projection for the entire business is necessary to determine if cash will be available from other parts of the business to make the loan payments on a new land purchase.

Legal Aspects

Purchasing land is a legal as well as financial transaction. As such, there are a number of possible legal pitfalls to be avoided. The legal description of the property should be checked for accuracy and the title examined for any potential problems. For example, there may be tax liens and mortgages on the property. The buyer should also be aware of any easements such as those for roads, pipelines, or power lines which might interfere with full and unrestricted use of the land. Zoning and other land use restrictions should also be checked, as they are becoming important factors in some areas.

Any water rights and mineral rights passing to the new owner should be carefully identified and understood. Rights to underground minerals do not automatically transfer with the rights to the land surface. Where oil, gas, coal, or other minerals are or may be important, the fraction of the mineral rights being received can have a large impact on land values. In the irrigated areas of the western United States, the right to use water for irrigation purposes is often limited and allocated on an individual farm basis. Obviously, the extent and duration of these water rights should be carefully determined.

When land is sold "subject to" a lease, the new owner cannot actually acquire full possession until the lease expires. This makes the terms and remaining length of the lease another factor in value and a legal restriction on full and immediate enjoyment of all ownership rights.

This is only a partial list of the many ways land buyers can receive less than they expected because of some unexpected legal problem. For these and other reasons, it is advisable for land buyers to retain the services of an attorney with experience in land transactions. This should be done before any verbal or written offer is made on the property.

LEASING LAND

Obtaining control of land through leasing has a long history in the United States and other countries. Not all this history has been good, as there has been exploitation of tenants and sharecroppers and poor land use. Full landownership has been advocated by some as a means of eliminating these problems. However, it is not likely that we will ever see an agriculture where all farmers own all the land they operate. The capital requirements are too large, and improvements in leasing arrangements have reduced many of the problems and inefficiencies.

Leases on agricultural land are strongly influenced by local custom and tradition. The type, terms, and length of leases tend to be fairly uniform within a given area or community but often differ from area to area. This reliance on custom and tradition results in fairly stable leasing arrangements over time, which is desirable. However, it can also mean lease terms which are slow to change in response to changing economic conditions and new technology. Inefficient land use can result from outdated leasing arrangements.

A lease is a legal contract whereby the landowner or landlord gives the tenant the possession and use of an asset such as land for a period of time in return for a specified payment. The payment may be cash, a share of the production, or a combination of the two. Oral leases are legal in most states but not recommended, as it is too easy for memories to fail, causing disputes over the terms of the original agreement.

A written lease should contain the following information: (1) the legal description of the land, (2) the term of the lease, (3) the rent to be paid as well as the time and place of payment, (4) the names of the landlord (lessor) and the tenant (lessee), and (5) the signatures of all parties to the lease. These are only the minimum requirements of a lease. A good lease will contain other provisions spelling out the rights and obligations of both the landlord and tenant. Many good leases contain a clause describing the arbitration procedure to be followed in case of an unresolved dispute. Dates and procedures for notification of lease renewal and cancellation should also be included, particularly if different from state law requirements.

A written lease form available through the Oklahoma Agricultural Extension Service is included at the end of this chapter. This is only one example of a lease. Blank lease forms are available through the Agricultural Extension

Service in many other states. It is important to use a lease adapted to a particular state, as farming conditions and legal requirements vary from state to state. As with all legal documents, the contracting parties may wish to obtain the advice of an attorney before signing a lease.

Three types of leases are commonly used in the leasing of agricultural land. They are cash rent, crop share, and livestock share, with each having some advantages and disadvantages to both landlord and tenant. Each type will be discussed in some detail in the following sections.

Cash Rent

A cash rent lease has the rent specified as a cash payment of either a fixed amount per acre or a fixed lump sum. If the rent is per acre, the number of acres should be specified in the lease to prevent later disagreements. Under a cash lease the landlord furnishes the land and buildings and the tenant receives all the income and typically pays all expenses except property taxes, insurance, and major repairs to buildings and improvements. The lease may contain restrictions on land use and require the tenant to use certain fertility practices and to maintain fences, waterways, terraces, and other improvements in their present conditions.

The characteristics of a cash lease create certain advantages and disadvantages. Some of the more important are:

1 *Simplicity.* There is less likelihood of disagreements, as the rent can be easily spelled out and understood by both parties. A cash lease is also easy for a landlord to supervise, as there are no management decisions to be made. For this reason, landlords who live a long distance from their farm or who have little knowledge of agricultural production may prefer a cash lease.

2 *Managerial Freedom.* Tenants are free to make their own decisions regarding crop and livestock programs and other management decisions. Tenants who are above-average managers often favor a cash lease, as they receive the total benefits from their management decisions.

3 *Risk.* A cash lease provides the landlord with a known, steady, and dependable rental income. The tenant stands all risk from yield and price variability. This division of risk is one reason cash rents tend to average lower than crop share rent on comparable land.

4 *Capital Requirements.* The landlord has a low capital requirement under a cash lease, as there is no sharing of the annual operating inputs. In addition to all annual operating inputs, the tenant has the cash rent to pay, which is another fixed, annual cash expense.

5 *Poor Land Use.* With all income accruing to them, some tenants may be tempted to exploit the land, particularly under short-term leases. This can be prevented with fair and proper land use restrictions included in the lease.

6 *Poor Improvements.* Landlords may be reluctant to invest in buildings and other improvements when using a cash lease, as they do not share in any additional income they provide.

7 *Rigid Rents.* Cash rents tend to become inflexible and slow to change. Unless they are renegotiated each year after considering changes in prices, land values, and technology, inequities can soon develop.

Crop Share

Crop share leases are popular in the Midwest and other areas where cash grain farms dominate. These leases specify the landlord is to receive a certain share of the crops produced, with the proceeds from their sale becoming the rent. Many crop share leases provide for the landlord to share in the cost of some of the variable crop inputs in the same proportion as the share of production. Fertilizer, seed, chemicals, and irrigation costs may be shared along with harvesting and other costs in some areas. Along with sharing production and expenses, landlords often participate in the management decisions.

The landlord's share will vary from one-half down to one-quarter or less depending on the type of crop, local custom, and whether or not any variable costs are shared. Soil productivity is an important factor, as many of the tenant's costs such as labor and machinery will be nearly the same regardless of soil type. Therefore, tenants must receive a larger share of the production on poorer soils to cover their production costs. Figure 14-5 shows how crop shares tend to vary by soil productivity level. Landlords whose farms contain poorer soils may find they have to take a smaller share and/or pay more of the variable costs to attract a good tenant.

The advantages and disadvantages of crop share leases fall into the following categories:

1 *Variable Rent.* The landlord's rent will vary with changes in yields and prices. This may be a disadvantage if the land rent is an important part of the landlord's total income, as it may be for retired persons. Variable rent is an advantage to the tenant, as the rental payment varies with the ability to pay as yields and prices fluctuate.

2 *Risk.* The sharing of production and some expenses divides the risk between landlord and tenant. Neither must stand the full brunt of yield and price fluctuations.

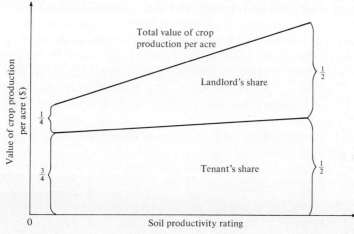

Figure 14-5 The relationship between divisions of crop shares and soil productivity rating.

3   *Management*. Landlords using a crop share lease usually maintain some direct or indirect control over crop selection and other management decisions. This may be an advantage to an inexperienced tenant and gives the landlord some control over land use. The tenant usually has complete freedom in the management of any livestock enterprises.

4   *Capital Requirements*. Because some crop production expenses are shared, the landlord's capital requirements increase while the tenant's decrease when compared with a cash lease.

5   *Expense Sharing*. A problem with crop share leases is determining a fair and equitable sharing of expenses. As a general rule, variable expenses should be shared in the same proportion as the production, but this rule is little help in determining which expenses should be shared. The adoption of new technology often creates new problems on the proper share of its costs and benefits.

6   *Building and Pasture Rent*. Since the landlord receives no direct benefits from buildings (except grain storage) and livestock pasture, problems can arise concerning a fair rent for these items. A cash rent supplementing the crop share is often paid by the tenant for use of buildings and livestock pasture.

7   *Buildings and Improvements*. Crop share leases do not encourage a landlord to invest in buildings other than grain storage. This is particularly true of livestock buildings, since the landlord does not share in that income. With a crop share lease, a tenant may be restricted on the type and size of the livestock operation that can be carried out.

Livestock Share

A livestock share lease is much like a crop share lease except livestock income is also shared between landlord and tenant. The tenant typically furnishes all labor and machinery and a share of the livestock and operating inputs, with the landlord furnishing land, buildings, and a share of the livestock and operating inputs. Most livestock share leases are 50-50 shares, although other share arrangements are possible depending on the major livestock enterprise and how many and which expenses are shared.

Livestock share leases can be complex, and there is considerable latitude in the number and type of expenses to be shared. Since the livestock income is shared, livestock expenses such as feed, utilities, health expenses, and marketing costs should be shared. In addition, the landlord may share in the cost of machinery and equipment related to livestock production such as milkers, feed grinders, feed wagons, feeders, waterers, and forage harvesting equipment. The lease should contain a full and detailed list of the expenses to be shared and the sharing ratio.

The advantages, disadvantages, and potential problems with a livestock share lease are as follows:

1   *Rent*. Landlords have typically received a higher average rent with livestock share leases than with the other types. The rent will be more variable, however, as it is subject to fluctuations in prices and yields of both crops and livestock. Tenants may feel the rent is too high, as the landlord receives a

share of the livestock income which may be produced entirely with the tenant's own or hired labor.

2 *Risk.* A livestock share lease divides the risk in a more equal manner than other leases. Both parties are directly affected by all price and yield fluctuations.

3 *Capital Requirements.* The sharing of livestock investment increases the landlord's capital requirements and decreases the tenant's when compared with a crop share lease with the same livestock numbers. A tenant with limited capital may find this an advantage, as a livestock share lease will allow a larger livestock operation on a larger farm.

4 *Buildings and Pasture.* A livestock share lease provides the landlord with some rent on these items through livestock production with no need to negotiate a cash payment for them. Landlords are more likely to furnish and maintain a good set of buildings since they help generate livestock income. Tenants may desire additional building improvements to reduce their labor requirements in the shared livestock production.

5 *Management.* There is a need and opportunity for sharing management decisions under a livestock share lease, and this requires a good working relationship between the landlord and tenant. The tenant has less freedom in making management decisions and an above average manager may feel restricted, but an inexperienced tenant can benefit from advice and counsel of an experienced landlord.

6 *Records.* The sharing of both crop and livestock income and expenses requires good records to ensure the proper division. There should be a periodic accounting of income and expenses with compensating payments made to balance the accounts.

7 *Lease Termination.* Terminating a livestock share lease can be complex and time-consuming. All livestock and any shared equipment must be divided in a fair and equitable manner. Because of the difficulties that can arise, the lease should contain an agreed upon method for making the division and an arbitration procedure for any unresolved disputes.

Efficiency and Equity in Leases

With many leases based on local custom and tradition, inefficiencies, poor land use, and a less than equitable division of income and expenses can become part of rigid leasing arrangements. There have been many critics of a land tenure system based on leasing because of the existence of these problems. It may not be possible to write a perfect lease, but improvements can be made. There are two broad areas of concern in improving the efficiency and equity of a lease. The first is the length of the lease, and the second is the cost sharing arrangements.

Farm leases are typically written for a term of 1 year, with some livestock share leases written for 3 to 5 years. Most 1-year leases contain a clause providing for automatic renewal on a year-to-year basis if neither party gives notice of termination before a certain date. Many such leases have been in effect for long periods of time, but the possibility always exists that the lease may be canceled on rather short notice if the landlord sells the farm or finds a better tenant. This places the tenant in a state of constant worry and insecurity. It also tempts the tenant to plant only the more profitable, soil-depleting crops rather than those which would help build up the soil over time.

Short leases also discourage a tenant from making soil and building improvements, as the lease may be terminated before the cost can be recovered. Soil conservation practices are an example. These problems can be at least partially solved by longer-term leases and agreements to reimburse the tenant for the unrecovered cost of any improvements. Building improvements at the tenant's expense, application of limestone and rock phosphate, soil conservation expenses, and other soil-building practices can be covered under an agreement of this type.

Inefficiencies can also arise from poor cost-sharing arrangements. Farm management specialists recommend that the cost of those inputs which directly affect yield be shared in the same proportion as the income or production. Seed, fertilizer, chemicals, and irrigation water are examples. If these are not shared on the same basis as production, inefficient input use, reduced profits, and disagreements on input levels can easily occur.

Table 14-3 is an example of what can happen. Profit maximization from fertilizer use is where its marginal value product is equal to its marginal input cost, which occurs at 140 pounds of fertilizer. However, if the tenant receives only one-half the crop but pays all the fertilizer cost, the marginal value product for the tenant is only one-half the total. This is shown in the last column of Table 14-3. Under these conditions the tenant will use only 100 pounds of fertilizer per acre to maximize profit. While this amount will maximize profit for the tenant under these conditions, it reduces the total profit per acre from what it would be at 140 pounds of fertilizer.

The potential conflict between landlord and tenant over fertilizer use is magnified even more by fertilizer having a zero marginal input cost to the landlord. Additional fertilizer use does not increase the landlord's costs but does increase yield which is shared. The landlord would like to fertilize for

Table 14-3   Example of Inefficient Fertilizer Use under a Crop Share Lease (Landlord Receives One-Half of Crop but Pays No Fertilizer Cost)

Fertilizer (lbs)	Yield (bu)	Marginal input cost, at 20¢/lb ($)	Total marginal value product, corn at $2 per bu ($)	Tenant's marginal value product ($)
60	95			
80	100	4	10	5
100	104	4	8	4
120	107	4	6	3
140	109	4	4	2
160	110	4	2	1

maximum yield as the way to maximize profit. This would be at 160 pounds of fertilizer per acre in the example in Table 14-3.

These types of conflicts can be eliminated by sharing the cost of yield-determining inputs in the same way the production is shared. If fertilizer cost was equally shared in this example, both parties would pay one-half the marginal input cost and receive one-half the marginal value product. They would both independently arrive at 140 pounds of fertilizer as the profit-maximizing level. Tenants are understandably reluctant to adopt any new yield-increasing technique or technology if they must pay all the additional cost but receive only a share of the yield increase.

Determining Proper Lease Shares

The objective of any lease should be to provide a fair and equitable return to both parties for the inputs they contribute to the total farm operation. Lease terms and rental rates should be designed to encourage maximum profit given the productivity potential for the farm. This is equally as important as the sharing rate, as it is obvious that either party is better off with 40 percent of a $50,000 income than with 50 percent of a $30,000 income.

Most people agree that a fair and equitable sharing arrangement exists when *each party is paid for the use of their inputs according to the contribution those inputs make toward generating income.* Application of this principle requires the identification and valuation of all inputs contributed by both the landlord and tenant.

One method for determining the proper shares for a crop share lease is shown in Table 14-4. This same procedure could be used for a livestock share lease, but it would contain more detail, as livestock investment and expenses would also be shared. The example in Table 14-4 starts from an assumed 50-50 sharing of production; so crop production expenses for seed, fertilizer, and lime and other crop expenses are also shared equally. Other costs are allocated to the landlord or tenant based on who owns the asset or provides the service.

The most difficult part of this procedure is placing a value on assets such as land and machinery and selecting the interest rates. A different value for these assets and/or different interest rates could substantially change the results. All these values should be carefully considered and agreed to by both parties. The values placed on tenant's labor and management and unpaid family labor are also subject to negotiation and will greatly influence the tenant's share. Most of the other values can be easily obtained from either the landlord's or tenant's past records with adjustments made for expected future price changes.

This example has a cost sharing very close to the assumed 50-50 sharing of production. It may be so close that neither party feels any adjustments are necessary. If the cost shares are substantially different, one of two methods can be used to make adjustments. First, the party contributing the smaller part of the costs can agree to furnish more of the capital items or pay for more of

Table 14-4 Determining Shares under a Crop Share Lease

Item of Expense	(A) Estimated Total Value	(B) Estimated Interest Rate	ESTIMATED ANNUAL COST		
			(C) Whole Farm	(D) Landlord's Share	(E) Tenant's Share
	Dollars	Percent	Dollars	Dollars	Dollars
Interest Charges:					
1. Land and buildings	400,000	8	32,000	32,000	
2. Tractor and workstock	50,000	9	4,500		4,500
3. Machinery & equipment	40,000	9	3,600		3,600
4. Productive livestock					
5. Feed and Supplies					
6. Other					
7.					
Farm Operation Expenses:					
8. Labor:					
(a) Tenant, Labor and Management			12,000		12,000
(b) Landlord, Labor and Management			1,000	1,000	
(c) Unpaid family			1,500		1,500
(d) Hired			2,000		2,000
9. Repairs:					
(a) Buildings, fences, etc.			1,500	1,500	
(b) Machinery			3,000		3,000
10. Depreciation:					
(a) Buildings, fences, etc.			2,500	2,500	
(b) Tractor & workstock			8,000		8,000
(c) Machinery			6,000		6,000
11. Tractor fuel			2,000		2,000
12. Machine work hired					
13. Seed purchased			1,200	600	600
14. Fertilizer and lime			6,000	3,000	3,000
15. Other crop expense			2,000	1,000	1,000
16. Feed purchased					
17. Other livestock expense					
18. Insurance:					
(a) Buildings			500	500	
(b) Personal property			400		400
19. Taxes:					
(a) Land and Buildings			1,500	1,500	
(b) Personal property			600		600
20. Miscellaneous					
21. Total Interest Charges and Farm Operating Expenses			91,800	43,600	48,200
22. Percent Contributed			100%	47.5 %	52.5 %

the variable costs. Appropriate adjustments can be made to make the cost sharing 50-50 to correspond with the production shares.

If the calculated cost shares are too far from the planned production shares, it may be difficult to make the necessary adjustments in cost shares. As a second alternative, the production shares can be changed to 60-40 or some other division to more nearly match the cost shares. This should include changing the cost sharing on the variable inputs to the same ratio to prevent the inefficiencies discussed earlier. Whichever alternative is used to match the cost and production shares, the final result should have the tenant and landlord sharing farm income in the same proportion as they contribute to the total cost of production.

SUMMARY

The decision to buy or lease land is an important one which will affect the financial condition of the business for many years. Capital availability, personal goals, land availability, and other factors will influence the decision. Land has been a good investment in the past as land prices have more than kept pace with inflation. However, purchasing land requires a strong capital position and adequate cash flow potential to make interest and principal payments on any loan. In spite of high land prices, a larger proportion of farmers own all the land they operate, and a smaller proportion are full tenants than in the past. A mixture of owned and leased land exists in many farm and ranch businesses.

Leasing arrangements can take many forms with cash rent, crop share, and livestock share being the more common types of leases. Each lease type has advantages and disadvantages to both the tenant and landlord in terms of the capital position of each party, the amount of price and yield risk to be shared, the farm type, and the desires and goals of each party. The final choice of lease type and rental rate may depend on the relative bargaining position of the landlord and tenant. Share leases should provide for the sharing of income in the same proportion as each party contributes to the total cost of production.

QUESTIONS FOR REVIEW AND FURTHER THOUGHT

1 List as many reasons as you can to explain why people buy land. Would your list or the importance of each reason be different for an operating farmer than for a nonfarm investor?
2 Using the capitalization method, how much could you afford to pay for an acre of land with an estimated net return of $70 per year if you wanted a 6 percent return on your investment? A 10 percent return?
3 Use the data in Table 14-1 to calculate the farm's value if machinery fixed cost and labor were both zero. How would you explain why farmers buying land to add to their existing operation are sometimes willing to pay a premium if the additional land can be farmed without any additional machinery or labor?
4 Why is a cash flow analysis important in a land purchase decision?
5 What common goals and conflicting goals might exist between a tenant and landlord when negotiating a lease?
6 List three advantages and disadvantages of each lease type for both the tenant and the landlord.
7 Suggest some changes in costs in Table 14-4 which would help make the cost shares closer to 50-50.

REFERENCES

American Society of Farm Managers and Rural Appraisers: *Rural Appraisal Manual*, 4th ed., Stipes Publishing Co., Champaign, Ill., 1974.

Davis, K. C., and Cecil D. Maynard: *The Oklahoma Farm Lease Agreement,* Oklahoma State University Extension Facts No. 121.

Kletke, Darrel D., and James S. Plaxico: "Farm Land Profitability and Feasibility Appraisals: New Concepts and Procedures," *Journal of the American Society of Farm Managers and Rural Appraisers,* October 1978, pp. 51–58.

Osburn, Donald D., and Kenneth C. Schneeberger: *Modern Agriculture Management,* Reston Publishing Co., Reston, Va., 1978, chap. 17.

Reiss, Franklin J.: "Decision Making in the Farmland Market," *Journal of the American Society of Farm Managers and Rural Appraisers,* October 1976, pp. 35–43.

Reiss, F. J.: *Farm Leases for Illinois,* Illinois Cooperative Extension Service Circular 960, 1972, revised.

Stoneberg, E. G.: *Improving Your Farm Lease Contract,* Iowa Cooperative Extension Service, FM 1564, 1968.

Wise, James O.: "Some Needed Modificatons to the Capitalization of Income Approach to Farm Appraisal," *Journal of the American Society of Farm Managers and Rural Appraisers,* April 1977, pp. 42–45.

OKLAHOMA FARM LEASE AGREEMENT

I. NAMES OF PARTIES AND DESCRIPTION OF PROPERTY.

This lease is entered into this _____ day of_____, 19_____, between

_____, landlord, of_____
                                                                    ADDRESS

and _____, tenant, of _____
                                                                    ADDRESS

hereinafter called the landlord and tenant respectively, under the terms and conditions that follow, a farm of

approximately _____ acres, situated in _____ county, Oklahoma, and described as follows:

II. TERM OF LEASE

The term of this lease shall be _____ year (s) from _____ _____, 19_____,
                                                                    MONTH   DAY

to _____ _____, 19_____, and this lease shall continue in effect from year to year
        MONTH   DAY

thereafter until written notice of termination is given by either party to the other on or before the _____
                                                                                                            DAY

day of _____, before the expiration of this lease or any renewal thereof.
            MONTH

III. RENTAL RATES AND ARRANGEMENTS (Options not applicable to be stricken)

Option A. *Crop Share Rent*

As rent the tenant agrees to pay or give shares or quantities of the following crops:

	Crop	Approximate No. Acres	Landlord's share	Tenant's share	Distribution of landlord's share
1.					
2.					
3.					
4.					

Option B. *Livestock Share Rent.*

As rent the tenant agrees to pay or give shares or quantities of the following livestock:

	Kind	Approximate No. to be kept on farm	Landlord's share	Tenant's share	Distribution of Increase
1.					
2.					
3.					
4.					
Note:					

Option C. *Cash Rent*

As rent or partial rent for the farm, the tenant agrees to pay the total sum of _____ dollars

($_____) per year. Cash rent will be paid at (place) _____, _____,

and as follows: (time) _____.

IV. FARM OPERATION.

A. The necessary equipment shall be furnished and farm operating expenses divided between the landlord and tenant as follows:

Equipment	Furnished by		Operating Expenses	Proportionate Share	
	Landlord	Tenant		Landlord	Tenant
All Equipment			All Operating Expenses		
Exceptions			Exceptions		

Note:

V. CONSERVATION AND IMPROVED FARMING PRACTICES:

A. *Soil Conservation District Plan for Farm.* The farm is covered in a Cooperative agreement between the

landlord and the _____ Soil Conservation District, and the tenant agrees to operate the farm in accordance with the complete soil conservation and land use prepared under the said cooperative agreement.

B. *Conservation and/or other practices.* Payments which can be earned by participation in the Government Farm Programs shall be carried out as follows:

Practice and Extent	Contributions		Share of Government Payments	
	Landlord	Tenant	Landlord	Tenant
1.				
2.				
3.				
4.				

C. *Other Improved Practices*: Other improved farming practices which the landlord and tenant agree will be mutually beneficial to both parties:

Practices and Extent   Contributions by landlord

1. _____   _____

2. _____   _____

3. _____   _____

4. _____   _____

VI. IMPROVEMENTS AND REPAIRS

A. The landlord agrees to furnish materials for normal maintenance and repairs to maintain the farm in its customary condition. The tenant will furnish ordinary labor and haul the materials for these repairs, it being mutually agreed that skilled labor will be provided by the landlord.

B. Additional major improvements to be provided by the landlord are as follows:

Kind	Date

C. Construction and Removal of Fixtures by Tenant: With the written consent of the landlord, the tenant may add improvements at his own expense. He shall have the right to remove them even though they are legally fixtures, but shall have no right to compensation for them except as mutually agreed.

D. Compensation to Tenant for Unexhausted Value of Improvements: In event of termination of this lease, the tenant shall be entitled to payment for the unexhausted value of his contribution to the cost of improvements made with the consent of the landlord according to the following schedule:

Proportion remaining unexhausted after:

Improvement	1 Year	2 Years	3 Years	4 Years	5 Years
Rock Phosphate					
Ground Limestone					
Terraces					

VII. RECORDS.

Records on all matters of joint interest shall be kept by the tenant and shall be available to the landlord upon request. The records shall specify the following items:

A. _____   C. _____

B. _____   D. _____

VII. NONPARTNERSHIP AGREEMENT

This lease does not give rise to a partnership. Neither party shall have authority to bind the other without his written consent.

IX. RIGHT OF ENTRY.

The landlord shall have the right, in person or by agent, to enter upon the farm for inspections, repairs, or improvements. In case this lease is not to be renewed, the landlord or the incoming tenant shall have the right before it expires to do plowing or other work on the farm when doing so will cause no damage or interference to the present tenant.

X. ARBITRATION.

If parties to this lease cannot reach an agreement on any matter, or problem, the question shall be submitted to an Arbitration Committee. This committee shall be composed of three disinterested persons, one selected by each party hereto and the third by the two thus selected.

XI. IT IS MUTUALLY AGREED THAT

(a) This lease shall bind and shall inure to the benefits of the heirs, executors, administrators, and assigns of both parties.

(b) If either party willfully neglects or refuses to carry out any material provision, the other party shall have the right, in addition to compensation for damage, to terminate the lease. He shall do so by written notice on the party at fault, specifying the violations of the agreement. If violations are not corrected within 30 days, the lease shall be terminated.

XII. ADDITIONAL AGREEMENTS AND MODIFICATIONS:

Any additions to this contract or changes therein shall be in writing, and when so signed and executed before witnesses and attached hereto shall become a part hereof.

XIII. In testimony whereof witness our hands at_____, Oklahoma, on this_____

day of _____, 19_____ A. D.

Witnesses as to both signatures,

_____   _____ (Seal)
                                                (Landlord)

_____   _____ (Seal)
                                                (Tenant)

Chapter 15

Labor Management

CHAPTER OBJECTIVES

1 To outline the characteristics of agricultural labor and the factors which affect its use and cost

2 To discuss the economics of labor use for different situations regarding the type and amount of labor available

3 To illustrate the methods and procedures for measuring labor efficiency

4 To suggest ways to improve labor efficiency

5 To emphasize the importance of managing hired labor including hiring procedures, training, and improving labor retention

Labor has been one of the few and perhaps the only agricultural input (with the exception of draft horses and mules) whose use has declined substantially over time. There has been a steady decline in farm labor use since the 1930s, and the total change has been dramatic. Many factors have contributed to this decline, including the decrease in the number of farm operators whose labor is included in the total.

The decline in the number of farm operators is only one of the reasons for the decline in agricultural labor. Mechanization and new technology in many forms have contributed to the decline and have allowed agricultural production to increase in spite of the decrease in labor. Energy in the form of electrical and mechanical devices has replaced much of the physical energy provided by labor in the past. A relatively greater amount of the labor input on today's farms is spent operating, supervising, and monitoring these devices and less on physical effort. This change in the tasks performed by agricultural labor explains much of the increased emphasis on the quality, skills, and training of the labor force.

Table 15-1 documents the changes in labor and tractor use on United States farms since 1950. In 28 years, labor use has declined to less than one-third of what it was in 1950, while mechanical power has been increasing. The number of tractors peaked in about 1965, but the total horsepower used has continued to increase. Fewer but more powerful tractors have been the trend since the mid-1960s.

The mere availability of new technology such as larger tractors does not adequately explain its rapid and widespread adoption. There has to be an economic justification before farmers will use any new technology or it will simply "sit on the shelf." However, much of the new technology has been adopted as a substitute for labor. Larger tractors and equipment have reduced labor requirements, herbicides have replaced most hand hoeing, and mechanical harvesters have replaced a large amount of hand harvesting. Adoption of new technology can be explained by the input substitution principle discussed in Chapter 2.

Input substitution occurs because of a change in the physical marginal rates of substitution and/or a change in the relative prices of inputs. Both factors have been important in the substitution of capital-using technology for labor in agriculture. Marginal rates of substitution change as the new or improved technology alters the shape of the relevant isoquant to encourage the use of less labor and more of the new technology. Much of the new technology requires a capital investment, making the relevant prices the price of capital (the interest rate) and the wage rate for labor. Since 1950 the wage rate for hired farm labor has increased over 400 percent while interest rates have in-

Table 15-1 Comparison of Labor and Tractor Power Use on United States Farms (1950–1977)

Year	Labor (million hrs)	Tractors	
		Number (thousands)	Total horsepower (millions)
1950	15,137	3,394	93
1955	12,808	4,345	126
1960	9,795	4,688	153
1965	7,335	4,787	176
1970	5,896	4,619	203
1975	4,990	4,469	222
1977	4,659	4,402	232

Source: Changes in Farm Production and Efficiency, 1977, U.S. Department of Agriculture Statistical Bulletin 612, November 1978.

creased by approximately 50 percent. While both prices have increased, labor has become relatively more expensive than capital, changing the price ratio in favor of using more capital and less labor.

This substitution of capital for labor in production agriculture has had an important effect on labor productivity or output per labor hour. As shown in Figure 15-1, output per labor hour has increased rather sharply and fairly steadily since 1967. This increase is particularly impressive when contrasted with the same values for all nonfarm businesses as is done in Figure 15-1. The increase in farm labor productivity further emphasizes the role new technology has played in permitting fewer farm workers to produce an increasing amount of agricultural products.

CHARACTERISTICS OF AGRICULTURAL LABOR

A discussion of agricultural labor must recognize its unique characteristics which affect its use and management on farms. Labor is a continuous flow input, meaning the service it provides becomes available hour by hour and day by day. It cannot be stored for later use and must be used as it becomes available or it is lost. One month's labor supply cannot be placed in storage for use the following month along with that month's labor. This characteristic

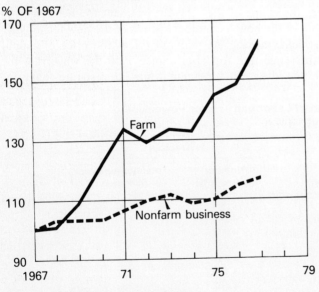

OUTPUT PER MAN-HOUR, FARM
AND NONFARM BUSINESS

1977 preliminary. Source: Bureau of Labor Statistics.

USDA   NEG. ESCS 8858-C-78 (10)

Figure 15-1 Change in farm labor productivity. (*Economic, Statistical and Cooperative Service, U.S. Department of Agriculture.*)

emphasizes the need for a manager to provide productive, year-round work for full-time employees to take advantage of the continuous flow of labor services.

Full-time labor is also a "lumpy" or "indivisible" input, meaning it is available only in whole and indivisible units. Part-time and hourly labor is often used, but a majority of agricultural labor is provided by full-time, year-round employees. If labor is available only on a full-time basis, the addition or loss of an employee is a major change in the labor supply on a farm with only a few employees. For example, a farmer hiring the first employee is increasing the labor supply by 100 percent, and the second employee represents a 50 percent increase. A problem facing a growing business is how to time and finance properly the acquisition of the additional resources needed to keep a new worker fully employed. When other resources such as land and machinery also come in "lumpy" units, it becomes very difficult to organize a business to prevent a shortage or excess of one or more resources.

The operator and other family members provide all or a large part of the labor used on many farms and ranches. This labor does not generally receive a direct cash wage; so its cost and value can be easily overlooked or ignored. However, as with all resources, there is an opportunity cost on operator and family labor which can be a large part of the total fixed cost in a whole farm plan. Compensation for operator and family labor is received indirectly through expenditures for family living expenses. This indirect wage or salary may vary widely, particularly for nonessential items, as net farm income varies from year to year. Cash income must first go to pay the fixed cash expenses of the farm business.

The human factor is another characteristic distinguishing labor from other resources. If an individual is treated as an inanimate object, productivity and efficiency suffer. The hopes, fears, ambitions, likes, dislikes, worries, and personal problems of both the owner/operator and employees must be considered in any labor management plan. Farm managers supervising several employees would find training in psychology, sociology, and personnel management very useful, but it is generally missing from their education.

ECONOMICS OF LABOR USE

An important principle in labor use is to keep all labor fully and productively employed throughout the year. This is often difficult in agriculture because of the seasonal nature of many enterprises. For example, labor requirements may exceed available labor during the months when planting, harvesting, calving, and farrowing take place. Longer workdays, overtime for hired employees, or temporary help may be necessary to perform these required tasks on time. At other times of the year there may be an excess labor supply.

A chart similar to the one in Figure 15-2 is useful for improving labor utilization. This labor profile, or calendar of operations, shows the total monthly labor requirements for all farm enterprises and the monthly labor provided by the farm operator and from the addition of a full-time employee.

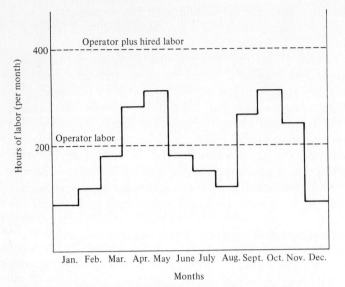

Figure 15-2 Profile of labor requirements and availability.

The farm operator in this example has a problem not uncommon on many farms and ranches. Operator labor will not meet the requirements in several months, but the addition of a full-time employee results in large amounts of excess labor during several months.

If the employee is not hired, the peak labor requirements will have to be met by part-time labor or hiring some field work done on a custom basis. Another alternative would be to study a change in the enterprise combination. A different combination might cause the labor requirements to be more evenly distributed during the year. However, a partial or total budgeting analysis should be performed to be sure profit would not be reduced by more than the cost of the additional labor.

Hiring a full-time employee more than meets the peak monthly labor requirements but results in considerable excess labor. In this situation, some expansion of present enterprises or the addition of new enterprises should be considered to take advantage of the available labor. However, capital limitations may prevent the acquisition of the other resources, and budgeting procedures should be used to confirm the profitability of any planned expansion.

The economic principles studied in Chapters 2 and 3 are also useful in managing labor use and allocation. Selection and application of the appropriate principle depends upon the nature of the available labor supply.

Labor Fixed but Plentiful   The total labor supply of the operator and/or full-time employees may be fixed but not fully utilized. If this labor is being paid a fixed sum regardless of the hours worked, there is no *additional* cost for utilizing another hour. Any productive use of otherwise idle labor does not increase labor cost, making the marginal input cost of otherwise idle labor equal to zero. In this situation, labor use should be increased in each activity or enterprise until its marginal value product is zero to equate it with marginal input cost.

If labor has an opportunity cost greater than zero from either leisure or off-farm employment, the marginal value product in each use should be equated with the opportunity cost. Any remaining labor should then go to the alternative use, be it hunting, fishing, or off-farm employment, whichever has the highest opportunity cost in terms of earnings or personal satisfaction. In this application, the opportunity cost might also be a reservation price. This is the minimum acceptable earning rate or marginal value product, and whenever marginal earnings are below this value, the individual would choose leisure over work.

Labor Variable but Plentiful   When the manager can hire an unlimited amount of labor on an hourly or monthly basis, its use should be analyzed like any other variable input. The economic rule for selecting the profit-maximizing input level is applicable, and labor should be hired until its marginal value product equals its marginal input cost or the wage rate. This decision rule applies to labor hired for any and all uses. It is important to include the cost of any extras or fringe benefits in the wage rate, as these items affect the marginal input cost.

Limited Labor   If the total labor available is less than the amount necessary to equate marginal value product and marginal input cost in all uses, the equal marginal principle should be used to allocate labor between alternative uses. Profit from the limited labor supply will be maximized when labor is allocated between alternative uses in such a way that the marginal value products of the last hour used in each alternative are all equal.

GOVERNMENT REGULATIONS AND LABOR USE

Federal and state regulations affecting the employment of agricultural labor have become an important factor in labor management. They have increased in number in recent years, and this increase is expected to continue. The net effect of these regulations is to increase the cost of hired labor through higher wages and fringe benefits, increases in required labor records, and additional investments for safety and environmental protection.

It is not possible to list and describe all the federal regulations pertaining to agricultural labor in a few pages. In addition, state labor regulations vary from state to state, all have been and will continue to be revised, and they will probably increase in number. Only the more important and general regulations will be described here.

Minimum Wage Law   All agricultural employers who use more than 500 person-days of labor in any calendar quarter of the preceding year must pay the federal minimum wage. The minimum wage has been increasing over time and is \$3.35 per hour effective January 1, 1981. However, further increases are likely, and employers should carefully monitor future legislation to ensure compliance with any changes. Workers paid on a weekly, monthly, or piecework basis are also covered under the minimum wage law. Employers are required to keep detailed payroll records to prove compliance with minimum wage legislation.

Social Security   Employers must withhold social security or FICA (Federal Insurance Contributions Act) taxes from their employee's cash wages and match the employee tax with an equal amount. This regulation applies to farmers with one or more employees if the employee was paid \$150 or more in cash wages during the year *or* the employee worked 20 or more days for cash wages. Social security taxes are not withheld for children under 21 years of age employed by their father or mother or for a wife in the employ of her husband or vice versa.

The tax rate and the wage base, or the maximum earnings subject to this tax, have increased steadily over the years. Both may increase in the future, but current legislation includes the rates in the chart below. It is important to remember that the tax rate and maximum tax figures represent the amounts withheld from the employee's pay, and the employer must match them with an equal amount for remittance to the Internal Revenue Service.

Year	Wage Base (\$)	Tax rate (%)	Maximum tax (\$)
1979	22,900	6.13	1,404
1980	25,900	6.13	1,588
1981	29,700	6.65	1,975

Federal Income Tax Withholding   Farmers have been permitted but not required to withhold federal income taxes from wages paid to agricultural workers. An employee may request in writing that his employer withhold income tax, but acceptance of the request is voluntary on the part of the employer.

Workers' Compensation   This is an insurance system to provide protection for workers injured on the job which also frees the employer from liability for such injuries. Laws regarding workers' compensation insurance for farm employees vary from state to state, but it is required in some. Where required, the employer pays a premium based on a percentage of the total employee payroll.

Unemployment Insurance   This insurance temporarily replaces part of a person's income lost due to unemployment. Farm employers are included if during the current or previous calendar year they (1) employed 10 or more workers in each of 20 or more weeks or (2) paid $20,000 or more in cash wages in any calendar quarter. Benefits are financed by an employer-paid payroll tax.

Occupational Safety and Health Act (OSHA)   This act was designed to assure the health and safety of employees. Farmers employing 10 or fewer persons have been exempt from OSHA regulations, but changes have been proposed. Current requirements for farmer/employers should be carefully checked to ensure compliance.

Other federal and state regulations may apply to some farmer/employers. For example, farmers with 15 or more employees are subject to the Federal Civil Rights Act, which prohibits any discriminatory employment practices. There are also a number of regulations pertaining to the hiring, transporting, and housing of migrant workers. Future changes and additions to labor regulations should be carefully monitored.

MEASURING LABOR EFFICIENCY

Labor efficiency depends not only on the skills and training of the labor used but on the size of the business, enterprises, amount of mechanization, soil types, and many other factors. This makes it difficult and unwise to compare labor efficiency on different types of farms and ranches. Any measure of labor efficiency should be used to compare and evaluate results on farm businesses of approximately the same size and type. Comparing labor efficiency on a small, poorly mechanized crop farm with the same measure on a large, highly mechanized dairy farm is meaningless.

Labor efficiency measures often use the concept of person-years of labor employed. This is a procedure for combining operator, family, and hired labor into a total labor figure which is comparable across farms. The example below shows 21 months of labor

Operator labor	12 months
Family labor	4 months
Hired labor	5 months
Total	21 months

$$21 \div 12 = 1.75 \text{ person-years equivalent}$$

provided from three sources. Dividing this total by 12 converts it into 1.75 person-years, or the equivalent of 1.75 persons working full time during the year.

Labor efficiency measures convert some physical, cost, or income total into a value per person-year. The following measures are commonly used.

Value of Farm Production per Person   This measures the total value of agricultural products produced per person-year equivalent and is found by dividing the value of farm production by the person-year equivalent. This measure of labor efficiency will be affected by business size, type of enterprise, and the amount of machinery and other laborsaving equipment used. However, when farms are grouped by size and type of enterprise, meaningful comparisons can be made, with higher values indicating greater labor efficiency.

Tillable Acres per Person   Dividing the number of tillable or rotated acres in the business by the person-years equivalent gives tillable acres per person. The result will obviously be affected by machinery size, the type of crops being grown, and whether or not any livestock are included in the operation. Higher values indicate more efficient labor use.

Labor Cost per Tillable Acre   This value is found by dividing the total labor cost for a year by the number of tillable or rotated acres. The opportunity cost of operator and family labor is included in total labor cost. This measure will be affected by the same factors as tillable acres per person, with lower values resulting from greater labor efficiency.

Work Units per Person   This is perhaps the best measure of labor efficiency if good work unit standards are available. In some states, work unit standards are available in publications of the state land-grant university or state extension service.[1] The units are often the hours of labor needed per acre for crops or per head for livestock enterprises under average or typical conditions, but other standardized units may be used. Total standard work units required for the actual farm organization can be found by calculating the requirements for each enterprise and summing the results. This value can be used to measure labor efficiency.

One measure of labor efficiency is the work units per person calculated from the equation

$$\text{Work units per person} = \frac{\text{total work units required}}{\text{number of person-years}}$$

The result can be compared against the standard number of work units one person should be able to accomplish in a year. A higher value indicates above-average labor efficiency. An alternative measure of labor efficiency would consist of dividing the total work units required by the total work units available and multiplying the result by 100. This provides an index of labor efficiency, with values above 100 indicating above-average efficiency and vice versa.

The use of standardized work units allows measuring labor efficiency on diversified farms and comparing results between farms of different types. However, differences in farm size and degree of mechanization will still affect any measure of labor efficiency.

Table 15-2 contains some labor efficiency measures for cash grain farms

[1]As an example see *Farm Management Manual*, AE-4426, Department of Agricultural Economics, University of Illinois, January 1977.

Table 15-2   Labor Efficiency by Farm Size for Cash Grain Farms in Northern Illinois, 1977 (Soil Rating 86–100)

Item	Farm size (acres)					
	260–339	340–499	500–649	650–799	800–949	Over 950
Value of farm production per person ($)	66,501	86,152	90,346	100,243	106,914	116,889
Labor cost per tillable acre ($)	35.28	27.21	24.65	23.07	22.14	21.84
Labor cost per dollar of farm production (¢)	14.3	10.9	10.2	9.3	8.9	8.4

Source: 53rd Annual Summary of Illinois Farm Business Records, University of Illinois, Cooperative Extension Service Circular 1162, August 1978.

available in other states and provide a comparison of an individual farm's labor efficiency with an average for the same size and type of farm. An interesting feature of Table 15-2 is the relationship between labor efficiency and farm size. There are economies of size related to the labor input, with the largest farm size showing a considerable advantage over the smallest. However, difference in size is not the full explanation, as the larger farms also have a larger capital investment per person employed, which in part reflects the larger machinery being used.

IMPROVING LABOR EFFICIENCY

Correct use of the economic principles discussed earlier in this chapter is one way to improve labor efficiency, and changing enterprise combinations may also help. Full utilization of available labor was also stressed, as poor utilization will increase the labor cost per unit of output. Figure 15-3 emphasizes this point. If each person can care for up to 75 dairy cows, whatever number of people are employed, the labor cost per cow will be lowest if each is caring for the maximum number. Hiring an additional employee to care for only 10 or 20 additional cows will increase labor cost per cow and per hundredweight of milk. This is another example of the "lumpy" nature of the labor input when only full-time employees are hired. There must be a coordination of labor hiring and purchase of other productive inputs to prevent increases in per unit labor costs.

Labor efficiency can also be improved by increasing the capital investment per worker through the use of larger machinery and other forms of mechanization. However, the objective should be profit maximization and not just increasing labor efficiency at any cost. The principles of input substitution show that substitution of capital for labor cannot continue indefinitely without reducing profit. Marginal rates of substitution and the input prices determine the proper combination. Increasing the capital investment per worker will increase profit only if: (1) total cost is reduced while output remains constant,

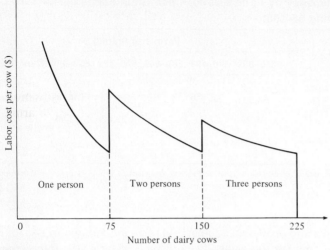

Figure 15-3   Labor cost per dairy cow for different herd sizes.

(2) the labor which is saved can be used to increase output and total business profit, or (3) a combination of the above is used. Partial budgeting can be a useful tool to check the profitability of a proposed capital for labor substitution.

Efforts to simplify working procedures and routines often have high pay-offs in terms of increasing labor efficiency. A stopwatch used to record productive vs. nonproductive time can identify areas where steps and time may be saved. Considerable time can be wasted moving from job to job, bringing tools and other supplies to the work area, opening and closing gates, etc. Changes in the farmstead layout, building design, field size and shape, and the storage site of materials relative to where they will eventually be used can save time and increase labor efficiency. As always, the additional cost of any changes must be weighed against the value and opportunity cost of the labor saved.

Routine tasks such as feeding and caring for livestock should be studied closely for ways to save steps and time. These tasks should be broken down into parts and a series of questions asked about each part. Why is it done? Can it be eliminated? Can several parts of the task be combined? Can it be done at a different time and location? Why is it done this way? Is there a better way? The answer to these questions will help identify any work simplification procedures that can be taken. Too often we become a victim of habit and never question many of our daily routines and working patterns.

Finally, the simple procedure of planning and scheduling work in advance will eliminate wasted time. Annual and daily schedules are both useful. On an annual schedule, tasks which must be done at a specific time can be scheduled in first and those that are not time-specific, such as building repairs and painting, planned for months of slack labor. A daily work schedule can be planned in a few minutes each morning or evening. Time spent organizing the next day's tasks and their order of importance is time well spent.

MANAGING HIRED LABOR

Hired labor is becoming a larger proportion of the total labor supply on farms and ranches. Acquisition, training, and retention of hired workers is a common subject of conversation whenever managers of medium- to large-sized farms get together. Managers are finding that skills in human relations and personnel management are valuable assets because of increasing problems in managing hired labor.

Hiring Labor

Many farmers report they cannot find farm labor to hire and/or they cannot afford to pay the going wage rate. Obviously, the second part of the statement may explain the first part. Equally obvious is the fact that additional labor should not be hired unless it will generate the additional income necessary to pay the extra cost. It is the manager's responsibility to obtain the required information and perform the budgeting analysis needed to determine if it will be profitable to pay the going wage rate for additional labor.

A competitive basic wage rate is the first essential in a successful labor hiring program. The actual cash wages are important, but the prospective employee should be made aware of any fringe benefits and their value. In the final analysis, it is the spendable income left after food, shelter, and salary deductions which should be compared against comparable figures in other employment. Fringe benefits such as housing, garden space, meat, and milk will make a lower cash wage for farm work competitive with nonfarm employment with a higher cash salary.

A Louisiana study[2] indicated total annual salary depended on (1) amount of paid vacation, (2) annual hours worked, (3) education and skill levels, (4) tenure, (5) type of farm, and (6) marital status. This same study showed fringe benefits and incentive payments averaged from 17 to 31 percent of total wages, depending on farm size and type. An Oklahoma study[3] found fringe benefits and incentive payments were from 37 to 47 percent of total wages for employees on an incentive program.

These studies emphasize the importance of fringe benefits and incentive programs in the total wage package. Prospective employees should be made aware of their value so they can fairly compare farm and nonfarm employment.

[2]W. F. Woolf and R. Craig Brown, *Wages and Other Economic Factors Affecting Recruitment, Retention and Productivity of Full-Time Hired Farm Workers*, D.A.E. Research Report 506, Department of Agricultural Economics, Louisiana State University, September 1976.

[3]John Wolfe, Michael Boehlje, and Vernon Eidman, *An Economic Evaluation of Wage Rates and Incentive Agreements for Full-Time Hired Labor on Oklahoma Farms*, Oklahoma Agricultural Experiment Station Bulletin B-713, April 1974.

However, it is important that everyone agree on their value, as employers are prone to value fringe benefits higher than employees. For this reason, some farm employers are dispensing with some or all of the fringe benefits and increasing the basic cash salary. Where fringe benefits are provided, it is advisable periodically to give employees a list of them along with their value.

Training Hired Labor

Farm and ranch managers often hire unskilled labor and expect the employee to perform highly skilled tasks in livestock management and with expensive machinery. The result is often disappointment, frustration, high repair bills, poor labor productivity, and employee dissatisfaction.

Studies of employment practices on farms and ranches show little evidence of formalized training programs for new employees. Even a skilled employee will need some instruction on the practices and routines to be followed. Employees with lesser skills should receive complete instructions and proper supervision during a training period, as satisfactory performance cannot be expected without proper training. Employers need to develop the patience, understanding, and time necessary to train and supervise new employees. Unfortunately in production agriculture, the training period may need to last as long as a year or until the new employee has had a chance to perform all the tasks in a complete cycle of crop and livestock production.

Periodic training may be necessary for even long-time employees. The adoption of new technology in the form of larger machinery, new chemicals, feed additives, seed varieties, and the introduction of a new enterprise may require additional training for all employees. Extension short courses, field days, and other short-term educational programs available in the community can be used for employee training. Participation in these activities will not only improve employees' skills but will also improve their self-esteem.

Labor Retention

Hiring and training new employees is costly in terms of both time and money. If labor turnover is high, these costs can become excessive, and labor efficiency will be low. Employers should be aware of the reasons for poor employee retention and take action to improve it.

A study of labor management practices on New York dairy farms[4] asked employees to list the disadvantages of their work. In order, the reported disadvantages were long hours and little time off, and early morning/late evening work was tied with low pay for third place. Other studies indicate more farm workers quit because of poor working conditions, including poor personal relationships with the employer, than because of poor pay. These studies confirm the existence of personal goals other than obtaining the highest pay.

[4]David M. Kohl, *Labor Management Practices on Selected New York Dairy Farms*, A.E. Res. 77-10, Department of Agricultural Economics, Cornell University, Agricultural Experiment Station, May 1977.

Employers, on the other hand, commonly report good pay as the most important factor in labor retention. This disparity indicates farm and ranch employers need to work at improving working conditions and human relationships. While good pay is undoubtedly important, other factors may contribute more to retaining good labor. Overtime pay can help reduce complaints of long hours during rush seasons. A set policy for adequate vacations and time off is important to employees, as is the opportunity to work with good buildings and equipment. Job titles can also be important, as the title "hired hand" contributes little to an employee's personal satisfaction and self-image. Herdsman, crop manager, foreman, and machine operator are examples of titles most people associate with a higher status than hired hand.

Good human relations may be the most important factor in labor management. This includes such things as a friendly attitude, loyalty, trust, mutual respect, the ability to delegate authority, and the willingness to listen to employee suggestions and complaints. Work instructions should be in sufficient detail that both parties know what is to be done, when, and how. We all respond to public praise for a job well done but appreciate receiving criticism and suggestions in private. Unpleasant jobs should be shared by all employees, and all should be treated equally. Employers who reserve the larger air-conditioned tractor for their own use while employees drive smaller tractors without cabs are likely to have labor problems.

Incentive programs and bonuses are often used to supplement base wages, improve labor efficiency and productivity, and help retain good employees. However, bonuses may do little to increase labor productivity, as they are not generally tied to performance. Employees soon come to expect the bonus and consider it part of the basic cash salary. If the size of the bonus is tied to annual profit, an employer may find it difficult actually to decrease the bonus in a poor year after employees have experienced several years with a substantial bonus.

Incentive programs of various kinds have been tried by a number of farm employers with mixed success. Some have continued with them while others have dropped their incentive program after becoming dissatisfied with the results. Incentive programs are intended to increase profit by: (1) reducing employee turnover, (2) increasing employee interest in the job, and (3) increasing productivity. Payments under incentive programs can be based on: (1) exceeding some level of physical production for crops and/or livestock, (2) a percentage of gross income, (3) a percentage of net income, (4) equity in or partial ownership of the business, (5) income from some crops or livestock raised by the employee on business property, or (6) a stipulated amount to be received when the employee has worked a specified period of time.

Each type of incentive program has advantages and disadvantages. A program based on physical production may encourage production at any cost and do little to increase profit. The same disadvantage applies to paying a percentage of gross income. Paying a percentage of net income makes an employee cost-conscious but gives the employee knowledge of farm profit which may not be acceptable to an employer. Both 2 and 3 above require complete agreement on exactly how the gross income or net income figures are to be calculated. Alternative 4 is attractive to some employees but requires the owner to give up some equity in the business and can create problems when and if an employee quits or retires. Other advantages and disadvantages can be listed for each of the possible incentive programs.

A successful incentive program is the result of carefully specifying the desired objectives. Some alternatives are more useful than others for certain objectives. However, there are some basic principles which will increase the effectiveness of any incentive program.[5]

1   The program should be simple and easily understood by the employee.
2   The program should be based on factors largely within the control of the employee.
3   The program should aim at rewarding work that is in the best interest of the employer.
4   The program should provide a cash return large enough to provide motivation for improved performance.
5   The incentive payment should be made promptly or as soon after the completion of work as possible.
6   The incentive program should be written, contain provisions for arbitration of misunderstanding, and indicate the duration of the program.
7   The incentive program should set forth employee responsibility and be administered equitably.
8   The incentive payment should not be considered as a substitute for competitive base wages and good labor relations.

After a proposed incentive program is developed and before it is put into effect, the potential size of the incentive payment should be calculated. This can be done by applying the proposed payment procedure to past production and financial records and also by projecting this information into the future. Some incentive programs have been discontinued because they were too expensive to the employer or provided so little cash payment to the employee that they were ineffective in meeting the objectives.

SUMMARY

Labor remains an important resource in the production of agricultural products even though total agricultural labor is declining. Fewer farms and ranches and increased mechanization have lowered the total labor required to produce an increased amount of food and fiber in this country. The end result has been a continual increase in labor productivity. These changes should continue as

[5]John Wolfe, Michael Boehlje, and Vernon Eidman, *An Economic Evaluation of Wage Rates and Incentive Agreements for Full-Time Hired Labor on Oklahoma Farms,* Oklahoma Agricultural Experiment Station Bulletin B-713, April 1974.

farm numbers continue to decline and technology provides an even wider array of new products and techniques.

A relative increase in the use of hired labor and increasing labor costs place labor management and use in a new and different position. These trends are also expected to continue. Wage rates, incentives, bonuses, fringe benefits, personnel management, and labor supervision and training will demand more of the farm manager's time in the future.

QUESTIONS FOR REVIEW AND FURTHER THOUGHT

1 Why are the training and skills needed by agricultural workers greater today than in the past?
2 Observe an actual routine farm chore such as milking or feeding livestock. What suggestions would you have for simplifying the chore to save labor? Would your suggestions increase costs? Would they be profitable?
3 Why are there wide variations in the monthly labor requirements on a crop farm and less variation on a dairy farm?
4 Assume the standard work unit for corn production is 4 hours per acre and 20 hours per litter of hogs. What is the number of standard work units per person for a farm with 400 acres of corn and 100 litters of hogs that uses 1.3 person-years of labor per year? How would you judge the labor efficiency on this farm if the standard work units per person per year are 2,500 hours?
5 Give as many reasons as you can to explain why the labor cost per acre is generally less for larger farms than for smaller.
6 What type of incentive program would be most effective on a dairy farm if the objective was to increase milk production per cow? If the objective was to retain the better employees for a longer time?

REFERENCES

Barnard, C. S., and J. S. Nix: *Farm Planning and Control,* Cambridge University Press, Cambridge, 1972, chap. 5.
Castle, Emery N., Manning H. Becker, and Frederick J. Smith: *Farm Business Management,* 2d ed, The Macmillan Company, New York 1972, chap. 13
Erven, Bernard, et al.: *Ohio Farm Labor Handbook,* Ohio State University Cooperative Extension Service, July 1978.
Herbst, J. H.: *Farm Management Principles, Budgets, Plans,* 4th ed., Stipes Publishing Co., Champaign, Ill., 1976, chap. 8.
Kohl, David M.: *Labor Management Practices on Selected New York Dairy Farms,* A.E. Res. 77-10, Department of Agricultural Economics, Cornell University, Agricultural Experiment Station, May 1977.
Wolfe, John, et al.: *An Economic Evaluation of Wage Rates and Incentive Agreements for Full-Time Hired Labor on Oklahoma Farms,* Oklahoma Agricultural Experiment Station Bulletin B-713, April 1974.
Woolf, W. F., and R. Craig Brown: *Wages and Other Economic Factors Affecting Recruitment, Retention and Productivity of Full-Time Hired Farm Workers,* D.A.E. Research Report 506, Department of Agricultural Economics, Louisiana State University, September 1976.

Chapter 16

Machinery Management

CHAPTER OBJECTIVES

1 To note the importance of machinery use and machinery management on the commercial farms of today

2 To identify the fixed and variable costs associated with owning and operating machinery

3 To demonstrate procedures for calculating machinery costs

4 To show the relationships between per hour and/or per acre machinery costs and the amount of annual use

5 To discuss some factors important in machinery selection including size, timeliness of operation, used machinery, leasing, and custom hiring

6 To suggest leasing and custom hiring as alternatives to machinery ownership

7 To outline methods and procedures for increasing the efficiency of machinery use

Mechanization in its many forms has had a dramatic effect on costs, production levels, production techniques, and labor requirements in United States agriculture. The latter effect was discussed in the last chapter. Table 15-1 documented the increase in tractor use, showing a nearly one-third increase in the number of tractors and a 150 percent increase in total horsepower since 1950. With the increase in tractor sizes, the size of other machinery has increased to keep pace. Tractor-drawn machinery continues to get bigger and wider, with 12-row planters, 28-foot tandem disks, and 40-foot field cultivators being widely used but certainly not the largest being used.

Discussions on the increased use of mechanization in agriculture are often in terms of tractors and other equipment used in crop production. Perhaps no less dramatic has been the increased use of other types of power and equipment in livestock production and materials handling. Physical labor requirements have been reduced in all areas by the use of small engines, electric motors, augers, elevators, conveyors, etc. Grain handling, manure collection and disposal, livestock feeding, feed grinding and mixing, and hay handling have all been greatly mechanized to reduce labor requirements and costs.

Not only has machinery use been increasing in both number and size but it has been increasing relative to other farm inputs. Figure 16-1 shows the changes in the use of selected farm inputs since 1967. During this time period only the use of agricultural chemicals has increased faster than the use of power and machinery. As discussed in the last chapter, the decline in the relative importance of the labor input is partially explained by the rapid increase in power and machinery use.

IMPORTANCE OF MACHINERY MANAGEMENT

Machinery and motor vehicles represent the second largest investment on our nation's farms and ranches. Only the investment in real estate (land and build-

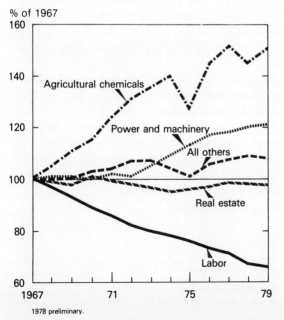

1978 preliminary.

Figure 16-1 Changes in use of selected farm inputs, 1967–1979. (*Economic, Statistical and Cooperative Service, U.S. Department of Agriculture.*)

ings) is higher. This large investment in machinery presents an opportunity for the manager perhaps to greatly increase profit by improving the efficiency of machinery use, reducing machinery costs, or increasing production from the available machinery.

Machinery costs are a large part of the total cost of production for crops, and therefore the potential exists for substantial cost savings in this area. Crop enterprise budgets often show that 50 percent or more of the total cost of production can be accounted for by costs which are directly related to machinery, equipment, motor vehicles, and the labor to operate them. If the land charge is omitted, this percentage will be even higher. Irrigated crop production increases both the absolute and relative machinery costs because of the wells, engines, pumps, and water distribution equipment and the additional labor required to monitor and operate this equipment.

Machinery and equipment costs in livestock production are a smaller percentage of total costs than for crop production but are still significant. They are becoming increasingly important in livestock production because of the increased use of mechanical devices for feed grinding and distribution, manure handling, and environmental control in livestock confinement buildings and feedlots.

Machinery management should be an important area of managerial concern because machinery costs can be a large part of the total cost of operating a farm business. A manager may also have greater control over these costs than over land and building costs, as machinery is typically purchased and sold more frequently. Control over machinery costs is accomplished by efficient use and management decisions regarding the number, type, and size of machinery to be used, purchasing new or used machinery, and the extent to which machinery requirements arc met by leasing machines or hiring custom operators.

Machinery management is the application of decision-making principles to a specific resource, machinery, with the objective of increasing profits. However, machinery management and use is related to enterprise combinations and the other resources used in the farm business. This makes it difficult to separate a discussion of machinery management completely from an analysis of the total business. The remainder of this chapter will concentrate on the use of economic principles and budgeting in machinery management, but wherever necessary, the relationships between machinery, other resources, and the production enterprises will be mentioned and discussed.

ESTIMATING MACHINERY COSTS

Machinery is costly to purchase, own, and operate. A manager must be able to calculate the cost of owning and operating a machine, as good machinery management requires a knowledge of these costs and how they are related to machinery use. It is easy to underestimate machinery costs, as a large proportion may be noncash and therefore easy to overlook.

Both fixed and variable costs are important in machinery management. Machinery fixed costs are often called *ownership or overhead costs,* and variable costs may be referred to as *operating or running costs.* Fixed and variable costs were discussed in Chapter 3 but will be reviewed in the following sections as they apply to estimating machinery costs.

Fixed Costs

Fixed or ownership costs are those which do not change with changes in the annual use of the machine. They begin with the purchase of the machine, continue as long as it is owned, and cannot be changed by the manager except by selling the machine. For this reason it is important to know what the resulting fixed costs will be before a machine is purchased.

Fixed costs are a large part of the total cost of machinery ownership and use. They can represent 60 to 80 percent of the total annual costs, with the smaller figure applicable to motorized machinery and the larger to tractor-drawn implements. As a very general rule of thumb, annual fixed costs will be about 20 percent of the original cost, depending on the type of machine, opportunity cost of capital, and the expected useful life. The components of machinery fixed costs are discussed below.

Depreciation   Depreciation is a noncash expense to reflect a loss in value from age, wear, tear, and obsolescence. It is also an accounting procedure to recover the cost of an asset over time by matching its expense against revenue. Since most of the depreciation is expected from aging and obsolescence and is affected little by annual use, it is considered a fixed cost.

Depreciation can be calculated using either the straight-line, declining balance, or sum-of-the-year's digits method. However, we are interested in finding the average annual depreciation in order to calculate the average annual fixed cost of owning the machine. For this reason, the straight-line method is used, as it gives the same depreciation for each year.

It is important to remember that depreciation is an accounting procedure to estimate the decline in value. The results may or may not reflect the actual decline in market value depending on use, inflation rates, maintenance policy, and other factors. However, a consideration of these factors in the selection of a useful life and salvage value will increase the accuracy of the estimated depreciation.

Interest   Investing in a machine ties up capital and prevents it from being used for an alternative investment. Capital has an opportunity cost, and this cost is part of the actual or true cost of machine ownership. The opportunity cost used for machinery capital should reflect the expected return in its next best alternative use, which will depend on the relative shortage or abundance of capital and any risk considerations in its use. A conservative opportunity cost would be the interest rate on savings accounts or the current interest rate on borrowed capital.

The interest component of annual fixed costs is calculated from the equation[1]

$$\text{Interest} = \frac{\text{cost} + \text{salvage value}}{2} \times \text{opportunity cost interest rate}$$

Since the machine is declining in value over time and depreciation is also being charged, its average value is used to determine the interest charge and not its purchase cost. The first part of the equation gives the average value of the machine over its life, or its value at midlife, which is then used to find the interest charge. This procedure recognizes that capital equal to the full purchase price is not tied up over the entire life, as it is being recovered over time by the depreciation charge.

Taxes   Some states levy a property tax on farm machinery, which is another fixed cost, as it will not change with changes in the annual use of the machine. The actual charge will depend on the evaluation procedure and tax rate in a particular location. Machinery cost studies often use a charge of about 1 percent of the average machine value as an estimate of annual property taxes. This rate would need to be adjusted upward for pickups and trucks to cover the cost of license and any other road use fees.

Insurance   Another fixed cost is an annual charge for insurance to cover the loss of the machine from fire, theft, windstorm damage, and any liability coverage. A charge for insurance should be included in fixed costs even if the owner carries no formal insurance and personally stands the risk. Some loss can be expected over time, and some recognition of this personal risk needs to be included in the total fixed costs. The proper charge for insurance will depend on the amount and type of coverage and insurance rates for a given location. Machinery cost studies estimate the annual insurance charge at 0.4 to 0.6 percent of the machine's average value. This charge will again need to be higher for pickups and trucks because of the higher insurance premiums for property damage, collision, and liability coverage.

Repairs   While repairs are typically listed as a fixed cost, machinery repairs have both a fixed and a variable cost component. Some repairs are often necessary to maintain and get an unused machine back into operating condition, but repair costs will also increase with increases in annual use. Figure 16-2 illustrates this relationship. If the fixed cost component can be estimated, it should be included as part of total fixed costs, with the repairs associated with use allocated to variable costs. Because of the difficulty in dividing repairs into the two components, most machinery cost studies include all repairs as a variable cost. This procedure will be used in this chapter.

[1]This equation only approximates the actual cost but is widely used. For an accurate method of determining the combined depreciation and interest charge which fully includes the time value of money see Easley S. Smith and J. Dale Oliver, *Farm Machinery Performance and Costs,* Virginia Cooperative Extension Service Publication 510, August 1972.

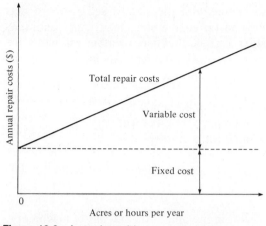

Figure 16-2 Annual machinery repair costs.

Housing Some machinery cost studies include an annual fixed cost for housing the machine. A properly housed machine will have fewer repair bills and may last longer; so the annual repair charge should take into account whether or not the machine will be housed. A housing charge can be estimated by calculating the annual cost per square foot for the machine shed (possibly including a prorated charge for any shop area) and multiplying this by the number of square feet the machine occupies. Cost studies have found annual housing costs to be about 1.5 percent of the average value.

Variable Costs

Variable costs are directly related to use. They are zero if the machine is not used and tend to increase directly with the amount of annual use. Unlike fixed costs, they are under the manager's control either by varying the amount of annual use, by improving efficiency, or by the maintenance program followed.

Repairs As indicated earlier, the annual costs are difficult to estimate, as they will vary with use, machine type, age, preventive maintenance programs, soil type, and enterprise. Some mathematical equations have been developed to estimate average annual repair costs for various machine types and level of annual use.[2] As a rule of thumb, machinery cost studies often use a charge of 3 to 5 percent of new cost as an annual charge for repairs. However, any rule of thumb needs to be used with caution. The best source of information is detailed, on-the-farm records of actual repair costs for each type of machine under the existing use, cropping pattern, and maintenance program.

Fuel and Lubrication Gasoline, diesel fuel, oil, oil filters, and other lubricants are included in this category. These costs will be minor for nonpow-

[2]See American Society of Agricultural Engineers, *1978 Agricultural Engineers Handbook,* or Wendell Bowers, *Modern Concepts of Farm Machinery Management,* Stipes Publishing Co., Champaign, Ill., 1970.

ered equipment, increasing in importance with the size of self-powered machinery. Fuel use per hour will depend on engine size, load, and condition. Farm records can be used to estimate average fuel use, or other estimates are available. Data from the University of Nebraska tractor tests indicate average fuel consumption in gallons per hour is as follows:

Gasoline = 0.06 × maximum rated p.t.o. horsepower
Diesel   = 0.044 × maximum rated p.t.o. horsepower
LP gas   = 0.072 × maximum rated p.t.o. horsepower

Costs for lubricants and filters average about 15 percent of fuel costs for self-powered machines.

Labor   Labor is a necessary factor in the operation and use of machinery, with the amount needed dependent upon the type of operation being performed and the size of the machinery used. Labor costs are generally estimated separately from machinery costs but need to be included in any estimate of the total cost of performing a given machine operation. Machine-related labor costs are often underestimated by including only the time actually spent in operating the machine in the field. The total labor charge should also include time spent fueling, lubricating, repairing, adjusting, and traveling between fields.

Other Variable Costs   Some specialized machines have additional variable costs associated with their use. Items such as twine, baling wire, and bags may need to be included in variable costs.

Cash and Noncash Machinery Costs

Machinery costs can be easily underestimated because a relatively large part of total costs are or may be noncash expenses. Depreciation is always a noncash expense, and part or all of some of the other costs may be noncash expenses. They are easy to overlook, as they do not appear in the checkbook or cash expense ledger.

The following is a breakdown of the various machinery costs into their possible cash and/or noncash categories:

Type of cost	Cash	Noncash
Depreciation		X
Interest on the investment	X	X
Property taxes	X	
Insurance	X	X
Housing	X	X
Repairs and maintenance	X	
Fuel and lubricants	X	
Labor	X	X

Interest may be a cash expense to the extent that interest is being paid on borrowed money, or it may be entirely a noncash expense if the machine was purchased with the owner's equity capital. Insurance may be a cash expense if formal insurance is carried with an insurance company or a noncash expense if the risk is assumed by the owner. In a like manner, labor may be a cash expense if hired labor is employed or a noncash expense if it is furnished by the owner. A complete accounting of all expenses including noncash expenses is necessary for an accurate estimation of total machinery costs.

MACHINE COSTS AND USE

Annual fixed costs are constant regardless of the amount of machine use during the year. Variable costs increase with the amount of use, and they often increase at a constant rate per acre or per hour. Adding fixed and variable costs results in total costs also increasing at a constant rate. These relationships are shown in Figure 16-3a.

For decision-making purposes it is often necessary to express machine costs in terms of the average cost per acre, per hour, or per unit of output. Average fixed costs will decline as the acres, hours, or units of output increase while average variable costs will be constant if the total variable costs increase at a constant rate. Since average total cost is the sum of fixed and variable, it declines like average fixed cost. These relationships are shown in Figure 16-3b, where the vertical distance between the average fixed cost and average total cost curves is constant and equal to average variable cost.

A problem with estimating machinery cost per unit is also evident in Figure 16-3b. Average variable cost is constant regardless of use, but average fixed cost declines continuously. As a result average total cost will depend on the assumed annual use of the machine and will decline as use increases. This

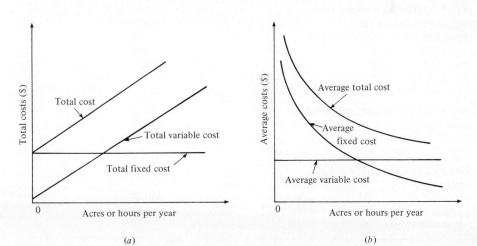

Figure 16-3 Relationships between total and average machinery costs.

makes machinery cost estimates only as accurate as the estimate of annual use. As much effort should go into estimating this value as in estimating the cost components. Again, actual farm records and the use of tractor-hour meters provide useful estimates. Without good records, it is very easy to overestimate actual machine use, particularly for machines with a small annual use.

Examples of Machinery Cost Calculations

Table 16-1 is an example of the steps and procedure used to calculate total machinery costs and average costs per hour, per acre, or per unit of output. The first step is to list the machine's cost and other data needed in the cal-

Table 16-1   Calculating Machinery Costs for a New Combine

Step 1—List basic data
New combine, 20-foot header, 120 hp diesel engine:

Cost	$40,000
Salvage value	$ 8,000
Average value $= \dfrac{\$40,000 + 8,000}{2}$	$24,000
Useful life	8 years
Estimated annual use	250 hrs
Opportunity cost on capital.........................	10 %

Step 2—Calculate fixed costs

Depreciation (straight-line) $= \dfrac{\$40,000 - 8,000}{8 \text{ years}}$	$ 4,000	
Interest $= \dfrac{\$40,000 + 8,000}{2} \times 10\%$	2,400	
Taxes and insurance (1½% of average value)	360	
Total annual fixed costs		$6,760
Fixed costs per hour ($6,760 ÷ 250 hrs)		$27.04

Step 2—Calculate variable costs

Repairs (4% of new cost)	$1,600	
Diesel fuel (0.044 gal/hp-hr at 75¢)	990	
Lubrication and filters (15% of fuel cost)	148	
Labor (300 hrs at $4)*	1,200	
Total annual variable costs		$3,938
Variable cost per hour ($3,938 ÷ 250 hrs)		$15.75

Step 4—Calculate total cost per hour

Fixed cost per hour	$27.04	
Variable cost per hour	$15.75	
Total cost per hour		$42.79

Step 5—Calculate cost per acre
Performance rate:

4 acres per hour ($42.79 ÷ 4 acres)	$10.70
5 acres per hour ($42.79 ÷ 5 acres)	8.56
6 acres per hour ($42.79 ÷ 6 acres)	7.13

*Labor requirements increased by 20 percent for time spent servicing, adjusting, repairing, and traveling between fields.

culations. Total fixed costs are calculated next and converted into average fixed cost per hour of annual use. Housing was not included as a fixed cost in this example. Based on the assumed 250 hours of annual use, the average fixed cost per hour is $27.04. Remember that this value will change if the actual use is different.

Total variable cost and variable cost per hour were calculated next, with labor cost included in this example. The labor requirement was increased by 20 percent over the estimated machine use to account for time required to service, adjust, and repair the machine. Average variable cost per hour was estimated at $15.75. Notice that fuel, lubrication, and filters and labor costs are directly related to hours of use. If repair costs were also directly proportional to hours of use, the average variable cost per hour would be constant regardless of the hours of annual use.

The total cost per hour is estimated at $42.79 based on 250 hours of annual use. This figure can be converted to a cost per acre or per unit of output if the capacity or production per hour is known or can be estimated. In this example, three performance rates are used to show how the cost per acre is affected by different performance rates.

The importance of some of the estimates used in the calculations must be stressed. Estimated hours of annual use affects the cost per hour and therefore the cost per acre. Increasing the hours of annual use will decrease these costs because average fixed cost per hour will be less and vice versa. A manager may wish to calculate cost per hour for several levels of annual use to find the range of costs which may occur as the amount of use varies. This procedure can be used by a custom operator to help determine a per acre or per hour charge which will cover all costs for different amounts of custom work which may be performed during a given year.

The example in Table 16-1 illustrates the tedious and time-consuming effort involved in calculating machinery costs. This is particularly true if costs are desired for a number of machines of different sizes or various amounts of annual use and when using one of the more sophisticated methods of computing repair costs. For this reason, computers are being widely used to compute machinery costs for enterprise budgets and other uses. Once the basic data and program are stored in the computer, estimates of machinery costs can be quickly and easily computed for a wide range of machine types, performance rates, and annual use.

Table 16-2 is an example of machinery costs generated by a computer for a specific crop enterprise budget. They are not shown separately, but tractor costs are included in the costs for each tillage operation. The costs shown are for specific assumptions about machine size, speed, field efficiency, number of tillage operations required, and the crop. All these factors will vary by the farm type and size, soil type and condition, area of the country, and crop. By utilizing a computer, machine costs for different combinations of these factors can be quickly and easily determined and compared.

A different application of a computer to calculate machinery costs is shown in Table 16-3. These costs are for just one machine, a 100-horsepower tractor, but cover a wide range of annual use. The last column shows the typical decline in cost per hour as annual use increases. This is the expected result from spreading the total fixed cost over a greater number of hours.

FACTORS IN MACHINERY SELECTION

One of the more difficult problems in farm management is proper machinery selection. Not only is the selection process complicated by the wide range of types and sizes available, it is also closely related to and dependent upon capital availability, labor requirements and availability, crop and livestock enterprises in the farm plan, and other factors. There is also the need to match the size of tillage equipment properly with tractor sizes to get maximum use of the tractor without overloading it. A few of the factors to be considered in machinery selection will be discussed in this section.

Machinery Size

The basic rule in selecting machinery sizes is to purchase the machine which will perform the required task within the time available at the lowest possible total cost. This will not always result in the purchase of the smallest machine, as labor and other costs must be considered. A first step is to determine the capacity in acres per hour for each possible machine size. The results can be

Table 16-2 Machinery Costs for an Enterprise Budget

GRAIN SORGHUM, IRRIGATED, (NATURAL GAS), TEXAS HIGH PLAINS II REGICN
ESTIMATED COSTS AND RETURNS PER ACRE
TYPICAL MANAGEMENT

OPERATION		ITEM NC.	DATE	TIMES OVER	LABOR HOURS	MACHINE HOURS	FUEL,OIL, LUB.,REP. PER ACRE	FIXED COSTS PER ACRE
SHREDDER 4R	TM	3,57	NOV	1.00	0.354	0.197	1.29	1.72
TANDEM DISC	TM	3,40	NOV	2.00	0.606	0.337	2.03	2.60
CHISEL	TM	3,44	DEC	1.00	0.215	0.119	0.82	1.14
PICKUP 1/2 TON		10	DEC	1.00	1.250	1.000	2.68	1.89
OFFSET DISC	TM	3,42	FEB	1.00	0.303	0.168	1.10	1.47
TANDEM DISC	TM	3,40	FEB	1.00	0.303	0.168	1.02	1.30
BOX FLOAT	TM	3,60	MAR	2.00	1.212	0.673	3.73	4.50
LISTER 6R	TM	3,54	MAR	1.00	0.221	0.123	0.71	C.88
ROLLING CULT	TM	3,30	APR	1.00	0.212	0.118	0.72	0.92
RODWEEDER	TM	3,50	MAY	1.00	0.141	0.079	0.50	0.65
LISTER-PLNT6R	TM	3,36	MAY	1.00	0.371	0.206	1.38	1.88
FURROW OPENER	TM	3,52	JUNE	1.00	0.200	0.111	0.57	0.86
TOTALS					5.389	3.300	16.64	19.82

Source: Texas Ag. Ext. Service, *Texas Crop Budgets*, 1978.

Table 16-3   Cost Estimates for a 100-Horsepower Tractor

WHEEL TRACTOR 100 HP CAB

PROJECTED ANNUAL COSTS AND COST PER HOUR OF USE

HOURS OF USE	YRS TO TRADE	DEPREC- IATION	THII [a]	REPAIRS	FUEL & OIL	TOTAL	COST PER HR
200	10.0	1367.	1508.	158.	591.	3625.	18.12
250	10.0	1367.	1508.	221.	739.	3835.	15.34
300	10.0	1367.	1508.	291.	887.	4053.	13.51
350	10.0	1367.	1508.	367.	1035.	4276.	12.22
400	10.0	1367.	1508.	448.	1183.	4506.	11.26
450	10.0	1367.	1508.	535.	1331.	4740.	10.53
500	10.0	1367.	1508.	626.	1479.	4979.	9.96
550	10.0	1367.	1508.	722.	1626.	5224.	9.50
600	10.0	1367.	1508.	823.	1774.	5472.	9.12
650	10.0	1367.	1508.	928.	1922.	5725.	8.81
700	10.0	1367.	1508.	1037.	2070.	5982.	8.55
750	10.0	1367.	1508.	1150.	2218.	6243.	8.32
800	10.0	1367.	1508.	1267.	2366.	6508.	8.13
850	10.0	1367.	1508.	1388.	2514.	6776.	7.97
900	10.0	1367.	1508.	1512.	2661.	7048.	7.83
950	10.0	1367.	1508.	1640.	2809.	7324.	7.71
1000	10.0	1367.	1508.	1771.	2957.	7603.	7.60
1050	10.0	1367.	1508.	1905.	3105.	7885.	7.51
1100	10.0	1367.	1508.	2043.	3253.	8171.	7.43
1150	10.0	1367.	1508.	2184.	3401.	8460.	7.36
1200	10.0	1367.	1508.	2328.	3549.	8751.	7.29
1250	9.6	1404.	1519.	2425.	3696.	9045.	7.24
1300	9.2	1440.	1531.	2522.	3844.	9337.	7.18
1350	8.9	1475.	1541.	2619.	3992.	9628.	7.13
1400	8.6	1510.	1551.	2716.	4140.	9918.	7.08
1450	8.3	1545.	1561.	2813.	4288.	10207.	7.04
1500	8.0	1579.	1570.	2910.	4436.	10495.	7.00
1550	7.7	1612.	1579.	3007.	4584.	10782.	6.96
1600	7.5	1646.	1588.	3104.	4731.	11068.	6.92
1650	7.3	1678.	1596.	3201.	4879.	11354.	6.88
1700	7.1	1711.	1603.	3298.	5027.	11639.	6.85
1750	6.9	1743.	1611.	3395.	5175.	11924.	6.81
1800	6.7	1775.	1618.	3492.	5323.	12208.	6.78

[a] Taxes, housing, interest, and insurance

Source: Gayle S. Willett et al., *The Cost of Owning and Operating Farm Machinery in Washington*, EM 4035, Washington Cooperative Extension Service, March 1976.

compared against the number of acres to be covered and the time available to determine which sizes can perform the task within the allotted amount of time.

The formula for finding capacity in acres per hour is

$$\text{Effective field capacity in acres per hour} = \frac{\text{speed in miles per hour} \times \text{width in feet} \times \text{field efficiency}}{8.25}$$

Field efficiency is included in the equation to recognize that a machine is not used at 100 percent of its theoretical capacity because of time spent turning, adjusting, repairing, work overlap, and materials handling. Operations such as planting which require frequent stops to refill seed, chemical, and fertilizer boxes may have field efficiencies as low as 50 percent. Field efficiencies may be as high as 85 to 90 percent for some tillage operations, particularly in large fields when turning time and work overlap is minimized.[3]

Once the minimum machine size is identified, the next question should be: Can a larger machine be justified? A larger machine will have a larger purchase price and annual fixed costs but will save labor and reduce field time. The important factor is often the additional costs of the larger machine vs. the value of the labor saved, which is an application of the substitution principle. If labor has a high opportunity cost, the larger machine may be justified.

Partial budgeting is a useful tool to use when making decisions about machinery sizes. Table 16-4 is an example which emphasizes the importance of the opportunity cost of labor. The value of the labor saved by switching to the larger planter was left blank intentionally, as this is the pivot point for the decision. With no value on this labor, the budget shows a loss of $475 from changing to the larger planter. To justify the larger planter, the opportunity cost of labor must be at least $9.50 per hour ($475 ÷ 50 hours). This may not be an unreasonable opportunity cost during the busy planting season. There will also be a slight decrease in tractor operating costs and an increase in timeliness to be considered in this decision.

Machinery selection may also involve the choice of one large machine or two smaller ones. Purchase cost and annual fixed costs will be higher for two machines, as the same capacity can usually be obtained at a lower cost in one large machine than in two smaller ones. Two tractors and two drivers will also be needed for tractor-drawn equipment. The primary advantage of two machines is an increase in reliability. If one machine breaks down, work is not completely stopped but can continue at half speed utilizing the remaining machine.

Timeliness

Another important factor in machinery selection is the relationship between machinery size and timeliness of field operations. Small machine sizes may mean certain field operations cannot be completed during the optimum time period, causing a reduction in yields. A yield reduction reduces profit, which should be included as part of the cost of utilizing the smaller machine. Operations such as planting and harvesting must often be completed within a narrow time period to avoid yield losses. Figure 16-4 shows a typical relationship between planting time and potential yield where planting too early or too late reduces yield. A larger planter may be economically justified to avoid delayed planting and the associated lower yield.

The dollar cost of poor timeliness is difficult to estimate, as it will vary from year to year depending on weather conditions. However, some estimate

[3]Average field efficiencies may be found in Wendell Bowers, *Modern Concepts of Machinery Management,* Stipes Publishing Co., Champaign, Ill., 1970.

Table 16-4   Example of Partial Budgeting Used For Selecting Machine Size

PARTIAL BUDGET

Adjustment: Changing from a 4-row planter ($4,000 cost) to an 8-row planter ($6,000 cost).
Assumes 10% salvage value, 8-year life, 10% opp. cost.

Additional Receipts:

None

Total additional receipts $0

Reduced Costs:

	Annual Ownership*	Operating
Depreciation	$450	
Interest	220	
Taxes and insurance	80	
Repairs		$200
Labor (50 hours)		?
Subtotal	750	200

Total reduced costs $950

Total of additional receipts and reduced costs $950

Additional Costs:

	Annual Ownership*	Operating
Depreciation	$675	
Interest	330	
Taxes and insurance	120	
Repairs		$300
Subtotal	$1125	300

Total additional costs $1425

Reduced Receipts:

None

Total reduced receipts $0

Total of additional costs and reduced receipts $1425

Net Change in Farm Income:

(Total of additional costs and reduced receipts subtracted from total of additional
receipts and reduced costs.)   ($475)

---

*Annual ownership costs are taxes, insurance, interest, depreciation, and possibly storage.

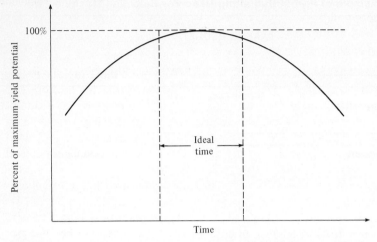

Figure 16-4 A possible relationship between time of planting and yield.

should be included in the cost of owning machines of different sizes. Figure 16-5 is a hypothetical example of how timeliness can be included in the costs when selecting machine sizes. The lower curve includes only the machine and tractor costs while the upper curve includes these costs plus the cost of timeliness or the value of the yield reduction due to delayed field operations.

The distance between the curves represents the cost of timeliness, which decreases with larger machine sizes. An interesting and typical result is the different location of the minimum cost point on each curve. The implication is that a larger machine size can be economically justified when the cost of timeliness is included in total costs. This factor combined with the reduced

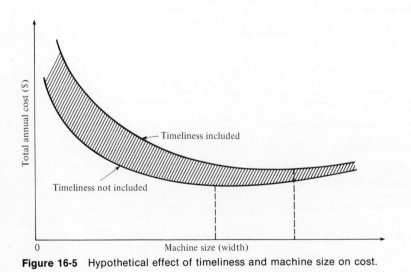

Figure 16-5 Hypothetical effect of timeliness and machine size on cost.

labor requirements has contributed to the larger machine sizes being purchased by many farmers today.

New vs. Used Machines

Farm machinery, like new cars, declines in market value most rapidly during the first few years of its useful life. This is particularly true for tractors and other self-powered machinery. Used machinery can therefore be an economical purchase and a way to lower machinery costs. Purchasing a machine is essentially the purchase of the service it can provide over time. If a used machine can provide the same service at a lower cost, it is an economical alternative.

The purchase of a used machine represents a lower investment and therefore lower annual fixed costs for depreciation and interest. Balancing off some of the lower fixed costs may be higher variable costs because of higher repairs and decreases in reliability and timeliness. A used machine may become obsolete sooner than a new one and also challenge the owner's ability as a mechanic.

Used machinery should be considered when capital is limited and/or its opportunity cost is high. This is particularly true when the machine will have a relatively small annual use and where a lower reliability and poor timeliness will have little effect on profit. The importance of the lower capital investment and its opportunity cost is shown in Table 16-5. Before interest is included in the annual costs, the new machine has the lower cost. The smaller investment in the used machine results in a lower annual interest cost, making the used machine the least-cost alternative when interest is included.

A little experimenting with different opportunity costs for capital shows a rate of about 7 percent is the break-even point. The used machine has a lower annual cost when the opportunity cost of capital is above 7 percent, and the new machine has the advantage when it is 7 percent or lower. As in this

Table 16-5   Example of Cost Comparison for a New and Used Machine

	New machine	Used machine
Purchase price	$10,000	$5,500
Useful life	10 years	6 years
Annual costs:		
Depreciation (no salvage value)	$ 1,000	$ 917
Taxes and insurance	200	150
Repairs	500	800
Total annual cost without interest	$ 1,700	$1,867
Interest at 10%	500	275
Total annual cost	$ 2,200	$2,142

example, the opportunity cost of capital combined with differences in repair costs and reliability is important in the decision.

Own, Lease, or Custom Hire

Alternatives to machinery ownership are leasing machinery and hiring custom operators to perform certain operations. They may be preferred to owning the necessary machinery when capital is limited and/or the machine will receive little use. A smaller machinery investment is an advantage of leasing or custom hiring, making the opportunity cost of capital an important consideration. When the machine will receive little use, these alternatives may also be less costly.

A lease is a formal agreement whereby the machine owner, which may be a machinery dealer or leasing company (the lessor), grants control and use of the machine to the user (the lessee) for a specified period of time for an agreed-upon payment. Short-term leases may cover several days to several months while long-term leases are for one or more years. As with any formal agreement, the lease should be in writing and should cover such items as payment rates and dates, who pays taxes, insurance, etc., responsibilities for loss or damage, and cancellation provisions.

Some leases allow the lessee to purchase the machine at the end of the lease period for a specified sum. However, any lease-purchase agreement must be carefully written to maintain the income tax deductibility of the lease payments. A lease which is improperly written may be termed a sales contract. The full deductibility of lease payments from taxable income can be an important advantage of leasing depending on the income tax bracket of the lessee.

There are several disadvantages to leasing. First, the leasing of farm machinery is not well established in many areas, and machinery may not be available for lease. Lease rates may also be relatively high compared with loan payments, but the total lease payment is tax-deductible compared with only the interest on debt repayments. A third disadvantage of leasing is its effect on the lessee's net worth statement. The leased machine does not show up as an asset, and the lessee does not have a claim to any residual or salvage value at the end of the lease period. Advantages of leasing are the smaller capital investment required, no reduction in available credit, and possible tax advantages.

Custom hiring is an important practice in some areas for operations such as hay baling and grain combining. The decision to own a machine or custom hire depends on the cost involved, which in turn depend upon the amount of work to be done. For machines which will be used very little, it is often more economical to hire the work done on a custom basis. The availability and dependability of custom operators must be considered. A manager may not want to rely on a custom operator for a task such as planting where timeliness is important.

Total cost per acre or per unit of output should be compared when deciding between machine ownership or custom hiring. Custom charges are typically a flat rate per acre or per unit of output while total ownership costs will decline with increased use as average fixed costs decline. The relationships are shown in Figure 16-6. At low levels of use hiring a custom operator has the lower cost per unit, while beyond some point the cost is lower if the machine is owned. The point where the cost advantage changes, or the break-even point, is output level *a* in Figure 16-6.

When the necessary cost data are available, the break-even point can be found from the following equation:

$$\text{Break-even units} = \frac{\text{total annual fixed costs}}{\text{custom rate minus variable costs per unit}}$$

For example, if machine ownership would incur $2,000 in total fixed costs, the custom rate is $8 per acre, and the variable cost for operating the owned machine would be $3 per acre, the break-even point would be

$$\frac{\$2,000}{\$8 - \$3} = 400 \text{ acres}$$

If the machine would be used on less than 400 acres, it would be less costly to hire the work done, while above 400 acres it would be less expensive to own the machine. A determination of the break-even point provides a useful guide for managers when choosing between machine ownership and custom hiring.

Labor use should be another consideration in custom hiring. The custom operator typically provides the labor necessary to operate the machine, which frees the farm operator's labor for other uses. This can be an advantage of custom hiring if it reduces the amount of hired labor needed or if the owner's

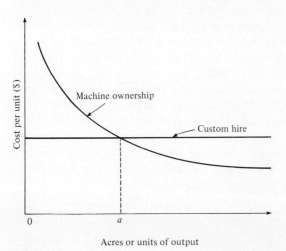

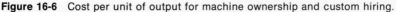

Acres or units of output

Figure 16-6 Cost per unit of output for machine ownership and custom hiring.

labor has a high opportunity cost at the time the custom work is being performed.

CALCULATING MACHINERY EFFICIENCY

Two values are often used to measure the efficiency of machinery use. The
first is *investment per rotated acre* (or per tillable acre), which is calculated by
dividing the current value of all machinery by the number of rotated or tillable
acres.

$$\text{Investment per rotated acre} = \frac{\text{current value of all machinery}}{\text{number of rotated acres}}$$

Current value of all machinery for a given year can be found by taking the
average of beginning and ending machinery inventory values. Ideally, this
should be the current market value, but this is not readily available in most
cases. Current book or depreciated value (cost less accumulated depreciation)
is commonly used, as these figures can be obtained from the depreciation
schedule or balance sheet.

The second measure of machinery efficiency is *cost per rotated acre* (or
tillable acre). It is found by dividing the total annual machinery cost by the
number of rotated acres. Total annual machinery cost should include all machinery fixed and variable costs, and most farm record analyses include all
pickup and truck expenses, the farm share of automobile expenses, the farm
share of utilities, machinery lease payments, and custom hiring expenses.

Lower values are desirable for both these efficiency measures, but they
should be used and compared with caution. Numerous studies have shown
that cost per acre and investment per acre will decline with increases in farm
size, and they will also vary with farm type. It is important to compare values
only with those calculated in the same manner for farms of the same approximate size and type. Any other comparison will be meaningless and misleading.

Values which are too high or too low compared with similar farms or past
records indicate machinery investment and cost problems. Investment per acre
can be kept low by leasing, by custom hiring, and by using old, small machinery, but these practices may increase machinery cost per acre. Labor use is
important to consider in a proper interpretation of machinery efficiency. Using
old, small machinery will lower machinery investment per acre but will increase labor cost and reduce labor efficiency. Machinery which is too large
will have poor machinery efficiency values but will reduce labor cost per acre.
With the interaction between machinery and labor costs, it is advisable to
consider both when analyzing machinery efficiency.

INCREASING MACHINERY EFFICIENCY

A number of techniques can be employed to improve machinery efficiency.
They will be discussed in the following four categories: selection, maintenance,
operation, and replacement.

Selection

Machinery selection is determining the proper size and type of machine for a given type and size of farm. As discussed above, errors can be made in selecting machinery which is either too small or too large, and both types of errors can be costly. Leasing, custom hiring, and purchasing used machinery should all be considered in the selection process.

A number of questions should be asked in machinery selection decisions.

1 Will the machine perform the desired job satisfactorily and increase farm profit?

2 Does the machine have enough capacity to complete the job on time with little loss from timeliness and meet any increases in capacity needed for planned farm growth?

3 Is the machine likely to become obsolete within a short time?

4 Are custom operators available and reliable? Is this a less costly alternative than purchasing the machine?

5 Is leasing a possible alternative? Would it be less costly?

6 Would a used machine have the reliability and capacity to do the job?

7 Would the capital saved by leasing, custom hiring, or purchasing a used machine produce greater returns in some other use?

8 Would the labor saved by purchasing a larger machine produce greater returns in another use?

9 Can a larger machine be justified by increased timeliness?

With the large capital investment required for some machines, the answers to these questions need to be considered carefully. They can do much to aid and improve machinery selection decisions.

Maintenance

Repairs are a large part of machinery variable costs, but they are a cost which can be controlled by proper use and maintenance. Agricultural engineers report that excessive repair costs can generally be traced to (1) overloading or exceeding the rated capacity, (2) excessive speed, (3) poor daily and periodic maintenance, and (4) abuse. All these items can be corrected by constant attention and proper training of machine operators.

A system of scheduling and recording repair and maintenance is essential to control repair costs. Adherence to the manufacturer's recommended maintenance schedule will keep warranties in effect, prevent unnecessary breakdowns, and reduce lifetime repair costs. Complete records of repairs on individual machines will help identify machines with a higher than average repair cost. When these machines are identified, they should be considered for early replacement.

Operation

How a machine is operated affects both repair costs and field efficiency. Speed should be adjusted to load a machine to capacity without overloading it or lowering the quality of the work being done. Improving field efficiency reduces cost by allowing more work to be done in a given time period or permits the same work to be done in less time or by a smaller machine. Small and irregular-shaped fields requiring frequent turns, frequent stops, and work overlap all reduce field efficiency. For example, a 20-foot disk operated with a 2-foot overlap loses 10 percent of its potential efficiency from this factor alone.

A factor which often contributes to high machinery cost is small annual use of an expensive, specialized machine. Fixed costs per unit of output remain high unless the annual use can be increased. Some farmers are purchasing these types of machines jointly with one or more neighbors. This not only decreases per unit fixed costs but decreases the investment required from each individual. Jointly owned machinery can reduce machinery costs for each individual owner, but it is important that the partners be compatible and agree on the details of the machine's use. Whose work will be done first and the division of expenses such as repairs, insurance, and taxes should be agreed to before the machine is purchased.

Machine cost per unit of output can also be reduced by performing custom work for neighbors. If custom work does not interfere with timely completion of the owner's work, it will lower machine costs and provide additional income which may be important on smaller farms. The custom rate charge should include the cost of the labor being provided, as the opportunity cost of labor in the operator's own business is important when contemplating custom work.

Replacement

One of the more difficult decisions in machinery management is the optimum time to replace or trade a machine. There is no simple, easy to use decision rule applicable to all types of machines under a wide range of conditions. Any replacement decision must also include the income tax effects, which adds additional complexity to the decision.

Replacement decisions can be made for any one of the following reasons:[4]

1 The present machine is worn out—the age and accumulated use is such that the machine is no longer capable of performing the required task.

2 The machine is obsolete—new developments in machinery technology or changes in cropping patterns make the present machine no longer suitable for the job.

3 Costs are increasing with the present machine—repair and timeliness costs are increasing rapidly in total and per unit of output.

4 The capacity is too small—the acreage has increased or timeliness has become so critical that the old machine cannot complete the job on time.

5 The old machine is not dependable—breakdowns are becoming so frequent that repair and timeliness costs are exceeding acceptable limits.

6 Income taxes—this factor is related to the overall after-tax profit of the farm. In a high-profit year, machines may be replaced to take advantage of the tax-reducing benefits of additional first-year depreciation and investment credit.

[4]William K. Waters and Donald R. Daum, *Farm Machinery Management Guide,* Pennsylvania State Cooperative Extension Service Special Circular 192.

7 Pride and prestige—there is a certain "pride of ownership" involved in the purchase of new and larger machinery. While this may be important to some individuals, it can be a costly reason and one which is difficult to include in an economic analysis.

The first five reasons can be used individually or in combination to determine the replacement age for a specific machine. Cost and repair records on each machine can greatly aid the replacement decision. Income taxes, pride, and prestige can be easily overemphasized, resulting in a costly decision.

A study of machinery investment practices by Washington farmers found the following reasons given as being important in replacement decisions:[5]

1 Dependability of the old machine.
2 Repairs on the old machine make a new one cheaper to own.
3 Obsolescence of the old machine in terms of efficiency and capacity.
4 Current needs exceed the capacity of the old machine.

The first reason recognizes the need for reliability and its relation to timeliness. This answer was given by 42 percent of the farmers in the survey, while the next three responses were obtained from only 11 to 14 percent of the farmers.

SUMMARY

Machinery investment is the second largest investment after real estate on most farms, and machinery costs are a large part of the total annual operating costs. Both machinery investment and annual cost are under the direct control of the manager and represent an important area for improving farm efficiency and profits. Management efforts should be directed toward establishing actual machinery costs, proper selection of machine sizes considering cost and timeliness of operations, and improving efficiency of machinery use. Leasing and custom hiring are machinery management alternatives which fit some farm types and sizes, particularly for specialized machines with small annual use.

Machinery costs and labor costs are inversely related and should be analyzed together. Larger machinery means higher machinery fixed costs but lower labor costs and vice versa. The opportunity cost of any labor saved and timeliness are the two most important factors when considering larger machine sizes. If labor has a low opportunity cost, the larger machine can be justified only by increases in timeliness.

QUESTIONS FOR REVIEW AND FURTHER THOUGHT

1 What is the total annual fixed cost for a $30,000 tractor with an 8-year life and an $8,000 salvage value when insurance and taxes are 2 percent of average value and there is a 9 percent opportunity cost on capital? What is the average fixed cost per hour if the tractor is used 500 hours per year? If it is used 800 hours per year?

[5]Dwaine E. Umberger et al., *Machinery Investment Practices of Washington Farmers,* Washington Agricultural Experiment Station Bulletin 737, 1971.

2   What is the field capacity in acres per hour for a 28-foot tandem disk operated at 4 miles per hour with 80 percent field efficiency? How much does it change if the field efficiency could be increased to 90 percent? How much time would be saved on 400 acres?

3   Owning a certain machine would have a cost of $10 per acre on 250 acres. Leasing a machine to do the same work would cost $25 per hour and would have a field capacity of 2.2 acres per hour. Hiring the work done on a custom basis would cost $12 per acre but would free 120 hours of labor which has an opportunity cost of $4 per hour. Which alternative has the lowest total cost?

4   Assume a self-propelled windrower would have annual fixed costs of $3,850 and variable costs of $3 per acre. A custom operator charges $7.50 per acre. What is the break-even point in acres per year?

5   List ways to improve the field efficiency of machine operations such as planting, disking, and combining small grain.

6   How does the opportunity cost of capital enter into the decision to purchase, lease, or custom hire a machine?

7   What factors are important in a machinery replacement decision? How would you rank them in order of importance? Might your ranking be different for different types of machines?

REFERENCES

Barnard, C. S., and J. S. Nix: *Farm Planning and Control,* Cambridge University Press, Cambridge, 1973, chap. 4.

Castle, Emery N., Manning H. Becker, and Frederick J. Smith: *Farm Business Management,* 2d ed. The Macmillan Company, New York, 1972, chap. 14.

Herbst, J. H.: *Farm Management Principles, Budgets, Plans,* 4th ed., Stipes Publishing Co., Champaign, Ill., 1976, chap. 9.

Schlender, John R,, and D. Leo Figurski: *Examining Your Machinery Costs,* Kansas Cooperative Extension Service, C-375, 1971 revised.

Schwart, R. B.: *Farm Machinery Economic Decisions,* Illinois Cooperative Extension Service Circular 1065, 1972.

Smith, Easley S., and J. Dale Oliver: *Farm Machinery Performance and Costs,* Virginia Cooperative Extension Service Publication 510, 1972.

Umberger, Dwaine E., Norman K. Whittlesey, and M. E. Wirth: *Machine Investment Practices of Washington Farmers,* Washington Agricultural Experiment Station Bulletin 737, 1971.

Waters, William K., and Donald R. Daum: *Farm Machinery Management Guide,* Pennsylvania Cooperative Extension Service Special Circular 192.

Part 5
ADDITIONAL
MANAGEMENT TOPICS

Part 5
ADDITIONAL MANAGEMENT TOPICS

HIGHLIGHTS

A review of the topics covered in the previous chapters illustrates the breadth of farm management as an academic discipline. However, there are any number of additional topics which might be properly discussed in a farm management textbook. Several of these topics have been selected for inclusion in this final part. While no less important than some of the earlier material, these topics either did not fit well in the previous parts or require a basic understanding of management principles.

Income tax payments were identified as a cash outflow when cash flow budgeting was discussed in Chapter 6. Because tax payments are a cash outflow and it is only after-tax income which is finally available for debt payment, new investment, and consumption, income taxes are important in managerial decision making. Many decisions will affect income taxes in both the short and long run. This requires a manager to have some fundamental knowledge of tax regulations to control income taxes and properly analyze new investments. Chapter 17 discusses the more important topics in tax management.

Risk and uncertainty are a part of most managerial decisions because future events and prices are not known with perfect certainty. The economic principles of Chapters 2 and 3 were presented under the assumption that all prices and yields were known with perfect certainty to simplify their presentation and understanding. Rarely will a farm manager have the luxury of having perfect information for use in decision making. Chapter 18 discusses risk and uncertainty and its effect on decision making and presents some methods for minimizing its effects.

Part 5 and the text conclude with Chapter 19, which discusses professional management services which are available to farmers and landowners. This chapter was included for two reasons. First, farm management companies are a source of management advice and counsel to farmers and landowners and have been increasing in number and importance. Second, these companies provide employment opportunities for college graduates interested in using and improving their management skills. This brief discussion of farm management companies and the services they provide should be of interest to both groups.

Chapter 17

Managing
Income Taxes

CHAPTER OBJECTIVES

 1 To discuss the importance of income tax management on farms and ranches
 2 To identify the objective of tax management
 3 To analyze the advantages and disadvantages of the cash and accrual tax accounting methods
 4 To show how income leveling and income averaging can be used to reduce income taxes
 5 To explain how a net operating loss can be used to offset past and/or future taxable income
 6 To illustrate how regular and additional first-year depreciation can be used in tax management
 7 To note the importance of investment tax credit and the effect it has on income taxes
 8 To emphasize the effect of capital gain income on taxes, particularly as it affects the owners of breeding herds

Federal income taxes have been imposed since 1913 and affect all types of businesses including farms and ranches. Income taxes are an unavoidable result of operating a profitable business. However, the management decisions made during the year can have a large impact on the amount of income tax due. For this reason, a farm manager needs an understanding of the basic tax regulations in order to analyze the possible tax consequences of management decisions. Since these decisions are made throughout the year, tax management is a year-round problem and not something to be done only when the tax return is completed.

Farm managers need not and cannot be expected to have a complete knowledge of the tax regulations in addition to all the other knowledge they need. However, a basic understanding and awareness of the tax topics to be discussed in this chapter enables a manager to recognize the possible tax consequences of each business decision. This basic information also has another function. It should help the manager identify those decisions which may have large and complex tax consequences. This should be the signal to obtain the advice and opinion of a tax accountant or attorney who is experienced in farm tax matters. Expert advice *before* the management decision is implemented can be well worth the cost and save time, trouble, and taxes at a later date.

The income tax regulations are numerous, complex, and subject to change as new tax legislation is passed by Congress. Only some of the basic principles and regulations can be covered in this chapter. They will be discussed primarily as they affect a farm business operated as a sole proprietorship. Farm partnerships and corporations are subject to different regulations in some cases, and anyone contemplating using these forms of business organization should obtain competent tax advice. The reader is also advised to check for any changes in the tax regulations which may have been enacted since the Revenue Act of 1978.

OBJECTIVES OF TAX MANAGEMENT

Profit maximization has been the assumed management goal throughout this text. With the introduction of income taxes, this goal needs to be modified to "the maximization of *after-tax* profit." Income tax payments represent a cash drain or outflow for the business, leaving less cash available for other purposes. The cash available after paying income taxes is the only money which can be used for family living expenses, debt payments, and new business investment. Therefore, the goal should be the maximization of after-tax profit, since it is this amount which is finally available for use at the manager's or owner's discretion. Notice the goal is not minimization of income taxes. This goal can be met by arranging to have little or no taxable income.

A very short run objective of tax management is to minimize the taxes due on a given year's income at the time the tax return is completed and filed. However, this income is the result of decisions made throughout the year and perhaps in previous years. It is too late to change these decisions. Therefore, good tax management requires a continuous evaluation of how each decision will affect income taxes not only in the current year but in future years. It should be a long-run rather than a short-run objective and certainly not something to be thought of only once a year at tax time. Therefore, tax management should be *the managing of income, expenses, and purchases and sales of capital assets in a manner which will maximize long-run after-tax profits.*

Tax management is not tax evasion but is avoiding the payment of any taxes which are not legally due and postponing the payment of taxes whenever possible. Several tax management strategies are available which tend to postpone or delay tax payments but not necessarily reduce the amount paid over time. However, any tax payment which can be put off until later represents additional cash which can be used in the business for one or more years.

Tax management or minimizing taxes is sometimes equated with identifying and using "tax loopholes." This is generally an unfair assessment. While some inequities undoubtedly exist in the tax regulations, what some people refer to as tax loopholes were often legislated by Congress intentionally for a specific purpose. This purpose may be to encourage investment and production in certain areas or to increase investment in general as a means of promoting an expanding economy and full employment. Taxpayers should not be reluctant or feel guilty about taking full advantage of these regulations.

TAX ACCOUNTING METHODS

A unique feature of farm business income taxes is the choice of tax accounting methods allowed. Farmers and ranchers are permitted to report their taxable income using either the *cash* or *accrual* method of accounting. All other taxpayers engaged in the production and sale of goods where inventories may exist are required to use the accrual method, while farmers and ranchers may elect to use either one. The choice is made when the individual or business files the first farm tax return. Whichever method is used on this first tax return must be used in the following years.

It is possible to change tax accounting methods by obtaining permission from the Commissioner of Internal Revenue. The request must be filed on a special form within 180 days from the beginning of the tax year in which the change is desired. It must also include a reason for the desired change along with other information. A request may be denied and, if granted, may add complexity to the accounting procedures during the change-over period. Therefore, it is advisable to study the advantages and disadvantages of each method carefully and make the best choice when the first farm tax return is filed.

The Cash Method

Under the cash accounting method, income is taxable in the year it is received as cash or "constructively received." Income is constructively received when it is credited to your account or was available for use before the end of the taxable year. An example of the latter situation would be a check for the sale of grain which the elevator was holding for the customer to pick up. If the check was available on December 31 but was not picked up until several days later, it would still be income constructively received in December. The check was available in December, and the mere fact it was not picked up does not make it taxable income in the following year.

Expenses under cash accounting are tax-deductible in the year they are actually paid regardless of when the item was purchased or used. An example would be a December feed purchase which was charged on account and not paid for until the following January. This would be a tax-deductible expense in the next year and not in the year the feed was actually purchased and used. An exception to this rule is the cost of items purchased for resale, which includes feeder livestock. These expenses can be deducted only in the taxable year in which they were finally sold. This means the expense of purchasing feeder cattle or other items purchased for resale will need to be held over a year if the purchase and sale do not occur in the same year.

Inventories are not used to determine taxable income with the cash method of tax accounting. Income is taxed when received as cash and not as it accumulates in an inventory of crops and livestock. The cash method has several advantages and disadvantages.

Advantages A large majority of farmers and ranchers use the cash method for calculating taxable income. There are a number of advantages which make this the most popular method.

1 *Simplicity*. The use of cash accounting requires a minimum of records, primarily because there is no need to maintain inventory records.

2 *Flexibility*. Cash accounting provides maximum flexibility for tax planning at the end of a year. Taxable income for any year can be adjusted by the timing of sales and payment of expenses. A few days' difference can put the income or expense into one of two years.

3 *Capital Gain from the Sale of Raised Breeding Stock*. Income from the sale of raised breeding stock will often qualify as capital gain income under cash accounting, and this income is taxed at a lower rate than ordinary income. This subject will be discussed in detail in a later section.

4 *Delaying Tax on Growing Inventory*. A growing business with an increasing inventory can postpone paying tax on the inventory until it is actually sold and converted into cash.

Disadvantages There are several disadvantages to cash accounting which may make it less desirable in certain situations.

1 *Poor Measure of Income*. As discussed in Chapter 8, changes in inventory values are needed to measure net farm income accurately for an accounting period. Because inventory changes are not included when determining taxable income under cash accounting, the resulting figure does not accurately reflect net farm income for the year.

2 *Potential for Income Variation*. Market conditions may make it desirable to store one year's crop for sale the following year and sell that year's

crop at harvest. The result is no crop income in one year and income from two crops in the following year. Because of the progressive nature of the income tax rates, more total tax will be paid than if the income had been evenly distributed between the years.

3 *Declining Inventory.* During years with declining inventory values more tax will be paid because there is no inventory decrease to offset the cash sales from inventory.

The Accrual Method

Income under the accrual method of tax accounting is taxable in the year it is earned or produced. Accrual income includes the value of crops and livestock in inventory at the end of the taxable year as well as any cash income received. Therefore, any inventory increase during the tax year is included in taxable income, and inventory decreases are treated as an expense and reduce taxable income. Cash income from the sale of crops and livestock is also taxable income in the year of sale, even though payment may not be received until the following year.

Expenses under the accrual method are deductible in the tax year in which they are incurred whether or not they are paid. In essence this means any accounts payable at the end of the tax year are deductible as expenses, since they represent expenses which have been incurred but not yet paid. Another difference from cash accounting is the cost of items purchased for resale which can be deducted in the year of purchase even though the items have not been resold. Their cost is offset by the ending inventory value for the same items.

Advantages Accrual tax accounting has several advantages over cash accounting which should be considered when choosing a tax accounting method.

1 *Better Measure of Income.* Taxable income under accrual accounting is calculated like the net farm income calculated in Chapter 8. For this reason, it measures net farm income better than cash accounting and keeps income taxes paid up on a current basis.

2 *Reduces Income Fluctuations.* The inclusion of inventory changes prevents wide fluctuations in taxable income if the marketing pattern results in the production from two years being sold in one year.

3 *Declining Inventory.* During years when the inventory value is declining, as might happen when a farmer is slowly retiring from the business, less tax will be paid under accrual accounting because the decrease in inventory value offsets some of the cash receipts.

Disadvantages The disadvantages of accrual accounting more than offset any advantages for most farm businesses, which makes cash accounting the more popular method.

1 *Increased Record Requirement.* Complete inventory records must be kept for proper determination of accrual income. They should also be kept for

use in calculating net farm income, but the additional complexity of a tax inventory and valuation discourages many farmers from using accrual accounting.

2 *Increasing Inventory.* When the inventory is increasing, accrual accounting results in tax being paid on the inventory increase before the actual sale of the products. As no cash has yet been received for these products, this can cause a cash flow problem.

3 *Loss of Capital Gain on Raised Breeding Stock.* Accrual accounting will result in losing much of if not all of the capital gain income from the sale of raised breeding stock. This factor alone generally makes accrual accounting inadvisable for taxpayers with a breeding herd who raise most of their herd replacements.

4 *Less Flexibility.* Accrual tax accounting is less flexible than cash accounting for adjusting taxable income at year-end through the timing of sales and paying of expenses.

Tax Record Requirements

Regardless of the accounting method chosen, complete and accurate records are essential for good tax management and properly reporting taxable income. Both farming and the tax regulations have become too complex for records to be a collection of receipts and canceled checks tossed in a shoe box. Poor records often result in two related and undesirable outcomes—the inability to verify receipts and expenses in case of a tax audit and paying more taxes than may be legally due. In either case, good records do not cost; they pay in the form of lower income taxes.

Record books suitable for farm and ranch use are generally available through county or state agricultural extension service offices. Several states offer a computerized record-keeping service through their agricultural college or state extension service. These services may also be available from a local bank, other private businesses, or a farm cooperative.

Adequate records should include a listing of receipts and expenses for the year. A depreciation schedule is also needed for all depreciable property to determine annual depreciation and to calculate any gain or loss when the item is sold. Permanent records should be kept on real estate and other capital items including purchase price, depreciation taken, cost of any improvements, investment credit taken, and selling price. These items are important to determine any gain or loss from sale or for gift and inheritance tax purposes.

FARM TAX RETURN

Taxable income and tax-deductible expenses for a farm or ranch business are reported on Schedule F (Form 1040). A copy of this form is shown in Table 17-1. The net farm profit or loss on line 58 is transferred to the basic Form 1040, where it is combined with any income from other sources to determine the taxpayer's total taxable income.

Schedule F uses a single section (Part II) to record expenses for both cash

Table 17-1   Schedule F (Form 1040) Used for Filing a Farm Tax Return

SCHEDULE F (Form 1040)
Department of the Treasury
Internal Revenue Service

Farm Income and Expenses

► Attach to Form 1040 or Form 1065.   ► See Instructions for Schedule F (Form 1040).

1978

Name of proprietor(s)

Social security number

Farm name and address ►

Employer identification number (See instructions)

Part I   Farm Income—Cash Receipts and Disbursements Method

Do not include sales of livestock held for draft, breeding, sport, or dairy purposes; report these sales on Form 4797.

Sales of Purchased Livestock and Other Items Purchased for Resale

a. Description	b. Amount	c. Cost or other basis
1 Livestock:		
2 Other items:		
3 Totals		

4 Profit or (loss), subtract line 3, column c from line 3, column b . . . . ►

Sales of Raised Livestock and Produce and Other Farm Income

Kind	Amount
5 Cattle	
6 Calves	
7 Sheep	
8 Swine	
9 Poultry	
10 Dairy products	
11 Eggs	
12 Wool	
13 Cotton	
14 Tobacco	
15 Vegetables	
16 Soybeans	
17 Corn	
18 Other grains	
19 Hay	
20 Straw	
21 Fruits and nuts	
22 Machine work	
23 Patronage dividends (see Schedule F instructions) . .	
24 Per-unit retains (see Schedule F instructions) . .	
25 Nonpatronage distributions from exempt cooperatives . .	
26 Agricultural program payments:	
a Cash	
b Materials and services	
27 Commodity credit loans under election (or forfeited) . .	
28 Federal gasoline tax credit	
29 State gasoline tax refund	
30 Other (specify):	

31 Add lines 5 through 30 . . . .

32 Gross profits* (add lines 4 and 31) . . . . ►

58 Net farm profit or (loss) (subtract line 57 from line 32). Enter here and on Form 1040, line 19 or on Form 1065, line 9. **ALSO** enter on Schedule SE, Part I, line 1a. (For "at risk" provisions, see page 30 of Instructions.) . ►

Part II   Farm Deductions—For Cash and Accrual Method Taxpayers   **F**

Do not include personal or living expenses (such as taxes, insurance, repairs, etc., on your home), which do not produce farm income. Reduce the amount of your farm deductions by any reimbursement before entering the deduction below.

Items	Amount
33 a Labor hired (see Schedule F instructions)	
b New Jobs credit . . .	
c Balance (subtract line 33b from line 33a)	
34 Repairs, maintenance . .	
35 Interest	
36 Rent of farm, pasture . .	
37 Feed purchased	
38 Seeds, plants purchased .	
39 Fertilizers, lime, chemicals .	
40 Machine hire	
41 Supplies purchased . . .	
42 Breeding fees	
43 Veterinary fees, medicine .	
44 Gasoline, fuel, oil . . .	
45 Storage, warehousing . .	
46 Taxes	
47 Insurance	
48 Utilities	
49 Freight, trucking	
50 Conservation expenses . .	
51 Land clearing expenses . .	
52 Pension and profit-sharing plans (see Schedule F instructions)	
53 Employee benefit programs other than line 52 (see Schedule F instructions) .	
54 Other (specify):	
55 Add lines 33c through 54 . . . . . ►	
56 Depreciation (from line 61, Part III) . . . . ►	
57 Total deductions (add lines 55 and 56) . . . . ►	

*Use amount on line 32 for optional method of computing net earnings from self-employment. (See Schedule SE, Part I, line 3.)

263–059–1

Table 17-1   Schedule F (Form 1040) Used for Filing a Farm Tax Return
(Continued)

Schedule F (Form 1040) 1978   Page **2**

Part III Depreciation (Do not include the home you and your family live in, its furnishings, and other items used for personal purposes.)
If you need more space, use Form 4562.

a. Description of property	b. Date acquired	c. Cost or other basis	d. Depreciation allowed or allowable in prior years	e. Method of computing depreciation	f. Life or rate	g. Depreciation for this year
59 Total additional first-year depreciation (do not include in items below) ⟶						
60 Other depreciation:						
Buildings						
Animals						
Transportation equipment .						
Machinery and other equipment .						
Other (specify):						
61 Totals		Enter here and in Part II, line 56 . . ▶				

Part IV Farm Income—Accrual Method (Do not include sales of livestock held for draft, breeding, sport, or dairy purposes; report these sales on Form 4797 and omit them from "Inventory at beginning of year" column)

Kind	Inventory at beginning of year	Cost of items purchased during year	Sales during year	Inventory at end of year
Cattle				
Calves				
Sheep				
Swine				
Poultry				
Dairy products				
Eggs				
Wool				
Cotton				
Tobacco				
Vegetables				
Grain				
Fruits and nuts				
Other (specify):				
......				
62 Totals (enter here and in Part V below)	(Enter on line 71)	(Enter on line 72)	(Enter on line 64)	(Enter on line 63)

Part V Summary of Income and Deductions—Accrual Method

63 Inventory of livestock, crops, and products at end of year		
64 Sales of livestock, crops, and products during year		
65 Agricultural program payments: **a** Cash		
b Materials and services		
66 Commodity credit loans under election (or forfeited)		
67 Federal gasoline tax credit		
68 State gasoline tax refund		
69 Other farm income (specify): _____		
_____		
70 Add lines 63 through 69		
71 Inventory of livestock, crops, and products at beginning of year		
72 Cost of livestock and products purchased during year		
73 Total (add lines 71 and 72) . . . . ▶		
74 Gross profits* (subtract line 73 from line 70) . . . . ▶		
75 Total deductions from Part II, line 57		

76 Net farm profit or (loss) (subtract line 75 from line 74). Enter here and on Form 1040, line 19 or on Form 1065, line 9. **ALSO** enter on Schedule SE, Part I, line 1a. (For "at risk" provisions, see page 30 of Instructions.) . ▶

* Use amount on line 74 for optional method of computing net earnings from self employment. (See Schedule SE, Part I, line 3.)

Table 17-2   Tax Rate Schedule for Married Taxpayers Filing a Joint Return

If the amount of taxable income is		The tax is	
Over	But not over		Of the amount over
$ 3,400	$ 5,500	$ 0 plus 14%	$ 3,400
$ 5,500	$ 7,600	$ 294 plus 16%	$ 5,500
$ 7,600	$ 11,900	$ 630 plus 18%	$ 7,600
$ 11,900	$ 16,000	$ 1,404 plus 21%	$ 11,900
$ 16,000	$ 20,200	$ 2,265 plus 24%	$ 16,000
$ 20,200	$ 24,600	$ 3,273 plus 28%	$ 20,200
$ 24,600	$ 29,900	$ 4,505 plus 32%	$ 24,600
$ 29,900	$ 35,200	$ 6,201 plus 37%	$ 29,900
$ 35,200	$ 45,800	$ 8,162 plus 43%	$ 35,200
$ 45,800	$ 60,000	$ 12,720 plus 49%	$ 45,800
$ 60,000	$ 85,600	$ 19,678 plus 54%	$ 60,000
$ 85,600	$109,400	$ 33,502 plus 59%	$ 85,600
$109,400	$162,400	$ 47,544 plus 64%	$109,400
$162,400	$215,400	$ 81,464 plus 68%	$162,400
$215,400	———	$117,504 plus 70%	$215,400

Source: *Your Federal Income Tax: 1980 Edition*, Internal Revenue Service Publication 17.

and accrual basis taxpayers. However, income is reported in Part I for cash basis taxpayers and in Parts IV and V for accrual basis taxpayers. The inclusion of inventory value changes in taxable income when using accrual accounting can be seen by careful study of these parts of Schedule F.

INCOME LEVELING

Farm and ranch income is very dependent on prices and yields and therefore tends to vary widely. The high-income years put the taxpayer into a higher marginal tax bracket because of the progressive nature of the tax rates, as shown in Table 17-2. Therefore, a highly variable taxable income will result in paying more tax over time than a level income of the same average amount. The following example shows what can happen using taxable incomes and tax rates from Table 17-2.

	Situation 1		Situation 2	
	Taxable income ($)	Tax ($)	Taxable income ($)	Tax ($)
Year 1	35,200	8,162	20,200	3,273
Year 2	35,200	8,162	50,200	14,876
Average income	35,200		35,200	
Total tax paid		16,324		18,149

Even though the average income was the same for both situations, the variable income increased income taxes by $1,825 over the two years. Similar results can be shown for any level of taxable income.

One tax management strategy is to level out taxable income from year to year. Many good tax managers make an estimate of taxable income in early December of each year and compare it with that of past years and projections for the future. If it is above normal, sales can be delayed until the next year, bills paid by the end of December, and items needed early next year such as feed, seed, and fertilizer purchased and paid for by December 31. When the taxable income is expected to be below normal, additional sales can be made in December and purchases and payments delayed until next year whenever possible. This flexibility in adjusting annual taxable income was one of the advantages of cash accounting. It is very difficult using accrual accounting because most transactions are offset by a change in inventory value.

INCOME AVERAGING

One of the recent changes in the tax regulations reduces some of the undesirable results of widely fluctuating incomes. Taxpayers whose income varies widely from year to year are allowed to use a technique called *income averaging* to minimize taxes. It can be used for any tax year when the taxable income is more than 20 percent higher than the average taxable income for the four preceding years and the "averageable income" is more than $3,000. Averageable income is that portion of the current year's taxable income which is greater than 120 percent of the average income for the previous 4 years. Income averaging is not mandatory but should be considered in any year taxable income is greater than normal.

NET OPERATING LOSS

The wide fluctuations in farm prices and yields can cause a net operating loss some years despite the best efforts to level out annual taxable income. Special provisions relating to net operating losses allow them to be used in a way which also helps level out taxable income. Any net operating loss from a farm business can first be used to offset taxable income from other sources. If the loss is greater than the nonfarm income, any remaining loss can be carried back for 3 years or forward for up to 7 years.

When carried back, the net operating loss is used to reduce taxable income for these years, and a tax refund is requested. If carried forward, it is used to reduce taxable income and therefore income taxes in future years. A taxpayer can elect to forgo the 3-year carry-back provision and apply the net operating loss only against future taxable income for up to 7 years. However, this election must be made at the time the tax return is filed, and it is irrevocable for that tax year. In making this election, care should be taken to receive maximum advantage from the loss by applying it to the years with above-average taxable income.

A net operating loss is basically an excess of allowable tax-deductible expenses over gross income. However, there are certain adjustments and special rules which apply when calculating a net operating loss. Expert tax advice may be necessary to calculate properly and use a net operating loss to its best advantage.

DEPRECIATION

Depreciation plays an important role in tax management for two reasons. First, it is a noncash expense but tax-deductible; so it reduces taxable income without also being a cash outflow. Second, considerable flexibility is permitted in calculating depreciation, making it another tool which can be used for income leveling and postponing taxes. A working knowledge of the types of depreciation allowed, depreciation methods, and the rules for their use is necessary for good tax management.

Tax Basis

Every asset has a *tax basis*, and it must be calculated before any depreciation method is applied. The tax basis is simply the asset's value for tax purposes at any point in time. Any asset purchased directly, either new or used, has a beginning tax basis equal to its purchase price. When a used asset is traded in as partial payment on a new purchase, the beginning tax basis on the newly acquired asset is equal to the latest basis on the trade-in *plus* any cash difference or "boot" paid. For example, if a used tractor with a current basis of $10,000 plus $30,000 cash is exchanged for a new tractor with a list price of $50,000, the beginning basis on the new tractor is $40,000 and *not* $50,000. Since the beginning basis represents the value of an asset for tax purposes, it is the starting point for calculating depreciation.

An asset's basis is adjusted downward each year by the amount of depreciation taken to find its *adjusted* or *current tax basis*. In the example above, if $5,000 depreciation is taken the first year, the tractor would have an adjusted tax basis of $35,000 at the end of the year. The basis would be adjusted downward each following year by the amount of depreciation taken until the assigned salvage value is reached, and the basis would remain equal to salvage value as long as the asset is owned.

The basis on a nondepreciable asset such as land generally remains at its original cost for as long as it is owned. An exception would be some capital improvement to the land itself when the cost of the improvement is not tax-deductible in the current year or depreciable. In this case, the cost of the improvement is added to the original basis to find the adjusted basis.

An accurate record of the basis of each asset is important when it is sold or traded. The current or adjusted basis is used to determine the profit or loss on the sale or to determine the beginning basis for the newly acquired asset when a trade-in is a part of the transaction. Cost and basis information on assets such as land and buildings which have a long life and are sold or traded infrequently may need to be kept for many years. This is another reason for a complete, accurate, and permanent record-keeping system.

Regular Depreciation

The term regular depreciation is used here to differentiate it from another type of depreciation to be discussed in the next section. Regular or normal depreciation is calculated using one of the methods discussed in Chapter 7, either straight-line, declining balance, or sum-of-the-year's digits. A taxpayer can use a different method for different types of assets and may even use two different methods for two assets of the same type. However, the depreciation method cannot be changed during the life of the asset without permission from the Internal Revenue Service. An exception is a change from double declining balance to straight-line, which can be done without permission. There are, however, some restrictions on the type of assets eligible for some of the depreciation methods.

Declining Balance   Double declining balance depreciation is limited to tangible personal property with a useful life of 3 years or more. In farm and ranch businesses, this would include machinery, equipment, and breeding livestock. Another requirement is that the asset be put to its "original use" by the taxpayer, which essentially limits this method to new assets. Used assets are not eligible for double declining balance, but a rate equal to 150 percent of the straight-line rate can be used or 150 percent declining balance. This same rate can also be used on new farm buildings, but used buildings are not eligible for any type of declining balance depreciation.

Sum-of-the-Year's Digits   New machinery and breeding stock are eligible for the sum-of-the-year's digits depreciation method if they have a useful life of 3 years or more. New farm buildings and used property of any kind are not eligible.

Straight Line   Straight-line depreciation can be used on any depreciable property, new or used, provided the useful life is 2 years or more.

Additional First Year Depreciation

New or used tangible personal property with a useful life of 6 years or more is eligible for an additional 20 percent depreciation in the year of purchase. On farms and ranches, tangible personal property would consist of machinery, equipment, and breeding livestock. Additional first-year depreciation (AFYD) is an addition to any regular depreciation which can be taken, and unlike regular depreciation, it is not prorated the first year according to the length of time the asset was owned. The full 20 percent can be taken on eligible items even though they were purchased toward the end of the year. There is a limit of $4,000 (20 percent of $20,000) that can be claimed any year on a joint tax return and $2,000 on an individual tax return.

The 20 percent AFYD is taken on the beginning tax basis without subtracting the assigned salvage value. It is then subtracted from the beginning basis to determine the adjusted basis to be used for calculating the regular depreciation. When the new asset was acquired with a trade-in, AFYD can be taken only on the cash difference or boot.

Additional first-year depreciation is optional, making it a useful tax management tool. A manager can elect to take AFYD or not depending on the level of taxable income for the year, which makes it another tool for income leveling. If AFYD is not taken, the regular depreciation will be greater for each year of the asset's life.

As an example of how AFYD is calculated, assume a new $15,000 asset was purchased during the year. If the taxpayer files a joint return and elects to claim AFYD, it would be $3,000 (20 percent of $15,000). This $3,000 would be subtracted from the cost, leaving a $12,000 basis to use when calculating regular depreciation. Note that claiming AFYD does not increase the total amount of depreciation that can be taken over the asset's useful life. It simply allows a larger part of the total lifetime depreciation to be claimed the first year.

Depreciation and Income Leveling

The choice of depreciation method and the optional nature of AFYD provide flexibility and another means of income leveling which is available to both cash and accrual basis taxpayers. Assume a new machine is purchased on January 1 for $15,000 and assigned a salvage value of $3,000 and a useful life of 8 years. Table 17-3 shows the various amounts of depreciation which can be taken the first year depending on the choice of depreciation method and whether or not AFYD is claimed. In this example, total depreciation the first year can be as little as $1,500 using straight-line depreciation and no AFYD or as much as $6,000 using double declining balance and AFYD. These choices can be used to adjust or level out taxable income in the year a new asset is purchased. Of course, the choice also reflects the amount of depreciation which can be claimed in future years, as can be seen by the year-end adjusted basis. After the $3,000 salvage value is accounted for, $10,500 in depreciation remains in the first column but only $6,000 if the choice represented by the last column is selected.

Depreciation Recapture

Taxpayers generally select fast depreciation methods and elect to take AFYD because this combination is a way to postpone tax payments. This large deduction for depreciation in the first few years reduces taxable income, but it is increased in later years when smaller amounts of depreciation remain. However, another factor to be considered is *depreciation recapture,* which becomes important should the asset be sold before the end of its assigned useful life.

Whenever a depreciable asset is sold for more than its current adjusted basis, the difference between the selling price and the adjusted basis represents excess depreciation taken in previous years, and it must be "recaptured." This amount is included in taxable income for the year the asset was sold to account

Table 17-3   An Example of the Effect of Depreciation Choices on Total Depreciation in Year of Purchase (Useful Life of 8 Years and $3,000 Salvage Value)

	Straight line only	Double declining balance only	Double declining balance plus 20% AFYD
Beginning basis	$15,000	$15,000	$15,000
20% AFYD			3,000
Adjusted basis	15,000	15,000	12,000
Regular depreciation	1,500	3,750	3,000
Total depreciation taken first year	1,500	3,750	6,000
Year-end adjusted basis	13,500	11,250	9,000

for the excess depreciation deducted from taxable income in earlier years. Some depreciation recapture may be necessary on many assets because of the difficulty in accurately predicting salvage values and useful lives. However, the depreciation recapture can be substantial when a large amount of depreciation is taken the first few years and the asset is sold before the end of its assigned useful life.

INVESTMENT TAX CREDIT

Congress enacted the first investment tax credit in 1962 as a means of stimulating investment and economic activity. The tax credit rate was initially 7 percent, but it was reduced to 0 percent in 1969–1970 and then reinstated at 7 percent. It was then increased to 10 percent on a temporary basis, and this rate was made permanent in 1978. However, the rate is always subject to change by future legislation.

Investment tax credit is computed by taking 10 percent of the asset's beginning basis, and this amount is a direct credit on a dollar-for-dollar basis against any income tax which may be due and payable. Unlike depreciation and other expenses which reduce taxable income, investment tax credit is subtracted directly from any tax liability. Also unlike additional first-year depreciation, investment tax credit is not optional and must be claimed the year the asset is purchased even though no income tax may be due. However, any unused investment tax credit can be carried back up to 3 years and forward up to 7 years as a credit against past or future taxes.

Investment tax credit can be taken only on qualified property, which is defined as tangible personal property, depreciable in nature, having a useful life of at least 3 years and placed in service during the year. Applied to farms and ranches, this includes machinery, equipment, and breeding stock (other than horses). General-purpose buildings are not eligible, although storage facilities such as silos and grain bins are eligible. Fences, paved barnyards, wells, and drainage tile are other examples of eligible property.

The Revenue Act of 1978 added "single-purpose" agricultural structures to the list of eligible assets. This addition permits investment credit to be taken on buildings such as greenhouses, confinement buildings for raising livestock, and milking parlors. However, general-purpose buildings such as barns and sheds are still not eligible.

Eligible property must have a useful life of at least 3 years but must have a 7-year or longer useful life to qualify for the full credit. The relationship between useful life and the portion of the investment qualifying for investment credit is as follows:

    1- to 2-year useful life: investment does not qualify
    3- to 4-year useful life: one-third of the investment qualifies
    5- to 6-year useful life: two-thirds of the investment qualifies
    7 years or longer useful life: the entire investment qualifies

For example, if qualified property is purchased for $12,000 and assigned a 3- or 4-year useful life, the 10 percent investment credit can be taken on only $4,000. It can be taken on $8,000 with a 5- or 6-year life and on the full $12,000 only if the useful life is 7 years or longer. Investment credit does not affect the beginning basis of the property and therefore does not in any way reduce the amount of additional first-year depreciation or regular depreciation that can be claimed.

There is no limit on the amount of new property which is eligible for investment tax credit in any single year. However, there is a limit on the amount of investment tax credit which can be *used* in any year. This limit is the total tax for the year *or* $25,000 plus 90 percent of the tax liability in excess of $25,000, whichever is *less*. Any remaining credit can be carried back or forward as discussed earlier. While there is no limit on the amount of new property eligible for investment tax credit, there is a $100,000 limit on the amount of used property eligible in any year.

Like depreciation, investment tax credit is subject to recapture to prevent taxpayers from assigning each asset a 7- or 8-year life, taking investment credit on the full investment, and then selling the asset in a few years. For example, if investment credit is taken on the full investment but the asset is sold after 5 or 6 years, one-third of the investment credit taken is recaptured and added to the income tax liability for the year of sale. A sale after 3 or 4 years would cause two-thirds of the investment credit to be recaptured. Since any investment credit recapture is added directly to any income tax due, it can have a substantial impact on taxes in any given year.

EXAMPLE

The total effect of depreciation and investment tax credit on the tax liability in the year a new asset is purchased is best illustrated by an example. Assume a taxpayer with a taxable income of $35,200 who would pay $8,162 of income tax according to Table 17-2. Now assume this same taxpayer had purchased a $15,000 machine on July 1 and assigned it an 8-year life, making it eligible for both additional first-year depreciation and full investment tax credit.

Additional first-year depreciation would be $3,000 (20 percent of $15,000), and regular depreciation using double declining balance would be $1,500 (25 percent of the adjusted basis of $12,000 times one-half for the half year). This depreciation reduces the taxable income to $30,700, resulting in a tax liability of $6,497 (Table 17-2). Investment credit can be taken on the full investment, providing a $1,500 direct tax credit. The final tax liability is $4,997 ($6,497 minus $1,500 investment credit), or $3,165 less than it was without the purchase of the new machine.

The calculations show why farmers and other businesspeople who are anticipating a taxable income higher than normal often purchase new machinery and equipment during the year. This is used as a year-end tax management strategy, as full additional first-year depreciation and investment tax credit can be claimed on items purchased late in the year. However, in an effort to reduce taxable income and tax liability, care should be taken to avoid unwise and untimely purchases. The objective of tax management should be maximization of long-run, after-tax profit. Purchasing unneeded and unnecessary items in an effort to reduce taxes in one year can result in additional expenses and low profits in future years.

CAPITAL GAINS

The tax regulations recognize two types of income, ordinary income and capital gain. Ordinary income includes wages and salaries, interest, dividends, cash rents, and revenue from the sale of crops and feeder livestock. Capital gain can result from the sale or exchange of certain types of qualified assets. In simple terms, capital gain is the gain or profit made by selling an asset at a price which is higher than the original purchase price. However, there may be some depreciation recapture and other adjustments to determine the extent of the gain. A capital loss can occur if the selling price is less than the purchase price.

Two types of assets can qualify for capital gain treatment. "Capital assets" include primarily nonbusiness investments such as stocks and bonds. Of more importance to most farmers and ranchers are "Section 1231 assets," which are defined as property used in a trade or business. In a farm or ranch business, Section 1231 assets would include land, buildings, fences, machinery, equipment, and breeding livestock. Both types of assets must be owned for at least 1 year to be eligible for capital gains, with two exceptions. Commodity futures contracts need to be owned for only 6 months, and there are special rules pertaining to breeding livestock which will be discussed later.

As an example of capital gain income, assume farmland was purchased for a total of $100,000 and sold 3 years later for $150,000. A $50,000 capital gain would result from this transaction. In a similar manner, there can be a capital gain (or loss) from the sale or exchange of other assets provided they have been owned long enough to qualify. Any gain or loss from a sale or exchange of an asset owned for less than the required holding period would be a *short-term* gain or loss. *Long-term* gains or losses result when the holding period has been met which qualifies the sale or exchange for capital gain tax treatment.

Taxation of Long-term Capital Gains

The distinction between ordinary income and long-term capital gain is important because of the different way the two types of income are taxed. Special rules applicable to capital gains result in this type of income being taxed at a lower rate than ordinary income. If there is a net long-term capital gain after adjustment for long-term losses, the taxpayer calculates taxable income in the following manner. The Revenue Act of 1978 stipulates that 40 percent of net long-term capital gain should be added to any ordinary income and the remaining 60 percent is to be *excluded* from taxable income. In other words, 60 percent of capital gain income is not taxed and becomes essentially tax-free income. It is obvious that there is a substantial tax advantage to capital gain as opposed to ordinary income, and the higher the individual's marginal tax bracket the greater the advantage.

If there are short-term gains and losses as well as long-term gains and losses in a given tax year, special rules apply for offsetting the various gains with the losses. These rules should be carefully studied to obtain maximum advantage from the losses.

Capital Gain and Livestock

Farmers and ranchers will generally have more frequent opportunities to receive capital gain income from livestock sales than from selling other assets. Livestock are classified as Section 1231 assets, and their sale or exchange may result in a capital gain or loss *provided they were held for draft, dairy, breeding, or sporting purposes. In addition, cattle and horses must have been owned 24 months and hogs and sheep for 12 months.* Eligibility for capital gains depends on both requirements, the purpose and the holding period.

The above tax provision is of special importance to cash basis farmers and ranchers who raise their own replacements for a breeding or dairy herd. Raised replacements do not have a tax basis established by a purchase price nor do they have a basis established by an inventory value as would occur with accrual accounting. Therefore, cash basis taxpayers have a zero basis on raised replacement animals. If they are used for draft, dairy, breeding, or sporting purposes *and* are held for the required length of time, the entire income from their sale is capital gain (sale price minus the zero basis). Only 40 percent of this income is taxed, and the other 60 percent is tax-free.

This provision of the tax law makes cash basis accounting very desirable for taxpayers with beef, swine, or dairy breeding herds who raise their own replacements. In addition, the expenses of raising and maintaining these animals in the herd are tax-deductible in the year they occur. An accrual basis taxpayer loses most of this capital gain on raised animals because they have a tax basis equal to their last inventory value.

It is possible to receive capital gains upon the sale of purchased breeding stock but only if the selling price is above the original purchase price. For example, assume a beef cow was purchased for $400 and depreciated $50 per year for 3 years, making the current basis $250. If this cow was then sold for $500, the sale would result in $150 of depreciation recapture ($400 minus $250) and $100 of capital gain ($500 minus $400).

The capital gain cash basis taxpayers can receive from selling raised breeding and dairy animals does not necessarily mean replacements should be raised rather than purchased. There are also some tax advantages from purchasing replacements. Purchased replacements can be depreciated including the use of additional first-year depreciation, and they are eligible for investment credit. A replacement method should be selected after carefully considering the costs and production factors as well as the income tax effects. This is another example of the importance income taxes and the various tax regulations play in a manager's decision-making environment. To maximize long-run after-tax profit, a manager is forced to consider income taxes along with the costs and technical production factors of the various alternatives being considered.

SUMMARY

A business can spend or invest only that portion of its profit remaining after income taxes are paid. Therefore, the usual goal of profit maximization should become maximization of long-run after-tax profit. For a farm or ranch business, the tax management necessary to achieve this goal begins with selecting either the cash or accrual tax accounting method. It should continue on a year-round basis because of the many production and investment decisions which have tax consequences.

One aspect of tax management is income leveling utilizing income averaging, proper use of any net operating losses, and careful timing of sales and purchases toward the end of the taxable year. The choice of depreciation method and possible use of the optional additional first-year depreciation are other alternatives for leveling and reducing taxable income. Investment credit is a direct tax credit equal to 10 percent of the cost of a qualified investment. In combination with regular and additional first-year depreciation, it can substantially reduce taxes in any year new investments are made.

Long-term capital gains are taxed at a lower rate than ordinary income and may result from the sale or exchange of a capital asset or a Section 1231 asset. A common source of capital gain for a cash basis taxpayer is income from the sale of raised breeding or dairy animals. This and other sources of capital gains may require careful planning to qualify the sale or exchange for the reduced tax rates applicable to capital gains.

QUESTIONS FOR REVIEW AND FURTHER THOUGHT

1 How does a farmer choose a tax accounting method? Can it be changed? How?
2 Which accounting method would you recommend for each of the following? Why?
   a A crop farmer whose marketing policies cause wide variations in cash receipts and inventory values from year to year.
   b A rancher with a beef breeding herd who raises all the necessary replacement heifers.
3 Which will cause the greatest reduction in taxes: (*a*) an additional $100 of depreciation or (*b*) an additional $100 of investment credit? Why?
4 Assume Fred Farmer purchases a new business pickup for $6,000 on July 1 and wants to use this purchase to the fullest extent to reduce taxes in the purchase year. Does it make any difference if the pickup is assigned a 4-, 6-, or 8-year life? How much difference? (*Hint*: Remember the eligibility requirements for double declining balance depreciation, additional first-year depreciation, and investment credit.)
5 In a year when farm prices and yields are above average, machinery and equipment dealers often experience very brisk sales toward the end of the year. How would you explain this increase in sales?
6 Explain how a cash basis farmer can raise or lower annual taxable income by purchase and selling decisions made in December. Can an accrual basis farmer do the same thing? Why?

REFERENCES

Brown, R. Edward, Jr.: *Income Tax Management for Livestock Producers*, Georgia Cooperative Extension Service Bulletin 744, 1974.

Farmer's Tax Guide, 1980 Edition, Publication 225, Department of the Treasury, Internal Revenue Service.

O'Byrne, John C.: *Farm Income Tax Manual*, 5th ed. The Allen Smith Co., Indianapolis, 1977.

O'Byrne, John C., Charles Davenport, and James D. Keast: *Doane's Tax Management Guide*, Doane Agricultural Service, Inc., St. louis, 1973.

Weigle, R. N., R. Edward Brown, Jr., and Robert S. Smith: *Income Tax Management for Farmers*, Southern Farm Management Extension Publication 17, 1977.

Chapter 18

Managing Risk
and Uncertainty

CHAPTER OBJECTIVES

    1 To define risk and uncertainty and discuss their importance in decision making
    2 To identify the sources of risk and uncertainty which affect farmers and ranchers
    3 To illustrate the different methods for forming expectations about uncertain and risky events
    4 To discuss the importance of variability and its effect on decision making under risk and uncertainty
    5 To show how decision making is affected by individual attitudes toward risk and uncertainty
    6 To list and discuss the various alternatives for reducing risk and uncertainty

Decision making was discussed in Chapter 1 as the principal activity of management. Chapters 2 through 6 introduced some principles and techniques useful in management decision making, but the discussion implicitly assumed all the necessary information was available, accurate, and known with complete certainty. In other words, complete and perfect knowledge was assumed for input prices, output prices, yields, and other technical data. This assumption of perfect knowledge simplifies the understanding of a new principle or concept, but it seldom applies in the real world of agricultural production.

We live in a world of uncertainty. There is an old saying which states that nothing is certain "except death and taxes." To those two certain events we might add "change." Managers find their best decisions often turn out to be less than perfect because of changes which have taken place between the time the decision was made and the time the outcome of that decision is finalized or known. Many agricultural decisions have outcomes months or years after the initial decision is made.

Crop farmers must make decisions on crops to be planted, seeding rates, fertilizer levels, and other input levels early in the cropping season. The crop yield obtained as a result of these decisions will not be known with certainty for several months or even several years in the case of perennial crops. A rancher who has decided to expand a beef cow herd by raising replacement heifers must wait several years before the first income is received from the heifers kept for the herd expansion. Changes in weather, prices, and other factors between the time the decision is made and the first or final outcome is known can make a previously good decision look very bad. Unfortunately farmers and ranchers can do little to speed up Mother Nature's biological processes in crop and livestock production.

Because of this time lag in agricultural production and our inability to predict the future accurately, there are varying amounts of risk and uncertainty in all farm and ranch management decisions. Even if production was instantaneous the information and data acquired during the decision-making process may be of uncertain accuracy and reliability. If everything was known with certainty, most of us could be a successful manager. Decisions would be relatively easy. However, in the real world the more successful managers are the ones with the ability to make the best possible decisions, and the courage to make them, when surrounded by risk and uncertainty. They must also be ready to change and modify previous decisions when changes and/or new information indicate the outcome can be improved. This is an application of the control function discussed in Part 3. Each decision should be monitored, and if the outcome begins to deviate too far from the one expected or additional and better information becomes available, the decision needs to be reevaluated.

DEFINITION OF RISK AND UNCERTAINTY

Some writers make a distinction between risk and uncertainty. They define risk as a situation where all possible outcomes are known for a given management decision and the probability associated with each possible outcome is also known. Simple examples would be tossing a coin or rolling a die. All possible outcomes of each event are known by the decision maker before the toss or roll. If it is a fair coin and a balanced die, the probability or the odds for each possible outcome are also known before the toss or roll.

Probabilities are often assigned to other events such as the probability of rain in a weather forecast or the outcome of a sporting event. However, they are *subjective probabilities* based on the judgment and experience of an individual. In many situations the true or actual probabilities cannot be determined. Subjective probabilities are the only ones available, and they may vary from individual to individual.

Uncertainty is said to exist when one or both of two situations exist for a management decision. Either all the possible outcomes are unknown, the probability of the outcomes are unknown, or neither the outcomes nor the probabilities are known. With this distinction between risk and uncertainty, most agricultural decisions would be classified as involving uncertainty. Even if all possible outcomes could be listed, the associated probabilities can seldom be accurately determined. The best that can be done is to assign subjective probabilities. These are the decision maker's best estimate of the true probabilities based on the limited information available and past experience with the same or similar events and decisions.

The above distinction between risk and uncertainty has only limited usefulness for an individual farm or ranch manager. A pure risk situation will seldom exist because the true probabilities will not be known. Therefore, some authors have argued that farm and ranch managers are always making decisions in an environment where uncertainty prevails. Another line of reasoning is used to argue that all decisions involve risk. The basis for this argument is that even though the true probabilities are not known managers somehow formulate a set of subjective probabilities which are used in the decision-making process. This latter argument can also be used to explain why two managers, faced with the same problem under the same conditions, may make two different decisions. If their experience, background, and interpretation of the available information cause them to formulate different subjective probabilities, different decisions are very possible.

These arguments have tended to blur much of the definitional distinction between risk and uncertainty. Both terms are often used interchangeably, with the proponents of subjective probability favoring the use of risk. This chapter will use both terms interchangeably to describe the usual situation faced by a farm or ranch manager—a decision must be made with something less than perfect information regarding the possible outcomes and/or their probabilities.

SOURCES OF RISK AND UNCERTAINTY

There are a number of sources or types of risk and uncertainty, with one or more applying to most farm management decisions. What are the risks associated with selecting a crop or livestock enterprise, determining the proper levels of feed and fertilizer to be used, and borrowing additional money? What makes the outcomes of these decisions something that cannot be perfectly and accurately predicted? The more common sources of risk can be described in five categories.

Production and Technical Risk

Some types of manufacturing firms know that the use of a certain collection of inputs will always result in a fixed and known quantity of output. This is not the case with most agricultural production processes. Crop and livestock yields are not known with certainty before harvest or final sale. Weather, diseases, insects, weeds, and infertile breeding livestock are examples of factors which cannot be accurately predicted and cause yield variability. Even if the same quantity and quality of inputs are used every year, these and other factors will cause yield variations which cannot be predicted at the time most input decisions must be made. These yield variations are an example of production risk.

One type of production risk is illustrated in Figure 18-1, where weather is an important factor affecting yield. Production functions for three possible weather conditions are shown. Inputs such as seed and fertilizer must be applied before the weather is known, and regardless of the input level selected, weather will affect the output level. This creates uncertainty about the output which will be received for any input level as well as uncertainty about what input level to use.

Technical risk also contributes to the problem of determining the proper input level. It exists when the production function and other technical relationships are not known with certainty. This creates uncertainty about input levels and corresponding output levels even in the absence of other uncertain yield-influencing factors such as weather. In Figure 18-1, the three production functions were assumed to be known with certainty. If they are not, the manager must make decisions under conditions of both production and technical risk.

Price Risk

A major source of risk in agriculture is price variability. While farmers feel they may have some influence on yields through their decisions, prices are generally beyond their control except possibly through some type of cooperative effort or government action. Both input and output prices are variable, but output price variability is the most important. Input prices have been more stable although rising over time and can usually be determined with certainty at the time a purchase is made. Because of the time lag in agricultural pro-

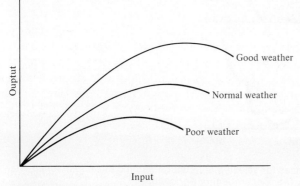

Figure 18-1 Production risk due to weather.

duction the price received for a commodity may be greatly different from the price at the time the production decisions were made.

The prices of most agricultural commodities vary seasonally within a year as well as changing from year to year. Both production and marketing decisions are made under uncertainty because of this price variability. Figure 18-2 shows the average annual prices for some of the major agricultural commodities. The price fluctuations shown in the graphs illustrate the difficulty of making management decisions where a future output price is important to the decision.

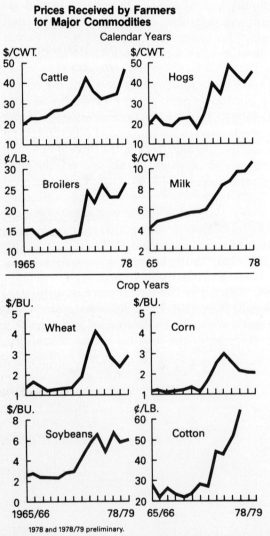

Figure 18-2 Average annual prices for selected agricultural commodities. (*Economic, Statistical and Cooperative Service, U.S. Department of Agriculture.*)

Keep in mind that the prices shown in Figure 18-2 are average annual prices. If seasonal variations were included, the price fluctuations would be even more extreme.

Financial Risk

Financial risk was discussed in Chapter 12 using the principle of increasing risk. This principle stated that there is an increasing risk of losing equity due to a decline in income as borrowing and the debt/equity ratio increases. Yield and price uncertainty combine to generate financial risk or uncertainty about the firm's ability to repay debt. A combination of lower than expected prices and yields can make debt repayment difficult, put a strain on the firm's cash flow, and possibly reduce equity. A series of such events can result in bankruptcy.

Government Policies

Many government policies, programs, rules, and regulations are subject to change, creating another source of uncertainty for farmers and ranchers. Basic farm programs generally expire after 2 to 4 years, requiring Congress to pass new farm program legislation or have no farm program. Even under a given program, acreage allotments, set aside requirements, target prices, and loan rates often change from year to year. Income tax regulations change, as do regulations issued under the Occupational Safety and Health Act (OSHA) and various U.S. Department of Agriculture regulatory agencies. Government policies regarding inflation, unemployment, money supply, and foreign trade influence price levels and are other factors contributing to price uncertainty.

Individuals

Individuals and their changeable nature also generate some uncertainty. Farmers and ranchers must deal with spouses, neighbors, bankers, suppliers, dealers, and landlords, any of whom can change their attitude, policy, or business relationship. The normally "friendly" banker who refuses a new loan request or the landlord who declines to renew a lease can upset past and current decisions. Such events may be infrequent, but they can and do happen. Unfortunately they often seem to happen at the most inopportune time and make long-run planning an even more uncertain activity.

DECISION MAKING UNDER RISK

The existence of risk and uncertainty adds complexity to many problems and to the decision-making process. However, decisions must still be made, and the manager is faced with making the best decision given the uncertainty associated with the available information. A basic part of the problem is that most decision-making principles require information in the form of a single value rather than a range of values. Use of the economic principles in Chapter 2 to determine the optimum amount of fertilizer requires a single value for the price of the output as well as a price for fertilizer and knowledge of the production function. Different output prices give different answers, and the manager must finally select only one fertilizer level. Therefore, the manager must form an "expectation" about the output price and somehow arrive at an "expected" value to use in the decision-making process.

Forming Expectations

Several methods can be used to form an expectation about future prices, yields, and other values which are not known with certainty. Once an expected value is obtained it can be used for planning and decision making, as it becomes the "best estimate" of some unknown value which will only be determined by future events.

Averages Two types of averages can be used to form an expected value. A series of actual past prices or yields can be used to find the simple average over some specified time period. This is a relatively simple method to use if past data are available. The primary problem is selecting the length of the data series to use in calculating the simple average. Should the average be for 3, 5, or 10 years? There are no simple rules to answer this question, and the choice will depend on the subjective estimate of the decision maker.

A weighted average can also be used to arrive at an expected value. This method usually weights the more recent values heavier than the older ones using some predetermined weighting system. Two problems are encountered with this system. First, how many years should be used, and, second, what weighting system is best? Again, the experience, judgment, and preferences of the decision maker along with a knowledge of the data provide the only guidelines that can be easily applied.

Table 18-1 is a simple example of using both averaging methods to arrive at an expected value. Four years of price information is used, which gives a simple average of $2.96. To calculate a weighted average, each price is multiplied by its assigned weight, and the results are summed and divided by the

Table 18-1   Using Averages to Form an Expected Value

Year	Average annual price	Weight	Price × weight
4 years ago	$2.43	1	2.43
3 years ago	3.02	2	6.04
2 years ago	2.94	3	8.82
Last year	3.46	4	13.84
Summation	$11.85	10	31.13

Expected value			
Simple average	$11.85 ÷ 4 = $2.96		
Weighted average			$31.13 ÷ 10 = $3.11

sum of the weights. The expected price would be $3.11 using the weighted average method. Notice this is higher than the simple average. In this example, the highest price was in the last year and the lowest 4 years ago. The assigned weight for the last year is four times that for the earliest year, making the weighted average higher than the simple average. This difference is also a result of the simple average implicitly assigning equal weights to all values. Obviously, a different set of weights would give a different weighted average.

Some research studies have shown that farmers may actually use some type of weighted average to form price expectations. These studies have had some success predicting crop acreages by assuming farmers make this decision using an expected price derived from some type of weighted average.

Most Likely Another way to form an expectation is to choose the value most likely to occur. This procedure requires a knowledge of the probabilities associated with each possible outcome, either actual or subjective. The outcome with the highest probability would be selected as the most likely to occur. An example is contained in the first two columns of Table 18-2 (ignore the last column for the moment) where four possible wheat yields are shown along with the probabilities of obtaining each yield. Using the most likely method to form an expectation, a yield of 24 bushels per acre would be selected. This yield has the highest probability and is therefore the most likely to occur. There is no assurance this yield will occur in any given year, but if the probabilities are correct, it will occur 40 percent of the time over a long period.

The procedure illustrated in Table 18-2 is difficult to apply when the uncertain or risky outcome is a continuous variable and can take on any value over some range. One possibility is to divide the range of possible outcomes into a number of subgroups, find the midpoint of each subgroup, and then determine the probability for each. Table 18-2 might be thought of as four subgroups representing a continuous yield distribution with the 18-bushel yield the midpoint for the 15- to 21-bushel subgroup. Accuracy can be increased by using a larger number of groups or by a direct use of the continuous probability distribution if it is known.

Figure 18-3 contains three examples of continuous probability distributions each with different characteristics. The higher the curve for any expected outcome the greater the probability of that outcome's occurring. In Figure

Table 18-2   Using Probabilities to Form Expectations

Possible wheat yields	Probability	Probability × outcome
12	0.1	1.2
18	0.3	5.4
24	0.4	9.6
30	0.2	6.0
Total	1.0	22.2

18-3a, the most likely outcome is at point M, as this outcome has the highest probability. This outcome is also the average outcome, since the probability distribution is symmetrical.

The probability distribution in Figure 18-3b is skewed to the left similar to the discrete distribution shown in Table 18-2. Again the most likely outcome is the one with the highest probability as shown by point M. However, the average outcome for this probability distribution is lower than the most likely because of the skewness. The average outcome is represented by point A.

Figure 18-3c is an example of a uniform distribution of expected outcomes. Since it is another symmetrical distribution, the average outcome is in the center at point A. However, the most likely method cannot be used to form an expectation with this distribution. All outcomes have the same probability, and no one is more likely than another.

Mathematical Expectation   When either the true or subjective probabilities of the expected outcomes are available, it is possible to calculate the mathematical expectation. The mathematical expectation is the average outcome of conducting the experiment or repeating the event many times and is the same as the average outcome discussed for the probability distributions in

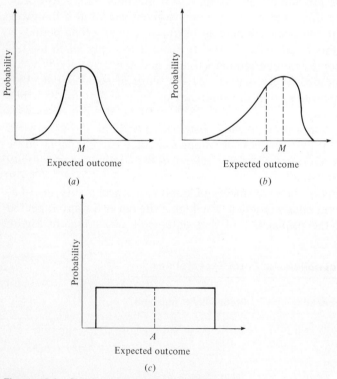

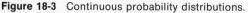

Figure 18-3 Continuous probability distributions.

Figure 18-3. The accuracy of the mathematical expectation using subjective probabilities depends on the accuracy of these relative to the true but unknown probabilities.

The method for calculating a mathematical expectation is shown in the right-hand column of Table 18-2. Each possible outcome is multiplied by its associated probability, and the results are summed to find the mathematical expectation. Notice the mathematical expectation of 22.2 bushels per acre is less than the most likely yield of 24 bushels because the probabilities are not symmetrical, being skewed toward the lower yields.

Variability

A manager who must select from two or more alternatives may consider another factor in addition to the expected values. The variability or dispersion of the possible outcomes around the expected value may also be important. For example, if two alternatives have the same expected value, most managers would choose the one whose potential outcomes have the least variability.

Range A simple measure of variability is the difference between the lowest and highest possible outcome or the range. Alternatives with a smaller range are preferred over those with a wider range provided that their expected values are the same. The range is not considered a good measure of variability because it does not consider the probabilities associated with the extreme values in the distribution of outcomes.

Standard Deviation A common statistical measure of variability is the standard deviation. It can be calculated for a continuous probability distribution or for a random sample of values drawn from the total population of some random variable.[1] A larger standard deviation indicates a greater dispersion of possible outcomes and therefore a greater probability that the actual outcome will be further from the mean or expected value. Figure 18-4 shows two probability distributions with the same expected value at x. However, distribution 1 has the smaller standard deviation because the possible outcomes are clustered about the expected value in a fairly narrow band. Distribution 2 has the greater standard deviation even though both distributions have the same mean or expected value. In this example, distribution 2 would also have the greater range.

Coefficient of Variation The standard deviation is difficult to interpret when the probability distributions have different expected values. Probability distributions with higher expected values might be expected to have greater variability and often do. An important consideration in this situation is the relative variability. Does the probability distribution with the higher expected value really have greater variability relative to its larger expected value?

---

[1]The equation for calculating the standard deviation can be found in any basic statistics textbook.

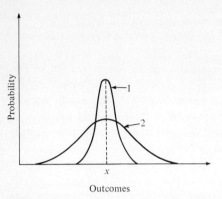

Figure 18-4 Variability of two probability distributions.

The coefficient of variation measures variability *relative to* the expected value or mean of the probability distribution. This measure of variation is found by dividing the standard deviation by the mean or expected value of distribution.

$$\text{Coefficient of variation} = \frac{\text{standard deviation}}{\text{expected value or mean}}$$

It provides a method of assessing the relative variability of any number of probability distributions which may have greatly different expected values. Smaller coefficients of variation mean the distribution has less variability in relation to its expected value than other distributions.

ATTITUDES TOWARD RISK

Once the expected values of all alternatives have been calculated we would expect the profit-maximizing manager to select the alternative with the highest expected value. However, using maximization of expected profit as the criterion for decision making under risk and uncertainty ignores the greater variability often associated with alternatives having the higher expected profits. The alternative selected by different managers will depend upon their attitudes toward risk. In other words, are they willing to accept an increase in risk for a higher expected profit and if so, how much?

Three possible attitudes toward risk are illustrated in Figure 18-5. The risk-averse manager is not willing to accept additional risk unless the expected profit is also greater. Those who are risk-indifferent do not require any increase in expected profit before they will accept a riskier alternative. They essentially ignore risk when making a decision. Managers with a preference for risk are willing to select an alternative with a lower expected profit in order to assume (enjoy?) more risk. They are sometimes referred to as "risk lovers."

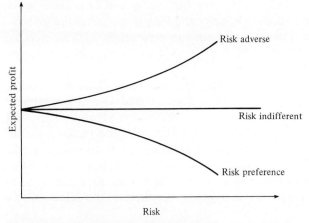

Figure 18-5 Possible attitudes toward risk.

While there are people who prefer riskier alternatives or are indifferent toward risk, most are risk-averse. They are aware of and consider the trade-off between increased risk and higher expected profits when making a decision. An example of this trade-off is shown in Figure 18-6, where the expected profit and risk for each of five alternatives have been plotted and connected with a smooth curve.

Some measure of variability is plotted as risk on the vertical axis. Each alternative might be thought of as a different farm plan each containing a different combination of crops and livestock. Plan A represents doing nothing—no profit but no risk or income variability. Adopting Plan B increases expected profit with some increase in risk. Moving to Plans C and D increases

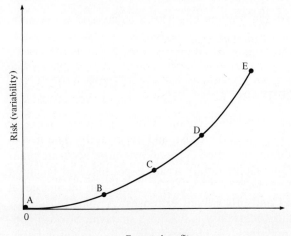

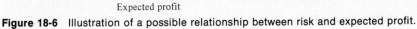

Figure 18-6 Illustration of a possible relationship between risk and expected profit.

expected profit even more, but risk is also increasing and at a faster rate. Expected profit would be maximized by selecting Plan E, but it has the greatest risk or variability of profit. Plan E might contain enterprises such as growing vegetables or feeding heavy cattle, both of which tend to have high expected or average profits but profits which are also highly variable.

A risk-averse manager would be likely to select from Plans B, C, or D. There is a large reduction in risk between Plans E and D and a relatively smaller decrease in expected profit. Each successive movement to the left reduces risk but by decreasing amounts. At some point the manager is un-willing to accept any additional decrease in expected profit to decrease risk any further. However, different managers may well select different plans when faced with the same curve with its risk and profit trade-offs. Risk-averse man-agers may differ in their degree of risk aversion, resulting in the selection of a different farm plan.

Another example may serve to illustrate further why managers may not always maximize expected profit without regard to the risk involved. Assume a manager is faced with choosing between the following two alternatives. The manager who maximizes expected profit would choose Alternative II. How-ever, this alternative has a one-fourth probability of a negative profit while the worst that can happen with Alternative I is a profit of zero. If the negative profit would cause severe financial difficulty or even bankruptcy, the manager may prefer Alternative I even with its lower expected value. Business survival is also an important goal or objective, and many managers would not be willing to risk a one-fourth chance of business failure for a higher expected profit.

Alternative I		Alternative II	
Profit ($)	Probability	Profit ($)	Probability
0	1/3	−5,000	1/4
5,000	1/3	10,000	1/2
10,000	1/3	20,000	1/4
Expected value = $5,000		Expected value = $8,750	

REDUCING RISK AND UNCERTAINTY

There are three general and perhaps related reasons why a risk-averse manager would be interested in taking steps to reduce risk and uncertainty. The first is to reduce the variability of income over time. This allows more accurate plan-ning for items such as debt repayment, family living expenses, and business growth. Second, there may be a need to assure some minimum income level to meet family living expenses and other fixed expenses. A third reason for reducing or minimizing risk and uncertainty is business survival. Several con-secutive years of low income may threaten business survival or result in bank-ruptcy. Some recent studies show many managers rate business survival as their most important goal. They would be willing to accept a lower expected income if it reduces income variability and hence the risk of business failure.

Several techniques can be used to reduce the risk and uncertainty associated with variable income. Some tend to reduce overall variability, and others are an attempt to ensure a minimum price or income. Each has some type of direct or indirect cost associated with its use.

Diversification

Many business firms diversify or produce more than one product to avoid having their income totally dependent on the production and price of one product. If profit from one product is poor, profit from producing and selling other products may prevent total profit from falling below acceptable levels. In agricultural production, diversifying by producing two or more commodities may reduce income variability if all prices and yields are not low or high at the same time. Table 18-3 is an example of how diversification can work to reduce income variability. To simplify the discussion, assume the only choices are producing all of either crop or dividing the available land equally between the two crops.

Based on the average income for the past 5 years, specialization in crop B would provide the greatest average income. However, this crop also has the greatest variability as measured by the range. Producing only crop A would reduce income variability but also the average income. The remaining possibility is to diversify. This results in an intermediate average income but a large reduction in income variability as measured by the range. Variability is reduced because of the relationship or correlation between the annual income for the two crops. Notice that whenever the income for crop A is below average the income for crop B is above average and vice versa. This negative correlation "smooths out" the annual income under diversification and reduces income variability.

To what extent will diversification reduce income variability in an actual farm situation? The answer depends on the price and yield correlation for the enterprises selected. If both prices and yields for the enterprises tend to move

Table 18-3   Theoretical Example of Diversification

Year		Crop A	Crop B	Diversification (½ of each)
		Annual income ($)		
1		5,000	50,000	27,500
2		20,000	0	10,000
3		5,000	30,000	17,500
4		50,000	−5,000	22,500
5		10,000	25,000	17,500
	Average:	18,000	20,000	19,000
	Range:	45,000	55,000	17,500

up and down together, little is gained by diversifying. The more these values tend to move in opposite directions the more income variability will be reduced by diversifying.

Weather is the primary factor influencing crop yields. Crops with the same growing season experience the same weather, and their yields tend to have a strong positive correlation. The yield correlation for crops with different growing seasons and susceptible to different insects and diseases will be somewhat less. Little information is available on the correlation of livestock yields, but intuitively we would expect little correlation. Why should the average pigs per litter, milk per cow, and eggs per hen tend to increase and decrease together? Disease may be one answer, but few diseases affect all classes of livestock. There is also little reason to expect a strong correlation between crop and livestock yields.

Most studies on the price correlation for major agricultural commodities show a positive and, for some commodities, a strong positive correlation. In other words, the prices for many agricultural commodities tend to move up and down together. This obviously does not happen every year but is the long-run tendency. Some specialty crops such as fruits and vegetables may show a weak or even negative price correlation, particularly with some of the major field crops.

There appear to be some opportunities to reduce income variability through diversification. For example, one study reported negative net income correlation between sugar beets and alfalfa, cotton, barley, and potatoes for some areas in California.[2] However, careful study is needed to select the proper combination of enterprises. Diversification may mean giving up specializing in a highly profitable but highly variable enterprise, making the manager's risk aversion an important factor in the final decision.

The above discussion has been in terms of product diversification, but there can also be diversification in marketing. This can be accomplished by selling part of the annual production at several times during the marketing year. For example, one-fourth of the crop might be sold every third month. This marketing strategy eliminates the possibility of selling the entire crop at the lowest price for the year. Of course, it also eliminates the possibility of selling the entire crop at the highest price. Diversification in marketing eliminates some of the seasonal variations in product prices and results in receiving about the year's average price for the total production marketed.

Insurance

A manager can provide insurance for a business in one of two ways. Formal insurance can be obtained through an insurance company to cover many types of risks which, if they occur, could have serious impact on business equity and survival. The alternative is for the business to provide its own insurance or be

[2]H. O. Carter and G. W. Dean, "Income, Price and Yield Variability for Principal California Crops and Cropping Systems," *Hilgardia,* vol. 30, no. 6, October 1960.

self-insured. In the latter option, some type of readily available or liquid financial reserves must be available in case a loss does occur. Without these financial reserves, a crop failure, major windstorm, or fire may be such a financial setback that the business will fail.

The choice between formal insurance and self-insuring is influenced by the difference in the annual premium paid to an insurance company and the cost of maintaining the liquid financial reserve. This choice can be formalized by the following equation:

$$g = R\,(r - i) - P$$

where g = gain from insuring

R = financial reserve needed

P = annual insurance premium

r = opportunity cost for the financial reserve (percent)

i = actual earnings on financial reserve (percent)

If g is greater than zero, the decision should be to use formal insurance, as the cost (in terms of income sacrificed) of maintaining the financial reserve is greater than the cost of the insurance premium.

Some formal insurance is carried by most farmers and ranchers. The above equation can be used to provide several explanations. First, the opportunity cost of the financial reserve will often be greater than the reserve will earn in a safe, liquid investment such as a savings account. Second, there is the problem of determining the size of the financial reserve. Acquiring and maintaining a reserve large enough to cover losses from all possibilities can be very costly. Yet as the reserve is decreased in size there is an increasing probability that it will be inadequate to cover the possible losses that might occur at any given time. There is also the problem of acquiring the cash to replenish the reserve any time it must be used.

Many types of risks are insurable. A manager may choose a combination of formal and self-insurance. Attitude toward risk and the financial condition of the business will determine the combination selected.

Property Insurance Property insurance is one of the more common types of insurance coverage. It protects against the loss of buildings, machinery, livestock, and stored grain from fire and lightning. A policy with extended coverage provides additional protection against loss from windstorm, theft, hail, explosion, falling aircraft, and certain other perils. Property insurance is relatively inexpensive, and the loss from a serious fire or windstorm can be devastating. Therefore, most farmers and ranchers choose to carry at least a minimum level of property insurance on their more valuable assets.

Liability Insurance This type of insurance protects the insured against lawsuits by third parties for personal injury and property damage for which the insured and/or employees may be liable. For example, the liability coverage on an automobile insurance policy pays for injuries and damages to third parties when the insured driver is at fault. Liability claims on a farm may occur when livestock wander onto a road and cause an accident or when a third party is injured on the property. The risk of a liability claim may be small, but some of the claims awarded by the courts in recent years have been very large. Most people find liability insurance an inexpensive method to provide some "peace of mind" and protection against the possible loss of business equity.

Crop Insurance   Two types of crop insurance are available. The first is crop hail insurance, which protects the insured crop only against losses caused by hailstorms. A number of private insurance companies provide this type of coverage, and the cost will depend on the amount of coverage desired and the past frequency and intensity of hailstorms in the local area.

The other type of crop insurance is "all-risk" insurance. As the name implies, this insurance provides protection against crop loss caused by everything except neglect, poor management practices, and theft. The largest payments under all-risk insurance have been made because of drought, with excess moisture, early freezes, hail, and insect damage following in that order. At present the only source of all-risk crop insurance in many areas is the Federal Crop Insurance Corporation (FCIC), which is an agency of the U.S. Department of Agriculture. Several private companies are experimenting with all-risk crop insurance on a limited scale.

Because hail and drought affect all crops and either one can cause a total crop failure, many farmers purchase hail or all-risk crop insurance. This is particularly true for beginning farmers and others with a low business equity and heavy debt. Lenders may require some borrowers to have crop insurance, particularly if the debt repayment is dependent upon the income from the insured crop.

Life Insurance   Many types of life insurance are available to provide protection against losses that might result from the untimely death of the farm owner/manager or a member of the family. The insurance proceeds can be used to meet family living expenses, pay off existing debts, pay inheritance taxes, and meet other expenses related to transferring management and ownership of the business.

Two basic types of life insurance are available—term and permanent. Term insurance provides only protection at relatively low cost but has no savings or cash value features. It provides protection for a specified period of time such as 5 or 10 years and makes payment if the insured dies within that period. At the end of the period or term the insurance lapses and a new policy must be taken out if continued coverage is desired. Premiums for term insurance increase with the age of the insured.

There are many types of permanent insurance each having some combination of protection, savings, and cash value buildup. Most feature level periodic premiums for a specified period such as 20 years, until age 65 or for life, and remain in force until the death of the insured. Endowment policies provide protection as well as returning the face value of the policy at a specified time if the insured is still living. The cash value of some permanent types of life insurance provides collateral for borrowing from the insurance company to meet future financial emergencies. Because of the cash value and other features of permanent insurance, premiums will be higher than for term insurance.

General Comments   Anyone contemplating the purchase of insurance is well advised to become familiar with insurance terminology, determine exactly what type and amount of coverage is desired, and then shop around. Competitive premium rates, good service, and a history of prompt and fair claim adjustments are factors to consider in selecting an insurance company. Both too much and too little insurance can be costly. The right amount is an individual choice based on risk attitude and the financial condition of the business.

Unused Credit

Studies have found that many farmers do not borrow up to the limit imposed upon them by their lender. This unused credit is a borrowing reserve to provide additional funds in the event of an unfavorable outcome. Utilizing this technique does not reduce risk and uncertainty, but it does provide a measure of protection against years of low income. However, it has a cost equal to the additional profit this unused capital would have earned in the business.

Pricing Contracts

Price uncertainty can be eliminated or reduced by using one of two types of procedures to set a selling or purchase price before the actual date of delivery. A selling price can actually be established before harvest or even before planting. The first type is a cash contract, which is an agreement with a buyer who agrees to pay a set price for a certain quantity and quality of a commodity to be delivered at a later date. A legal cash contract is binding on both parties regardless of price changes between signing the contract and delivery date for the commodity.

Futures contracts can be purchased or sold on one of the commodity exchanges through an established broker and are a second way to set a price. Attempting to set a price utilizing futures contracts is called *hedging*. The theory and techniques of hedging are covered in most basic textbooks on marketing. Before attempting to hedge, a manager should become thoroughly familiar with the theory and techniques of hedging and with the workings of the futures market. Only rarely can an exact price be established through hedging, as the prices of futures contracts and local cash market prices do not always move together. However, a price can normally be established within a fairly narrow range.

Other Methods

There are several other methods which can be used to reduce income variability. Participation in government commodity programs has been a way to guarantee a minimum price for the commodity. This minimum price may be determined by a target price, support price, loan rate, or some combination depending on the commodity and current farm program.

Flexibility has also been recommended. This refers to acquiring and organizing resources in a way to allow a relatively easy, rapid, and inexpensive move from one enterprise to another. When the profitability of one enterprise becomes too low, the farm plan can be easily changed to include another enterprise(s) which is now relatively more profitable. However, modern technology has made it difficult to maintain flexibility. Many of the newer machines, buildings, and production techniques are very specialized for use in one enterprise. For example, it is very difficult to convert a cotton picker, milking parlor, or a total-confinement hog house to some other use.

Finally, the choice of enterprises included in the farm plan will affect income variability. Enterprises such as dairying and irrigated crop production have a history of more stable income than raising vegetables or feeding heavy cattle, for example. However, there is always the problem of the trade-off between risk and expected profit. Enterprises with greater income variability typically have higher expected profit over the long run.

SUMMARY

We live in a world of uncertainty. Rarely do we know the exact what, when, where, how, and how much of any decision and its possible outcomes. Decisions must still be made, however, and one measure of management is its "batting average" in an uncertain environment. No one will make a perfectly correct decision every time, but decision making under uncertainty can be improved. Good information and a working knowledge of probabilities, forming expectations, and estimating variability of possible outcomes and methods to reduce risk and uncertainty will help to increase the "batting average." The decision maker should also perform some self-analysis concerning attitudes toward risk to make decisions which are more compatible with personal preferences and goals and the financial condition of the business.

QUESTIONS FOR REVIEW AND FURTHER THOUGHT

1 What are the sources of risk and uncertainty for farmers in your area? Which would you rank as the most important? Why?
2 What are subjective probabilities? How are they formed? How do they differ from true probabilities?
3 Suppose you had developed the data in Table 18-1 for a crop you grow and want to use it to make production and marketing decisions. You are offered a contract which will guarantee you a price of $3. Would you accept it? Why or why not?

4 Select five prices which you feel might be the average price for choice fed steers next year, being sure to include both the lowest and highest average price you would expect. Ask a classmate to do the same thing.
   a Who has the greatest range of expected prices?
   b Calculate the simple average for each set of prices. How do they compare?
   c Independently assign your own subjective probabilities to each price on your list, remembering the probabilities must sum to 1. Compare them.
   d Calculate the mathematical expectation for each set of prices and compare them.
   e Would you expect everyone in class to have the same set of prices and subjective probabilities? Why?
5 How might a young farmer with heavy debt view risk compared with an older, established farmer with little debt?
6 Might these same two farmers have different ideas about the amount of insurance they need? Why?

REFERENCES

Doll, John P., and Frank Orazem: *Production Economics: Theory with Applications,* Grid, Inc., Columbus, Ohio, 1978, chap. 8.

Halter, Albert N., and Gerald W. Dean: *Decisions under Uncertainty,* South-Western Publishing Co., Cincinnati, Ohio, 1971.

Osburn, Donald D., and Kenneth C. Schneeberger: *Modern Agriculture Management,* Reston Publishing Co., Reston, Va., 1978, chap. 20.

Upton, Martin: *Agricultural Production Economics and Resource-Use,* Oxford University Press, London, 1976, chap. 4.

Walker, Odell L., and A. Gene Nelson: *Agricultural Research and Education Related to Decision-Making under Uncertainty: An Interpretative Review of Literature,* Oklahoma Agricultural Experiment Station Research Report P-747, March 1977.

Chapter 19

Professional
Farm Management

CHAPTER OBJECTIVES

  1 To identify the three types of farm and ranch managers as self-employed farm owner/operators, private farm managers, and professional farm managers
  2 To outline the history of professional farm management
  3 To describe the services provided by professional farm management companies and the fees they charge for these services
  4 To discuss the qualifications needed to enter the field of professional farm management
  5 To note the existence of organizations which promote and enhance the profession of farm management

A large number of managers are classified as owner/operators or those who own, operate, and manage their own farm or ranch business. They may own all the land they operate, rent it all, or have a combination of owned and rented land, but they are self-employed in the business of producing agricultural commodities. Except for the larger operations with several employees, their time is divided between making management decisions and implementing them. In other words, the owner/operator managers also provide some or all of the labor input for their business in addition to the management.

Another group of managers might be classified as private farm managers. They are employed by an individual or firm to manage one farm or a group of farms all under the same ownership. These managers are employees who receive their income in the form of salaries, profit-sharing arrangements, bonuses, or some combination. As a group, private managers differ from other managers by being employees rather than self-employed and by providing management services for a single landowner. However, their duties are similar to those of farm owner/operators except that typically a larger part or all of their time is spent on management activities.

A third group of farm managers includes those known as professional farm managers. They provide management services for a number of farms and for many different farm owners. Professional farm managers either own or work for a firm whose business is providing farm management services for a fee. They differ from the other two classifications by providing management services for a large number of landowners. Their income is received directly or indirectly through management fees paid to the farm management company for the services provided.

Professional farm management has been a growing career field and one of interest to farm management students who do not have the opportunity to become owner/operators of their own farm or ranch business. The remainder of this chapter will discuss some of the history of professional farm management and other topics related to professional farm managers and farm management companies.

HISTORY

The beginning of professional farm management was in the Midwest during the 1910s and 1920s. This was about the same time that farm management was becoming widely recognized as an academic discipline in state land-grant universities. The need for professional farm management as it developed in Illinois has been traced to two factors.[1] First was the decline in the productivity of the land and the need to increase income following the decline in agricultural prices after World War I. Second, the original settlers and landowners were retiring and their land was passing on to the second generation. Widows of the first generation and sons and daughters in the second generation often rented out their land under a share lease, creating a need for someone to manage their farm. This was particularly true if they no longer lived close to the farm.

The first factor primarily created an awareness of the importance of sound farm management to maintain farm productivity and farm income. Professional farm management probably owes its beginnings more to the second factor. The 1930s generated another need for professional farm management. Insurance companies and other lenders had to foreclose on many farms when farmers

[1]"History of the American Society of Farm Managers and Rural Appraisers," *Journal of the American Society of Farm Managers and Rural Appraisers*, vol. 36, no. 2, October 1972.

could not make the mortgage payments. These farms were often rented back to the same farmer, and the lenders found themselves managing a number of farms being operated under some type of lease agreement.

From these beginnings, professional farm management has grown steadily over the years, with management services now available in nearly every state. Professional management is provided for a large number of farms and ranches, but the largest concentration is in the area from Ohio westward. As landownership passes into the second, third, and fourth generations, the owners often live some distance from the farm and recognize they do not have the time and knowledge to manage a farm with today's modern and changing technology. These absentee owners form a large part of the clientele for farm management companies. In addition, many farm management companies manage farms for trusts, estates, and investors in farmland.

THE FARM MANAGEMENT BUSINESS

A number of farm management companies of various sizes provide professional farm management services throughout the country. Several of the larger companies are Doane's Agricultural Services, Inc.,[2] Farmers National Company, and Western Farm Management Company. All operate in several states. The first two are primarily Midwestern companies, and the latter operates in 15 western states. There are also a large number of smaller firms ranging in size from one manager up to perhaps a dozen. They typically provide management services within one state or within a part of a state.

A large number of banks have entered the farm management business over the years. Bank trust departments often have farm and ranch land included in one or more trusts under their management, creating a need to employ a professional farm manager. Some banks have chosen to expand their management business to other than trust property to provide an additional service to their customers and for the additional income it provides.

Consulting services, rural appraisals, feasibility studies, and real estate sales are additional services provided by many farm management companies, as they generally complement the farm management services. They provide additional services to current customers and often provide contacts useful in expanding the farm management business.

Professional Farm Management Services

A landowner typically arranges for management services by signing a contract or agreement with a farm management company. This contract specifies the farm to be managed and the management fee, length, and termination procedure for the agreement and outlines some of the basic management services to be provided. It may also include sections on the type and amount of insur-

---

[2]This firm was founded in 1919 by D. Howard Doane. Mr. Doane was very active in early farm management work and is sometimes referred to as the "father of farm management."

ance coverage to be maintained, who will pay for insurance premiums and property taxes, and any limits on the amount the manager can spend without the owner's approval.

The professional farm manager's first step after receiving a new farm for management is to inventory the property and begin working on the whole farm plan. This physical inventory was discussed in Chapter 5 and includes field layout, soil maps, past cropping history, drainage, erosion and fertility problems, the number, size, capacity, and condition of buildings, and any other information necessary to develop a whole farm plan. With the owner's goals in mind, the manager uses this information to develop a whole farm plan including recommendations for capital improvements and their cost. A cash flow budget must be included to complete the planning phase of management.

These plans and budgets are submitted to the owner for approval, particularly if they include capital expenditures. Once approved, these plans become the plan of operation for the farm until new circumstances require that they be changed. The manager's duties and the services provided after this point are many and varied and cannot be listed here in any detail. However, the following list will provide a general outline.[3]

1 Select and supervise the best farm operator available for the farm. (This may be either an operator under a lease agreement or a farm supervisor if direct operation is deemed most appropriate for the farm and for the owner's goals.)

2 Visit the farm frequently enough to ensure that good management practices and the plans are being followed.

3 Make recommendations to the operator and owner concerning cropping systems, seed selection, seeding rates, fertilizer and chemical use, livestock feed rations, livestock management, harvesting, marketing, etc.

4 Arrange for and supervise repairs and maintenance of buildings, fences, water systems, land drainage systems, etc.

5 Prepare accurate and complete reports on a periodic basis and submit them to the owner. These reports should include results of the operation, current status of crops and livestock, and recommendations for changes and improvements.

6 Supervise the purchase of materials and supplies such as seed and fertilizer, passing any price discounts received because of volume purchasing along to the owner and farm operator.

7 Supervise the selling of the owner's share of crops and livestock and collect any cash rent.

8 Pay all proper expenses for the operation of the farm and periodically provide the owner with an accurate accounting of income and expenses.

9 Check and monitor the insurance coverage and represent the owner in adjusting any insurance losses.

10 Represent the owner in any situation affecting the farm such as drain-

[3]Adapted from American Society of Farm Managers and Rural Appraisers, *Professional Farm Management Manual*, January 1972.

age and irrigation district hearings, property tax assessments, and disputes over maintaining line fences.

    11 Provide the owner with information and assistance for income and estate tax planning and management.

    The first item on the above list is perhaps the most important from the standpoint of its long-term effect on the farm and its profitability. Selection of a good farm operator or farm supervisor who is in agreement with the farm plan and who is operating under a fair and equitable lease or contract can make a manager's job much easier.

    Farm visits and effective communication with the owner are also essential. The frequency of farm visits will depend on the type of farm, the time of year, and other factors. Whatever the number of visits during the year they should be frequent enough to ensure the farm operator is following the agreed upon management practices and to keep the manager current with the operation. Often the owner's only real feel for the adequacy of the management services being provided comes through the written reports. Therefore, frequent and accurate reports to the owner will do much to build and maintain confidence in the manager's ability and performance.

Professional Management Fees

Professional farm managers and management companies receive their income in the form of fees charged for the services provided. The more common fee arrangements are a flat fixed fee for the farm, a flat fee per acre, or a percentage of the owner's gross rental income. Fees may vary by region, farm type, farm size, and the range of management services provided. Combinations of fee types are also used such as a flat fixed fee plus some percentage of the gross income, as this arrangement provides a minimum annual fee for the manager. Percentage fees are commonly used in the Midwest for farms rented on a crop share basis. The fees charged are typically between 6 and 10 percent of the owner's share of the gross crop income, with 10 percent the most common fee. Fees based on a share of the owner's net income are not widely used.

Manager Qualifications

Professional farm managers need a combination of training, experience, and personal characteristics similar to those of other professions which provide a service to clients. Managers must have a technical knowledge of agricultural production and marketing, business management skills, and many other qualifications including high ethical and moral standards. The latter is important when potential clients are entrusting the management of an investment of several hundred thousand dollars or more to an individual. That individual must be completely honest and trustworthy in managing the owner's property and in handling the financial transactions for the farm.

    Most professional farm managers were born and reared on a farm or ranch and have a college degree in agriculture. While neither of these qualifications may be absolutely necessary, it is difficult to gain the trust and confidence of potential clients without some combination of experience and academic training in agriculture. Few people would be willing to place the management of any business in the hands of someone with no experience or training in the management of that type of business.

Agricultural training and experience alone will not guarantee success as a professional farm manager. Many other skills and talents are desirable, as illustrated by the following quote:

> To perform at a superior level he must be a businessman and may be required to be a master educator, a practical psychologist, a public relations expert, an engineer, a soil scientist, an entomologist, an animal husbandryman and a marketing specialist. A capable professional farm manager is a builder of land and a builder of character. To approach satisfactory accomplishment these basic qualities must prevail: (1) high ethical and moral standards, (2) business ability and good judgment, (3) intellectual and unbiased attitude, (4) an ever present drive for knowledge and accomplishment, (5) a desire to work with people.[4]

Skills in human relations and communication are often more important than the beginning manager realizes. Much of a manager's time is spent dealing with farm operators, input suppliers, buyers, contractors, and people in other professions such as attorneys and bankers. In addition, the manager must communicate periodically with the owner to obtain approval for plans, budgets, and capital improvements, to report the current status of crop and livestock production, and to summarize periodically as well as annually the financial affairs for the farm. The ability to communicate effectively both orally and in writing is necessary for the manager to implement management decisions and to keep the owner informed on the results of these decisions.

PROFESSIONAL FARM MANAGEMENT ORGANIZATIONS

The early professional farm managers felt a need to meet as a group to discuss common problems and learn new management and production methods. Managers in Illinois met informally several times, and in 1929 managers from Illinois, Iowa, and Missouri met to organize the American Society of Farm Managers. This group evolved into the present American Society of Farm Managers and Rural Appraisers in 1936 when rural appraisers were recognized as part of the organization. Membership is not limited to just professional farm managers but is also open to private farm managers, the owner/operators of larger farms, and those involved in farm management teaching, research, or extension activities at the university level.

[4]American Society of Farm Managers and Rural Appraisers, *Professional Farm Management Manual,* 1972, p. 2.

Professional farm managers and rural appraisers have also organized a large number of state and regional chapters. These state and regional chapters typically hold one or two meetings a year and organize workshops, tours, and other educational activities to help members keep up to date with the latest management, production, and appraisal techniques.

The American Society of Farm Managers and Rural Appraisers conducts a winter and summer meeting each year and sponsors other activities to promote and enhance the image of professional farm management. These other activities include the development of a code of ethics, conducting educational schools and workshops for managers and appraisers, the publication of a professional journal, publication of both a farm management and rural appraisal manual and granting the titles of Accredited Farm Manager® (AFM)® and Accredited Rural Appraiser® (ARA)®. These accredited titles are awarded only to those individuals who meet certain qualifications. For example, the title of Accredited Farm Manager is awarded only to individuals who (1) have at least 5 years of experience managing farms or ranches for others for a fee or salary, (2) have a university degree, (3) furnish affidavits of satisfactory performance of their management duties, (4) pass rigid written and oral examinations conducted by a committee of the society, and (5) subscribe to the society's code of ethics.

Meeting dates, membership requirements, and other information about the state or regional chapters can usually be obtained by contacting a state farm management extension specialist in the College of Agriculture at the appropriate state land-grant university. Addresses for state and regional chapters as well as information about the society can also be obtained by writing:

American Society of Farm Managers and
   Rural Appraisers, Inc.
P.O. Box 6847
Denver, Colorado 80206

REFERENCES

American Society of Farm Managers and Rural Appraisers, Inc.: *Professional Farm Management Manual,* 1972.
Hertz, Carl F.: "Development and Diversification of a Professional Management, Rural Appraisal and Farm Real Estate Business," *Journal of the American Society of Farm Managers and Rural Appraisers,* vol. 32, no. 2, October 1968.
"History of the American Society of Farm Managers and Rural Appraisers," *Journal of the American Society of Farm Managers and Rural Appraisers,* vol. 36, no. 2, October 1972.
Holcomb, J. M.: "Managerial Services," *Journal of the American Society of Farm Managers and Rural Appraisers,* vol. 29, no. 2, October 1965.
Wallace, James J., and Raymond R. Beneke: *Managing the Tenant-Operated Farm,* Iowa State College Press, Ames, Iowa, 1956.

Appendix

Table 1 Amortization Factors for Annual Payments on Amortized Loans with Equal _Total_ Payments

Years	Interest rate						
	4%	5%	6%	7%	8%	10%	12%
1	1.040	1.050	1.060	1.070	1.080	1.100	1.120
2	0.530	0.538	0.545	0.553	0.561	0.576	0.592
3	0.360	0.367	0.374	0.381	0.388	0.402	0.416
4	0.275	0.282	0.289	0.295	0.302	0.315	0.329
5	0.225	0.231	0.237	0.244	0.250	0.264	0.277
6	0.191	0.197	0.203	0.210	0.216	0.230	0.243
7	0.167	0.173	0.179	0.186	0.192	0.205	0.219
8	0.149	0.155	0.161	0.167	0.174	0.187	0.201
9	0.134	0.141	0.147	0.153	0.160	0.174	0.188
10	0.123	0.130	0.136	0.142	0.149	0.163	0.177
11	0.114	0.120	0.127	0.133	0.140	0.154	0.168
12	0.107	0.113	0.119	0.126	0.133	0.147	0.161
13	0.100	0.106	0.113	0.120	0.127	0.141	0.156
14	0.095	0.101	0.108	0.114	0.121	0.136	0.151
15	0.090	0.096	0.103	0.110	0.117	0.131	0.147
16	0.086	0.092	0.099	0.106	0.113	0.128	0.143
17	0.082	0.089	0.095	0.102	0.110	0.125	0.140
18	0.079	0.086	0.092	0.099	0.107	0.122	0.138
19	0.076	0.083	0.090	0.097	0.104	0.120	0.136
20	0.074	0.080	0.087	0.094	0.102	0.117	0.134
21	0.071	0.078	0.085	0.092	0.100	0.116	0.132
22	0.069	0.076	0.083	0.090	0.098	0.114	0.131
23	0.067	0.074	0.081	0.089	0.096	0.113	0.130
24	0.066	0.072	0.080	0.087	0.095	0.111	0.128
25	0.064	0.071	0.078	0.086	0.094	0.110	0.128
30	0.058	0.065	0.073	0.081	0.089	0.106	0.124
35	0.054	0.061	0.069	0.077	0.086	0.104	0.122
40	0.051	0.058	0.066	0.075	0.084	0.102	0.121
45	0.048	0.056	0.065	0.074	0.083	0.101	0.121
50	0.047	0.055	0.063	0.072	0.082	0.101	0.120

Table 2   Compound Interest Table or Future Value of a $1 Investment

Years	\multicolumn{7}{c}{Interest rate}
	4%	5%	6%	7%	8%	10%	12%
1	1.040	1.050	1.060	1.070	1.080	1.100	1.120
2	1.082	1.103	1.124	1.145	1.166	1.210	1.254
3	1.125	1.158	1.191	1.225	1.260	1.331	1.405
4	1.170	1.216	1.262	1.311	1.360	1.464	1.574
5	1.217	1.276	1.338	1.403	1.469	1.611	1.762
6	1.265	1.340	1.419	1.501	1.587	1.772	1.974
7	1.316	1.407	1.504	1.606	1.714	1.949	2.211
8	1.369	1.477	1.594	1.718	1.851	2.144	2.476
9	1.423	1.551	1.689	1.838	1.999	2.358	2.773
10	1.480	1.629	1.791	1.967	2.159	2.594	3.106
11	1.539	1.710	1.898	2.105	2.332	2.853	3.479
12	1.601	1.796	2.012	2.252	2.518	3.138	3.896
13	1.665	1.886	2.133	2.410	2.720	3.452	4.363
14	1.732	1.980	2.261	2.579	2.937	3.798	4.887
15	1.801	2.079	2.397	2.759	3.172	4.177	5.474
16	1.873	2.183	2.540	2.952	3.426	4.595	6.130
17	1.948	2.292	2.693	3.159	3.700	5.055	6.866
18	2.026	2.407	2.854	3.380	3.996	5.560	7.690
19	2.107	2.527	3.026	3.617	4.316	6.116	8.613
20	2.191	2.653	3.207	3.870	4.661	6.728	9.646
21	2.279	2.786	3.400	4.141	5.034	7.400	10.804
22	2.370	2.925	3.604	4.430	5.437	8.140	12.100
23	2.465	3.072	3.820	4.741	5.871	8.954	13.552
24	2.563	3.225	4.049	5.072	6.341	9.850	15.179
25	2.666	3.386	4.292	5.427	6.848	10.835	17.000
30	3.243	4.322	5.743	7.612	10.063	17.449	29.960
35	3.946	5.516	7.686	10.677	14.785	28.102	52.800
40	4.801	7.040	10.286	14.974	21.725	45.259	93.051
45	5.842	8.985	13.765	21.002	31.920	72.890	163.988
50	7.107	11.467	18.420	29.457	46.902	117.391	289.002

Table 3   Amount of an Annuity or Future Value of $1 Invested at End of Each Year

Years	Interest rate						
	4%	5%	6%	7%	8%	10%	12%
1	1.000	1.000	1.000	1.000	1.000	1.000	1.000
2	2.040	2.050	2.060	2.070	2.080	2.100	2.120
3	3.123	3.153	3.184	3.215	3.246	3.310	3.374
4	4.246	4.310	4.375	4.440	4.506	4.641	4.779
5	5.416	5.526	5.637	5.751	5.867	6.105	6.353
6	6.633	6.802	6.975	7.153	7.336	7.716	8.115
7	7.898	8.142	8.394	8.654	8.923	9.487	10.089
8	9.214	9.549	9.897	10.260	10.637	11.436	12.300
9	10.583	11.027	11.491	11.978	12.488	13.579	14.776
10	12.006	12.578	13.181	13.816	14.487	15.937	17.549
11	13.486	14.207	14.972	15.784	16.645	18.531	20.655
12	15.026	15.917	16.870	17.888	18.977	21.384	24.133
13	16.627	17.713	18.882	20.141	21.495	24.523	28.029
14	18.292	19.599	21.015	22.550	24.215	27.975	32.393
15	20.024	21.579	23.276	25.129	27.152	31.772	37.280
16	21.825	23.657	25.673	27.888	30.324	35.950	42.753
17	23.698	25.840	28.213	30.840	33.750	40.545	48.884
18	25.645	28.132	30.906	33.999	37.450	45.599	55.750
19	27.671	30.539	33.760	37.379	41.446	51.159	63.440
20	29.778	33.066	36.786	40.995	45.762	57.275	72.052
21	31.969	35.719	39.993	44.865	50.423	64.003	81.699
22	34.248	38.505	43.392	49.006	55.457	71.403	92.503
23	36.618	41.430	46.996	53.436	60.893	79.543	104.603
24	39.083	44.502	50.816	58.177	66.765	88.497	118.155
25	41.646	47.727	54.865	63.249	73.106	98.347	133.334
30	56.085	66.439	79.058	94.461	113.283	164.49	241.333
35	73.652	90.320	111.435	138.237	172.317	271.02	431.663
40	95.026	120.800	154.762	199.635	259.057	442.59	761.091
45	121.029	159.700	212.744	285.749	386.506	718.90	1,358.230
50	152.667	209.348	290.336	406.529	573.770	1,163.9	2,400.018

Table 4   Present Value of $1 To Be Received at End of a Specified Time Period

Year	Interest rate						
	4%	5%	6%	7%	8%	10%	12%
1	0.962	0.952	0.943	0.935	0.926	0.909	0.893
2	0.925	0.907	0.890	0.873	0.857	0.826	0.797
3	0.889	0.864	0.840	0.816	0.794	0.751	0.712
4	0.855	0.823	0.792	0.763	0.735	0.683	0.636
5	0.822	0.784	0.747	0.713	0.681	0.621	0.567
6	0.790	0.746	0.705	0.666	0.630	0.564	0.507
7	0.760	0.711	0.665	0.623	0.583	0.513	0.452
8	0.731	0.677	0.627	0.582	0.540	0.467	0.404
9	0.703	0.645	0.592	0.544	0.500	0.424	0.361
10	0.676	0.614	0.558	0.508	0.463	0.386	0.322
11	0.650	0.585	0.527	0.475	0.429	0.350	0.287
12	0.625	0.557	0.497	0.444	0.397	0.319	0.257
13	0.601	0.530	0.469	0.415	0.368	0.290	0.229
14	0.577	0.505	0.442	0.388	0.340	0.263	0.205
15	0.555	0.481	0.417	0.362	0.315	0.239	0.183
16	0.534	0.458	0.394	0.339	0.292	0.218	0.163
17	0.513	0.436	0.371	0.317	0.270	0.198	0.146
18	0.494	0.416	0.350	0.296	0.250	0.180	0.130
19	0.475	0.396	0.331	0.277	0.232	0.164	0.116
20	0.456	0.377	0.312	0.258	0.215	0.149	0.104
21	0.439	0.359	0.294	0.242	0.199	0.135	0.093
22	0.422	0.342	0.278	0.226	0.184	0.123	0.083
23	0.406	0.326	0.262	0.211	0.170	0.112	0.074
24	0.390	0.310	0.247	0.197	0.158	0.102	0.066
25	0.375	0.295	0.233	0.184	0.146	0.092	0.059
30	0.308	0.231	0.174	0.131	0.099	0.057	0.033
35	0.253	0.181	0.130	0.094	0.068	0.036	0.019
40	0.208	0.142	0.097	0.067	0.046	0.022	0.011
45	0.171	0.111	0.073	0.048	0.031	0.014	0.006
50	0.141	0.087	0.054	0.034	0.021	0.009	0.003

Table 5 Present Value of an Annuity or $1 To Be Received at the End of Each Year

Years	Interest rate						
	4%	5%	6%	7%	8%	10%	12%
1	0.962	0.952	0.943	0.935	0.926	0.909	0.893
2	1.886	1.859	1.833	1.808	1.783	1.736	1.690
3	2.775	2.723	2.673	2.624	2.577	2.487	2.402
4	3.630	3.546	3.465	3.387	3.312	3.170	3.037
5	4.452	4.329	4.212	4.100	3.993	3.791	3.605
6	5.242	5.076	4.917	4.767	4.623	4.355	4.111
7	6.002	5.786	5.582	5.389	5.206	4.868	4.564
8	6.733	6.463	6.210	5.971	5.747	5.335	4.968
9	7.435	7.108	6.802	6.515	6.247	5.759	5.328
10	8.111	7.722	7.360	7.024	6.710	6.145	5.650
11	8.760	8.306	7.887	7.499	7.139	6.495	5.938
12	9.385	8.863	8.384	7.943	7.536	6.814	6.194
13	9.986	9.394	8.853	8.358	7.904	7.103	6.424
14	10.563	9.899	9.295	8.745	8.244	7.367	6.628
15	11.118	10.380	9.712	9.108	8.559	7.606	6.811
16	11.652	10.838	10.106	9.447	8.851	7.824	6.974
17	12.166	11.274	10.477	9.763	9.122	8.022	7.120
18	12.659	11.690	10.828	10.059	9.372	8.201	7.250
19	13.134	12.085	11.158	10.336	9.604	8.365	7.366
20	13.590	12.462	11.470	10.594	9.818	8.514	7.469
21	14.029	12.821	11.764	10.836	10.017	8.649	7.562
22	14.451	13.163	12.042	11.061	10.201	8.772	7.645
23	14.857	13.489	12.303	11.272	10.371	8.883	7.718
24	15.247	13.799	12.550	11.469	10.529	8.985	7.784
25	15.622	14.094	12.783	11.654	10.675	9.077	7.843
30	17.292	15.372	13.765	12.409	11.258	9.427	8.055
35	18.665	16.374	14.498	12.948	11.655	9.644	8.176
40	19.793	17.159	15.046	13.332	11.925	9.779	8.244
45	20.720	17.774	15.456	13.606	12.108	9.863	8.283
50	21.482	18.256	15.762	13.801	12.233	9.915	8.304

Index